The Georgic Revolution

The Georgic Revolution

Anthony Low

Princeton University Press
Princeton, New Jersey

Copyright © 1985 by Princeton University Press

Published by Princeton University Press, 41 William Street,
Princeton, New Jersey 08540
In the United Kingdom: Princeton University Press, Guildford, Surrey

All Rights Reserved

Library of Congress Cataloging in Publication Data will be
found on the last printed page of this book

ISBN 0-691-06643-4

Publication of this book has been aided by a grant from
The Abraham and Rebecca Stein Faculty Publications Fund of
New York University, Department of English.

This book has been composed in Linotron Sabon

Clothbound editions of Princeton University Press books
are printed on acid-free paper, and binding materials are
chosen for strength and durability

Printed in the United States of America by Princeton University Press
Princeton, New Jersey

Agricola incurvo terram dimovit aratro:
hinc anni labor, hinc patriam parvosque nepotes
sustinet, hinc armenta boum meritosque iuvencos.
(*Georgics*, 2.513-15)

Contents

CONTENTS

List of Illustrations

Figure 1 is used with permission of the Houghton Library, Harvard University. Figures 2-5 are used with permission of the Beineke Rare Book and Manuscript Library, Yale University. Figure 6 is used with permission of the Huntington Library, San Marino, California.

Acknowledgments

IN WRITING this book, I have benefited from a great number of secondary works, only the most relevant of which could be mentioned in the notes. I am happy to acknowledge here a threefold additional debt. Louis L. Martz inadvertently started me in pursuit of the georgic mode. During a lengthy argument with him at a meeting of The Milton Seminar at Yale some years ago, I first began thinking about *Paradise Regained* in georgic terms. The eventual result was an article on that poem that was an early version of part of chapter 7, the first part of this book to be written. My next debt is to William A. Sessions, whose splendid essay on "Spenser's Georgics" (cited in chapter 2) reinforced my thinking about Milton and heartened me to proceed. Since then I have frequently corresponded with him, and he has been magnanimous in his encouragement. My third debt is to Raymond Williams, whose brilliant book, *The Country and the City*, showed me a methodology that could relate poetry to its cultural and ideological origins. I am not sure whether Professor Williams will approve of my own ideology—or rather my typically American lack of one— yet I hope he will be entertained by some of my findings.

My colleague Ernest B. Gilman has read the typescript in its formative stages and responded with encouraging sympathy and a great number of good suggestions. Any writer should wish for such a reader. Diana Benet and Dustin Griffin also gave useful advice. Bert S. Hall of Toronto and Robert R. Raymo, another colleague, both were helpful when I inquired about medieval technology; in addition, Professor Raymo has read the typescript with an eye toward my treatment of the Middle Ages. Walter R. Davis, Albert C. Labriola, and Annabel Patterson read the book as it was drawing toward its final form, and their advice on various matters has helped me decide where to prop and where to prune. At an earlier stage, John T. Shawcross and Janel M. Mueller gave aid and comfort to the chapter on Milton. Needless to say none of these generous volunteers is responsible for errors that remain.

I thank the editors of *PMLA* and *English Literary Renaissance* for their many kindnesses and for permission to reprint two articles that are revised and incorporated as parts of chapters 7 and 4 respectively. Another part of chapter 4 was presented to the Conference on Science, Technology, and Literature at Long Island University in February 1983, where it elicited some useful reactions from the audience. Parts of chapters 2 and 7 were used in a paper on Spenser and Milton read at the December 1983 convention of the Modern Language Association, at a session jointly sponsored by the Spenser Society and the Milton Society of America.

New York University granted me sabbatical leave for 1982-83, which allowed me to finish the book much sooner than would otherwise have been possible. I am grateful to the Dean and Chairman for giving me that opportunity to work without official interruption. I am also deeply grateful to Mrs. Arthur Sherwood in her role as Princeton's Literature Editor.

Finally I want to express my sorrow that Douglas Bush, with whom I originally studied some of the poets discussed in this book, will not be at 3 Clement Circle to read it and send me his comments. I like to think that he would have enjoyed one or two of the amusing bits.

New York University   A. L.

A NOTE ON THE TEXT

IN QUOTING from primary sources of the sixteenth and seventeenth centuries, I have silently regularized *i, j, u, v,* and expanded contractions. I also follow customary practice and omit place of publication for books published in London between 1500 and 1700. Biblical quotations are from the Authorized Version.

The Georgic Revolution

Introduction

VIRGIL'S immense influence on poets of the Middle Ages and the Renaissance is well known. Not even Homer or Ovid exerted an authority anywhere nearly equal to his. He was the chief guide of the major epic writers: Dante, Ariosto, Tasso, Camoens, Spenser, Milton. He was also the chief progenitor of thousands of pastoral poems, in Neolatin and in all the vernaculars of Europe. The universal use of Latin in the Church, education, and diplomacy assured that he would be more accessible than any of the major Greek writers, and it happened that many of the basic mythic and imaginative patterns underlying his poems proved especially amenable to the continuing Christian intellectual synthesis. The doings of Virgil's shepherds and the sufferings and triumph of Aeneas were allegorized and otherwise continually modernized so that they bore directly on the present concerns of his many interpreters in their times. Thus, as old Rome became new Rome, and Britain became new Troy, the Virgilian vision was adapted and carried over into succeeding ages.

The Middle Ages, which regarded Virgil as a godlike figure—magician, necromancer, and prophet—sought to find some deep significance in the stages of his career and especially in his having produced three basically different genres or modes of poetry. Virgil's commentators were encouraged in their speculations by the discarded introduction to the *Aeneid*, which preceded the presently accepted opening and may be translated: "I am he who once tuned my song on a slender reed; then, leaving the woods, I forced the nearby fields to obey the ever-greedy tiller of the soil, a work pleasing to farmers; but now for the roughness of Mars." Out of these lines and the threefold Virgilian œuvre to which they call attention—pastoral, georgic, epic—the Middle Ages developed the *rota Vergilii* or wheel of Virgil, a scheme that divided

3

not only poetry but life, society, and human personality into three interrelated parts. According to these theories, pastoral, georgic, and epic are written in three styles: low, middle, and high. They correspond to three social ranks or occupations: shepherd, farmer, and soldier. They may take place in three locales: pasture, field, and castle; and they may be symbolized by three kinds of tree: the beech, the fruit-tree, and the laurel.[1] Further elaborations on the scheme might be mentioned, for the Middle Ages loved such details, but it is more important to stress that, above all, the three kinds of poetry correspond to three basic human activities, into which almost everything we do in life may be divided: pastoral celebrates play and leisure, georgic celebrates work, and epic celebrates fighting.

A fundamental characteristic of the Renaissance was the determination of many to remake and control their lives, an activity that Stephen Greenblatt has called, in his book of the same title, "Renaissance self-fashioning." Not only did Sir Walter Ralegh and Sir Philip Sidney write gracefully crafted poems; they also produced deliberate and lasting works of art by shaping their own lives. A poet who wished to write great poetry, Milton thought, "ought him selfe to bee a true Poem." A considerable number of poets, engaged in the process of fashioning their lives and characters, took Virgil as a chief model. They began with pastoral and they aimed at epic as their crowning achievement. But, as we shall see, there was a curious anomaly. Even though the Virgilian pattern was a commonplace about which everyone talked, and which served important poets as a pattern for their careers, few georgics were apparently written in England between 1500 and 1700. The middle term in the Virgilian series, a third part of the *rota* and for that matter an important part of human existence, was unaccountably absent.

That absence poses a considerable problem. Why would an

---

[1] On the *rota Vergilii*, see Ernst Curtius, *European Literature and the Latin Middle Ages*, trans. Willard R. Trask (New York: Pantheon Books, 1953), pp. 231-32; and Richard Neuse, "Milton and Spenser: The Virgilian Triad Revisited," *ELH*, 45 (1978), 606-32.

age that consciously imitated and strove to outdo the classics, and that considered Virgil the greatest model for imitation and rivalry, simply ignore one of his three major works? The answer that I shall propose is twofold. First, English poets did not ignore georgic altogether during this period. The seventeenth century witnessed a "georgic revolution" in poetry and also in forms of thought and social relationship: a revolution that some poets helped to further and others strenuously resisted. Second, an answer must be sought not in literary theory alone, but in the social, political, and even economic assumptions of English Renaissance culture. The great enemy of the georgic spirit was the courtly or aristocratic ideal, which dominated the thinking of Tudor and Elizabethan poets, but which some later poets threw off during the seventeenth century in favor of other modes of thought and hierarchies of relative value. The absence of georgic was a function of a fundamental contempt for labor, especially manual and agricultural labor, on the part of England's leaders. As it happens, their attitude in some ways resembles a more recent phenomenon, which European economists refer to, appropriately, as "the English disease."

Even in our time poetry is a valuable indicator of cultural patterns, and it anticipates cultural transformations almost as often as it closely follows them. In an age when political and social leaders regularly read and often wrote poems themselves, poetry provides us with an even more significant means of investigating attitudes and especially of digging into those underlying assumptions that are too basic for any culture to discuss openly or in some cases even to bring to conscious awareness. In this way, an interpreter who proceeds with caution and requisite tact may learn a great deal about the implicit or unacknowledged attitudes of the author and his presumptive readers and thus about the society to which they belong. For example, it has often been asserted that the agricultural and industrial revolutions, which have their roots in England of the sixteenth and seventeenth centuries, were in part products of a "Protestant work ethic." Somehow Protestantism, and especially Calvinism, led the English of that time to place a high value on commercial activity and productive labor. Yet English poetry, when examined closely, reveals an entirely different story. If anything, the Protestant Reformation swept all positive views about work out of England, and it took more than a hundred years of effort to reintroduce them. Some refinement of the existing historical models is therefore indicated.

As is well known, research into such fields as regional history, agricultural and industrial archeology, the historical sociology of ordinary people, and the statistical study of populations, crops, finances, pollen deposits, and similar topics, has given us the means of drawing ever more accurate, though still admittedly imperfect, pictures of the objective past. Still, at some point a historian must subordinate these masses of facts to an interpretive theory, if he is to make them comprehensible. Just at the interface of objective historical forces with subjective desires—that is to say, of harvests, wars, or population growth with individual opinions or the cultural consensus—human history is produced. It so happens that Virgilian georgic, with its stress on obscure private individuals who perform small tasks the cumulative effect of which is to transform society, is an especially apt mode for a poetry that reflects on the making of history. Two poets who played a dominant part in the georgic revolution, Spenser and Milton, both were notably historical-minded, and both were determined to persuade their readers to take hold of events in order to transform their individual and collective futures.

The subject of this book is the georgic revolution that took place in England between about 1590 and 1700, as it is reflected in poetry and was brought about both by poets and by scientists and religious reformers. The nature of the subject is such that I have been obliged to look backward briefly at attitudes toward work, technology, and reform in the Middle Ages and early English Renaissance. I have also had to look forward to the Agricultural Revolution and the "New Husbandry" of the eighteenth century, which were the products of the georgic revolution of the seventeenth. For the most part, the book moves forward chronologically, but occasionally it has seemed best to begin with a known outcome and to trace that outcome back to its causes. Therefore, as far as possible, I have provided dates for the works under discussion. Unless otherwise indicated, these are dates of publication (or of the provenance of a manuscript), although in some cases it has been desirable to indicate when a poem was probably written as well as published. It will be evident from the discussion thus far that I have sometimes had to venture beyond my nominal area of expertise, not only into other periods of literature but also into domains of classics, history, sociology, political theory, economics, theology, and psychology. Since the subject is almost untouched, I have also had to draw up rules and boundaries without much in the way of precedent. So I can only hope that readers will find that the pursuit of this significant topic—which I, at least, have found fascinating—is sufficiently novel to excuse such slips and revelations of ignorance as a study of this kind must inevitably entail.

Like pastoral, georgic is primarily a mode rather than a genre. It is an informing spirit, an attitude toward life, and a set of themes and images rather than anything so definite, say, as a four-book, didactic poem of two thousand lines on the subject of agriculture. Unlike georgic, pastoral has been much studied, and literary historians recognize that there are pastoral plays, elegies, romances, satires, political allegories, and love lyrics, and that although at its most basic pastoral may be defined as short eclogues having to do with sheep and shepherds, or with goats and goatherds, many a poet has dispensed with the sheep, the sheep-hook, and the pipes in pursuit of more rarefied interests. I use "georgic" in the same general sense that literary critics have agreed to use "pastoral," except that I would not wish to claim for the term liberties as extensive as some pastoral theorists have proposed. Some of the poems discussed in this book are georgic in every way, perhaps even generically, but most are georgic or anti-georgic in varying degrees of mode, spirit, theme, character, and imagery.

As recent criticism has recognized, the *Georgics* is more than a simple didactic poem or an instruction manual for farmers. Just how much more is still in dispute among classicists, yet scholars have long recognized certain important qualities of georgic spirit. For one thing, the poem is preeminently about the value of hard and incessant labor. "Labor omnia vicit / improbus et duris urgens in rebus egestas," "Toil has conquered all things, ruinous toil, and want that presses when life is hard" (1.145-46).[2] Farming is a heroic activity, a kind of constructive warfare in which farmer and ox may labor together as fellow-soldiers. Anticipating the opening of the *Aeneid*, Virgil announces, "Dicendum et quae sint duris agrestibus arma," "I must tell, too, of the hardy farmers' weapons" (1.160). These are the plow, the wain, the sledge, the drag, the hoe, the basket. Farming is also a cultural and a civilizing activity, a means of building up the state and ensuring its peaceful prosperity. Various etymological puns

---

[2] Latin text is from *Virgil*, ed. H. Rushton Fairclough, Loeb Classical Library, 2 vols. (Cambridge, Mass.: Harvard Univ. Press, 1953); translations of Virgil are mine except where otherwise indicated. Studies of the *Georgics* I have found especially useful include L. P. Wilkinson, *The* Georgics *of Virgil* (Cambridge: Cambridge Univ. Press, 1969); and Gary B. Miles, *Virgil's* Georgics (Berkeley: Univ. of California Press, 1980). Important studies with views somewhat divergent from mine include Heinrich Altevogt, "Labor Improbus," *Orbis Antiquus*, 7 (1952); and Michael C. J. Putnam, *Virgil's Poem of the Earth* (Princeton: Princeton Univ. Press, 1979). On Virgil's mind and art I have found two books on the *Aeneid* especially valuable: Mario A. Di Cesare, *The Altar and the City* (New York: Columbia University Press, 1974); and J. William Hunt, *Forms of Glory* (London: Feffer & Simons, 1973). W. R. Johnson, *Darkness Visible* (Berkeley: Univ. of California Press, 1976), carries revisionism to a powerful extreme; those who consider Virgil to be a single-minded imperialist may find this an eye-opening study. That Virgil's is a world of confusion, ambiguity, and divided consciousness is indisputable; his vivid portrayal of *lacrimae rerum* was well known to the Renaissance and much admired. Yet in my view the Virgilian hero, whether of epic or georgic, must like the Spenserian or Miltonic hero learn to go forward, however seemingly insuperable the doubts and difficulties that confront him. To put it very crudely, the implied message to the reader is not "give up," but "press on in spite of everything."

on *cultus*, meaning both tilled and civilized, permeate the *Georgics* and belong to the texture of Western language.

Virgil touches on other arts and crafts in the *Georgics*, showing that husbandry is not only basic to civilization but also paradigmatic for other professions. In the great "Jupiter theodicy," which many consider to be at the heart of the *Georgics*, Virgil reveals the important interconnections among farming, the constructive arts, divine providence, and civilization itself. Here is C. Day Lewis's translation:

> for the Father of agriculture
> Gave us a hard calling: he first decreed it an art
> To work the fields, sent worries to sharpen our mortal wits
> And would not allow his realm to grow listless from
>   lethargy.
> Before Jove's time no settlers brought the land under
>   subjection;
> Not lawful even to divide the plain with landmarks and
>   boundaries:
> All produce went to a common pool, and earth
>   unprompted
> Was free with all her fruits.
> Jove put the wicked poison in the black serpent's tooth,
> Jove told the wolf to ravin, the sea to be restive always,
> He shook from the leaves their honey, he had all fire
>   removed,
> And stopped the wine that ran in rivers everywhere,
> So thought and experiment might forge man's various crafts
> Little by little, asking the furrow to yield the corn-blade,
> Striking the hidden fire that lies in the veins of flint.
> Then first did alder-trunks hollowed out take the water;
> Then did the mariner group and name the stars—the
>   Pleiads,
> Hyads and the bright Bear:
> Then was invented the snare for taking game, the tricky
> Bird-lime, the casting of hounds about the broad wood-
>   coverts.

One whips now the wide river with casting-net and
  searches
Deep pools, another trawls his dripping line in the sea.
Then came the rigid strength of steel and the shrill saw-
  blade
(For primitive man was wont to split his wood with
  wedges);
Then numerous arts arose. Yes, unremitting labour
And harsh necessity's hand will master anything.
                                        (1.121-46)[3]

At the root of all these beneficial activities, and therefore of
civilization itself, was Jove's initiative, which brought the
Golden Age to an end and compelled human beings by the
driving force of want to labor, to think, and to invent.

The Roman ancestors who founded the state saw no shame
in farming. Cincinnatus, whom Romans and their spiritual
heirs down through history never cease to extol, easily ex-
changed his plow for weapons and the tactics of war when
he was called on to save the state. Andrew Marvell recalls the
tradition in his praise of Cromwell:

> Who, from his private Gardens, where
> He liv'd reserved and austere,
>   As if his highest plot
>   To plant the Bergamot,
> Could by industrious Valour climbe
> To ruine the great Work of Time,
>   And cast the Kingdome old
>   Into another Mold.
>   (29-36)[4]

One could scarcely find a phrase more Virgilian in spirit than
"industrious Valour"; it perfectly suggests the continuity that
characterizes all the labors of a dedicated man like Cromwell,

[3] *The Georgics of Virgil*, trans. C. Day Lewis (New York: Oxford Univ.
Press, 1947), p. 7.

[4] *The Poems and Letters of Andrew Marvell*, ed. H. M. Margoliouth, 2d
edn., 2 vols. (Oxford: Clarendon Press, 1967), 1:88.

who is forcefully consistent in every sphere, restless, never ceasing, and so, finally, irresistible. True, under the pressures of English culture the Roman farm has become a country gentleman's estate, and labor has been raised and assimilated into the heroic from activities more nearly pastoral than georgic. Yet Marvell's lines show how the arts of peace might suddenly and even apocalyptically give place to the arts of war and then be transformed yet again into the georgic activity of nation building. Just so, Virgil takes the values he painfully builds up in the *Georgics* and without essential contradiction transforms them into the values of the *Aeneid*, an epic in which—by grim necessity—suffering, toil, and war lead to foundation.

Virgil's georgic theodicy, with its double vision of labor as both a curse and a blessing and its assumption that a historical devolution took place from a primal Golden Age of pastoral ease and abundance at the same time that an evolution took place in human thought, art, and invention, is readily and variously accommodated to a Christian world view. Some commentators stress the positive, others the negative. Henry Reynolds, in *Mythomystes* (1632) represents traditional opinion when he argues that Virgil's theodicy reflects the Christian doctrine of the fall of man and borrows from the *Georgics* (1.125-28) his clinching proof-text:

> What could they meane by their *Golden-Age*, when
> > *Nulli subigebant arva coloni,*
> > > *Ipsaque tellus*
> > *Omnia liberius nullo poscente ferebat,*
> But the state of Man before his Sin? and consequently,
> by their Iron age, but the worlds infelicity and miseries
> that succeeded his fall?[5]

To account for the present state of the world, Virgil even posited a primal crime, variously given as the killing and eating

---

[5] "No farmers subdued the plowland . . . and the Earth herself bore everything more freely when no one demanded"; *Mythomystes*, in *Critical Essays of the Seventeenth Century*, ed. J. E. Spingarn, 3 vols. (Bloomington: Indiana Univ. Press, 1957), 1:175-76.

11

of the plow ox (2.536-37) or the Trojan Laomedon's offense against Apollo and Neptune (1.501-504). (At about the same time, Horace suggested in Epode 7 that Roman civil strife began with the murder of Remus by Romulus, a theme that St. Augustine was to take up again in the *City of God*.) Thus Virgil might be Christianized by portraying man's prelapsarian state as pastoral and his postlapsarian state as georgic— when it is not something considerably worse.

We shall refine our understanding of georgic as we go on. The genre is rich; moreover, as the book proceeds it will be evident that georgic is more than simply a literary genre or mode, for it entails a way of living and seeing as well as of writing. The revolution mentioned in the title of this study was a real one, with social, ideological, economic, and technological ramifications as well as literary consequences. Therefore the aim of the book is both to describe a social history as it is revealed in the barometer of poetry and in turn to elucidate that poetry by placing it more accurately in a living context. As an initial working definition, however, we may say that georgic is a mode that stresses the value of intensive and persistent labor against hardships and difficulties; that it differs from pastoral because it emphasizes work instead of ease; that it differs from epic because it emphasizes planting and building instead of killing and destruction; and that it is preeminently the mode suited to the establishment of civilization and the founding of nations. Early modern Britain might be said to have been born with the overthrow of Richard Plantagenet by Henry Tudor, to have reached greatness and national self-consciousness under Queen Elizabeth, and to have entered the modern world during the traumatic struggles of the Civil War. It would seem that georgic is a mode or an ideal peculiarly suited to a nation at such a stage: why, then, did England's poets so conspicuously avoid it?

ONE

Resistance to Georgic

In the October Eclogue of *The Shepheardes Calender* (1579), Spenser has Cuddie recall the Virgilian paradigm of the poet's career, the *rota Vergilii*, which serious poets since the Middle Ages had much admired and imitated, and on which Spenser will largely model his own career:

> Indeede the Romish *Tityrus*, I heare,
> Through his *Mecœnus* left his Oaten reede,
> Whereon he earst had taught his flocks to feede,
> And laboured lands to yield the timely eare,
> And eft did sing of warres and deadly drede,
> So as the Heavens did quake his verse to here.
>
> (55-60)[1]

The pattern was still familiar in 1659, when Lovelace's translation of an epigram by Sannazaro was posthumously published:

> A Swain, Hind, Knight; I fed, till'd, did command
> Goats, Fields, my Foes; with leaves, a spade, my hand.[2]

---

[1] *The Works of Edmund Spenser*, ed. Edwin Greenlaw, C. G. Osgood, and F. M. Padelford, 11 vols. (Baltimore: Johns Hopkins Press, 1932-49), 7:97. On the *rota Vergilii* see Ernst Curtius, *European Literature and the Latin Middle Ages* (New York: Pantheon Books, 1953), pp. 231-32.

[2] *The Poems of Richard Lovelace*, ed. C. H. Wilkinson (1930; Oxford: Clarendon Press, 1963), p. 203. Sannazaro also refers to the *rota* in his *Arcadia* (1.10); and see Mantuan:

> Tityrus (ut fama est) sub Maecenato vestuto
> rura, boves, et agros et Martia bella Canebat.
>
> (5.86-88)

13

Of the three modes of poetry—pastoral, georgic, and epic—
over which Virgil was thought to have thrown the mantle of
his immense authority, pastoral was clearly the most popular
in England during the sixteenth and seventeenth centuries,
and epic the most honored. But literary historians have found
that georgic, the middle term in the series, was unaccountably
absent.[3] "Virgilian pastoral thrives," notes James Turner, "but
true Georgics are hard to find."[4] As Turner and Raymond
Williams have argued and thoroughly documented, the Eng-
lish literary mentality during the Tudor and Stuart reigns was,
on the whole, so antipathetic to manual labor and to the
"base" work of husbandry that poets either scorned the ag-
ricultural laborer or, more usually, ignored him completely.[5]
In pastoral fields, lovely nymphs abound but farm laborers
are apt to be banished.

Not that the English were uninterested in farming. Most of
the country still made its living from the land, and a profusion
of legal documents reveals that everyone from the Lord Chan-
cellor and members of Parliament to cottagers with customary
rights to graze their stock on the village commons were con-
stantly involved in vexing questions of agricultural law.[6]
Nearly all that class of men who were sufficiently advantaged
to be literate would have hoped to end their days as landed
proprietors on at least a small scale or, if they belonged to
the clergy, as the holders of benefices that were ordinarily

[3] See L. P. Wilkinson, *The Georgics of Virgil: A Critical Survey* (Cambridge:
Cambridge Univ. Press, 1969), pp. 270-313.

[4] *The Politics of Landscape* (Cambridge, Mass.: Harvard Univ. Press,
1979), p. 185.

[5] Turner, esp. pp. 53, 85; Williams, *The Country and the City* (London:
Chatto & Windus, 1973).

[6] See Eric Kerridge, *Agrarian Problems in the Sixteenth Century and After*
(London: George Allen & Unwin, 1969); also useful is *The Agrarian History
of England and Wales*, ed. H.P.R. Finberg (Cambridge: Cambridge Univ.
Press, 1967–). A study still influential in its theories if outmoded in its data
is R. H. Tawney, *The Agrarian Problem in the Sixteenth Century* (London:
Longmans, Green, 1912).

supported by agricultural tithes. We may suspect that Herrick was not wholly disinterested when he wrote his epigram "Upon *Much-more*":

> *Much-more*, provides, and hoords up like an Ant;
> Yet *Much-more* still complains he is in want.
> Let *Much-more* justly pay his tythes; then try
> How both his Meale and Oile will multiply.[7]

Similarly, the fellows of an Oxford or Cambridge college often dealt with such matters as the quarterly rents from college properties and with how the college holdings might best be improved or, it might be, enclosed. Sir Richard Weston, author of *A Discours of Husbandrie used in Brabant and Flanders* (1650), speaks with uncommon bluntness:

> If you observ the common Cours of things, you will finde that Husbandrie is the end, which men of all Estates in the world do point at: For to what purpose do Souldiers, Scholars, Lawyers, Merchants, and men of all occupations and trades, toil and labor with great affection, but to get monie; and with that monie when they have gotten it, but to purchase Land; and to what end do they buy that Land, but to receiv the fruits of it to live; and how shall one receiv the fruits of it, but by his own Husbandrie, or by a Farmers? So that it appear's by degrees, that what cours soëver a man taketh in this world, at last hee cometh to Husbandrie, which is the most common occupation amongst men.[8]

Such were the facts; yet it is surprising how infrequently those facts are reflected in the literature of the period. Poets generally prefer the fiction that the country gentleman and his ancestors have always owned his estates, and that the chief function of

---

[7] *The Poetical Works of Robert Herrick*, ed. L. C. Martin (1956; Oxford: Clarendon Press, 1963), p. 73.

[8] I quote from the second edn., "Corrected and Inlarged," of 1652, pp. 2-3.

those estates is to afford rural ease to the host and hospitality to guests.

Between the Augustan Age of Rome and that of England, literary historians have noticed a few scattered imitations of the *Georgics*, not very like the original, and in England they have noted that Renaissance schoolmasters sometimes set the *Georgics* as a text.[9] Of course, if at any time during this supposed hiatus a writer had occasion to speak of style, he would automatically cite the formula that assigned low style to pastoral, middle to georgic, and high to epic. Still, the trope might be thought to have become little more than a reflex. Poets with Virgilian pretensions often leapt straight out of pastoral into epic, without troubling to serve out an apprenticeship at the georgic level. Therefore in English poetry the georgic is usually said to begin with Dryden's translation of Virgil's *Eclogues* and *Georgics*, which was published in 1697 along with Dryden's laudatory preface and Addison's influential essay on the georgic kind.[10] For the first time in the seventeenth century, save for a remarkable compliment by the iconoclastic Montaigne,[11] Dryden argued that the *Georgics* was Virgil's finest poem, and that he wrote it, "in the full strength and vigour of his Age, when his Judgment was at the height, and before his Fancy was declining." Addison agreed, calling the poem "the most Compleat, Elaborate, and finisht Piece of all Antiquity."[12]

[9] L. P. Wilkinson, pp. 270-313.

[10] For the georgic in England beginning with Dryden (1697), see Dwight L. Durling, *Georgic Tradition in English Poetry* (New York: Columbia Univ. Press, 1935), and John Chalker, *The English Georgic: A Study in the Development of a Form* (London: Routledge & Kegan Paul, 1969).

[11] "Of Books," *Essays*, 2.10: "I have always thought, that in Poesie, *Virgil*, *Lucretius*, *Catullus* and *Horace* do many degrees excel the rest; and signally, *Virgil* in his *Georgicks*, which I look upon for the most accomplished piece of Poetry"; *Essays of Michael Seigneur de Montaigne*, trans. Charles Cotton, 3 vols. (1685), 2:134.

[12] Dryden, *The Works of Vergil* (1697); see *The Poems of John Dryden*, ed. James Kingsley, 4 vols. (Oxford: Clarendon Press, 1958), 2:913; and Joseph Addison, *Miscellaneous Works*, ed. A. C. Guthkelch, 2 vols. (London, 1914), 2:11.

Three earlier English translations of the *Georgics* were published, the first by "A.F.," probably Abraham Fleming, in 1589.[13] Still it was Dryden's genius that enabled him, as so often, to discover and proclaim a new fashion. Not even the appearance of his much-admired *Aeneid* the following year could prevent his *Georgics* from touching off a new mode that was to last through much of the eighteenth century, reaching its acknowledged peak in Thomson's *Seasons* before it petered out among a new "mob of gentlemen who wrote with ease."

Aside from frequent but usually perfunctory appeals to the middle style, the *Georgics* survived most obviously in seventeenth-century poetry in a few important but fragmented motifs and topoi. The popular myth of Orpheus, symbol of the artist, of the harmonizer and civilizer, although it owes much to the *Metamorphoses*, achieved its most notable statement in *Georgics* 4. The myth of Proteus, so important to the age as a symbol for changeable matter in the phenomenal world, while it originates in the *Odyssey*, likewise takes vivid form in *Georgics* 4. A still more prominent topos, the idea or image of the Golden Age, though it owes much to Hesiod, Horace, Ovid, and Virgil's "Messianic" Eclogue, persistently echoes and alludes to the *Georgics*. Yet these golden-age allusions seldom adhere to the georgic spirit of the Virgilian original. Thus Montaigne's seminal essay "Of Cannibals," which was to bear fruit in Rousseau's potent doctrine of primitive man, turns to the *Georgics* for its single supporting citation;[14] but Montaigne draws his Virgilian distinctions between labor and ease, property and community, invention and indolence, hierarchy and brotherhood, injustice and justice, in order to move away from a georgic world of work, invention, and civilization into precisely the pastoral idyll that Virgil had

---

[13] A. F., *The Buckolicks of Publius Vergilius Maro . . . together with his Georgicks* (1589); Thomas May, *Virgil's Georgicks* (1628); John Ogilby, *The Works of Publius Vergilius Maro* (1649; 1650, 1654, 1665, 1668, 1684).
[14] *Essays*, 1.30; trans. Cotton, 1:368-69.

invoked to provide a contrast with the hard and laborious world of his farmers.

In the *Georgics*, Virgil suggests that the Golden Age of ease and communistic justice is gone forever. Instead, he proposes an alternative, exemplified by the "happy husbandman." This figure Virgil associates with a more recent past, when Roman ancestors lived a simpler and nobler life as farmers, before the city was cursed with luxury and civil war. The whole course of the *Georgics* suggests that this ideal, unlike the Golden Age, may actually be reattainable. Under the enlightened leadership of Octavius and by means of the exertions of individual citizens, typified by but not necessarily limited to the husbandman, Rome may once more be entering a period of happiness and prosperity, which is characterized not by a miraculous transformation back to primal *otium*, as Virgil had earlier prophesied in *Eclogue 4*, but by the performance of equitable labor for the common welfare.[15] In such circumstances, work is transformed from a curse into a blessing.

Ironically, though Virgil's happy husbandman proved highly popular throughout the seventeenth century, in title-page epigraphs, translations, and verse paraphrases, social conditions and assumptions were such that this figure was persistently transformed from a georgic exemplar into what amounted to simply another variation on the theme of pastoral ease.[16] The georgic mode was not congenial. When Christopher Johnson took his schoolboys at Winchester through the *Georgics* in 1563, he felt obliged to warn them not to despise agricultural labor, which the Romans obviously valued much more highly than did the English.[17] But warnings of this kind had little effect on those schoolboys who grew up to be poets

[15] See, e.g., Patricia A. Johnston, *Vergil's Agricultural Golden Age: A Study of the* Georgics (Leiden: E. J. Brill, 1980).

[16] For a brief history of the motif, see Maren-Sofie Røstvig, *The Happy Man* (Oslo: Akademisk Forlag, 1954), pp. 69-116.

[17] British Library MS. Add. 4379, fol. 79; cited by T. W. Baldwin, *William Shakspere's Small Latine and Lesse Greek*, 2 vols. (Urbana: Univ. of Illinois Press, 1944), 1:327, and see pp. 321-32.

version of his life that is offered in Horace's second epode, *Beatus ille*. Notoriously, it turns out in the end that the body of this poem has been spoken by the usurer Alphius, who has just finished collecting his rents and is toying with the idea of retiring to a country villa. But, in the closing stanza, "avarice again gains the upper hand," and he decides to remain in Rome.[20] In other words, seductive as Horace's poem is, it represents the vision of a city-dweller dreaming of the country life, and it reflects few of the nagging realities. It is also notorious that most of the English translators and paraphrasers of these popular lines dropped Horace's ironic stance along with his final stanza and thus essentially revealed themselves as gentlemen amateurs. Ben Jonson is a notable exception. William Browne, whose pastorals Milton extensively annotated and who deserves credit for being more realistic than most, nevertheless can insert a leisured stanza such as this into his paraphrase of Horace:

> By some sweet stream, clear as his thought,
> He seats him with his book and line;
> And though his hand have nothing caught,
> His mind hath whereupon to dine.[21]

Obviously these are not the reveries of a laborer or a subsistence farmer. Browne's "Happy Life" is not wholly without labor, but it is a labor that is well under control:

> His afternoon spent as the prime
> Inviting where he mirthful sups;
> Labour, or seasonable time,
> Brings him to bed and not his cups.

Perhaps Browne's vision is Stoic as well as Epicurean; yet there is nothing in it of Virgil's constant and even terrifying toil, which is better captured, although rejected, in Barnfield's

[20] Røstvig, p. 71.
[21] *Poems of William Browne of Tavistock*, ed. Gordon Goodwin, 2 vols. (London: Routledge & Sons, n.d.), 2:299-300.

22

and writers. In a hierarchical society it was proper for a schoolboy to work hard, or an agricultural laborer, but not a full-grown man of the educated classes. "[G]oe chide / Late schoole boyes, and sowre prentices," Donne's lover tells an intrusive, taskmaster sun; "Call countrey ants to harvest offices." An English gentleman might readily imagine himself sitting on a hillside at his ease, dressed in shepherd's garb, playing on his pipes or making love to the local shepherdesses, but ordinarily he was unlikely to imagine himself a plowman.

THE PASTORAL VIEWPOINT

The prejudices with which the age began, which were as much political and social as they were literary, are typically represented by Richard Barnfield. "The Shepherds Content, or The hapines of a harmless life" (1594) begins: "Of all the kindes of common Countrey life, / Me thinkes a Shepheards life is most Content" (1-2).[18] Not surprisingly, Barnfield's shepherd has few labors or duties to perform, but is put into the world chiefly to enjoy himself. The only threats to his happiness are ambition, which might take him to court, and all-conquering love, which not even a shepherd can escape (216-73). His only chore is to see that those sheep that contravene the rules of hierarchy are "pounded" (155-61). A more idyllic life could scarcely be imagined:

> He sits all Day lowd-piping on a Hill,
> The whilst his flocke about him daunce apace,
> His hart with joy, his eares with Musique fill:
> Anon a bleating Weather beares the Bace,
> A Lambe the Treble; and to his disgrace
> > Another answers like a middle Meane:
> > Thus every one to beare a Part are faine.
> > > (141-47)

[18] In *The Affectionate Shepheard* (1594); rpt. in *Poems, 1594-1598*, ed. Edward Arber (Westminster: Archibald Constable, 1896), pp. 25-33.

19

Quite opposite to this pleasant *otium* is the lot of the hus-
bandman, who is somewhat illogically lumped together with
courtiers, scholars, merchants, and soldiers as an instance of
how "low degree" as well as too much ambition can lead to
trouble and unrest:

> The painfull Plough-swaine, and the Husband-man
> Rise up each morning by the breake of day,
> Taking what toyle and drudging paines they can,
> And all is for to get a little stay;
> And yet they cannot put their care away:
> > When Night is come, their cares begin afresh,
> > Thinking upon their Morrowes busines.
> > > (99-105)

This realistic husbandman, unlike those pretended figures in
translations of Virgil and Horace who are really courtly shep-
herds in disguise, is not a "happy husbandman." How could
he be, in the common Elizabethan view, when he is base-born,
rude, poor, and condemned to endless labor?

What many poets really thought about rustics is docu-
mented by James Turner. Alexander Brome (1661) pretends
to retire from polite society to country contentment, but he
thinks very little of his real country neighbors:

> Here, if we mix with *company*, 'tis such
> As can say *nothing* though they talk too *much*.
> Here we learn *georgicks*, here the *Buckolicks*,
> Which buildings cheapest, *timber*, *stone*, or *bricks*.
> Here *Adams* natural Sons, all made of *Earth*—
> *Earth's* their *Religion*, their *discourse*, their *mirth*.

The unknown author of *Honoria and Mammon* (1659) pro-
vides us with an even more unsparing portrait, which indicates
with full vividness how an aristocratic "shepherd" might view
a real countryman who happened to cross his path:

> thou horrid Lumpe
> Of leather, coarse wooll, ignorance, and husbandry,

20

Most pitifully compounded, thou that
Hast liv'd so long a dunghill, till the weeds
Had over-grown thee, and but ten yards off
Cosen'd a horse that came to graze upon thee.[19]

For the most part, however, poets preferred not to sp(
landscapes with such ugly objects; better to ignore th
laborer entirely, keep him in the background, or tra
him from a georgic into an acceptably pastoral figure.
One may notice the characteristic psychological impe(
in coming to terms with the profession of husbandry (
a manual on choosing a trade. Thomas Powell, who
his *Tom of All Trades* (1631) to the hopeful parents of
men looking for work appropriate to their means and ab
of necessity touches on the commonest profession of a
he cannot refrain from the customary note of comic s(

> Your sonne whom you intend for a *Husbandman*, m
> be a disposition part gentile, and rustike equally m
> together, for if the Gentleman be predominant: his r
> ning Nagge will out run the *Constable*. His extraordin
> strong Beere will be too headstrong in office of *Chur*
> *Warden*. And his well mouthed dogges will make h
> out-mouth all the Vestrie. But if the clowne be predo
> inant he will smell all browne bread and garlicke. (si
> F2ᵛ-F3ʳ)

In other words, the gentleman is too well-bred and high-
ited to farm, but the rustic is beneath contempt. That i
esting hybrid, the gentleman-farmer, who in later years
be the commonest of sights and of literary ideals, is only ba
conceivable to Powell and his readers—as an impossible
adox or a bad joke.

Not too surprisingly, therefore, English poets who pr
the happy husbandman prefer the milder and less labori

[19] Brome, *Songs and Other Poems* (1661), p. 191; *Honoria and Mam*
(1659), p. 7; both cited by Turner, p. 176; *The Politics of Landscape* qu
much similar illustrative material.

21

brief portrait. To be truly georgic, a poem should come face to face with the realistic details of farming life, see them for what they are, yet accept them and even glorify them. Apparently most writers in England found such concepts impossible to think about, and even in the eighteenth century poets seem to find it difficult not to sink back into the repose of the gentleman amateur, all of whose work is performed for him by his laborers—including the work of supervision.

Thus, as Raymond Williams aptly points out, Herrick is able to admire the sweaty laborers of "The Hock-cart," yet in the end he puts them back firmly into their proper social position:[22]

> Come Sons of Summer, by whose toile,
> We are the Lords of Wine and Oile:
> By whose tough labours, and rough hands,
> We rip up first, then reap our lands. . . .
> And, you must know, your Lords word's true,
> Feed him ye must, whose food fils you.
>
> (1-4, 51-52)

A modern reader, however conservative, is likely to feel Herrick's politics sticking in his throat; still we can admire him for his poetic realism and for the greater than usual openness with which he depicts country living as it was. It may be that Virgil would not have approved of this latter-day version of latifundian agriculture, yet there is georgic energy absolutely typical of Virgil in Herrick's rough, tough manual labor and his ripping and reaping of the land.

A much more typical "establishment" attitude (taking the word mostly in its old Erastian sense) is expressed by Isaac Walton's Venator, after he has been tutored and converted by his master Piscator.[23] Sitting under a willow by a stream, he contemplates a farmer's meadow across the way, and he pities its lawsuit-ridden owner. Better to sit and look at such

---

[22] *The Country and the City*, pp. 33-34.
[23] *The Compleat Angler*, 1.16.

a field than to own or to farm it. Better to be an angler than a farmer. His attitude is understandable; in 1653, when *The Compleat Angler* first appeared, Royalists had good reason to take a Stoic view. Land sequestrations and fines were at their height, and rural England was in turmoil. Still, fishing had always been a preferred activity for gentlemen who, with Venator, might sometimes feel that the exertions of hunting came rather too close for comfort to hard work. Henry Peacham, in *The Complete Gentleman* (1622), confirms that fishing is a properly gentle accomplishment, a suitable "pastime for all men to recreate themselves at vacant hours."[24] At the height of Walton's vision, fishing rises to the dignity of religious contemplation; yet it still is associated with familiar conservative social and political prejudices.

For a more extensive illustration of the typical view that country life should be a life of leisure, we can hardly do better than to turn to Henry Vaughan. Vaughan's love of nature is, of course, well known. "Upon the Priorie Grove" and "To the River *Isca*" demonstrate what is obvious enough, that he liked to stroll about quietly and contemplate nature's beauties, and that he was a gentleman in retirement rather than a man with an interest in living off the land, or for that matter in observing others living off it. His paraphrase of Boethius's "Metrum 5" celebrates, in the traditional terms, the Golden Age. Among his paraphrases of Casimir Sarbiewski, the Polish Neolatinist, is "The Praise of a Religious life . . . In Answer to that Ode of *Horace*," in which he dismisses even the modicum of work that Horace had allowed into *Beatus ille*:

> *Flaccus* not so: That wordly *He*
> Whom in the Countreys *shade* we see
> Ploughing his own *fields*, seldome can
> Be justly stil'd, *The Blessed man.*
> That title only fits a *Saint*,
> Whose free thoughts far above restraint

---

[24] *The Complete Gentleman*, ed. Virgil B. Heltzel (Ithaca: Cornell Univ. Press, 1962), p. 171 (ch. 20).

And weighty Cares, can gladly part
With *house* and *lands* . . .
Sits in some fair *shade*, and doth give
To his *wild thoughts* rules how to live.
(1-8, 19-20)

Vaughan's poem reflects two facts of English social life: the separation of the gentleman from close contact with the land, and the separation of the contemplative "saint" from his original monastic foundation—where, according to the ancient Benedictine formula, prayer was to be balanced by work. The result of this separation is a rootless and etiolated rural spirituality, toward which not only the pleasure-seekers and the urban cynics of the day are drawn, but even the most dedicated and ascetic of Englishmen. Vaughan, who was certainly not a lazy or an idle man, was in the habit of rising at midnight for his prayers. He can praise a country diet of "thin *beere*," "*fresh berries*," and "the *Bean* / By Curious *Pallats* never sought" (72-81), yet he cannot seem to imagine himself doing the work of brewing, planting, or gathering these humble comestibles. His attitude may be influenced by Casimir's but it is perfectly consonant with his thinking elsewhere.

The personal views of a translator like Vaughan are revealed by what he chooses to translate as well as by what he changes from the original. Another work he admired is *The Praise and Happinesse of the Countrie-Life* (1651), which he translated from the Spanish of Antonio de Guevara, Bishop of Carthagena and adviser to Charles V. Vaughan takes his title-page epigraph from the familiar opening of Virgil's praise of the happy husbandman in *Georgics* 2, *O fortunatos nimium*, and a closing dash presumably signals the assumption that readers will recall the rest of this often-quoted passage. In the light of the present discussion, the interesting thing about this little treatise is how it mingles and confuses the lives of the country gentleman and of the country laborer.

In the Country the *Gentleman* aswell as the *Ploughman* may live, to please himself, and is not bound to a charge-

able Imitation of the *fashions* and *foppery* of others. . . .
A *bill* to walk his grounds with, a *fish-basket*, an *angling-rod*, or *birding-piece* are his chiefest accoutrements. . . .
Yea, more *blessed* is he, that living honestly in the *sweat of his face*, rides his own simple *Asse*, than a rich un-conscionable *Tyrant* that furnisheth his great *stable* or *dairie* with the *Cattel* and *Horses* of an innocent, honest *man*. . . . (pp. 126-27)[25]

The Husbandman is alwaies up and drest with the morning, whose dawning light . . . chaseth away the dark-nesse (which would hinder his early labours) from every *valley*. If his days task keep him late in the *fields*, yet *night* comes not so suddenly upon him, but he can returne home with the *Evening-star*. (p. 129)

O who can ever fully expresse the pleasures and hap-pinesse of the Country-life! with the various and delight-full sports of *fishing, hunting* and *fowling*, with *guns, Greyhounds, Spaniels*, and severall sorts of *Nets*! what oblectation and refreshment it is, to behold the *green shades*, the beauty and Majestie of the tall and antient *groves*, to be skill'd in *planting* and dressing of *Orchards, Flowres* and *Pot-Herbs*, to temper and allay these harm-lesse *imployments* with some innocent merry *song*, to ascend sometimes to the *fresh* and *healthfull hils*, . . . to heare the *musick* of *birds*, the *murmurs* of *Bees*, the *falling* of *springs*, and the pleasant discourses of the *Old Plough-men*, where without any impediment or trouble a man may walk. (p. 130)

[W]hen the *Sabbath day* comes . . . The poorest *Coun-try-labourer* honours that day with his best *habit*; their *families*, their *beasts*, and their *cattell* rest on that day, and every one in a decent and Christian *dresse* walks Religiously towards his *Parish Church*. (p. 131)

Towards *sun setting*, the *nightingale* and other pleasant

[25] *The Works of Henry Vaughan*, ed. L. C. Martin (Oxford: Clarendon Press, 1957), pp. 123-36.

birds caroll to him out of the *wood*, his *dogs* like faithfull
attendants walk about him; The *Rams* leap, the *kids* skip,
and his *Yard* abounds with *Pigeons, Turkeys, Capons,
ducks* and all sorts of *Poultrie*. . . . Though he should
rest no where else, but on *straw*, or the bare *Earth*, yet
are his sleeps unbroken, and far more sweet, than those
naps which are taken upon *silks*, and *beds* of *down*. (p.
134)

There is much in Vaughan's idyllic picture of the countryside
to soothe and attract a reader's imagination. A reader would
have to be very sour not to recognize and sympathize with
Vaughan's real love for the retired and unambitious life of a
country gentleman. When one recalls that this "Praise" was
published in 1651, the year Charles II lost the Battle of
Worcester and became a fugitive, and also a year when Roy-
alist estates were being sequestered in increasing numbers,
then Vaughan's nostalgia for a harmonious, peaceful, hier-
archical society, even if it never existed in such perfect and
universal contentment, becomes more understandable. In the
circumstances even the plowmen might have preferred Vaugh-
an's ideal. The small tenants and laborers on the estates were
suffering, like their masters, from the exactions of new owners,
local officials, and soldiers anxious for their pay. Two years
later, a report on expropriated lands notes that "the tennants
of those lands doe perfectly hate those who bought them, as
possibly men can doe; for these men are the greatest tyrants
every where as men can be; for they wrest the poore tennants
of all former imunitys and freedoms they formerly enjoyed."[26]

Still, there is undoubtedly moral confusion and failure of
vision in an idyll that turns its plowmen into pleasant fixtures
of the landscape, making their discourses one with the singing

[26] Letter of 14 December 1653 from "T. M." to the English merchant
"Rider" in Paris, *Thurloe State Papers*, ed. Thomas Birch, 7 vols. (1742),
1:633; see also Christopher Hill, "The Agrarian Legislation of the Revolu-
tion," *Puritanism and Revolution* (1958; New York: Schocken, 1964), pp.
153-96; Hill cites this letter p. 187.

of the birds and the murmuring of the bees, while the owner walks about his place from task to task "without any impediment or trouble." The confusion between plowman and landowner obscures a never-quite-stated distinction between what is good for the laborer—to rise with the sun, work all day, sleep on straw, and rest (like the farm animals) on Sundays— and what is good for the owner—to read, contemplate, stroll about, enjoy the landscape and the rural sports, and to turn even the supervision of chores into leisurely pleasures, secure in the illusion that his laborers are as content as he is, and that he has successfully escaped the guilt of being a "*Caterpiller*" upon society (p. 136) by the simple act of fleeing the city for the country. I do not mean that Vaughan should necessarily have taken up a spade to join the laborers of Breconshire at their tasks—although two years earlier others had called on the English to do just that—but rather that his writings are peculiarly blind to the moral and social value of labor of any kind. Like most of his fellow poets, Vaughan saw the countryside through the accustomed glasses of pastoral vision. Pastoral, of one sort or another, whether it was concerned with shepherds suffering from the pangs of love or with hermits breathing out their prayers in rural shades, was an almost universal preoccupation of writers. Georgic, to the contrary, had become an uncongenial mode, which most writers either ignored entirely or silently converted, in the alembic of imagination and prejudice, back into pastoral.

THE SIXTEENTH CENTURY

The husbandman is often a prominent and sometimes a sympathetic figure in Medieval poetry. One thinks of Chaucer and of that prototypical figure, Piers Plowman. But with the revival of English poetry in the age of Wyatt and Surrey, attitudes appear to have changed. There are few sympathetic depictions of country labor in the English Renaissance. Poets normally employ the country as a place on which they can project the psychological vicissitudes of love or of religious aspiration, or to which they can retreat in order to recoup their energies or tame their ambitions. The meadows, woods, and streams of the pastoral landscape offer the easy pleasures of *otium* as opposed to *negotium*, of ease and play as opposed to business and the striving for wealth and place that goes on continually at court and in the city. Nearly all the poetry during the period that touches on the country in any way is pastoral.

As a rule, if plowlands, pastures, or fields of grain appear, poets treat them as aspects of the natural landscape rather than as places where farmers are making their livings or their fortunes and laborers are hard at work. The general blindness to labor characterizes even those country poems that are otherwise more than usually realistic in spirit. For example, the speaker in Wyatt's satire "Myne owne John Poynz" (c. 1536) is an unusually energetic man who, most critics have found, presents us with a realistic view of rural activities. Yet although the poem is realistic in tone, and is a celebration of country living, it never for a moment is georgic:

> This maketh me at home to hounte and hawke
> And in fowle weder at my booke to sitt.
> In frost and snowe then with my bow to stawke;
> No man doeth marke where so I ride or goo. . . .
> Where if thou list, my Poynz, for to come,
> Thou shalt be judge how I do spend my tyme.
> (80-83, 102-103)[27]

One assumes that a gentleman staying in the country, even though he had a capable estate manager or bailiff, would spend at least some of his time overlooking his business affairs, but Wyatt makes no mention of this sort of concern. One also assumes that when Wyatt or his protagonist went out hunting or hawking there would be grooms, gamekeepers, and various other servants in attendance, yet Wyatt is able to claim: "No man doeth marke where so I ride or goo." Presumably he

---

[27] *Collected Poems of Sir Thomas Wyatt*, ed. Kenneth Muir and Patricia Thomson (Liverpool: Liverpool Univ. Press, 1969).

means no one worth mentioning, no one, unless Poynz should join him, who is equal to *judging* him (103). The servants in attendance are simply not seen, and still less those who are working in the fields.

Oddly, if one wants to find a glimpse of country laborers in Wyatt, he must turn to another satire, the one based on the fable of the town and country mice:

> My mothers maydes when they did sowe and spynne,
> They sang sometyme a song of the feld mowse. . . .
> She thought her self endured to much pain,
> The stormy blastes her cave so sore did sowse . . .
> To comfort her when she her howse had dight,
> Sometyme a barly corn, sometyme a bene,
> For which she laboured hard boeth daye and nyght,
> In harvest tyme whilest she myght goo and glyne;
> And [wher stoore] was stroyed with the flodd,
> Then well away! for she undone was clene.
>
> (1-15)[28]

On the evidence of these two country satires, we might be hard pressed not to conclude that Wyatt was able to feel a greater sense of solidarity with his fictional mouse than with his own servants, or at least that he found it easier to express his sympathy for the plight of agricultural laborers in a round-about way. Wyatt's reluctance to depict the country laborer more directly is not, of course, unusual for his time; what is unusual is that he should display such remarkable empathy for the farmworker's plight even under cover of a beast fable. Although Wyatt was a thorough aristocrat, we remember that he was something of a rebel who seldom saw eye to eye with the court. Significantly, the mouse fable appears in a context of exile and of the speaker's isolation from his peers; it is then that he remembers a piece of folk comfort that he heard as a

---

[28] In line 14 I substitute the Egerton MS's reading "wher stoore" for Muir's "when her stoore"; see Richard Harrier, *The Canon of Sir Thomas Wyatt's Poetry* (Cambridge, Mass.: Harvard Univ. Press, 1975), p. 174.

child from his "mothers maydes." Still, he applies the lesson to himself, not to his servants; the country mouse's story, like his own, is personal; so far as we are told she struggles to feed herself rather than to benefit her family or community. So, though some of Wyatt's details, especially the flood that destroys the harvest, are reminiscent of the plight of Virgil's husbandman, the mouse's labors lack the sort of public resonance that characterizes Virgilian georgic.

Of course, it is always possible to read the *Georgics* without noticing the spirit of labor and of social reform with which it is imbued. We have noted how seventeenth-century poets liked to tear Virgil's happy husbandman from his context in order to make him into the leisured hero of a succession of pastoral lyrics. Sir Thomas Elyot, whose humanist views and strenuous educational goals might have given him some insights into the georgic spirit, was similarly blinded by the assumptions of his time, and speaks of Virgil's poem as if it were a purely pastoral idyll: "In his Georgikes, lorde what pleasaunt varietie there is: the divers graynes, herbes, and flowres, that be there described, that reding therin hit seemeth to a man to be in a delectable gardeine or paradise."[29] L. P. Wilkinson indignantly demands, "How could anyone who really knew the poem characterise it in this way?"[30] A proper question, surely; yet if we take into account Elyot's aristocratic audience and the almost universal prejudices of his time, as well as the natural human tendency at any time only to see what the culture allows, then a different question arises: How could we expect Elyot to speak in any other way?

Indeed, for the most part, not even contemporary treatises on farming are georgic in spirit. The rise of the first printed farming manuals in England attests to the sixteenth century's interest in agriculture.[31] Fitzherbert's *Boke of Husbondrye*

[29] *The boke named the Governour* (1531; facs. Menston, Yorkshire: Scolar Press, 1970), fol. 32ᵛ.

[30] Wilkinson, p. 295.

[31] See, e.g., G. E. Fussell, *The Old English Farming Books, from Fitzherbert to Tull* (London: Crosby Lockwood & Son, 1947).

(1523) was followed by Thomas Tusser's *A hundreth good pointes of husbandry* (1557), which was sufficiently popular to appear in several more editions and to expand into *Five Hundreth good Pointes of Husbandry, united to as many of good Huswifery* (1573). When these writers digress from detailed advice in order to praise the country life, however, they focus on rural sports and pastoral beauties, and they treat husbandry as a means to private wealth, with no emphasis on the virtues of labor or the benefits it may bring to the nation as a whole. Tusser oscillates between anxiety to preserve the ancient hierarchies and concern for making a quick profit. Because he stresses the profit motive so heavily, some of his early readers drew ironic satisfaction from his failure to put his theories successfully into practice. Henry Peacham draws the appropriate moral in *Minerva Britanna* (1612):

> They tell me *Tusser*, when thou wert alive,
> And hadst for profit, turned every stone,
> Where ere thou cammest, thou couldst never thrive. . . .[32]

Once, however, Tusser touches on the georgic ideal, in a riddle poem (whose answer is husbandry) that is Virgilian in theme if not in skill:

> I Seeme but a drudge, yet I passe any King
> To such as can use me, great wealth I do bring.
> Since Adam first lived, I never did die,
> When Noe was shipman, there also was I.
> The earth to susteine me, the sea for my fish:
> Be readie to pleasure me, as I would wish.
> What hath any life, but I help to preserve,
> What wight without me, but is ready to sterve.
>
> In woodland, in Champion, Citie, or towne
> If long I be absent, what falleth not downe?
> If long I be present, what goodnes can want?
> Though things at my comming were never so scant.

[32] (Facs. Leeds: Scolar Press, 1966), p. 61.

So many as loove me, and use me aright,
With treasure and pleasure, I richly acquite.
Great kings I doe succour, else wrong it would go,
The King of al kings hath appointed it so.[33]

Tusser's conclusion suggests how easily the Virgilian vision of husbandry as a means of national prosperity, working together with such related civilizing skills as fishing and the conquest of the sea (*Georgics* 1.141-45), can be given a Christian turn. Husbandry seems "but a drudge" to most people, yet it has the sanction of the "King of al kings," and therefore it is worthy of honor and respect even from those at the top of the social scale. We search Tusser in vain, however, for any reappearance of this broad philosophic view. He quickly returns to his usual mixture of didacticism, forehead-knuckling, and greed, interspersed with characteristically pastoral moments of relaxation.

Minor poets seldom are capable of bringing about major changes in viewpoint. They are far more likely to follow the prevailing trends than to set new ones in motion. The honor of initiating a major revolution in attitudes concerning rural labor, and eventually of giving wide currency to a vision that flashes forth for one anomalous moment from Tusser's poem on husbandry, belongs to Edmund Spenser. Except for Spenser, there are few other traces of georgic in the sixteenth century. After all, nearly all the best poets of that time were courtiers, whose interest in practical country matters was evident only when they laid aside their lutes to peruse the bailiff's accounts, negotiate a marriage settlement, or take a neighbor to court. The poetic milieu at the century's end is summed up with considerable justice by *Englands Helicon* (1600), a collection that consists almost entirely of aristocratic pastoral, written either by courtiers or by their admirers. In "*Coridon to his Phillis*," Sir Edward Dyer gives us a perfect emblem of the outcome, so far, of the unequal contest between the georgic

---

[33] Rpt. *Five Hundred Pointes of Good Husbandrie (1580)*, ed. W. Payne and Sidney J. Herrtage (London: Trübner, 1878), pp. 15-16.

and the pastoral modes. Corydon, whose metaphors suggest that he is a plowman rather than the usual shepherd, has been sufficiently unwise or unlucky to have fallen in love with a nymph-goddess-shepherdess, thus aggravating the usual Petrarchan predicament by the further social disparity that poetry and custom assign to their respective ways of life:

> Her beautie, Natures pride, and Sheepheards praise,
> Her eye, the heavenly Planet of my life. . . .
> > My bud is blasted, withred is my leafe:
> > And all my corne is rotted in the sheafe. . . .
> Leave *Coridon* to plough the barren field,
> Thy buds of hope are blasted with disgrace:
> For *Phillis* lookes no harty love doo yeeld,
> Nor can she love, for all her lovely face.[34]

A moralist might notice in this situation an instructive contrast between pastoral sterility and georgic fruitfulness, which is at least potentially favorable to georgic; indeed, Bishop King was to write a georgic love poem to that effect some thirty years later. But in 1600, clearly it is georgic that lies blasted and defeated by the irresistible radiance, the sun-like power, of pastoral. If the lover presents himself in a guardedly georgic guise, it is only in order to emphasize the depths of his abasement.

[34] *Englands Helicon* (1600; facs. Menston, Yorkshire: Scolar Press, 1973), sig. L2.

TWO

Poet of Work: Spenser and the Courtly Ideal

AT THE MIDPOINT of the *Georgics* Virgil appropriately presents himself as a plowman-poet, laboring in the fields:

> Sed nos immensum spatiis confecimus aequor,
> et iam tempus equum fumantia solvere colla.
>
> (2.541-42)[1]

"But in our course we have crossed an immense plain, and now it is time to unyoke the steaming necks of our horses." Possibly Chaucer, a poet with a medieval sympathy for agricultural labor, echoes Virgil in "The Knight's Tale": "I have, God woot, a large feeld to ere, / And wayke been the oxen in my plough" (1.886-87).[2] Certainly Drayton alludes consciously to the *Georgics* at the close of the first song of *Poly-Olbion* (1612): "Heere I'le unyoke awhile, and turne my steeds to meat: / The land growes large and wide: my Teame begins to sweat."[3] A few brief passages in *Poly-Olbion* might be called georgic, on account of their subject matter, yet in each case Drayton subordinates any hint of labor to an essentially pastoral vision, a vision that looks on sheep, cattle, or grainfields simply as parts of the natural landscape. The maps printed with the poem are indicative: where the geographers of a later age would show the typical products of the

---

[1] *Virgil*, ed. H. Rushton Fairclough, Loeb Classical Library, 2 vols. (Cambridge, Mass.: Harvard Univ. Press, 1953); translations are mine.

[2] *The Works of Geoffrey Chaucer*, ed. F. N. Robinson, 2d edn. (Boston: Houghton Mifflin, 1957), p. 26.

[3] Michael Drayton, *Poly-Olbion*, ed. J. William Hebel, in *The Works of Michael Drayton*, 4 (1933; Oxford: Shakespeare Head, 1961), 15.

various regions—grain, dairy products, meat, lumber—the plates in *Poly-Olbion* show nymphs and shepherds, who are the personifications of rivers, mountains, and towns. The ingrained English tendency to pastoralize—we might almost say pasteurize—what would naturally be georgic is typified by Drayton's horses, which are only beginning to sweat, whereas Virgil's are steaming from their exertions. Thus Drayton echoes Virgil's metaphor for the hard labors of the poet, but he evades its essential spirit.

Sixteen years earlier, however, Spenser's poetry had already begun to combat the prevailing English prejudices against farming and against manual labor. In the second installment of *The Faerie Queene*, published in 1596, Spenser supplements the image of the poet as a mariner seeking the port, which he had used throughout the first three books, by Virgil's georgic image of the poet as a plowman. In Spenser's hands, the metaphor becomes not just a perfunctory echo, as it is in *Poly-Olbion*, but an essential constituent of the poet's self-image within *The Faerie Queene*, comparable to Milton's image of himself as the blind bard. The motif of the poet-plowman first appears in Book 4, at the end of Canto 5:

> But here my wearie teeme nigh over spent
> Shall breath it selfe awhile, after so long a went.[4]

The image reappears in Book 5, at the end of Canto 3:

> And turne we here to this faire furrowes end
> Our wearie yokes, to gather fresher sprights.

Spenser begins with what appears to be simply another conventional use of Virgil's metaphor, conventionally employed at the end of a narrative unit. Repetition with slight variation of the image of the poet as plowman not only marks another turning point in the narrative, however, but also begins to

---

[4] *The Works of Edmund Spenser, A Variorum Edition*, ed. Edwin Greenlaw, C. G. Osgood, F. M. Padelford, and Ray Heffner, 11 vols. (Baltimore: Johns Hopkins Press, 1932-49). See also 3.12.47 in *FQ* (1590).

reflect the character of the narrator. Thus Spenser subtly prepares the reader for a third, much fuller statement of his theme in Book 6, at the beginning of Canto 9:

> Now turne againe my teme thou jolly swayne,
>   Backe to the furrow which I lately left;
>   I lately left a furrow, one or twayne
>   Unplough'd, the which my coulter hath not cleft:
>   Yet seem'd the soyle both fayre and frutefull eft,
>   As I it past, that were too great a shame,
>   That so rich frute should be from us bereft;
>   Besides the great dishonour and defame,
> Which should befall to *Calidores* immortall name.

This greatly expanded version of the metaphor thoroughly establishes the poet's self-image as a plowman. And it does more. The tone of this passage, the reader will have noticed, is different from those quoted earlier. Spenser presents us not with a plowman tired by his labors and longing for rest, but with a "jolly swayne" who is cheerfully going about the systematic accomplishment of his work, and who is not wearily looking backward on the difficulty of the task, but rather is looking forward toward the future and the rich fruits that his labors will produce.

Even more remarkable, to one familiar with the period, is Spenser's importation of chivalric language into a context of realistic georgic. Farming is a base activity, yet here is Spenser the plowman saying that it would be "too great a shame" not to finish these particular furrows, or to break these particular clods with his plow-blade, and moreover that if he were to turn away from his task now, that would bring "dishonour and defame" to his hero. Spenser's use of such language in this context reveals a radical revision of the period's typical attitude toward agricultural labor, a revision that *The Faerie Queene* as a whole confirms. The plowman's humble task is no longer to be considered shameful or unmentionable, as most of Spenser's literate contemporaries would have judged it. Instead, the plowman's work is useful, it is honorable, it is even capable of glorious fruits; while the neglect of such painstaking labor is what Spenser condemns as unknightly.

Spenser drives home his point in the following stanza, when he turns to his hero:

> Great travell hath the gentle *Calidore*
>   And toyle endured, sith I left him last
>   Sewing the *Blatant beast*, which I forebore
>   To finish then, for other present hast.
>   Full many pathes and perils he hath past,
>   Through hils, through dales, throgh forests,
>   and throgh plaines
>   In that same quest which fortune on him cast,
>   Which he atchieved to his owne great gaines,
> Reaping eternall glorie of his restlesse paines.
>   (6.9.2)

The husbandman's imperative is transferred from the poet to his hero, who travails, toils, endures, and takes unceasing pains in his seemingly endless quest, and as a result will reap a reward appropriate to a husbandman: a harvest of endless glory. Within the broad genre of romance epic to which *The Faerie Queene* belongs, Spenser counterbalances the theme of pastoral retreat in Book 6 less by heroic warfare than by georgic labor.

The rationale behind Spenser's incorporation of the georgic mode into *The Faerie Queene* has been discussed with penetrating insight by William A. Sessions, in his powerful essay "Spenser's Georgic."[5] Spenser thought that Britain, like Virgil's Rome, was at a crux in history, a moment when, if men

---

[5] *ELR*, 10 (1980), 202-208. As my citations partly indicate, Sessions has written a well-nigh definitive article on Spenser and georgic. Some repetition is inevitable, but Sessions puts greater emphasis on Spenser's sources than I do, whereas I have emphasized his relation to contemporaries and his influence on successors. After this book was completed, another article that supports my case without much overlapping it came to my attention: Andrew V. Ettin, "The Georgics in *The Faerie Queene*," *Spenser Studies*, ed. Patrick Cullen and Thomas P. Roche, Jr., 3 (1982), 57-71.

and women seized the opportunity, civil strife and sectarian violence might give way to a just and fruitful imperial unity, a new *pax Romana*, a third Troy. As Sessions argues, "Vergil discovered his essential strategy in the *Georgics*. The message of the Maecenas-commissioned *Georgics* was to reclaim the imperial homeland by a series of difficult labors in historical time: 'Labor omnia vicit / improbus et duris urgens in rebus egestas' " (p. 204). This georgic vision Virgil also incorporated into the *Aeneid*, with its heavy stress on labor and foundation. "[T]antae molis erat Romanam condere gentem"; "So great was the effort to found the Roman race" (*Aeneid* 1.33; see Sessions, pp. 205, 219). The georgic mode descends to *The Faerie Queene* largely through the mediating influence of the *Aeneid*. Whereas most Renaissance admirers of Virgil speak exclusively of Aeneas' military prowess, Spenser was, for his time, unusually receptive to the georgic strain in Virgil's epic.

A further result of this aspect of Virgilian influence is to give new meaning and purpose to Spenser's Ariostan device of multiple heroes. "What is new about the Vergilian task i[s] that, unlike the earlier Hercules, the new collective hero will utilize all aspects of labor, even the most trivial, for the single purpose of directing the forces of history. Thus labors in time for the purpose of transforming history could hardly be less than a profound plurality, given the communal nature of history and the meaning of Vergilian destiny that includes trivial landscapes" (Sessions, p. 206). The *Georgics*, and to a lesser extent the *Aeneid*, emphasizes painstaking attention to detail, constant labor, deeds that are trivial and take place in obscurity; yet the sum total of these deeds over time will be to transform the nation irresistibly. Such too is the spirit and the intention of *The Faerie Queene*. Spenserian heroes must learn to be patient and persistent; the reader often observes them sweating and straining as they toil. Often they are deprived of their horses and their weapons, and they are forced to trudge across the faerie landscape on foot. Thus Spenser's poem celebrates not swift military conquest, or what Sessions calls "golden" moments, but long labor, constant struggle, and hard, cooperative effort by many heroes working together at a task that is never finished.

As early as the first book of *The Faerie Queene*, Spenser begins making the point that decisive military victory in battle is not enough. When Redcross defeats Sans Joy at the House of Pride, he merely entangles himself further in the deceptive snares of Lucifera. Constancy and persistence in his quest, together with the ability to discriminate between truth and seeming truth, are virtues more important than mere strength of arm, and he betrays those standards because of a misplaced confidence in his military abilities. Even after his victory over the dragon and his betrothal to Una, Redcross cannot rest; he must return to the "endlesse worke" in company with his fellow knights. Therefore it is fitting that, though his blood is royal, Redcross should have been brought up as a husbandman:

> Thence she thee brought into this Faerie lond,
>> And in an heaped furrow did thee hyde,
>> Where thee a Ploughman all unweeting fond,
>> As he his toylesome teme that way did guyde,
>> And brought thee up in ploughmans state to byde,
>> Whereof *Georgos* he thee gave to name;
>> Till prickt with courage, and thy forces pryde,
>> To Faery court thou cam'st to seeke for fame,
> And prove thy puissant armes, as seemes thee best became.
>
> (1.10.66)

Thus Spenser reveals that the premier knight of England, the patron of a chivalric society at the court of Elizabeth, derives his honorable name from the Greek word for husbandman. It is a notable piece of mythic propaganda, to which, it may be, Spenser resorts because he lacks Virgil's opportunity of appealing to a native tradition of work as exemplified by Cincinnatus or the Sabine farmers, who would lend an appropriate nobility to husbandry and to manual labor (see *Georgics* 2.532-40). The implication of the myth for Spenser's readers, and especially for courtiers, is that, while it is approriate that England's leaders should have good blood, they might best develop their inward virtues if they were to serve at least a spiritual apprenticeship under those who are acquainted with hard work.

In Book 2, Spenser emphasizes the importance of labor in the first words spoken by Belphoebe:

> Who so in pompe of proud estate (quoth she)
>   Does swim, and bathes himselfe in courtly blis,
>   Does waste his dayes in darke obscuritee,
>   And in oblivion ever buried is:
>   Where ease abóunds, yt's eath to doe amis;
>   But who his limbs with labours, and his mind
>   Behaves with cares, cannot so easie mis.
>   Abroad in armes, at home in studious kind
> Who seekes with painfull toile, shall honor soonest find.
>
> (2.3.40)

Since it is a prime concern of any courtier to be seen, and the only audience worthy of seeing him is at court, it follows that exile from the court is equivalent to oblivion. Castiglione's Federico Fregoso voices an attitude that most courtiers would have shared:

> [W]henever the Courtier chances to be engaged in a skirmish or an action or a battle in the field, or the like, he should discreetly withdraw from the crowd, and do the outstanding and daring things that he has to do in as small a company as possible and in the sight of all the noblest and most respected men in the army, and especially in the presence of and, if possible, before the very eyes of his king or the prince he is serving. . . . [H]e will strive to be as elegant and handsome in the exercise of arms as he is adroit, and to feed his spectators' eyes with all those things that he thinks may give him added grace; and he will take care to have a horse gaily caparisoned, to wear a becoming attire, to have appropriate mottoes

and ingenious devices that will attract the eyes of the spectators even as the loadstone attracts iron.[6]

Therefore, when Belphoebe argues that he who spends all his time at court "Does waste his dayes in darke obscuritee" and will be condemned to oblivion, Spenser is deliberately reversing common opinion among courtiers. For a gentleman to shut himself up in his study, even to pursue arms abroad at too great a distance from the royal eye, are not the usual roads to preferment, as Spenser surely knows.

Belphoebe continues her description of the right path to honor:

> In woods, in waves, in warres she wonts to dwell,
> And will be found with perill and with paine;
> Ne can the man, that moulds in idle cell,
> Unto her happie mansion attaine:
> Before her gate high God did Sweat ordaine,
> And wakefull watches ever to abide:
> But easie is the way, and passage plaine
> To pleasures pallace; it may soone be spide,
> And day and night her dores to all stand open wide.
>
> (2.3.41)

As Sessions suggests (pp. 224, 229), Spenser is here engaging in a reinterpretation of Genesis 3:19 as well as echoing Hesiod's *Works and Days* (287-91). God's injunction to Adam to go forth and earn his bread in the sweat of his face, which was traditionally taken to be a curse resulting from the fall, may instead be taken as an invitation, an opportunity to resist the consequences of the fall. Indeed, those noble souls who thirst for honor, glory, and renown must seek them by means of labor and sweat.

Spenser's fundamental revision of aristocratic ideals, away

---

[6] Baldesar Castiglione, *The Book of the Courtier* (2.8), trans. Charles S. Singleton (New York: Doubleday, 1959), pp. 99-100. See also Wayne Rebhorne, *Courtly Performances* (Detroit: Wayne State Univ. Press, 1978), esp. pp. 23-51.

from preoccupation with leisure, grace, and *sprezzatura* and toward what a later generation, whether rightly or wrongly, would think of as the middle-class virtues of effort, care, and labor, finds its fullest expression in the last completed book of *The Faerie Queene*. There are two obvious reasons for the concentration of georgic spirit in Book 6: first, because, as the biographical evidence and the poem itself suggest, Spenser was growing progressively disillusioned with the values represented by the Elizabethan court and society—as were many other thoughtful people in the Queen's last years; and second, because Calidore's quest exemplifies courtesy, precisely the virtue that Spenser is seeking to revise. Of course Spenser's critics have long been familiar with both of these matters, but (except for Sessions) they have been handicapped by the difficulty of accounting for Spenser's revisionism purely in terms of pastoral. For it is well known that Spenser's attitude toward pastoral in Book 6 is equivocal; not only, I would suggest, because pastoral may represent a wrongful postponement of the quest for the Blatant Beast (I doubt that it does), but because it is far too closely associated with the conventionally aristocratic to offer, in itself, a comfortable long-term alternative to courtly corruption. Pastorella's foster father Meliboe, although he seems to be a genuine shepherd, tells Calidore that he is actually a retired courtier (literally, a court gardener), and he voices the conventional aristocratic platitudes about escaping from wealth and ambition by retiring to the countryside. He proves wholly defenseless against the brigands, who make short work of him.

In the proem to Book 6, Spenser introduces his fundamental image for the knight of courtesy:

> Revele to me the sacred noursery
>   Of vertue, which with you doth there remaine,
>   Where it in silver bowre does hidden ly
>   From view of men, and wicked worlds disdaine.
>   Since it at first was by the Gods with paine
>   Planted in earth, being deriv'd at furst

From heavenly seedes of bounty soveraine,
And by them long with carefull labour nurst,
Till it to ripenesse grew, and forth to honour burst.

Amongst them all growes not a fayrer flowre,
Then is the bloosme of comely courtesie,
Which though it on a lowly stalke doe bowre,
Yet brancheth forth in brave nobilitie,
And spreds it selfe through all civilitie.
(6.Proem.3-4)

Spenser employs some familiar elements of pastoral in this allegory; in particular, his emphasis on secrecy and enclosure help to suggest that courtesy is born in a paradise meant to recall the garden of Eden, and that it has affiliations with the traditional enclosed garden of divine love and with what Milton will call the "paradise within."[7] Planted by the gods, courtesy may be said to have its roots in the Golden Age. Yet Spenser's gods also have planted courtesy in the earth "with paine" and have nursed it "long with carefull labour." Although its flower is hidden and shielded from the world, when it is ripe it will burst forth to honor. Spenser stresses the georgic cultivation of his garden as much as he admires its pastoral beauty.

Finally, when the lowly flower has branched forth and spread itself abroad, it will do so "through all civilitie." This emphasis on civility is as much as to say that courtesy is not just a private virtue, but that it is the very basis of the social

---

[7] For interpretations of Book 6 in pastoral terms, see esp. Kathleen Williams, *Spenser's* Faerie Queene: *The World of Glass* (London: Routledge & Kegan Paul, 1966), pp. 189-223; Humphrey Tonkin, *Spenser's Courteous Pastoral* (Oxford: Clarendon Press, 1972); Isabel G. MacCaffrey, *Spenser's Allegory* (Princeton: Princeton Univ. Press, 1976), pp. 343-422. On the enclosed garden, see Stanley Stewart, *The Enclosed Garden* (Madison: Univ. of Wisconsin Press, 1966); A. Bartlett Giamatti, *The Earthly Paradise and the Renaissance Epic* (Princeton: Princeton Univ. Press, 1966); Maud Bodkin, *Archetypal Patterns in Poetry* (1934; London: Oxford Univ. Press, 1965), pp. 90-152; James Nohrnberg, *The Analogy of* The Faerie Queene (Princeton: Princeton Univ. Press, 1976), pp. 655-66.

order. Starkey's *England* (1538) speaks of bringing "the hole
cuntrey to quyetnes and cyvylyte."[8] Sir Thomas Browne ad-
mires ants and bees because "the civilitie of these little Citi-
zens, more neatly set[s] forth the wisedome of their Maker."
These social insects are not just polite to one another but live
together in harmonious cooperation as ideal citizens. Like-
wise, in *The Reason of Church-government* (1641), Milton
writes that poetry has the power "to inbreed and cherish in
a great people the seeds of vertu, and publick civility."[9] Don-
ald Cheney comments that most of Book 6 "portray[s] Cour-
tesy as the principal motive in man's collective efforts toward
civilization," and Humphrey Tonkin that the book "deals
with social issues, with the life of the courtier and the stand-
ards of the court, [which] makes the sixth book itself a mirror
of Elizabethan society."[10] Courtesy cannot persist in a retreat
either to the pastoral life or to the paradise within; it must
eventually manifest itself in society and public life. It can be
bred and nurtured in pastoral gardens, but it cannot remain
there.

As Calidore sets forth on his quest, he encounters Artegal,
who is returning victorious from his:

> Now happy man (sayd then Sir *Calidore*)
> Which have so goodly, as ye can devize,
> Atchiev'd so hard a quest, as few before;
> That shall you most renowmed make for evermore.

> But where ye ended have, now I begin
> To tread an endlesse trace, withouten guyde,
> Or good direction, how to enter in,
> Or how to issue forth in waies untryde,
> In perils strange, in labours long and wide.
> (6.1.5-6)

[8] O.E.D., s.v. "civility," I.6.

[9] *Religio Medici*, 1.15 (1643; Menston, Yorkshire: Scolar Press, 1970), p.
31; *The Works of John Milton*, ed. Frank A. Patterson et al., 18 vols. (New
York: Columbia Univ. Press, 1931-40), 3:238.

[10] Cheney, *Spenser's Image of Nature* (New Haven: Yale Univ. Press, 1966),
p. 177; Tonkin, *Spenser's Courteous Pastoral*, p. 11.

Once more Spenser speaks of the quest in terms of endless labor. We think of Aeneas, who attempts again and again to refound the city of Troy, only to learn that he must continue on his unknown journey, "dum per mare magnum / Italiam sequimur fugientem et volvimur undis" (*Aeneid* 5.628-29), "while we pursue receding Italy over the great sea, and toss on the waves." Virgil's farmer too suffers under the burden of endless work:

> sic omnia fatis
> in peius ruere ac retro sublapsa referri,
> non aliter, quam qui adverso vix flumine lembum
> remigiis subigit, si bracchia forte remisit,
> atque illum in praeceps prono rapit alveus amni.
>
> (1.199-203)

"Thus all things are fated to rush toward the worst, and are borne backward to glide away; they are no different from one who can barely row his small boat upstream; if for a moment he rests his arms, the boat sweeps him away headlong down the swift current." Yet neither Virgil nor Spenser despairs. Although success in this world is unlikely to remain uncompromised, and any particular hero may not live to see his goals achieved, nevertheless those goals can be accomplished over the long run, if many heroes are willing to continue working toward them.

Virgil's image of the husbandman as a rower against the stream follows his observation that georgic labor must be continuous:

> vidi lecta diu et multo spectata labore
> degenerare tamen, ni vis humana quotannis
> maxima quaeque manu legeret.
>
> (1.197-99)

"I have seen seeds, though examined carefully with great labor, yet degenerate, unless human effort yearly picks out the largest ones by hand." The farmer must unremittingly plow, lop, prune, cull, or he will never bring about a successful

harvest. So too in Spenser's faerieland. In the encounter be-
tween Calidore and Artegal, Spenser counterbalances contin-
uing effort with success; yet Artegal too was subjected to the
difficulties of the georgic imperative:

> Though vertue then were held in highest price,
>> In those old times, of which I doe intreat,
>> Yet then likewise the wicked seede of vice
>> Began to spring which shortly grew full great,
>> And with their boughes the gentle plants did beat.
>> But evermore some of the vertuous race
>> Rose up, inspired with heroicke heat,
>> That cropt the branches of the sient base,
> And with strong hand their fruitfull rancknes did deface.
>
> . . . .
>
> And such was he, of whom I have to tell,
>> The Champion of true Justice *Artegall*.
>>> (5.1.1-3)

If a leader is determined to reform and cultivate a people, and
eventually to bring them to full ripeness, then the laws of
farming as well as those of war demand a certain ruthlessness.
Virgil's vinegrower is tender with his young plants, but at the
appropriate time he must adapt another manner:

> inde ubi iam validis amplexae stirpibus ulmos
> exierint, tum stringe comas, tum bracchia tonde
> (ante reformidant ferrum), tum denique dura
> exerce imperia et ramos compesce fluentis.
>> (2.367-70)

"When they have embraced the elms with their strong shoots,
then strip off their locks, then cut off their arms (before that,
they fear iron), then at last exercise a hard dominion, and
curb their flowing branches." Neither Virgil nor Spenser
shrinks from the unavoidable side effects that result from the
achievement of the vision: the farmer must often exert an iron
ruthlessness, and Artegal requires the flail of Talus.

The lesson of labor is hard for an aristocrat. He can understand fighting, but all his instincts shrink from the base contagion inherent in manual work. Therefore, one must admire the ingenuity with which Spenser invents various situations that force his noble heroes to work, whether they like it or not, until at length they have learned their lessons. A favorite device, of course, is to deprive them of their horses, which are the very symbols of knighthood. In a similiar spirit, Spenser obliges Calepine, who has put his sword aside, to kill a bear by stuffing a rock down its throat (6.4.21) and Calidore to kill a tiger, which is threatening to devour Pastorella, by stunning it with his shepherd's crook (6.10.36).

After a series of complicated rescues, Calidore finds himself alone in the woods with Priscilla and her wounded lover Aladine. They must get Aladine to his father's castle quickly, or he may die. But first Calidore and Priscilla must overcome any reluctance they may feel about taking on what amounts to rather an awkward chore:

> Yet could she not devise by any wit,
>> How thence she might convay him to some place.
>> For him to trouble she it thought unfit,
>> That was a straunger to her wretched case;
>> And him to beare, she thought it thing too base.
>> Which when as he perceiv'd, he thus bespake;
>> Faire Lady let it not you seeme disgrace,
>> To beare this burden on your dainty backe;
> My selfe will beare a part, coportion of your packe.
>
> So off he did his shield . . .
>> And twixt them both with parted paines did beare.
>> (6.2.47-48)

Cooperation, it will be noticed, allows them to carry Aladine with greater dignity: on the traditional shield. Christian pity, sympathy for a wounded man, and love overcome any reluctance Priscilla may still feel. As Calidore has told Briana earlier, "No greater shame to man then inhumanitie" (6.1.26).

Thus Spenser has arranged his action to demonstrate that cooperative manual labor need not be disgraceful.

Indeed it may be that Spenser began even earlier to reform his readers' understanding of what it means to be courteously heroic. No poetic technique contributes more immediately to a hero's stature than the epic similes a poet employs as he describes his hero going into combat. Yet the first two epic similes of Book 6 allude to an energy that is more georgic than epic:

> Like as a water streame, whose swelling sourse
> > Shall drive a Mill . . .
> Such was the fury of Sir *Calidore*
> > (6.1.21)

> But he them all from him full lightly swept,
> As doth a Steare, in heat of sommers day,
> With his long taile the bryzes brush away.
> > (6.1.24)

On the first of these similes, an allusion to the uncontrolled onslaught of Pyrrhus against the Trojan citadel, which Virgil represents as a stream overflowing its banks and sweeping away the herds and folds (*Aeneid* 2.496-99), Spenser superimposes a water mill, which civilizes the hero's energy and channels it into useful work. There are, of course, precedents for the use of epic similes of this kind in Homer; but they are scarce in Renaissance epic except where Homer is being directly imitated or where the poet has a satirical purpose, which is not the case here. Similarly georgic in spirit is the full epic simile that Spenser employs at the height of Calidore's battle against the Brigants, who have captured Pastorella:

How many flyes in whottest sommers day
> Do seize upon some beast, whose flesh is bare,
> That all the place with swarmes do overlay,
> And with their litle stings right felly fare;
> So many theeves about him swarming are,
> All which do him assayle on every side,

And sore oppresse, ne any him doth spare:
But he doth with his raging brond divide
Their thickest troups, and round about him scattreth wide.
(6.11.48)

Although the chief effect of this image is to diminish the Brigants, it also tends to turn Calidore's onslaught into an irksome barnyard episode.

Not long after Calidore has helped Priscilla to bear home her burden, Sir Calepine sets his beloved Serena, whom the Blatant Beast has mauled in passing, on his own horse, and walks alongside supporting her. Their appearance is emblematic of Spenserian courtesy, of chivalry willing to unhorse itself in order to bear its burdens. When Calepine comes to a river, he is unable to ford it on foot while still supporting Serena on his horse. At that moment a knight, later identified as Sir Turpine, appears at the ford with his lady. When Calepine asks Turpine, reasonably enough, for help, Turpine's response is a precise exemplar of the courtly attitude toward labor that, as we have seen, was so prevalent among the English:

To whom that other did this taunt returne.
Perdy thou peasant Knight, mightst rightly reed
Me then to be full base and evill borne,
If I would beare behinde a burden of such scorne.

But as thou hast thy steed forlorne with shame,
So fare on foote till thou another gayne,
And let thy Lady likewise doe the same,
Or beare her on thy backe with pleasing payne,
And prove thy manhood on the billowes vayne.
(6.3.31-32)

The enraged Calepine plunges into the river on foot and somehow manages to convey Serena safely across. When he reaches the far bank Turpine declines his challenge, perhaps because he is a coward, Spenser says, or perhaps because he scorns "the challenge of so base a thrall" (6.3.36)—that is, of a man on foot who is using his warhorse as a beast of burden.

This encounter, between the shell of courtesy and what Spenser conceived to be its true substance, is continued the following day. As Calepine trudges along beside Serena's horse after a night in the bushes, he is attacked by Turpine on horseback and forced to make a further spectacle of himself, skipping around Serena's horse (his only shelter from his mounted attacker) "like a wilde goate," and taking ignominious refuge "Behinde his Ladies backe" (6.3.49), until at length Turpine spears him through the shoulder and lays him out on the ground. Here, as earlier, Calepine's difficulties result not from cowardice but from courtesy. Because he has voluntarily unhorsed himself and has burdened himself with the wounded Serena, he has laid himself open to Turpine's attack. Turpine, in whom courtesy is pure appearance, so that he scorns to dismount or to take up a burden, is repeatedly able to discommode Calepine and to make him look like a fool in conventional courtly eyes (as well as those of some modern critics). But Providence, which allows this outward disgracing, analogous to the disgracing of the angels in Milton's war in heaven, sends the Salvage Man to rescue Calepine at the critical moment. This rescuer drives Turpine off and leads Calepine and Serena to his home deep in the woods.

As critics note, the Salvage Man represents a form of pastoral innocence underneath a fierce appearance. He is very similar to those noble savages whom Montaigne imagines in his essay "Of Cannibals." His connection with the Golden Age, and therefore his disconnection from any of the bonds, the arts, and the inventions of civilization, is revealed immediately when Spenser describes his crude home:

> But the bare ground, with hoarie mosse bestrowed,
> Must be their bed, their pillow was unsowed,
> And the frutes of the forrest was their feast:
> For their bad Stuard neither plough'd nor sowed,
> Ne fed on flesh, ne ever of wyld beast
> Did taste the bloud, obaying natures first beheast.
>
> (6.4.14)

This sort of life, which Virgil (and Montaigne quoting him) describes as having once been universal and radically communal (*Georgics* 1.125-28), has in the present age dwindled to a single, anachronistic savage. He has his virtues; nevertheless, Spenser calls him a "bad Stuard," precisely because he neither plows nor sows. Those, after all, are the primary arts of civilization. The Golden Age has gone from this world, and therefore the Salvage Man's state is reduced to something not unlike the plight of Virgil's bad farmer, who, having failed to obey the law of work, is parodically obliged to hunt for acorns, the prototypical golden-age food, in the woods:

> quod nisi et adsiduis herbam insectabere rastris
> et sonitu terrebis aves et ruris opaci
> falce premes umbram votisque vocaveris imbrem,
> heu magnum alterius frustra spectabis acervum
> concussaque famem in silvis solabere quercu.
>
> (1.155-59)

"So, unless you attack the weeds with constant hoeing, and scare off the birds with noise, and cut back the shade from the darkening fields with your pruning knife, and pray for rain, alas! you will gaze in vain on your neighbor's great harvest, and appease your hunger by shaking an oak in the forest."

The Salvage Man, who would have been commonplace in an earlier age, is clearly exceptional in a fallen world. Much more typical is the Salvage Nation, which Serena has the misfortune to encounter after her separation from Calepine:

> In these wylde deserts, where she now abode,
>> There dwelt a salvage nation, which did live
>> Of stealth and spoile, and making nightly rode
>> Into their neighbors borders; ne did give
>> Them selves to any trade, as for to drive
>> The painefull plough, or cattell for to breed,
>> Or by adventrous marchandize to thrive;

> But on the labours of poore men to feed,
> And serve their owne necessities with others need.
>
> (6.8.35)

These savages follow no trades and do no work, but live off the "labour" of others. The very first thing that Spenser says about them is that they refuse "to drive / The painefull plough"; from that refusal the rest of their way of life logically follows: their land is an unproductive desert, they steal unjustly from the labors of the poor, and they treat strangers inhospitably. Appropriately, therefore, Spenser allegorizes their fault of living by devouring the substance of others, of gaining their bread by the sweat of other men's brows, as cannibalism:

> Thereto they usde one most accursed order,
>   To eate the flesh of men, whom they mote fynde,
>   And straungers to devoure, which on their border
>   Were brought by errour, or by wreckfull wynde.
>
> (6.8.36)

Ease, the normal way of life in the prelapsarian order, becomes idleness in a world laboring under the curse; perversion "gainst course of kynde" (6.8.36) is the inevitable end result of a refusal to obey the georgic and biblical imperatives.

Spenser emphasizes the importance of this theme, the refusal to plow the earth, yet a third time. When he introduces the Brigants who capture Pastorella and destroy her village, once more the first thing that he stresses is their failure to follow the plow:

> It fortuned one day, when *Calidore*
>   Was hunting in the woods (as was his trade)
>   A lawlesse people, *Brigants* hight of yore,
>   That never usde to live by plough or spade,
>   But fed on spoile and booty, which they made
>   Upon their neighbours, which did nigh them border,
>   The dwelling of these shepheards did invade,

53

And spoyld their houses, and them selves did murder;
And drove away their flocks, with other much disorder.

(6.10.39)

Failure to live "by plough or spade" results once more in
murder, for people must feed on something, and these Brigants
feed on "spoile and booty" taken from their neighbors. In
contradistinction, Calidore is absent on proper and lawful
business, "hunting in the woods (as was his trade)." It cer-
tainly appears that Spenser intends to exonerate him from an
indirect responsibility for the catastrophe.

While Spenser makes a strong negative case against the sin
of refusing to live by the plow, he devotes less attention to
the positive case, which he might have made by showing his
readers a working estate. We may guess that the rulers of his
evil castles live by depredations on their neighbors and on
passing strangers—if, like Busirane or Lucifera, they are not
too far along the allegorical axis for such speculations even
to arise. In Book 6, Sir Bruin's tenure of his castle involves at
least some reference to economic realities. Bruin has gained
his estates by conquest from the giant Cormoraunt, evidently
another personification of devouring greed, and, as his wife
tells Calepine, he has succeeded in bringing the affairs of the
estate into some order:

> So is my Lord now seiz'd of all the land,
> As in his fee, with peaceable estate,
> And quietly doth hold it in his hand.
>
> (6.4.30)

But, "for want of heires it to defend," the estate will revert to
Cormoraunt when Bruin dies. Thus he will lose both his con-
quest, which gained him the estate, and all his labors, which
keep it:

> he does thinke
> That all this land unto his foe shall fall,
> For which he long in vaine did sweat and swinke.
>
> (6.4.32)

Fortunately, Calepine happens to have a spare baby with him, which he has just rescued from the bear. Probably the need for Bruin to "sweat and swinke" on his estate is about as much economic reality as one may expect in a fairy tale of this order; it would be too much to expect Spenser to show us Bruin's laborers working the fields.

But Spenser offers his reader at least one positive alternative to the ways of the Salvages and the Brigants: the example of his shepherds, and also of Calidore while he is living among them. While the shepherds, naturally, are living a pastoral existence, theirs is a pastoralism tempered by the exigencies of the world. Although they hold singing contests, enjoy country sports, and offer to strangers a haven of ease from the anxieties of worldly ambition, still they do not disdain honest work. For them even courtship is laborious, as the swain Corydon reveals when he fears that all his efforts to gain Pastorella have been in vain now that Calidore has intervened: "That this of all his labour and long paine / Should reap the harvest, ere it ripened were" (6.9.38). Calidore will not gain Pastorella without long pains of his own. He has been drawn to the shepherd's life not only by the sight of Pastorella but also by a legitimate desire to rest for a while from his heavy labors in pursuit of the Blatant Beast. When he first appears among the shepherds, he is conspicuously sweating from the relentless chase (6.9.5-6). He is rewarded by his first sight of Pastorella only because, as an exemplar of true courtesy, he is "nothing nice" (6.9.7), and therefore he does not disdain the shepherds' proffer of a humble hospitality. Here, it appears, is a heaven-sent opportunity for him to recuperate his energies before he continues on his quest. (If it is not heaven-sent, then why would Pastorella turn out to be an eligible lost princess, who might otherwise have made an unequal marriage with a common shepherd?)

Calidore puts his case to Pastorella's foster father. Since each individual must determine how "to fashion his owne lyfes estate," and he has grown tired and confused by the "stormes of fortune and tempestuous fate," the "seas of troubles and of toylesome paine" from which he has suffered so long, he asks permission to rest awhile among the shepherds (6.9.31). Having heard Meliboe's tale of retirement from the court, he acknowledges the temptation to rest in this pleasant refuge not just "awhyle" but permanently. Yet for the moment he seeks only the leisure to make a considered decision how best to shape his life. Certainly he suffers from no illusion that life with the shepherds will be merely idle. He gladly helps Pastorella herd and fold her sheep and keep watch against wolves, and he disdains no labor, however menial or seemingly foreign to his strength, rank, or blood:

> So being clad, unto the fields he went
>> With the faire *Pastorella* every day,
>> And kept her sheepe with diligent attent . . .
>> And otherwhiles for need, he did assay
>> In his strong hand their rugged teats to hold,
> And out of them to presse the milke: love so much could.
>
> (6.9.37)

Calidore's behavior does not conceal a blameworthy effeminacy, like that of Sidney's Pyrocles when he dresses himself up as an Amazon lady in order to pursue his love.[11] Rather, his deeds are comparable to his bearing up of the wounded Aladine and to Calepine's labors with Serena: they are shameful in the conventional aristocratic view, but they are honorable in a context of Christian charity, of communal obligation, and of courteous love. One hears the voice of the presiding poet in Spenser's last words: "love so much could."

Calidore has already shown himself prepared to labor in ways that convention would call shameful. Now he is apprenticed to Pastorella, a princess who has herself been apprenticed to the shepherds in order to learn lessons and at-

---

[11] See Mark Rose, "Sidney's Womanish Man," *RES*, 15 (1964), 353-63. Unlike Redcross, Calidore doffs an ordinary suit of armor, not St. Paul's armor of salvation; his change of garb is perfectly appropriate to his temporary change of vocation; it is analogous to Calepine's dismounting from his horse.

titudes she could not have been taught in her proud grandfather's castle. Just as Redcross is found, symbolically, in a furrow, Pastorella is found by her foster father Meliboe, as he grazes his sheep, lying abandoned "In th' open fields" (6.9.14), where her mother's handmaid has carefully placed her.[12] Thus the tragic quarrels within her family providentially become a blessing, as she is raised in a community that will redirect her life. By the time Calidore has arrived on the scene, Pastorella has learned the shepherds' customs and attitudes so well that she herself has come to epitomize their ways and to animate them in their tasks:

> Then all the rest about her rose likewise,
> And each his sundrie sheepe with severall care
> Gathered together, and them homeward bare:
> Whylest everie one with helping hands did strive
> Amongst themselves, and did their labours share.
>
> (6.9.15)

Under the spell of Pastorella's beauty, Calidore joins this community of laborers.

As C. S. Lewis has noted, Shakespeare and Spenser did much to transform English literary attitudes toward love, and in particular to transform courtly love into what we would now call romantic love leading to marriage.[13] Both poets argue, by the disposition of action, theme, and character, that legitimate love leading to marriage must serve out an apprenticeship, must prove itself over a period of time, and must act and labor in the world.[14] Although Calidore conventionally falls in love at first sight, he shows the quality of his love by his willingness to earn Pastorella's regard. It is for this reason, and not because he shrinks from his quest, that Calidore "continu'd there long time, / To winne the love of the faire *Pastorell*" (6.9.46).

---

[12] Twice more Spenser calls attention to the place where Pastorella is found, at 6.12.7 ("the emptie fields") and 6.12.16 ("in the open fields").

[13] *The Allegory of Love* (London: Oxford Univ. Press, 1936).

[14] See Barbara L. Parker, "Shakespeare's Theory of Love," diss., New York Univ. 1982, pp. 126, 233-35, 250-66.

He must win her love as Corydon had hoped to win it, by means of "labour and long paine," of a sort that one must undertake if he wishes to gain a "harvest" (6.9.38). So Calidore labors day by day,

> and in her mynde the seeds
> Of perfect love did sow, that last forth brought
> The fruite of joy and blisse, though long time dearely bought.
> (6.9.45)

At the moment of Calidore's eventual success, just before the appearance of the Brigants, Spenser repeats this georgic image:

> So well he woo'd her, and so well he wrought her,
> With humble service, and with daily sute . . .
> That of his love he reapt the timely frute.
> (6.10.38)

The georgic imagery is especially fitting, because it not only looks back on Calidore's long and painful labors, which have achieved this harvest, but also looks forward toward marriage and childbirth, since for Spenser the consummation of legitimate love necessarily entails fruition.

When the Brigants, who represent the savage desire to tear down and pillage the fruits of the georgic community, capture Pastorella, they carry her into a landscape where no harvest is possible:

> Their dwelling in a little Island was,
> Covered with shrubby woods, in which no way
> Appeard for people in nor out to pas,
> Nor any footing fynde for overgrowen gras.
> (6.10.41)

The shrubs and weeds that have overgrown productive pastures and fields are manifestations of a lack of cultivation and of true community among the Brigants, whose aversion to labor has uncivilized their tribe. At this point, Spenser finds another image for Pastorella, now in captivity to these anti-georgic forces, an image that contrasts vividly with the earlier one of ripe fruition:

> she nought did but lament
> Her wretched life, shut up in deadly shade,
> And waste her goodly beauty, which did fade
> Like to a flowre, that feeles no heate of sunne.
>
> (6.10.44)

Spenser derives this contrast from an antithesis of sun and shade, labor and idleness, which may be seen, with varying moral implications, in Virgil's admonition to prune back all excess growth that may shade the crops from the sun, in Marvell's invitation to abandon the heat and dust of the active life for cool retirement in his "Garden," and in Milton's insistence in *Areopagitica* that the true Christian must leave the cloistered shelter of youthful inexperience in order to try himself in the sun and dust of the world. The Brigants, who are less a community than "a sort of hungry dogs ymet / About some carcase by the common way" (6.11.17), burn the shepherds' cottages, drive off their sheep, and eventually murder most of the inhabitants. Then, in a battle that reduces the muzzling of the Blatant Beast to something of an anticlimax, Calidore destroys these destructive subhumans and rescues Pastorella. We may imagine that the two will marry, although, as is becoming habitual with him, Spenser leaves that particular strand for a later knotting that will never take place.

When, in Book 5, Spenser extols those vigorous heroes whose task it is to prune back and "deface" the tall growth of plants that have sprung from "wicked seed," before they can destroy the "gentle plants," he mentions two mythical heroes before he introduces Artegal. They are Bacchus and Hercules, figures who are appropriate to this task because one is a patron of agriculture and the other an accomplisher of great labors (5.1.1-3). Under his own name and that of his Roman equivalent Liber, Bacchus is a significant figure in the *Georgics* and the first of the great gods whom Virgil invokes

(1.7). Hercules reappears at the close of Spenser's Book 6, first in a comparison between the Blatant Beast and the Hydra:

> Or like the hell-borne *Hydra*, which they faine
> That great *Alcides* whilome overthrew,
> After that he had labourd long in vaine,
> To crop his thousand heads. . . .
> (6.12.32)

After this preparatory image, Spenser then compares Calidore to Hercules directly, in the last epic simile of the book, "Like as whylome that strong *Tirynthian* swaine" (6.12.35). Hercules is an odd exemplar with which to close the Book of Courtesy. As a fighter, he is no gentleman, since he dresses in hides and wields a club. John Harington, who with Spenser appears to have suffered from fools among the gentlemen of the court, notes that in his time one might find a "squint eyed *Zoilus*" in every corner, who "will not sticke to call *Hercules* himselfe a dastard, because forsooth he fought with a club and not at the rapyer and dagger."[15] We may be sure that Sir Turpine would have concurred with these gentlemen. But, as Spenser emphasizes, in his first simile especially, Hercules is appropriate to the kind of courtesy that is portrayed in *The Faerie Queene*, because he is unashamed of labor. His uncouth appearance will stop any reader from mistaking the outward shows of courtesy for its essence, which has been Spenser's point all along. Finally, Hercules, through his labors, is a notable reformer of society and destroyer of tyrants, which is the task of courtesy in its manifestation as public civility and good citizenship.

A recurrent theme of Book 6 is that proper conduct of the individual within society is similar to the role of the poet as maker. Spenser gives us two contrasting views about the nature of poetry within this book. The poet is a careful and

---

[15] Preface to Harington's trans. of *Orlando Furioso* (1591), in *Elizabethan Critical Essays*, ed. G. Gregory Smith, 2 vols. (1904; London: Oxford Univ. Press, 1967), 2:194.

methodical worker, the plowman or the careworn mariner who is tossed on the "stormie surges" of the wide ocean (6.12.1). At the same time, he is like Colin Clout, who effortlessly pipes forth the music for the dance on Mount Acidale, where the Graces signify not only grace and beauty but also the give-and-take of commerce between heaven and earth.[16] Those two apparently contradictory aspects of poetic composition, difficulty and ease, art and grace, are evident in the opening stanza of the Proem:

> The waies, through which my weary steps I guyde,
>> In this delightfull land of Faery,
>> Are so exceeding spacious and wyde,
>> And sprinckled with such sweet variety,
>> Of all that pleasant is to eare or eye,
>> That I nigh ravisht with rare thoughts delight,
>> My tedious travell doe forget thereby;
>> And when I gin to feele decay of might,
> It strength to me supplies, and chears my dulled spright.

Of course, the paradox in which Spenser takes such delightful comfort is ancient; it represents the traditional view that poetry is both made with effort—beaten laboriously on the Muses' anvil, Jonson would say—and freely given through the grace of divine inspiration (see 6.Proem.2). The two aspects of poetic composition happen to correspond to two of the Virgilian modes, georgic and pastoral. Spenser embodies the effort of making largely in georgic imagery, while he sets Colin Clout's secret and exalted rhapsody in a locus that is quintessentially pastoral. Just as both inspiration and labor have been thought necessary to the production of great poetry, so both the pastoral and the georgic mode (though I have naturally stressed the latter) are necessary for Spenser to achieve the complex balance of grace and effort that enriches his Book of Courtesy. Pastoral may be said to represent the grace and

[16] On the Graces, see Edgar Wind, *Pagan Mysteries in the Renaissance,* enlarged edn. (New York: Barnes & Noble, 1968), pp. 26-52.

the beauty of life, epic the necessity to defend what is good
in life against the perpetual incursions of evil, and georgic the
need to earn one's daily bread in the sweat of his face. A full
life can afford to neglect none of these three.

In this fallen world, pastoral ease ordinarily is available to
the hero only as a temporary refuge, one that offers him a
well-earned but necessarily impermanent respite from his la-
bors. If pastoral enclosure is legitimate, and not merely the
pleasant-seeming captivity to temptation offered by such
places as the Bower of Bliss, then it will allow the hero to
recuperate and to gather his strength for further efforts in the
outer world. For this reason, pastoral *otium* cannot last. Cal-
idore's intrusion dissipates the vision of Mount Acidale (which
could not have persisted in any case, any more than a poem
can survive without submitting itself to readers); and the in-
vading Brigants destroy the defenseless shepherds' paradise.
Yet at the same time, as many readers have felt, the pastoral
of Book 6 in some respects represents a superior state. That
is true because, although pastoral is frail on earth, having
disappeared into the irretrievable past along with Eden and
the Golden Age, nonetheless it is emblematic of man's future
too: that is, it foreshadows heaven and eternity. Georgic cor-
responds to the six days' labor of the creation and to the long
trials of human history, within which we must work; pastoral
corresponds to the great sabbath day of rest, which will bring
all history to a close. Therefore, it is just that Colin's visionary
dance should have the same place in Calidore's progress, as
a reward for patient labor under tutelage, that Redcross's
vision of the Heavenly Jerusalem has in his; although it rep-
resents a kind of experience that cannot endure in this life, it
anticipates the end. That ontological significance casts an aura
of otherworldly glory on the ring of dancing maidens, who
move to the measure of Colin's inspired song; it likewise ac-
counts, although less directly, for the measure of cheer with
which the poet plowman goes about his endless task. As Spen-
ser says in his ship simile, the poet has in his possession an
accurate compass, so no matter how widely and wearily he

must travel, he is confident of coming home to the port at last.

Although Spenser provides his courtly reader of Book 6 with abundant indications of how he wants him to redirect his thinking, the conclusion indicates that he was not very sanguine that the court would accept (or even understand) his advice. At the end of Book 6, Calidore finally subdues the Blatant Beast, but, as Spenser's critics have often noted, he is unable to make a permanent conquest. His failure does not discredit his deeds nor deprive him of the endless glory that he has deservedly reaped by his long labors; rather it reflects the equivocal nature of this world, and in particular of courtly society as Spenser now views it. Each individual hero is obliged to work against the prevailing currents of history and the biases of society, like Virgil's rower; yet, although the world resists his efforts, others come to his aid, laboring toward the same ends, taking up the unfinished work and carrying it forward. After the Blatant Beast has escaped, a succession of knights joins in the quest:

> The good Sir *Pelleas* him tooke in hand,
> And after him Sir *Lamoracke* of yore,
> And all his brethren borne in Britaine land;
> Yet none of them could ever bring him into band.
>
> (6.12.39)

Malory, who provides Spenser with the immediate source for this episode, mentions only a single knight; the addition of a whole company of knights in pursuit of the Beast is apparently Spenser's own invention.[17] It is evident that a knight who challenges the Blatant Beast must hope to earn his glory in the quest itself, in the long travail, for he is unlikely to gain a single, swift, decisive victory. Golden moments are not enough. When Calidore slays the tiger, his act brings him to

---

[17] See C. G. Osgood in the *Spenser Variorum*: "Whomever Spenser may be following here other than his own fancy, it is not Malory. Sir Palamides alone there has the quest of the Beast; neither Pelleas nor Lamorack nor any other takes part in it" (6:271).

Pastorella's favorable attention, but only the long labors of courtship can gain her heart.

At the close of this last completed book, the Blatant Beast seems to emerge from the fiction, to turn and rend the poet himself:

Ne may this homely verse, of many meanest,
    Hope to escape his venemous despite,
    More then my former writs, all were they cleanest
    From blamefull blot, and free from all that wite,
    With which some wicked tongues did it backebite,
    And bring into a mighty Peres displeasure,
    That never so deserved to endite.
    Therfore do you my rimes keep better measure,
And seeke to please, that now is counted wisemens threasure.

Since *The Faerie Queene* not only is rooted in British history, but intends to influence the future course of that history, Spenser's critics and biographers have rightly devoted considerable energy to identifying the "mighty Pere," who is usually thought to be Burghley, the Lord Treasurer. The intense irony of the last two lines in no way resembles the kind of language that Spenser's contemporaries were accustomed to use when they wanted to get back into the good graces of a political or social superior.[18] Spenser is not suing for forgiveness; he is challenging the system by throwing his glove down before the one person, after the Queen, most responsible for determining the nation's future course and the behavior of its court. Far from showing himself anxious to please, Spenser insists on his own hard-won beliefs concerning the true nature of heroism and the poetry that celebrates it. As he turns from the story of Calidore to the generations of knights who succeed him, and then to himself as a poet in the same chivalric line, his parting challenge to his readers does not simply vent a personal grudge but arises precisely and naturally from his

[18] See Frank Whigham, "The Rhetoric of Elizabethan Suitors' Letters," *PMLA*, 96 (1981), 864-82.

redefinition of knightly or courtly heroism. That redefinition, exemplified in Book 6 by a courtier who is rarely at court, is expressed in an unpretentious style that, in contrast with the conventions of military epic, Spenser expects to strike his readers as "homely verse, of many meanest."

On some issues, as Spenser matured as a poet he departed further and further from the common aristocratic assumptions of his time. As Daniel Javitch argues, he "shows an increasing disaffection with courtly behavior in the work that follows the publication of the first three books of *The Faerie Queene* in 1590."[19] Earlier, in company with most of the poets of his age, Spenser had praised the court as the fountain of all virtues, public and private. But as the decade of the 1590s progressed, as the Queen grew older and the corruption at court became increasingly evident, and as the dreams and plots of the Protestant-imperial faction with which he was associated seemed to recede ever further from realization, Spenser, in "Colin Clouts Come Home Againe" and the latter part of *The Faerie Queene*, began to intimate that the malaise was not incidental to the court but endemic. The problem was not that some individuals were falling away from the ideal, but that the ideal itself was flawed. Therefore a new strain of anti-courtliness began to stiffen his poetry. The idea that the poet might turn to the courtier for an appropriate model of behavior began to be reversed; instead, the poet might instruct the errant courtier and, using the sugared medicines of fiction, inform him how he ought to conduct himself.[20]

By 1596, although Spenser remained a political conservative by the standards of later history, he had ceased to follow aristocratic opinions blindly. Unlike Wyatt and others of the

---

[19] *Poetry and Courtliness in Renaissance England* (Princeton: Princeton Univ. Press, 1978), p. 132.

[20] This is Javitch's central argument. Another important discussion of Spenser as a public poet—but with a view of Book 6 very different from mine—is Richard Helgerson's "The New Poet Presents Himself: Spenser and the Idea of a Literary Career,"*PMLA*, 93 (1978), 893-911, reprinted in *Self-Crowned Laureates* (Berkeley: Univ. of California Press, 1983).

earlier generation of court poets, Spenser did not merely re-
treat from the court into the exile of privacy. Instead, his
poetry suggests, he determined to "fashion" his "gentleman
or noble person" along lines of his own devising. Javitch ar-
gues that his chief source for an alternative to the courtly
world-view was Cicero, whose writings, in contradistinction
to the aristocratic rhetoric of play and outward show, offered
Spenser a rhetoric based on moral purpose and humanistic
discipline (pp. 18-49). Certainly Cicero was the great patron
of the humanists, and his influence on Spenser was consid-
erable. Yet, as Spenser's ideal of heroic behavior grew less
dependent on contemporary values manifested at the court of
Elizabeth, which consciously imitated the manners of Castig-
lione's idealized court of Urbino, there was another writer to
whom he was able to turn, another instructor of courtiers,
one who had been his model for many years: Virgil.

Even Spenser's earlier poetry is not notable for that inor-
dinate love of play, of role-playing, and of leisure, that char-
acterizes much Elizabethan aristocratic pastoral. If no one in
The Shepheardes Calender is actually hard at work, neither
does any of the shepherds have much leisure for the popular
pastoral pursuit of *otium*. Spenser gives Palinode, who rep-
resents the pernicious Roman Catholic viewpoint, a praise of
idleness ("Maye," 35-36, 63-66), but needless to say he only
allows these views expression so he may rebuke and refute
them through the persona of Piers, who is the namesake of
Piers Plowman. The eclogues are, as they say they are, pas-
toral; yet the balance struck in the woodcuts, most of which
show shepherds singing and conversing in the foreground,
while in the background husbandmen wield axes and hoes
and gather in the harvest, is consonant with Spenser's moral
tone. From the first, Spenser had the instincts of a poetic
revolutionary who hoped to change his society; time and hard-
ship simply taught him that his attempts to hold a friendly
dialogue with the shapers of history, his readers, must give
place to a longer and much harder struggle.

Mother Hubberds Tale (1591) reflects Spenser's familiarity with a rural reformist tradition that can be traced back into the Middle Ages through such poets as Skelton and Langland (see ch. 5 below). In this tradition, virtue is associated with productive labor, and vice with economic parasitism. The Fox explains the relation between these two classes of men to the Ape: "For they doo swinke and sweate to feed the other, / Who live like Lords of that which they doo gather" (163-64). In the encounter between the Ape and the Husbandman, Spenser delineates the classic confrontation between labor and leisure. Invited to become a farm worker, "To plough, to plant, to reap, to rake, to sowe, / To hedge, to ditch, to thrash, to thetch, to mowe" (263-64), the Ape declines, preferring the easier trade of shepherd (and, with the Fox's help, devouring the flock with which he is entrusted). The sharpness of this social criticism is somewhat blunted, however, since the Ape is not a real gentleman, courtier, or soldier, but only a pretended one, who is unmasked and put back into his proper place. The criticism in Book 6 of *The Faerie Queene* is considerably more restrained and subtle, but necessarily so, since it is directed at actual courtiers and not mere social-climbing vagabonds or outsiders.

As we might expect, Spenser's discussion of the civilizing power of agriculture in *A View of the Present State of Ireland* (1596) is distorted by his eagerness to suggest ways of keeping the Irish firmly pacified by tying them to the soil (10:215-18). In the Mutabilitie Cantos, however—probably the last poetry Spenser wrote—he returns husbandry to its rightful place by incorporating it in the great zodiac of months (7.7.32-43). Again he shows his familiarity with Medieval as well as Classical traditions of rural labor.[21] In his mythological procession, seasonable labor becomes the perpetual and crowning concern

[21] On Spenser's zodiac see Sherman Hawkins, "Mutabilitie and the Cycle of the Months," in *Form and Convention in the Poetry of Edmund Spenser*, ed. William Nelson (New York: Columbia Univ. Press, 1961), pp. 76-102. On the Medieval background, see Emile Mâle, *The Gothic Image*, trans. Dora Mussey (New York: Harper, 1954); and Rosemond Tuve, *Seasons and Months* (Paris: J. Gamber, 1933).

of human life in the natural world; it is the best evidence that Spenser provides for Nature's verdict that time brings all things not to destruction but to "their owne perfection" (7.7.58). Thus the unfinished coda to *The Faerie Queene* triumphantly confirms the georgic values established in Book 6.

The georgic vision is reconcilable with any of a number of political systems. Virgil himself wrote at the turning-point in history between the Roman Republic, which collapsed after a long and bloody century of civil war, and the Empire, which was just beginning to take form. During the years that Virgil was working on the *Georgics*, however, it was far from clear that a Neronian empire of the sort we know was inevitable. Still, the georgic vision has at least potential affiliations with the imperial vision, as Spenser's treatise on Ireland and involvement with the British colonization of that country might suggest.[22] We may recall the only ground that More's Utopians found for declaring war:

> [W]herever the natives have much unoccupied and uncultivated land, they found a colony under their own laws. . . . By their procedures they make the land sufficient for both, which previously seemed poor and barren to the natives. The inhabitants who refuse to live according to their laws, they drive from the territory which they carve out for themselves. If they resist, they wage war against them. They consider it a most just cause for war when a people which does not use its soil but keeps it idle and waste nevertheless forbids the use and possession of it to others who by the rule of nature ought to be maintained by it.[23]

---

[22] For meditations on Virgilian imperialism in *The Faerie Queene*, see Angus Fletcher, *The Prophetic Moment* (Chicago: Univ. of Chicago Press, 1971), esp. pp. 76-90.

[23] Sir Thomas More, *Utopia*, ed. Edward Surtz, S.J. (New Haven: Yale Univ. Press, 1964), p. 76. On the right to use land efficiently and therefore to colonize, see also Donne's sermon to the Virginia Company, in *The Sermons of John Donne*, ed. George R. Potter and Evelyn M. Simpson, 10 vols. (Berkeley: Univ. of California Press, 1953-62), 4:274.

Such was the mechanism that operated when Europe settled the new world. More immediately, one might fear that not only Spenser's ragged mob of land agitators but also his Giant Cormoraunt (from whose greedy hands Sir Bruin has wrested his estates by right of his sword) are to be identified with the Irish, who were being driven off their land by British colonists. Spenser himself was both a propagandist of this procedure and one of the landholders. Thus georgic urges played at least some part in the imperial process; one may see as much in the title of an agricultural treatise published by Hartlib some sixty years later: *Irelands Natural History . . . with the severall way[s] of Manuring and improoving the same* (1652).[24]

Although Virgil hoped that Octavius would preside over the birth of a new and happier age, still his poem argues by force of example that the reformation will be brought about only by the efforts of many individual husbandmen (and, by implication, of artisans and craftsmen). The *Georgics* celebrates the small landowner, not the proprietor of a country villa or the owner of large estates worked by slaves. Virgil's heroes work as hard as the humblest day laborer or slave, yet they work for no one but themselves—and, by a happy paradox, for the nation as a whole. Virgil's basic vision, that a nation's citizens may unify their country and make it fruitful by working the land, eventually proved congenial to a variety of British ideologies: it was easily adaptable to the meliorist aims of the scientific land-improvers, such as Hartlib; it played a central role in the visionary politics of the agricultural revolutionists, such as Winstanley; it contributed to the long and stable reign of the Whig "landocracy"; and it helped to fashion the ideal of rural self-sufficiency urged by such populists as Cobbett. Although Spenser repudiated some of the worst failings of the aristocracy, especially its unreasoning horror of work, he remained generally sympathetic to the aristocratic ideal. Although he developed a powerful and, for his time,

---

[24] Although the author is Gerard Boate, this is one of a number of agricultural treatises solicited and published by Samuel Hartlib during the 1650s (on which see ch. 4).

remarkable doctrine of individual labor for the common wel-
fare, he never shows any signs of changing his views about
land ownership. Whether his democratic land redistributors
are based on the Irish or the English, Talus makes short work
of them. Most significantly, though Spenser abandoned the
Elizabethan courtier as a model for his heroes, he did not
abandon him as the most important constituent of his audi-
ence. He still hoped to convert the courtier to a respect for
labor and for public service, and thus to contribute to the
founding of a new society, into which Elizabeth's aristocrats
and gentry would lead the British people.

Spenser's program failed in his lifetime. When James I came
to the throne, he merely accelerated the progressive deterio-
ration of courtly energies. Yet Spenser's powerful myths and
his poetic images passed nonetheless over the heads of his
intended audience to reach a much wider and more receptive
readership during the following century. Gradually, with the
help not of courtiers but of scientists and religious leaders and
of such poets as Milton, the georgic vision took root in British
soil. For all his antique pageantry and his conservative politics,
Spenser was the first and in some ways the most revolutionary
propagator of that vision.

THREE

The New Century

DURING Elizabeth's last years and James's first, Robert Cecil, as Secretary of State, continued and confirmed the cautious policies of his father, the first Lord Burghley. Next to his learning and his horsemanship, the king liked to be praised for his wonderful abilities as a peacemaker, or in other words as a political compromiser among the contending continental powers. Except among a few of the more radical Protestants, imperial vision gave place for several decades to a more restricted version of nationalism. The Spenserian poets, encouraged by the success of several new editions of Spenser's works early in the century, drew their inspiration chiefly from their predecessor's pastoral vision, his sense of beauty, his use of moral and religious allegory, his interest in the trappings of chivalry, and his (occasional) use of a lush, archaic style. They were less observant of his underlying Virgilian strength or his commitment to national greatness. Even George Wither, although he was subsequently to develop a unique georgic voice of his own, retreated at first into pastoral. Having been censured for the publication of a collection of satirical poems, *Abuses Stript and Whipt* (1613), he made his apologies to the court by means of an "Epithalamion" in honor of the marriage of Princess Elizabeth to the Elector Frederick:

> Loe thy poore *Vassall*, that was erst so rude,
> With his most *Rusticke Satyrs* to intrude,
> Once more like a poore *Silvan* now drawes neare;
> And in thy sacred *Presence* dares appeare.
> (3-6)[1]

---

[1] *The English Spenserians*, ed. William B. Hunter, Jr. (Salt Lake City: Univ. of Utah Press, 1977), pp. 117-34.

With none of Spenser's irony, Wither promises that henceforth he will strive to write only to please: "My *Will* is ever, never to offend, / These that are good" (11-12). Pastoral is the proper garb for this penitent suitor, who has thrown off the costume of the hairy, satirical satyr to become a "poore *Silvan*." As he metaphorically approaches the mercy seat, he recollects his retreat from the court and from involvement in public life, in what may be termed a prototypical pattern of regression into pastoral privacy, such as we have noticed in the generation of court poets that preceded Spenser:

> Minding for ever to abandon sport,
> And live exilde from places of resort;
> Carelesse of all, I yeelding to securitie,
> Thought to shut up my *Muse* in darke obscuritie:
> And in content, the better to repose,
> A lonely *Grove* upon a *Mountaine* chose.
> East from *Caer Winn*, mid-way twixt *Arle* and *Dis*,
> True *Springs*, where *Britains* true *Arcadia* is.
>
> (15-22)

Even these obsequious protestations were insufficient to keep Wither out of Marshalsea prison, but they may have helped him to gain the king's good will and thus to speed his subsequent release.

For the most part, Spenser's imitators, like the Wither who speaks in "Epithalamion," steered clear of politics. Typically, Phineas Fletcher reserves his spleen in *The Locusts* for such safe targets as the Pope, the Jesuits, and the Gunpowder plotters. In his preface to *Poly-Olbion*, the first part of which appeared in 1612, Drayton complains: "[T]here is this great disadvantage against me; that it commeth out at this time, when Verses are wholly deduc't to Chambers, and nothing esteem'd in this lunatique Age, but what is kept in Cabinets, and must only passe by Transcription" (*Works*, 4: v*). Thus those poets who might have wished to write in Spenser's public mode found that the market and the political climate for such works were unfavorable. As a result of these various factors, the pastoral of the Spenserian poets lacks the pervasive political commitment that undergirds *The Shepheardes Calender*; their religious poetry too is usually personal and devotional. Not until Milton appeared on the scene, with the publication of "Lycidas" in *Justa Edouardo King Naufrago* (1638), did an important English poet again combine landscape, religion, and politics so as to hold up to the nation a new model for reform, as Spenser had done in *The Faerie Queene*. The Spenserian poets lacked Spenser's interest in a poetry of work. The exception is Wither, and it is arguable that Wither's later poetry is not stylistically Spenserian.[2] Like others in the early Stuart period, the Spenserian poets retreated from the dangerous and discouraging business of giving political advice to important people into a preoccupation with more fashionable and usually more private forms. Oddly, the chief immediate heir to Spenser in his role of anti-courtly gadfly and amender of aristocratic values was one of the two poets who were most responsible for the anti-Spenserian revolution in style: Ben Jonson. Perhaps the connection is not so odd, since both Spenser and Jonson were revolutionary innovators in their own times, and it is to the innovators that we must look for the development of a georgic spirit in England, against the prevailing currents. The reaction to the court of a second major innovator, John Donne, proved less fruitful for the georgic movement, although it was to have positive consequences for the poetry of private analysis and of personal relationships.

---

[2] See Hunter, *The English Spenserians*, pp. 111-15. Another important poem that exploits landscape in the service of ideology is *Coopers Hill* (1642). Yet although Brendan O Hehir argues in *Expans'd Hieroglyphicks* (Berkeley: Univ. of California Press, 1969), pp. 9-15 et passim, that Denham's poem is georgic, the plowmen appear only briefly and peripherally and the minor marks of georgic that O Hehir cites vanish on close inspection (the poet does not address or advise the plowmen, and the "weather prognostication" is rather simply a description of cloud formations). It is plausible that, as O Hehir argues, Denham learned how to use landscape politically from Virgil's *Georgics*, but Denham's views were too typically royalist to have inclined him toward either a georgic spirit or a georgic subject matter.

JOHN DONNE

Donne's feelings toward the court, so far as one can reconstruct them from his poetry, were deeply ambivalent. At the start, when he was filled with ambition for advancement and circulated his satires to Sir Thomas Egerton and others as proofs of his sophisticated wit and his promise in worldly affairs, he was unable to suppress an intensity of loathing and terror, coupled with irresistible fascination, that were disproportionate to his subject or his ostensible satirical purpose. Like a dog returning to its vomit, the speaker in these satires cannot keep away from the court, yet any contact with either court or courtiers fills him with deadly anxiety and disgust. Although the Donne of these satires speaks like a man who has lost his religious faith or his certitude in anything, his constant fearful references to spies and pursuivants and his insistent pursuit of the theme of betrayal imply that his upbringing as a Roman Catholic, which desire for advancement urged him to repudiate, exacerbated the already negative response of many of his fellows (including Egerton) to a court that no longer could be viewed as a model for imitation.[3] Donne's predecessors vented such feelings by resorting to pastoral. But in Donne, the strong urge to be different seems to have blocked this natural and rather harmless outlet. In all his poetry, the nearest he came to pastoral, or even to anti-pastoral, is his answer to Marlowe's "Passionate Shepherd," "The Baite." This poem earned Donne a place in Walton's *Compleat Angler*, but it is hardly typical of him. One might search the rest of his poetry (including his ironically titled "Ecclogue") in vain for even a single line in the pastoral mode—which is surely extraordinary at a time when pastoral

[3] On Donne as a private poet, see esp. Earl Miner, *The Metaphysical Mode from Donne to Cowley* (Princeton: Princeton Univ. Press, 1969); on Donne's Catholicism see John Carey, *John Donne: Life, Mind & Art* (New York: Oxford Univ. Press, 1981), and works cited in a summary article by Dennis Flynn, "The 'Annales School' and the Catholicism of Donne's Family," *John Donne Journal*, 2.2 (1983), 1-9; on Jacobean disillusionment see George Williamson's classic essay, "Mutability, Decay, and Seventeenth-Century Melancholy," *ELH*, 2 (1936), 121-50.

was invading comedies, romances, tragedies, epics, and sat-
ires, as well as lyrics.

Nevertheless, disgust with the court did not encourage
Donne to a public-spirited response, as it did Spenser and, to
a lesser degree, Jonson. Instead, Donne found new forms of
privacy: the microcosm of the two lovers, who exclude the
world, and the microcosm of the thinking and feeling self,
which also excludes the world. "Seeke wee then our selves in
our selves," Donne urges his friend Rowland Woodward.[4] In
Donne's hands, this impulse was more than the traditional
injunction to know oneself. For those who were unable to
enter into the spirit of James's court, two responses were
possible: commitment to reform and retreat into privacy. As
a secular poet—and, it might be argued, sometimes even as
Dean of St. Paul's—Donne chose the latter. On the 18th of
February, 1548, Hugh Latimer preached his Sermon of the
Plough from the shrouds of St. Paul: "Oh London London,
repente repente, for I thynke God is more dyspleased with
London, then ever he was with the citie of Nebo."[5] On the
12th of December, 1626, John Donne preached his sermon
at the funeral of Sir William Cockayne, Alderman of London:
"[W]hen we consider with a religious seriousnesse the man-
ifold weaknesses of the strongest devotions in time of Prayer,
it is a sad consideration. I throw my selfe downe in my Cham-
ber, and I call in, and invite God and his Angels thither, and
when they are there, I neglect God and his Angels, for the
noise of a Flie, for the ratling of a Coach, for the whining of
a doore; I talke on, in the same posture of praying. . . ."[6] Even
when Donne is acting in the most public of offices, we find

[4] Texts of the satires and verse epistles are from *The Satires, Epigrams and
Verse Letters of John Donne*, ed. W. Milgate (Oxford: Clarendon Press,
1967).

[5] *A notable Sermon of the reverende father Maister Hughe Latemer, whiche
he preached in the Shrouds at paules churche in London* (1548), Bii^v; for
background see Millar MacClure, *The Paul's Cross Sermons, 1534-1642*
(Toronto: Univ. of Toronto Press, 1958); and see ch. 5 below.

[6] *The Sermons of John Donne*, ed. Evelyn M. Simpson and George R.
Potter, 10 vols. (Berkeley: Univ. of California Press, 1953-62), 7:264.

him always internalizing, always looking within; and his advice to his congregation is frequently to do likewise.

Evidently Donne had no fondness for any of the Virgilian forms, whether pastoral, georgic, or epic. Virgil simply was not his poet. Donne mentions him seldom in his sermons, and mainly in order to attack his ready adaptability in support of the Catholic doctrine of purgatory (*Sermons*, 7:131, 177). Donne cites the *Georgics* only as exemplifying the lowest kind of poetry: "[T]ake but the *Georgiques*, the consideration of the *Earth*, a farme, a garden, nay seven foot of earth, a grave, and that will be book enough" (4:167). Surprisingly, however, considering how little Donne was interested in the country and how thoroughly he ignored the vogue for pastoral, his poems touch on various georgic subjects fairly often. Almost invariably the references are negative. As we shall see in a later chapter, at about the middle of the century a number of minor poets with Royalist sympathies began referring to georgic issues in order to satirize or attack them. These later writers were reacting to what by then was a well-established trend. Donne, with his sensitive antennae and his powerful instinct for setting trends rather than following them, seems almost to have anticipated the main georgic movement. He might have been reacting to the published ideas of Spenser, Ralegh, or Bacon, yet there are no obvious literary echoes. It seems more likely that he was reacting to the English passion for land and rents, of which he must have seen a great deal in life, though it had not yet found much expression in literature. Certainly his attitude toward agriculture and farming seems to be very closely connected to his ambivalent feelings about advancement and worldly success. Love, friendship, and poetry, which Donne regularly opposes to success, he also opposes to farming.

In "Satyre II," Donne's villain is a former poet who has turned successful lawyer and who, we may suspect, Donne resents precisely because he has succeeded in doing what he himself, in part at least, would like to do—leave impoverished art behind and grow rich. From Donne's jaundiced imagination, neither poetry nor law emerges unscathed:

When sicke with Poëtrie, 'and possest with muse
Thou wast, and mad, I hop'd; but men which chuse
Law practise for meere gaine, bold soule, repute
Worse then imbrothel'd strumpets prostitute.

(61-64)

Not to be ambitious is madness; to be ambitious is worse. Donne's lawyer, who had done what Donne himself patently both hopes and fears to do, has for his ultimate goal the ownership of land. His was a common aim, as we have seen, but one rarely so openly expressed:

Shortly ('as the sea) hee'will compasse all our land;
From Scots, to Wight; from Mount, to Dover strand. . . .
Peecemeale he gets lands, and spends as much time
Wringing each Acre, as men pulling prime.
In parchments then, large as his fields, hee drawes
Assurances, bigge, as gloss'd civill lawes.

(77-78, 85-88)

Land was for Donne something so desirable that it was sinful even to think about it. Land meant security, as the landless Donne knew, even before his disgrace put that security forever beyond his grasp. When the gossiping courtier of "Satyre IV" speaks of the plight of an acquaintance who "hath sold his land, and now doth beg / A license, old iron, bootes, shooes, and egge- / shels to transport" (103-105), Donne knows what it would feel like to find oneself in such a humiliating position.

In "The Curse," Donne reverts once more to the queasy pain of material loss, which is like the queasiness of sexual disgust:

In early and long scarcenesse may he rot,
For land which had been his, if he had not
Himselfe incestuously an heire begot.

(14-16)[7]

---

[7] Poems from the elegies and the *Songs and Sonets* are quoted from *The Poems of John Donne*, ed. H.J.C. Grierson, 2 vols. (1912; London: Oxford Univ. Press, 1951).

What could not a Freudian critic make of that particular image? And in "Loves diet," Donne associates sexual disgust with still another variation on the theme of the misfortune of landlessness:

> When she writ to me,
> And that that favour made him [Love] fat,
> I said, if any title bee
> Convey'd by this, Ah, what doth it availe,
> To be the fortieth name in an entaile?
>   (20-24)

If we may conclude that Donne felt little respect but rather more envy for the wealthy landowner, we may also say that his poems dismiss farm laborers and servants with far less ambivalence. His lover condemns farmwork obliquely in a phrase: "Call countrey ants to harvest offices." This image from "The Sunne Rising" he takes up again in "Obsequies to the Lord Harrington," expanding it and bringing the farm workers into the city with their produce.

> Now I grow sure, that if a man would have
> Good companie, his entry is a grave.
> Mee thinkes all Cities, now, but Anthills bee,
> Where, when the severall labourers I see,
> For children, house, Provision, taking paine,
> They'are all but Ants, carrying eggs, straw, and grain.
>   (165-70)

Although a religious sorrow may have provided the initial impetus for this passage, that impulse is soon buried under Donne's characteristic scorn for manual labor.

For Donne, something about the country and country people is antipathetic to love. He addresses the rural guests who have come to the wedding at Lincoln's Inn dismissively: "Yee country men, who but your beasts love none" (28). Of the possible forms that this love of beasts might take, and on which Donne is playing, probably the worst is to raise them for profit. In "The Canonization," landowners appear again,

among those worldlings whose materialism is opposed to the
protagonist's wholehearted dedication to love:

> Alas, alas, who's injur'd by my love?
>   What merchants ships have my sighs drown'd?
> Who saies my teares have overflow'd his ground?
>   (10-12)

A similar antipathy to georgic matters is to be found in the
elegies, which are generally thought to have been written in
the 1590s. In "Change," Donne anticipates Suckling's scorn-
ful use of georgic imagery to deprecate a certain kind of un-
romantic lovemaking. The speaker's point is that women are
naturally promiscuous, like foxes or goats, like clogs to which
men bind themselves, like galleys to which men are chained.
Such is the context for Donne's georgic image for lovemaking:

> Who hath a plow-land, casts all his seed corne there,
> And yet allowes his ground more corne should beare.
>   (17-18)

The potential of this image to suggest fruition is wholly dis-
placed by the speaker's repressed jealousy and cynical scorn.
A similar distaste marks Donne's use of plowing as a sexual
metaphor in "The Comparison": "Is not your last act harsh,
and violent, / As when a Plough a stony ground doth rent?"
(47-48). This is a sexual soil that is unproductive, resistant to
fruition. So too in a third elegy, "The Anagram," the speaker
once more reaches for georgic imagery to convey his disgust.
The poem, which consists of a string of Italianate paradoxes,
finds Donne mockingly praising what he means to condemn—
in the case of the relevant couplet, female ugliness and the use
of land to raise crops:

> Beauty is barren oft; best husbands say,
> There is best land, where there is foulest way.
>   (35-36)

"Husbands," of course, is a pun, but, whichever way one
turns it, it conveys a sense of opprobrium. Once more the

context implies a basic polarity between pleasure and pro-
creation, which is exemplified by a polarity between love and
farming.

To be sure, Donne condemns the city and the court as well
as the country. His beast-loving countrymen of the "Epitha-
lamion made at Lincolnes Inne" are accompanied by "frolique
Patricians" and the sons of rich city "Senators." In a verse
letter "To Sir Henry Wotton," Donne finds the act of corre-
sponding with his friend relief from "the tediousnesse of my
life," a tediousness which he expresses in georgic terms: "But
I should wither in one day, and passe / To'a bottle of Hay,
that am a locke of Grasse" (5-6). Lasting relief is nowhere to
be found:

> But Oh, what refuge canst thou winne
> Parch'd in the Court, and in the country frozen?
> Shall cities, built of both extremes, be chosen?
> Can dung and garlike be'a perfume? . . .
> The Country is a desert, where no good,
> Gain'd (as habits, not borne,) is understood.
> There men become beasts, and prone to more evils;
> In cities blockes, and in a lewd court, devills.
>   (14-17, 25-28)

Donne is working with a conventional theme in this epistle,
yet the intensity with which he puts the case suggests his
personal engagement.

Donne's fullest statement of his opinion of the georgic way
of life, however, is to be found in two early verse epistles
addressed "To Mr I. L." The identity of I. L. (or possibly
J. L.) has not been established. Milgate conjectures that he
had been a friend of Donne's at university or the Inns of Court.
Internal evidence suggests that the first of the two identically
titled epistles was written to I. L. after a period during which
the two had been out of touch; I. L. had recently married and
was living in the country somewhere north of the River Trent.
The second letter was written some time later—Bald argues
in August of 1594—when Donne's mistress had gone to I. L.'s

estate for a visit and Donne writes from the vicinity of London.[8] The first epistle clarifies the complaint to Wotton; the problem with living in the country is that it leaves no time for the more important business of life, which includes, in particular, friendship and the writing of poetry:

You doe not duties of Societies,
If from the'embrace of a lov'd wife you rise,
View your fat Beasts, stretch'd Barnes, and labour'd Fields,
Eate, play, ryde, take all joyes which all day yeelds,
And then againe to your embracements goe:
Some houres on us your frends, and some bestow
Upon your Muse, else both wee shall repent,
I that my love, she that her guifts on you are spent.

(7-14)

Friendship and poetry are the twin "duties of Societies"; Donne will not often write in this easy Jonsonian vein again. Yet his poem still reveals, though more good-naturedly than the later ones, his characteristic resistance to farming the land. Here the husbandman's life is idyllic, yet it is a life that is wholly material, self-centered, almost animalistic in its unselfconsciousness. As Donne's views of human nature grow more jaundiced, the descent from animal contentment to bestiality is predictable. In this first epistle to I. L., as in "Satyre II," Donne opposes the writing of poetry to working hard in a profession. Love, friendship, poetry are all impractical activities the pursuit of which the world may well consider mad; yet for Donne, it is better to be mad in these ways than to give oneself wholly to the selfish or thoughtless pursuit of profit. The idea that work may be beneficial to others as well as profitable to oneself does not seem to enter into his thinking.

In the second epistle to I. L., Donne writes almost as if he were an outcast from a georgic Eden. Ostensibly his reason

[8] Milgate, *Satires*, pp. 220-22; R. C. Bald, "Donne's Early Verse Letters," *Huntington Library Quarterly*, 15 (1952), 286, and *John Donne: A Life* (Oxford: Clarendon Press, 1970), pp. 75-76.

for doing so is his separation from his mistress, who is with
his friend in the country, a theme to which he refers in the
opening and closing couplets. Yet the separation of Donne
from the happy, unexamined, and prosperous life led by I. L.,
a "happy husbandman" if ever there was one, is, we might
think, a theme of equal if unintended prominence:

Blest are your North parts, for all this long time
My Sun [i.e. mistress] is with you, cold and darke'is our Clime. . . .
And since thou art in Paradise and need'st crave
No joyes addition, helpe thy friend to save.
So may thy pastures with their flowery feasts,
As suddenly as Lard, fat thy leane beasts;
So may thy woods oft poll'd, yet ever weare
A greene, and when thee list, a golden haire;
So may all thy sheepe bring forth Twins; and so
In chace and race may thy horse all out goe;
So may thy love and courage ne'r be cold;
Thy Sonne ne'r Ward; Thy lov'd wife ne'r seem old;
But maist thou wish great things, and them attaine,
As thou telst her, and none but her, my paine.
                                        (1-2, 11-22)

Donne delineates a productive, not a pastoral, landscape, al-
though in good-humoredly condescending to I. L.'s worldly
views he verges on that natural beauty that his poetry so
scrupulously avoids elsewhere. His tone and attitude are not
unlike those of the lover in "The Canonization," who also
tells his friend, in effect: You for your brand of happiness in
the world, and more power to you; I for my brand of happiness
in the counter-world of love.

   Just once, in the verse epistle "To Mr Rowland Woodward"
(c. 1597), Donne speaks of georgic activity in wholly favorable
terms. Evidently responding to a request from Woodward for
a copy of his latest poems, Donne turns to a farming metaphor
to belittle his earlier productions—presumably the satires and
elegies—and to describe a recent period of poetic inactivity:

Like one who'in her third widdowhood doth professe
Her selfe a Nunne, ty'd to retirednesse,
So'affects my muse now, a chast fallownesse;

Since shee to few, yet to too many'hath showne
How love-song weeds, and Satyrique thornes are growne
Where seeds of better Arts, were early sown.

(1-6)

Clearly poetry is an idle sort of husbandry; it produces a poor, postlapsarian crop of weeds and thorns. In the scales on which God weighs "Mens workes," such vanities lie as heavily as sin. "There is no Vertue, but Religion," Donne concludes; therefore, we must look first to the cultivation of our souls. Having begun with a dispirited application of georgic metaphor to his activities as a poet, Donne concludes with a much more satisfying application of the same metaphor to the inward activities of devotion:

Wee are but farmers of our selves, yet may,
If we can stocke our selves, and thrive, uplay
Much, much deare treasure for the great rent day.

Manure thy selfe then, to thy selfe be'approv'd,
And with vaine outward things be no more mov'd,
But to know, that I love thee'and would be lov'd.

(31-36)

Only in this special context, of what is usually called spiritual georgic, can Donne speak favorably about such activities as manuring. This taking in of rents and laying up of treasure is for once entirely legitimate, since the gospel commands it. Here, under the shadow of New-Testament paradoxy, one may put pride aside, and dirty one's hands working for the heavenly taskmaster.

If husbandry ordinarily provoked in Donne even more than the usual scorn and disinterest, the same may be said about work in general. Tough and energetic as Donne's verse may be, he seldom pictures himself in the act of working. "Some that have deeper digg'd loves Myne then I, / Say, where his centrique happinesse doth lie." Even such mock labor is soon blocked off by his innate sense of social snobbery: "Ends love in this, that my man, / Can be as happy'as I can [?]" Only at a moment of frustration, when he is penned in spiritually and can find no exit, does Donne turn in despair to work as a solution:

> On a huge hill,
> Cragged, and steep, Truth stands, and hee that will
> Reach her, about must, and about must goe;
> And what th' hills suddennes resists, winne so;
> Yet strive so, that before age, deaths twilight,
> Thy Soule rest, for none can worke in that night.
> To will, implyes delay, therefore now doe:
> Hard deeds, the bodies paines; hard knowledge too
> The mindes indeavours reach. . . .
> ("Satyre III," 79-87)

But this passage, though justly famous, is not really typical of Donne's thinking, and, although it advocates labor in the search for truth, it is scarcely optimistic. This is the labor of a man with his back to the wall, not of one who would encourage others to cooperate in the building of a new world—not, that is, a Virgilian, a Spenserian, or a Baconian sort of labor.

A critic might, of course, argue that in the case of the lyrics, and even in that of the satires and epistles, the views of a particular speaker need not represent those of Donne himself. Purist interpretations of poetry are less common than they once were, however, so we might rather think of Donne's poems in terms of the poet's wearing various masks of indirection and irony than as separable worlds containing personae wholly independent of their creator. With respect to georgic, however, the unanimity in tone and attitude of all the spokesmen in Donne's poems toward labor and agriculture is telling. Even if one wanted to argue that Donne himself was free of the scorn for labor that his poems persistently display (although there is no evidence to support such a position), it would remain true that the poems reveal his awareness of the prevalent gentlemanly view of georgic matters, and that he often plays on it. Thus, while in any particular poem it may be a "lover" or the spokesman of a satire who complains about farming, Donne evidently judged that his readers would understand the mood and attitude exemplified by such complaints. As the number and variety of instances increases, it becomes increasingly reasonable to assume that Donne, or at least one important side of him, felt and thought the same way.

Of course, Donne presumably knew that it was wrong for a good Christian to despise anyone, even a peasant farmer or a laborer. In a relatively late poem, "To Mr. Tilman after he had taken orders," Donne uses the biblical image of putting his hand to the plow to suggest both their joint commitment to the ministry and Donne's awareness that, from the typically aristocratic point of view, his chosen vocation would be thought more than a little shameful.[9] The same combination of shame with acceptance of shame is associated with the image of the plow in the sermons (4:170, 6:93). As an ordained priest, Donne continues to find labor demeaning, yet now he offers to embrace it for that very reason. Commenting on the injunction to act virtuously, *That they may see your works*," he picks up the laboring element implicit in "works": "which is a word that implies difficulty, and paine, and labour, and is accompanied with some loathnesse. ... Doe such workes, for Gods sake, as are hard for thee to doe" (10:94). In a similar spirit, Donne preached two sermons at Whitehall some time after 1625 on the rather unusual text of Ezekiel 34:19: "And as for my flock, they eate that, which yee have troden with your feet, and they drink that which yee have fouled with your feet." In both sermons (but seldom else-

[9] In her edition of *The Divine Poems of John Donne*, 2d edn. (Oxford: Clarendon Press, 1978), Helen Gardner dates the poem after Tilman took deacon's orders in December 1618; for further discussion, see ch. 5 below.

where), Donne adds georgic to pastoral imagery to suggest that, in laboring for the Church, a good minister embraces humiliation, so as not to "be a spunge, to drinke up the sweat of others, and live idly" (10:140-43). But to accept labor for God's sake is a duty belonging especially to the clergy and to works of charity, not to secular vocations (3:55-67). Even in the sermons, Donne continues to view labor and sweat as evils to be endured; nowhere does he suggest that work should be thought noble or socially respectable. And, if the sermons reveal a Donne beginning to wrestle with the problem of labor, still there is little in his poetry—most of which was written before his ordination—to suggest that he had begun to reconsider the prejudices that characterized his time.

Confronted by the collapse of early Elizabethan optimism and expansionism, the response of some poets, such as Spenser, was simply to dig in and work harder. Others spoke nostalgically about the world's decay. We may think of the disappointed Ralegh's unfinished poem to the queen: "My steapps are backwarde, gasinge on my loss."[10] The most deeply disillusioned poets turned from concern for the public welfare to private love and friendship and, even further inward, to the world that lay within themselves. Such a poet was Donne. Too proudly private, it would seem, to resort to the commonplace privacies of pastoral, Donne nevertheless was sensitive to and repelled by the public call represented by georgic. The georgic imperative—that is, the practical necessity to earn one's bread, the moral necessity usefully to multiply one's talents in the service of others, and the creative necessity to invent useful arts and discover new worlds—irritated him. As a result, more often than we might expect, he took up georgic themes and modes in order to give them the back of his hand.

> Let sea-discoverers to new worlds have gone,
> Let Maps to other, worlds on worlds have showne,

[10] "The 11th: and last booke of the Ocean to Scinthia," 1. 514, in *The Poems of Sir Walter Ralegh*, ed. Agnes Latham, The Muses' Library (Cambridge: Harvard Univ. Press, 1951), p. 43.

> Let us possesse one world, each hath one, and is one.
> ("The good-morrow," 12-14)

It is evident that Donne often worked, and that he worked hard: at his studies, at the composition of his poetry and his sermons, at the painful task of piecing together his broken career, and, it may be, even at his lovemaking. Yet, much as he feared and despised the court and what it stood for, he retained at least one courtly habit: the pretense of never working too hard. That pretense insured in turn that, although he was a notable reformer in poetry, he would reject the more public-spirited reform represented by the georgic vision of Spenser and Bacon. His satirical thrusts propose no practical cure for the world's malaise; rather, they succeed chiefly as psychological anatomies of his malcontented speakers.

Of course, Donne's greatest accomplishments lie elsewhere, in that private world of self-analysis and inward feeling that he shares with his mistresses and his God. The *Songs and Sonets* and the devotional poems, by which Donne is deservedly best known, need no recommending here, even if our theme permitted. Still, it is worth observing that his greatest positive accomplishments as a poet were impelled, at the beginning, not only by the failure of his career but also by his violent rejection both of the old public poetry of the court and of the new public poetry that was just beginning to emerge to take its place. As witness, we can do no better than simply to take the lines just quoted and look at them differently, as if they were an optical illusion in which a concave surface suddenly grows convex under one's eyes:

> Let sea-discoverers to new worlds have gone,
> Let Maps to other, worlds on worlds have showne,
> Let us possesse one world, each hath one, and is one.

In order to reverse the polarity of these lines, it is necessary only to stress not what Donne rejects but what he gains in its place: something that for him—and for many of his readers—is worth as much as all those lost "worlds on worlds." Approaching the *Songs and Sonets* thus, by the back door, may help explain, too, why Donne wrote love poetry of such intensity; until he found God again, a private life with a few friends and with women, or with one woman, were all he had left.

GEORGE HERBERT

Donne liked to extend his opinions to the same extremes to which he stretched his imagery; therefore, though the extent of his anti-georgic sentiment is somewhat surprising, its intensity is not. Because Donne is so individual a poet, his reactions might be thought atypical. Herbert, not Donne, is the poet whom most of the great devotional writers of the century acknowledged as their master.[11] As a rule, Herbert writes with a more communal spirit than Donne, and with more obvious charity toward others. His dedication to duty and to his chosen profession finds greater expression, too. Donne, for all his brashness, his technical innovations, and his interest in—or perhaps fear of—New Science, was temperamentally conservative and backward- or inward-looking, while Herbert, within the limits of his theology, was optimistic. Herbert wrote four, possibly five, poems that honored Francis Bacon. He celebrated the publication of the *Magna Instauratio* in what has been thought to be his best Latin poetry. As William A. Sessions persuasively argues, "Herbert's is, as far as one can judge, the first objective statement of Bacon's power to shape the future through his concepts of science and especially of technology."[12] One distich sums up Herbert's understanding

[11] Vaughan's remarks in the introduction to *Silex Scintillans* (1655) are well known, as are the many verbal echoes in his poetry; Crashaw's debt is suggested by his title, *Steps to the Temple*. See also *George Herbert and the Seventeenth-Century Religious Poets*, ed. Mario A. Di Cesare (New York: Norton, 1978).

[12] "Bacon and Herbert and an Image of Chalk," in *"Too Rich to Clothe the Sunne": Essays on George Herbert*, ed. Claude J. Summers and Ted-Larry Pebworth (Pittsburgh: Pittsburgh Univ. Press, 1980), p. 169. For a possible fifth poem on Bacon, see Hilton Kelliher, "A Latin Poem Possibly by George Herbert," *Seventeenth-Century News*, 35 (1977), 12.

that though the present age honors Bacon as Lord Chancellor, future ages will honor him for his scientific ideas: "Munere dum nobis prodes, Libróque futuris, / In laudes abeunt secula quaeque tuas" (1-2). "While you give [publish] to us today by your office, and tomorrow by your book, all times are lost in praise of you."[13]

Yet the only place we find Herbert recommending work in a cooperative, georgic spirit is in his translation of Luigi Cornaro's *Treatise of Temperance*, a work first published in Padua in 1558. According to John Ferrar, Herbert translated this work chiefly because he was interested in the spare diet that Cornaro recommends. Yet he was at least sufficiently sympathetic to Cornaro's enthusiasm for what might be called georgic works of corporal mercy not to have omitted the passages describing them from his version—as he omitted other material that he found displeasing or irrelevant, such as Cornaro's complaints about the prevalence in Italy of "sycophancy, Lutheranism, and drunkenness."[14] In connection with the power of temperance to improve health, Cornaro remarks that "the faults of Nature are often amended by Art, as barren grounds are made fruitfull by good husbandry" (p. 292). One way Cornaro keeps healthy is to stroll about the grounds of his house in the hills. Surrounding this country place are "fruitfull fields, well manured," which are the products of Cornaro's ambitious improvements:

> In former times, it was not so, because the place was moorish and unhealthy, fitter for beasts then men. But I drained the ground, and made the aire good: Whereupon men flockt thither, and built houses with happy successe. By this means the place is come to that perfection we

[13] My translation of Herbert's typically dense and gnomic lines; cf. Mark McCloskey and Paul R. Murphy, *The Latin Poetry of George Herbert* (Athens: Ohio Univ. Press, 1965), pp. 166-67.

[14] For John Ferrar's remarks and discussion of Herbert's omissions, see *The Works of George Herbert*, ed. F. E. Hutchinson (1941; Oxford: Clarendon Press, 1964), pp. 564-66; Herbert's prose is quoted from Hutchinson by page number and poetry by line.

now see it is: So that I can truly say, That I have both given God a Temple, and men to worship him in it: The memorie whereof is exceeding delightfull to me. . . .

But this chiefly delights me, that my advice hath taken effect in the reducing of many rude and untoiled places in my countrey, to cultivation and good husbandrie. I was one of those that was deputed for the managing of that work, and abode in those fenny places two whole moneths in the heat of summer. (pp. 301-302)

Word of Cornaro's civic-minded projects, which came to Herbert through the Latin version published by a Jesuit professor at Louvain (Antwerp, 1613), does not otherwise seem to have influenced Herbert's thinking or directly contributed to the growth of georgic consciousness in England. Still, these passages are a salutary reminder that the ideals of georgic benevolence and cooperation, not widely accepted in England until the eighteenth century, might be found in Italy as early as the middle of the sixteenth century. Draining of the fens and similar projects had already begun in England, but they left little reflection in the literature of that time. Of course the ideal of corporate land improvement could also be found in England before the monastic dissolution, but that is another story that will be discussed briefly in chapter 5.

Considering Herbert's communal spirit, his charity toward others as recounted by Walton, his dedication to his profession and to the ideal of a divine "calling," and his apparent interest in the Baconian plan for improving the human condition, it would not be surprising to find him making some use of the georgic mode.[15] Indeed, many fragments of georgic themes and images appear in *The Temple*. Yet in the end, the full

[15] On several of these topics, and especially Herbert's dedication to his profession or calling as reflected in the poetry, see Diana Benet's *Secretary of Praise: The Poetic Vocation of George Herbert* (Columbia: Univ. of Missouri Press, 1984). I agree (as against Helen Vendler) that the poems of *The Temple* have public and altruistic implications and are not simply private cogitations, but they are concerned to talk Herbert's readers and neighbors into seeking heaven rather than improving their material lot.

georgic spirit proves to be lacking; it is frustrated by Herbert's otherworldly theology and, in particular, by his Protestant emphasis on grace and on the impossibility of accomplishing anything positive by one's own efforts. In this regard, the opening lines of "Grace" are especially telling:

> My stock lies dead, and no increase
> Doth my dull husbandrie improve:
> O let thy graces without cease
> Drop from above!
> (1-4)

Plainly it will take a miracle to get this metaphorical farm going again; no amount of effort on the farmer's part is going to help. So it proves: if no solution is possible in this world, then it must be looked for in the next:

> O come! for thou dost know the way:
> Or if to me thou wilt not move,
> Remove me, where I need not say,
> *Drop from above.*
> (21-25)

For Herbert, paradise or the Golden Age is to be sought not in this world, but in heaven. It is to be achieved not by effort but by conformity to God's will. A reader may infer the same lesson from "The Flower." The divine gardener makes skillful use of the dews of grace and the heats and frosts of affliction to cultivate the soul, but the last lesson God teaches us is that "we are but flowers that glide," and that there is no "garden for us, where to bide" on this side of eternity (44-46). In this view, it would be a serious, indeed a damnable, mistake to devote too much energy to the illusory pursuit of worldly success. Further, as some of Herbert's other writings reveal, it would be a mistake even to seek too much worldly prosperity for others. What is true for the individual is true for society as a whole; neither should look to find its happiness in the goods of this present life.

Other poems in which God and not the protagonist is the

91

landlord or the active cultivator include "Redemption" and
"Love (II)." In the fifteenth poem of his sequence *Memoriae
Matris Sacrum*, Herbert names his mother "Θεοῦ γεώργιον,"
"Tilled field of the Lord" (p. 429). A second poem "on the
proud man" in *Lucus*, "In eundum," gives man the choice of
sterile rebellion or of fruitful submission to the divine tilling:

> Unusquisque hominum, Terra est; et filius arvi.
> Dic mihi, mons sterilis, vallis an uber eris?
>
> (p. 413)

"Each man is earth, and a child of the field. Tell me, will you
be a sterile mountain or a fertile valley?"

If we work, we work only to escape this world for the next.
"Coloss. 3.3" urges that we apply our "daily labour" in an
effort "To gain at harvest an eternall *Treasure*" (10). The
work has little value in itself. In "Sunday," Herbert writes
that "worky-daies" are only the "back-part" of the week,
mere laborious preparations or digressions from Sunday rest.
Herbert is, of course, working in the tradition that associates
the six days of the creation with historical time and the seventh
day with our eternal, eschatological rest with God in heaven.
Speaking of Sundays in "The Church-porch," Herbert is as
insistent as Herrick that we pay our tithes, though in this case
they are metaphorical tithes: "Restore to God his due in tithe
and time: / A tithe purloin'd cankers the whole estate" (385-
86). In the domain of this image, the tithe given to the landlord
is the true end and purpose of labor; other fruits are merely
byproducts of no permanent value. When Sunday comes
around, and it is time to enter the presence of God in church,
weekday business has no place:

> Let vain or busie thoughts have there no part:
> Bring not thy plough, thy plots, thy pleasures thither.
> Christ purg'd his temple; so must thou thy heart.
> All worldly thoughts are but theeves met together
>   To couzin thee.
>
> (421-25)

92

Without grace, it is beyond human power to cultivate the soul. The fate of the man from whom God turns his face is "ev'n in Paradise to be a weed" ("The Crosse," 30). "Employment (I)" delivers the same message:

> Let me not languish then, and spend
> A life as barren to thy praise,
> As is the dust, to which that life doth tend,
> > But with delaies.
>
> All things are busie; onely I
> Neither bring hony with the bees,
> Nor flowres to make that, nor the husbandrie
> > To water these.
>
> I am no link of thy great chain,
> But all my companie is a weed.
> Lord place me in thy consort; give one strain
> > To my poore reed.
> > > (13-24)

Again and again Herbert reverts to the twin themes that man is the passive field and not the farmer and that his true harvest is not of this world:

> Nothing but drought and dearth, but bush and brake,
> Which way so-e're I look, I see. . . .
>
> We talk of harvests; there are no such things,
> But when we leave our corn and hay:
> There is no fruitfull yeare, but that which brings
> The last and lov'd, though dreadfull day.
> > ("Home," 49-50, 55-58)

What all these various passages and poems have in common is that they depreciate the value of labor in the world and make God, not man, the active husbandman.

Herbert was too sensible not to contradict himself occasionally. One thing that inspires him to an advocacy of active spiritual georgic is his hatred of idleness and sloth. Since sloth is one of the seven deadly sins, it follows that there must be virtue in work, even though work may be valuable more because it keeps us out of the devil's hands than because it might produce something useful in itself. Herbert works out his thoughts concerning work and idleness most systematically in "The Church-porch." "Flie idlenesse," he exhorts his readers, "which yet thou canst not flie / By dressing, mistressing, and complement" (79-80). Everyone, whether a magistrate, a student, or a soldier, must play his part in life to the hilt (85-90). In a striking metaphor (which could not be more opportune for the purposes of this book), Herbert associates the endemic laziness of the English gentry with their proneness to sink into an easy, pastoral role that may be less noble than they imagine.

> O England! full of sinne, but most of sloth;
> Spit out thy flegme, and fill thy brest with glorie:
> Thy Gentrie bleats, as if thy native cloth
> Transfus'd a sheepishnesse into thy storie:
> Not that they all are so; but that the most
> Are gone to grasse, and in the pasture lost.
> (91-96)

Yet, as the next lines reveal, any expectation that Herbert is about to advocate a literally georgic solution to the nation's problems would be mistaken: "This losse springs chiefly from our education. / Some till their ground, but let weeds choke their sonne" (97-98). There is room in Herbert's scheme of things for a certain amount of spiritual georgic; but actually to plow the earth is to be distracted from the main business of life—getting oneself, one's children, and one's neighbors into heaven. The better husbandry is the interior husbandry. "Pick out of mirth, like stones out of thy ground, / Profanenesse, filthinesse, abusivenesse" (234-35). "Let thy minde still be bent, still plotting where, / And when, and how the businesse may be done. / Slacknesse breeds worms" (337-39). "Canst be idle? canst thou play, / Foolish soul who sinn'd to day?" ("Businesse," 1-2). With the help of God's grace, Herbert's protagonists occasionally have enough freedom to act on their own, evidently; but if they are wise they will limit their endeavors to self-cultivation.

Consideration of the georgic passages in Herbert's poetry leads us to the conclusion that the Protestant strain in his thinking was an important factor in turning him away from a possible interest in what is sometimes called the "work ethic." Both distrust of "the world" and emphasis on grace at the expense of confidence in one's ability to produce useful works reveal a degree of Calvinist influence on Herbert, as Joseph Summers has argued.[16] Thus Protestantism is not, as it has often been thought, in itself a sufficient motive for turning toward a georgic ideal or a "Protestant work ethic." Not Protestantism in its broad sense, but the impulse toward reform was the common motive force, as I shall attempt to show in subsequent chapters. That reforming impulse found expression in figures as different as the scientist, the humanist, and the Puritan sectary—and, on the continent, among the vanguard of the Counterreformation.

In *The Country Parson*, as in tales that are told about him in real life, Herbert reveals a sympathetic interest in plowmen, tradesmen, and the common people of his parish. But what he is apt to tell such people is not to commit themselves too deeply or whole-heartedly to their occupations. They should save their souls first, and plow their fields or attend to their business only second. One reason Herbert gives, for example, for the country parson to make the circuit of his flock is so he can see them not at their Sunday best but at their worldly worst: "most naturally as they are, wallowing in the midst of their affairs" (p. 247).

[16] *George Herbert: His Religion and Art* (Cambridge: Harvard Univ. Press, 1954), esp. pp. 49-69; also relevant is William H. Halewood, *The Poetry of Grace* (New Haven: Yale Univ. Press, 1970). Contrary to some recent critics, I do not believe that Herbert was by any means a thoroughgoing Calvinist, yet on the issue of faith and works his poetry inclines (with the institutional Church of his time) in that direction.

[T]hen he admonisheth them of two things; first, that they dive not too deep into worldly affairs, plunging themselves over head and eares into carking, and caring; but that they so labour, as neither to labour anxiously, nor distrustfully, nor profanely. Then they labour anxiously, when they overdo it, to the loss of their quiet, and health: then distrustfully, when they doubt God's providence, thinking that their own labour is the cause of their thriving, as if it were in their own hands to thrive, or not to thrive. *Then they labour profanely, when they set themselves to work like brute beasts, never raising their thoughts to God.* . . . Secondly, he adviseth them so to labour for wealth and maintenance, as that they make not that the end of their labour, but that they may have wherewithall to serve God the better, and to do good deeds. (pp. 247-48)

Although Herbert certainly was alive to the attractions of the courtly way of life, to the lullings of play and pleasure, it would not be fair to read into his disparagement of the farmer's work vestigial family pride or prejudice, still less an anachronistic class antagonism. Still, the views he expresses, in good conscience and with Christian orthodoxy, might readily be abused for the preservation of the status quo.

Herbert takes considerable pleasure in the power of divine providence to frustrate the most efficient georgic activities:

The Countrey Parson considering the great aptnesse Countrey people have to think that all things come by a kind of naturall course; and that if they sow and soyle their grounds, they must have corn; if they keep and fodder well their cattel, they must have milk, and Calves; labours to reduce them to see Gods hand in all things, and to beleeve, that things are not set in such an inevitable order, but that God often changeth it according as he sees fit, either for reward or punishment. . . . By his sustaining power he preserves and actuates every thing in his being; so that corne doth not grow by any other vertue, then by that which he continually supplyes, as the corn needs it; without which supply the corne would instantly dry up, as a river would if the fountain were stopped. . . . So that if a farmer should depend upon God all the year, and being ready to put hand to sickle, shall then secure himself, and think all cock-sure; then God sends such weather, as lays the corn, and destroys it: or if he depend on God further, even till he imbarn his corn, and then think all sure; God sends a fire, and consumes all that he hath. . . . Better were his corne burnt, then not spiritually improved. (pp. 270-72)

Scientific husbandry, which was to transform the English nation over the next two centuries, depends on precisely such faith: if one plants in such a way, or manures the ground in such a way, then such and such will be the results. The essence of scientific experimentation is predictability. As Bacon often argued, the God of science does not tamper with the chain of second causes. Therefore, while the Christian farmer will expect that God may, from time to time, thwart his efforts, he will, nonetheless, continue to follow a methodical course, which need not prevent him from praying or from cultivating his soul at the same time that he cultivates his soil.

Virgil describes heaven-sent storms, fires, droughts, and plagues very like Herbert's; but he gives these divine hardships a different, indeed an opposite, interpretation. Jupiter sends his plagues against humanity in order to stimulate them and force them to greater effort and inventiveness (1.121-46). A farmer who does not work all the harder in response to such setbacks may, as we have seen, end up hunting acorns in the forest for his supper (1.155-59). The farmer should "pray for rain" (157), but he must also do a good deal of hoeing and pruning at the same time. Virgil's farmer depends, like Herbert's, on divine favor; yet Virgil stresses precisely that attitude toward life that Herbert takes such pains to deny: first, that individual effort and labor are necessary and can produce a successful outcome or at least stave off the world's drift toward decay and chaos; and second, that the sum total of all such individual efforts is capable of transforming the whole of society into something better and happier. Certainly Virgil is fully aware of the difficulties; yet his georgic vision includes the hope of worldly progress and civil evolution—outcomes the very possibility of which Herbert prefers to ignore or deny. That it is not simply Christianity that makes the difference is revealed by the case of Spenser, whose God approves of hard work as thoroughly as Herbert's seems to look down on it—or, for that matter, by the case of Luigi Cornaro, whose God delights in the material improvement of the land and its inhabitants.

It is no secret that Herbert's poetry, like Donne's, turned inward. It may be that Herbert had a variety of personal reasons for giving up the pursuit of "State-employments";[17] yet the times also were such that a Spenserian vision of public service by means of public labors was no longer easily tenable. Herbert's example shows how little even a forward-looking and charitable member of the English establishment—himself a hard worker in his chosen vocation—was capable of understanding the importance of work, or of agricultural labor, or of the potential benefit to the nation inherent in land improvement. Herbert admired Bacon; for a man of his station he was unusually sympathetic to the problems of ordinary people; and he was drawn to a country parish by what he felt to be a special calling. At Bemerton he observed the countrymen about their work, and he based a number of his images on their activities. Yet not even Herbert could perceive, in the labor that he witnessed, much more than the negative spectacle of sinners busying their hands to avoid idleness or, far too often, "wallowing" in worldliness.

BEN JONSON

There is a familiar contradiction in Ben Jonson's relationship to his successors in English poetry. When, against the odds,

[17] The phrase is used by the author of "The Printers to the Reader," whom tradition associates with Nicholas Ferrar (Herbert, *Works*, p. 3).

the bricklayer's stepson became the court's chief poet and consorted on more or less equal terms with society's leaders, a paradoxical result was that this man with his "mountaine belly" and "rockie face," this laborious composer of deliberate verse and notorious burner of midnight oil, this professional writer for money, adopted and inspired a line of graceful, aristocratic, careless, and amateur sons, known as Cavaliers. The disjunction between Ben and the Sons of Ben is reflected in Jonson's writings; it is especially evident when we consider Jonson's attitude toward that bête noire of the typical courtier, hard work. Clearly Jonson was far more successful than Spenser in persuading the court to admire and in fact to pay for his views. While Spenser had to settle for patronage in exile, as an uncrowned laureate in distant Ireland, Jonson had the freedom of Westminster and fought with Inigo Jones for the honor of being chief artist to the king. Doubtless Jonson's greater immediate success was due to his tact. A strain of anti-courtliness imbues such poems as "On Some-thing, that Walkes Some-where" and "On Court-Worme," but these poems may be (and presumably were) interpreted as attacks on individual, aberrant courtiers and not on the court as an institution. More disturbing are those poems, such as the Cary-Morison Ode, which express Jonson's deep conviction that personal integrity may be achieved only strenuously, against the pull of almost universal corruption in society. Still, the masques and encomia in which Jonson offers models of conduct for readers and onlookers to emulate seldom openly advocate ideals that would too much trouble the tastes of a conservative aristocrat.

As far as the ideal of hard work as a virtue is concerned, Jonson no more attempted to foist it on the courtiers and ladies whom he praised than he succeeded in imposing it on his Sons and poetic heirs; yet, parodoxically, he made himself famous as a hard worker, and he made hard work a basic constituent of the self-portrait that runs through his poetry and his literary criticism. Raymond Williams has made us subversively aware of how Jonson removes work from such artistocratic celebrations as "To Penshurst," effecting a "magical extraction of the curse of labour" by the simple expedient of removing the laborers.[18] Only by indirection does Jonson suggest that courtiers may earn their positions and their perquisites by working, as when he praises Sir Henry Goodyere for his hawking but concludes: "Now, in whose pleasures I have this discerned, / What would his serious actions me have learned?" ("To Sir Henry Goodyere," 11-12).[19] The one exception, which proves the rule, is "An Epigram on William Lord Bur[ghley]," written to be presented to Robert Cecil engraved on a gold plate. Neither of these men affected the manners of a Ralegh or a Leicester or was likely to be thought of as the embodiment of *sprezzatura*; Jonson's poem fastens on precisely what differentiated Burghley from his less painstaking rivals:

> The only faithfull Watchman for the Realme,
> > That in all tempests, never quit the helme,
> But stood unshaken in his Deeds, and Name,
> > And labour'd in the worke; not with the fame.
>
> > > (9-12)

Unlike most courtiers, Cecil might be expected to take this particular form of praise as a compliment, both to his father and to himself. Most gentlemen would have preferred a more graceful compliment.

This is not to say, of course, that most of England's great men refused to work hard, since clearly the kingdom did not rise to greatness solely by means of accomplished *sprezzatura* on the part of its leaders. Rather, those leaders preferred to conceal their labors, as Castiglione had urged a courtier should do, by the use of social fictions, fictions that were elaborated in the poetry that celebrated their deeds or their way of life. Such a habit of concealment was bound to result in at least divided attitudes toward work, making even apparently well-

[18] *The Country and the City* (London: Chatto & Windus, 1973), p. 32.
[19] *The Complete Poetry of Ben Jonson*, ed. William B. Hunter, Jr. (1963; New York: Norton, 1968), p. 36. The non-dramatic poems are quoted from this text.

intentioned or public-spirited labor into something that one did secretly for one's profit or advancement, something one hesitated to admit, something best left, publicly at least, to one's social inferiors. As we have noted, everyone of importance was engaged in farming, directly or indirectly, but so long as literature chose to ignore that fact it would be difficult to regard agriculture as an activity beneficial to society. Similarly, everyone was engaged in work, of one sort or another, but, so long as few chose to admit it, hard labor for the common welfare would remain a clouded ideal. When an experienced printer, Richard Jones, offered *Brittons Bowre of Delights* (1591) "To the Gentlemen *Readers,*" he candidly admitted that his motives were "chiefly to pleasure you, and partly to profit my selfe."[20] That is to say, profit is the apt reward for this shrewd business practitioner, who abases himself by the very admission, but pleasure is the fit reward for his gentle readers. When Barnabe Barnes informed the Earl of Southampton in a dedicatory sonnet that the poems of *Parthenophil and Parthenophe* (1593) were "Sprong from a rude and unmanured lande," he may be suspected of tacitly boasting his role of gentleman amateur at the same time that he is working the standard modesty topos. In much the same way, Barnes is able to establish a measure of common ground with the great Earl of Essex in another sonnet by associating his largely pastoral collection of verse with leisure and aristocratic play:

Voutchsafe (thrise valiant Lord) this verse to reade,
    When time from cares of more importe permittes,
    The too deare charge of mine uncharged wittes:
    And that I do my lighter muses leade
To kisse your sacred handes, I myldely pleade
    For pardon, where all gracious vertue sittes.[21]

[20] *Brittons Bowre of Delights 1591*, ed. Hyder Edward Rollins (1933; New York: Russell & Russell, 1968), p. 3.

[21] *Parthenophil and Parthenophe*, ed. Victor A. Doyno (Carbondale: Southern Illinois Univ. Press, 1971), pp. 131-32.

The sharing of leisure, and therefore of a common gentility, is what enables Barnes to approach such a patron even humbly. This particular maneuver will be recognized as common; only the most confident poets, such as Spenser and Jonson, would risk hinting that they ought to be rewarded for working hard at their vocations, just as their noble patrons were working hard at theirs.

Jonson was not above celebrating leisured courtly ideals. In *The Golden Age Restored* (1615), for example, he allows British poetry and the king's beneficent presence, aided by the powers of dance, effortlessly to bring back Astraea, so that "earth unplough'd shall yeeld her crop, / Pure honey from the oake shall drop."[22] Like Montaigne in "Of Cannibals," Jonson is making an anti-georgic out of Virgil's description of the Golden Age in the *Georgics* (1.125, 131). In *Pleasure Reconciled to Virtue* (1618), Jonson brings in Hercules as a central character, not to work but to rest from his labors. Under the harmonious influence of the British court, the famous choice between easy pleasure and arduous virtue becomes unnecessary. Indeed, Jonson once more cites Virgil against himself, mocking in his antimasque the hard georgic necessity that gave rise to human civilization. Jove forced man to cultivate himself along with the soil and to invent the various arts, Virgil says, by means of *labor improbus* and *urgens egestas* (*Georgics* 1. 121-46). In his "Hymn" to Comus, Jonson parodies the whole process:

> Roome, roome, make roome for the bouncing belly,
> first father of Sauce, and deviser of gelly,
> Prime master of arts, and the giver of wit,
> That found out the excellent ingine, the spit,
> The plough, and the flaile, the mill, and the Hoppar,
> The hutch, and the bowlter, the furnace, and coppar.
> (7:479-80)

---

[22] *Ben Jonson*, ed. C. H. Herford, Percy and Evelyn Simpson, 11 vols. (Oxford: Clarendon Press, 1925-52), 7:426. The text of Jonson's masques is from vol. 7 of Herford and Simpson.

Of course, this is only the antimasquers who speak, with characteristically energetic insolence. After the revels, Jonson adds a final song that retracts what has seemed to be the message of the masque:

> [Virtue] will have you know,
>   That though
> hir sports be soft, hir life is hard.
>   You must returne unto the Hill,
>   and there advaunce
> With labour, and inhabit still
>   that height, and crowne.
>   (7:491)

As it happens, however, life impinged on art with peculiar aptness, so as to prevent Jonson from communicating this rather severe correction to the listening courtiers. As Orasio Busino, chaplain to the Venetian ambassador, reports, precisely as this final song was about to be sung, the king intervened in a well-known exhibition of his character:

> [T]he King, who is naturally choleric got impatient and shouted aloud, "Why don't you dance? What did you make me come here for? Devil take you all, dance." Upon this the Marquis of Buckingham, his Majesty's most favored minion immediately sprang forward cutting a score of lofty and very minute capers, with so much grace and agility that he not only appeased the ire of his angry Lord, but moreover rendered himself the admiration and delight of everybody.[23]

Thus did *sprezzatura* save the day. Incidents such as this must have discouraged Jonson from addressing the court on such subjects as work; indeed, when the masque was performed again, Jonson concluded it with a series of "merry speeches"

---

[23] G. E. Bentley, *The Jacobean and Caroline Stage*, 5 vols. (Oxford: Clarendon Press, 1941-56), 4:671; cited by Stephen Orgel, *The Jonsonian Masque* (Cambridge, Mass.: Harvard Univ. Press, 1967), pp. 70-71.

performed by counterfeit Welshmen. Doubtless the king and his court approved for political reasons of the defeat of Comus and his antimasquers; but that is not to say they did not in the meantime enjoy Jonson's amusing substitution, for Virgil's Jove, "Pater ipse colendi" (1.121), "the father of agriculture himself," of the fat figure of Comus, "first father of Sauce."[24]

By its very nature, the masque as a genre is prone to show the reduction of disorder to order without the visible expenditure of much fuss or effort, arriving at its denouement by means of dance, music, and clever machinery. The masque-writer assumes that the king's mere presence or his barest wish is sufficient to bring about a miraculous transformation—as indeed it often was, although in practice that wish had to exert itself through the toils of the bureaucracy. Besides (to raise another generic consideration) it is ill manners to call for hard work at a celebration. Still, it looks as if Jonson moderated or suppressed his personal views about the value of labor in favor of more typically courtly attitudes. For when he turns to the business of life, and especially to himself and his own profession, his tone is quite different.

According to common report, Jonson was well known, and often mocked, for his laboriousness—presumably by those who swore by the courtly vogue of *sprezzatura*. Thus Suckling draws the traditional contrast between "The sweat of learned *Johnsons* brain" and "gentle *Shakespear*'s eas'er strain,"[25] and Jonson's friend Carew reassured him in the face of common criticism:

> Let them the deare expence of oyle upbraid
> Suckt by thy watchfull Lampe. . . .
> Repine not at the Tapers thriftie waste. . . .

---

[24] For a more charitable view, with the suggestion that Jonson's more strenuous private valuation of labor might have been perceived by acute onlookers, see Richard S. Peterson, "The Iconography of Jonson's *Pleasure Reconcil'd to Virtue*," *Journal of Medieval and Renaissance Studies*, 5 (1975), 123-53 + plates.

[25] *The Works of Sir John Suckling: The Non-Dramatic Works*, ed. Thomas Clayton (Oxford: Clarendon Press, 1971), p. 70.

Thy labour'd workes shall live.
("To Ben. Johnson")[26]

The well-known lines in Jonson's praise of Shakespeare clearly reflect his own experience in composition. Their nervous energy makes them a quintessential statement of poetry as triumphant labor:

Who casts to write a living line, must sweat,
    (such as thine are) and strike the second heat
Upon the *Muses* anvile: turne the same,
    (And himselfe with it) that he thinkes to frame;
Or for the lawrell, he may gaine a scorne,
    For a good *Poet's* made, as well as borne.[27]

Jonson's imperious distortions of word order and of rhythm, the association that he forces between his muses and the crude blacksmith's anvil and furnace, his insistence on the need to sweat if one really wishes to achieve his goal, all are considerably different in tone from any of the various conventional portrayals of poetic composition.

But the fullest statement of Jonson's doctrine of labor may be found in *Timber* (1640). Here are a number of significant filiations: that the labor of writing is closely connected with the best methods of education; that it is connected with the Baconian search for truth; that it is inseparable simply from living, since the study of poetry "offers to mankinde a certaine rule, and Patterne of living well, and happily; disposing us to all Civill offices of Society."[28] The first requirement for a poet is "frequent . . . Exercise" of his abilities. If a poem will not come at first, "try an other time, with labour." Do not fly into a rage, but "bring all to the forge, and file, againe; tourne it a newe. . . . If it come, in a yeare, or two, it is well." The

[26] *The Poems of Thomas Carew*, ed. Rhodes Dunlap (Oxford: Clarendon Press, 1949), p. 65.

[27] *Complete Poetry*, ed. Hunter.

[28] *Ben Jonson*, ed. Herford and Simpson, 8:636. All quotations from *Timber* are from vol. 8.

"incomparable *Virgil* . . . brought forth his verses like a Beare, and after form'd them with licking." "I have met many of these Rattles, that made a noyse, and buz'de. They had their humme; and, no more. Indeed, things, wrote with labour, deserve to be so read, and will last their Age" (8:636-38). Shakespeare never blotted a line, it is said; Jonson wishes he had "blotted a thousand" (8:583).

Also in *Timber*, Jonson advises a nobleman, perhaps the Earl of Newcastle, on the education of his children. They should first learn how to write and speak well, for thus they will be enabled to find out and express their own true natures. Noble children should not be tutored privately at home, "in a shade," as was the usual custom, but should be taught with others in the "heate of the Sunne." "I would send them where their industry should be daily increas'd by praise; and that kindled by emulation." The child's natural desire to play should be encouraged, since "it is a signe of spirit, and live-linesse"; yet play should be balanced by work. Therefore the child should be nourished in ambition and honor and taught "never to bee suspected of sloath" (8:614-15).

If one wishes to write well, three things are necesary: to read the best authors, to listen to the best speakers, "and much exercise of his owne style." "No matter how slow the style be at first, so it be labour'd, and accurate." One should imitate the great writers, who "impos'd upon themselves care, and industry" (8:615-16). To illustrate his doctrine of laborious-ness, which, against tradition, he argues ought to be imposed even on the nation's young aristocrats, Jonson chooses georgic metaphors:

> And therefore these things are no more written to a dull disposition, then rules of husbandry to a barren Soyle. . . . There is a time to bee given all things for maturity; and that even your Countrey-husband-man can teach; who to a young plant will not put the proyning knife, because it seemes to feare the iron, as not able to admit the scarre. No more would I tell a greene Writer all his

faults, lest I should make him grieve and faint, and at last despaire. (8:617-18)

The country husbandman to whom Jonson refers is obviously Virgil's vinegrower, who refrains from using his knife on young shoots because, before they reach maturity, they "fear the iron" (1.369). Jonson's metaphor for training up young children to be hard but spirited workers echoes Virgil's general description as well as this particular phrase.

Jonson again echoes the *Georgics* when he insists that poverty is not a disgrace, as his detractors would claim, but a force that incites men to foundation and invention. "It was the ancient poverty, that founded Common-weales; built Cities, invented Arts, made wholesome Lawes; armed men against vices; rewarded them with their owne vertues; and preserv'd the honour, and state of Nations" (8:605). Jonson's poverty is equivalent to Virgil's *egestas* (1.146), need or want, the driving force behind man's hard labors, the spur that urges his progress toward civilization. For Jonson, as his poems continually reveal, it is what a man is and does that counts; riches and high birth have no value in themselves and may even impede a man if he rests on them. Virtue, which according to feudal opinion (still largely current) resided primarily in the blood, he would rather associate with active accomplishment and in particular with hard and ambitious labor.

Jonson's georgic sense of virtue is embodied in his preference for a workmanlike middle style. When Jonson speaks of the three levels of style in poetry, he conforms to traditional views when he calls on the writer to match his style to his subject matter. In a vivid comical metaphor, he writes that big men should pour out their words "all grave, sinnewye and strong," while dwarfs should speak "humble, and low, the words poore and flat." But Jonson then proceeds to break with tradition, and to insist not only that style and matter should suit one another, but that the middle style is simply the best. "The middle are of a just stature. There the Language is plaine, and pleasing: even without stopping, round without swelling. . . . [V]itious Language is vast, and gaping . . . full of Rocke, Mountaine, and pointednesse: as it affects to be low, it is abject, and creeps, full of bogs, and holes" (8:625-26). Even considering Jonson's implicit appeal to the familiar concept of an Aristotelian mean, this is a radical view, for all his fellow critics agreed that the greatest writing is that which treats high matter in a high style. Characteristically, for every brief mention of the *Georgics* in the sixteeth and seventeenth centuries in connection with style, there are a hundred fervent praises of the *Aeneid*.

Although he is not always given full credit, Jonson was in many respects a deeply innovative poet and theoretician, much more radical than the flamboyant Donne. He was as much a catalyst to his century as Ezra Pound was to ours. The significance, and possibly the source, of Jonson's support for the middle style becomes clearer if we consider its immediate context. Right after Jonson states his preference for the middle style, he evokes Francis Bacon on the distempers of language, which impede the search for rational and scientific truth. The astonishing implication is that the high and the low styles are nothing more than such distempers. Although there are rumors of planned or lost Jonsonian epics, nevertheless it remains true—and surprising—that throughout most of his long career Jonson avoided the two genres most popular in his time, pastoral and epic. His unfinished play, *The Sad Shepherd*, is a late and critically controversial exception. He often touched on the base and the heroic from various points of view; he wrote mock epic and pindaric; yet on the whole his poems adhere to a middle way. "By discrediting falshood, Truth growes in request," Jonson writes, and goes on to argue that the best way to accomplish such a transformation is to reform the language, to avoid both bombast and affected simplicity, to write in such a way as—in another georgic metaphor—"gently [to] stirre the mould about the root of the Question" (8:627).

For Jonson in his role as poet there are to be few instances of unmitigated heroics or of pastoral retreat, but instead constant labors. He repeats a tale about Plato, that foremost seeker of truth; dissatisfied with the learning he found in Athens, Plato traveled into Italy and Egypt. His arduous journey teaches Jonson this lesson: "Hee labour'd, so must wee." From the husbandman we may learn how best to support these necessary, constant labors with variety:

> As when a man is weary of writing, to reade; and then againe of reading, to write. . . . But some will say, this variety breeds confusion. . . . Why doe wee not then perswade husbandmen, that they should not till Land, helpe it with Marle, Lyme and Compost? plant Hop-gardens, prune trees, looke to Bee-hives, reare sheepe, and all other Cattell at once? It is easier to doe many things, and continue, then to doe one thing long. (7:619-20)

The image of the poet that Jonson fashions in *Timber* could not be further from the conventional pastoral image of the poet as shepherd or as gentleman amateur; after all, Jonson's poet, like the plowman of *The Faerie Queene*, is not afraid or ashamed of work.

Although Jonson reveals in *Timber* that he had developed definite theories concerning the relationship of poetry to life, theories that put a high, even a supreme, value on persistent labor, nonetheless it is also clear that he did not put those theories wholly into practice in his own poetry. His poems were labored, but they do not celebrate labor. The only poem in which Jonson unabashedly celebrates the value of hard work is his praise of Shakespeare, itself another piece of literary criticism. Although "To Penshurst" and "To Sir Robert Wroth" are both thoughtful philosophical poems about the nature of country living, neither has much if anything to say about country labor. Most of Jonson's poems are social poems, yet more often than not they show the people whom he admires interacting with one another in various situations of leisure, not of cooperative toil. "Inviting a Friend to Supper" is typical. Jonson has dispensed with that overworked

109

cliché of aristocratic leisure, the easy pastoral, but he cannot be said to have replaced the pastoral mode by the georgic, as Spenser had done. We can only speculate what were the reasons for this obvious discrepancy between Jonson's poetic theory and his practice. He seems to have felt a profound ambivalence about the value of labor. It was, essentially, labor that made him what he was; it was continuing labor that enabled him to remain what he was and to produce great poetry; yet it was also labor that subjected him to ridicule and that set him apart from those aristocrats whose way of life he so obviously admired and with whom he was anxious to consort on terms of equality.

I am reminded of Yeats, who said about the difficulties of poetic composition: "Better go down upon your marrow-bones /And scrub a kitchen pavement, or break stones," yet who was constantly putting that labor to the service of a graceful aristocratic ideal. The poem in which these lines appear is the one in which Yeats discusses the contradiction most explicitly; aptly he gave it the title "Adam's Curse."[29] Jonson too refers to that ancient curse, in his heartfelt, some have thought despairing, prayer, "To Heaven":

> Is it interpreted in me disease,
>> That, laden with my sinnes, I seeke for ease? . . .
> I know my state, both full of shame, and scorne,
>> Conceiv'd in sinne, and unto labour borne,
> Standing with feare, and must with horror fall,
>> And destin'd unto judgement, after all.
>> (3-4, 17-20)

Here is no honor for labor; work is the companion of ineradicable shame, of scorn and sin; it is the advance sign of fear, of horror, and of a fall into judgment. One may well see in these lines evidence that Jonson feels a deep personal

---

[29] *The Collected Poems of W. B. Yeats* (1940; New York: Macmillan, 1954), pp. 78-79. I am grateful to Michael Yeats, Macmillan London, Ltd., and Macmillan Publishing Co., Inc., New York, for permission to quote these lines.

identification with those old theological conventions, that he is telling his readers a story that concerns not only the general fall of man but some personal, psychological fall or early trauma. The full details about Jonson's much-ridiculed apprenticeship to his bricklaying stepfather are now beyond confirmation; still less can we know whether this rumored experience was for Jonson what working in the bottling factory was for Dickens. Yet the poetic evidence points in that direction.

Although Jonson wrote no unqualified praise of work except for his poem to Shakespeare, he did write a poem that is distinctly ambivalent in its praise, to Richard Brome, who had once been Jonson's servant but who had left to become a successful playwright and therefore potentially an equal and a rival for popularity. The story may have been rather similar to Jonson's own, except that it happened more unavoidably under society's eye. Spenser's Redcross and his Pastorella, whom he apprenticed respectively to a plowman and a shepherd, learned the value of honest work but experienced no shame, perhaps because they were secretly of noble blood and only the adopted children of their foster parents. Real life is seldom so obliging. People found it difficult to get over the impression that the really remarkable thing about Brome was not that he wrote so well but that (like Samuel Johnson's dog) a servant should write at all. Whether consciously or unconsciously, Jonson seems to have shared that attitude toward his friend and former servant. Ordinarily the distinction between Jonson's poems of praise and those of blame is sharp, but not in this instance:

> I Had you for a Servant, once, *Dick Brome*;
>> And you perform'd a Servants faithfull parts:
> Now, you are got into a nearer roome,
>> Of *Fellowship*, professing my old Arts.
> And you doe doe them well, with good applause,
>> Which you have justly gained from the *Stage*,
> By observation of those Comick Lawes
>> Which I, your *Master*, first did teach the Age.

So far, one might see nothing but a natural rivalry, revealed by the confident skill with which Jonson at once praises his friend yet puts him in his place relative to himself as master (in both senses of the word). But there is more:

> You learn'd it well; and for it, serv'd your time
>   A Prentise-ship: which few doe now a dayes.
> Now each Court-Hobby-horse will wince in rime;
>   Both learned, and unlearned, all write *Playes*.
> It was not so of old: Men tooke up trades
>   That knew the Crafts they had bin bred in, right:
> An honest *Bilbo*-Smith would make good blades,
>   And the *Physician* teach men spue, or shite;
>   The *Cobler* kept him to his nall; but, now
>   Hee'll be a *Pilot*, scarce can guide a Plough.

Here is apprenticeship, craftsmanship, and professionalism with a vengeance. At first Jonson seems to be saying that the problem is an invasion of the writer's craft by courtly amateurs, who try to write plays without having first labored through the necessary long and arduous preparation. But honorable professions quickly give place to dishonorable ones. We begin with the martial swordmaker, a fine contrast to courtly fribbles, but we soon descend, through the physician and the cobbler, to the mere plowman. People should stick to the crafts they have been "bred" in; this particular phrasing has reference to blood, rank, and station as well as to expertise. Oddly, Jonson ends his increasingly bitter "praise" with Spenser's two metaphors for the poet, pilot and plowman, but he leaves little doubt which of the two metaphors he considers to be the more honorable or admirable. Spenser thinks it no shame to compare himself to a plowman; obviously Jonson thinks otherwise.

More than simple contempt for Brome underlies the sudden eruption of scatological imagery into Jonson's previously friendly if characteristically measured panegyric.[30] The poem

[30] Contrary to Edmund Wilson's argument in "Morose Ben Jonson," *The*

moves from a subtext that touches on himself rather closely yet that Jonson is able to handle smoothly—the jealousy any playwright might feel toward a new rival—to one that for Jonson is far more intimate and troubling—the value and place of labor in the life of a self-made man. For Jonson, to repudiate labor would mean to repudiate the very essence of his Muse, yet to embrace labor would mean to confess to low origins. The shame Jonson attaches to the idea of the plowman-poet is revealed by the one instance in which he assumes the role; he does so with tellingly harsh self-mockery. He concludes his notorious mock-epic, "On the Famous Voyage," with a couplet that seems to glance satirically at Spenser as well as at Virgil and himself:

> And I could wish for their eterniz'd sakes,
> My *Muse* had plough'd with his, that sung *A-jax*.
> (195-96)

Only in such a context, safeguarded by the involutions of irony, will Jonson take up his plow. Given the social context in which he was operating and his desire to be an accepted member of the best society, the conflict between Jonson's high opinion of work and his sense that work was shameful would appear to have been irreconcilable. The result was that although he did not hesitate to give his aristocratic patrons and friends plenty of moral advice under the guise of praise in his poetry, unlike Spenser he was not sufficiently confident in himself, or sufficiently self-sacrificing, to advise his social betters to work, even though, as *Timber* repeatedly reveals, work was close to the heart of his own personal ethic. The closest he came to playing the part of a Spenserian adviser to courtiers was when he suggested that the children of aristocrats might be taught to work hard. Like Bacon, he saw that present

---

Triple Thinkers (1948; New York: Oxford Univ. Press, 1963), pp. 213-32, the scatological imagery in Jonson's works is usually functional in its context, as in Shakespeare, Milton, or Swift. That is, one can usually find an explanation for it in the poem rather than in Jonson's personality.

113

incomprehension and inertia might yet be turned to future success; unlike Bacon, he never pursued that insight further.

Nevertheless, one might think that any admirer who confronted Jonson's poetry, aware of the poet's reputation for laborious effort and witnessing the sheer energy and the massive authority of the verse itself, as well as its emphasis on self-fashioning, would learn the implicit lesson of labor in spite of Jonson's surface reticence. Such, however, was evidently not the case. Jonson drew back from a full exposition of labor's human and civic value; as a result, it must have been much easier for his Sons to imitate their father's ease and elegance but not his strenuousness. Of them all, only Carew shows much inclination to move in that direction in his verse style, and, lacking Jonson's overwhelming moral vision, he chose to exercise his capabilities only occasionally— as when he was praising the two poets, Jonson and Donne. Perhaps he perceived the stylistic but not the social utility of the labored mode. Few other poets early in the century practiced anything like a poetry of work. The cult of difficulty, as exemplified by Chapman, with its origins in the more pessimistic branches of Roman Stoicism, has a surface resemblance to some of the ideals that Jonson expressed in *Timber*, but it too lacks the Jonsonian sense of moral commitment. Even given Chapman's interest in Greek, it seems significant that he chose to translate Hesiod's *Works and Days* rather than Virgil's *Georgics*, for Hesiod has none of Virgil's sense that labor may contribute to national progress. Essentially the cult exemplified by Chapman reflects not an optimistic Baconian search for reformation and truth but a backward-looking, pessimistic despair at the corruption of the times. At the beginning of the century, Jonson alone was capable of taking up the task that Spenser had laid down. Perhaps for the reasons I have suggested, perhaps for others, he did so only partly. As a result, the new poetry that came in with the new century, even though it derived much of its energy from an impulse to revolt against the courtly style, posed no immediate threat to the courtly aversion to work. If that judgment applies to Jonson and his followers, it applies even more obviously to those other new voices in poetry, Donne and Herbert.

Donne was too private a poet to embrace the georgic vision, but from time to time the mixture of envy and contempt that he felt for land ownership and for the unexamined contentment of the husbandman led him to satirize or otherwise to pillory the georgic mode. His negative response is a fine example of how Donne could make good poetry out of bad feelings, as well as a revelation of the forces, psychological and political, that were driving him inward toward his characteristically private sort of poetry. In contrast with Donne, Jonson had an excellent understanding of the value of work, one that may be judged to have been the equal of Spenser's; but his ambition to associate himself with worldly greatness and, it may be, to escape the shame of his origins, led him to suppress open advocacy of labor except when discussing poetic composition. Jonson's divided treatment of the theme of work is intimately connected with his integrity as a poet and moralist, and it raises difficult questions about the location of that point where tact becomes compromise, or where poetic tension and complexity become complicity. Still, he deserves much credit for at least wrestling with those powerful social assumptions to which most other poets quietly surrendered.[31]

The early heirs of Spenser generally ignored his work ethic. The Sons of Ben, given comfort by their father's ambivalence to work, imitated only his ease. Marvell excepted, the Metaphysical heirs of Donne and Herbert, constrained by High-Church loyalties in a deteriorating political situation, retreated still further from engagement in public affairs. The proclamation of 1620 forbidding public discussion of state affairs, about which Drayton complains so bitterly in "To Master George Sandys" ("I feare, as I doe Stabbing, this word, State"),

---

[31] By the poet's choice, questions of moral integrity are more central to Jonson's work than they might be in other cases; on this issue see Richard S. Peterson's fine study, *Imitation and Praise in the Poems of Ben Jonson* (New Haven: Yale Univ. Press, 1981), and the suggestive review of that book by Arthur F. Marotti, *Renaissance Quarterly*, 35 (1982), 526-28.

was only one incident in the lengthy tale of the crown's al-ienation even of those poets who were disposed to be friendly. As Jonathan Goldberg points out, as early as 1584, when he was still James VI of Scotland, the king had written, in a treatise on the rules to be "observit and eschewit" in poetry: "Ye man [must] also be war of wryting any thing of materis of commoun weill, or uther sic grave sene subjectis . . . because . . . they are to grave materis for a Poet to mell in."[32] After the outbreak of the Civil War, other poets and writers, who rode the revolution, might hope according to their various lights to direct its forces into channels that would benefit the nation; those poets who resisted the revolution could only grit their teeth, rail against a world in which carters and plowmen trampled down their betters, or retreat into privacy and hope for the return of king and court. Virgil conceived the *Georgics* in the midst of civil war; the development of similar conditions in England gave his poem and its ideals new relevance to the nation's political and historical situation. In the meantime, however, the result of Jonson's reluctance to throw his full weight into the struggle begun by Spenser, of Donne's pro-phetic if sometimes petulant resistance to georgic ideas, and of Herbert's Christian scorn for worldly labor and material progress, was that the center of effort of the georgic movement passed, for a while, from the poets to the scientists.[33]

[32] James I and VI, *Ane Schort Treatise, Conteining Some Reulis and Cautelis to be observit and eschewit in Scottis Poesie* (ch. 7), in *The Essayes of a Prentise* (Edinburgh, 1584), sigs. Mii[v]-Miii[r]; cited by Goldberg, *James I and the Politics of Literature* (Baltimore: Johns Hopkins Univ. Press, 1983), p. 19.

[33] Like Spenser and Jonson, Shakespeare came to question the aristocratic view of poetry, but for the most part his disillusionment took other forms. See Alvin B. Kernan, *The Playwright as Magician* (New Haven: Yale Univ. Press, 1979).

FOUR

New Science and
the Georgic Revolution

As the first chapter noted, georgic is usually said to have been introduced into English poetry by Dryden's popular translation of 1697. At that time, Dryden and Addison gave wide currency to the view that the *Georgics* was Virgil's finest poem; that it was, in brief, "the most Compleat, Elaborate, and finisht Piece of all Antiquity."[1] No one would argue with the proposition that full-scale georgic as a strict genre in imitation of Virgil's poem was essentially a phenomenon of the early eighteenth century. But georgic, like pastoral, is a mode more than a genre: a mode capable of invading, modifying, and even becoming central to a variety of distinct poetic genres. In that sense, as we have seen, the georgic mode and spirit, together with georgic themes and imagery, entered English poetry in no casual manner as early as Spenser, and began to inform or trouble the works of Jonson, Donne, and Herbert. Since standard theory held the *Georgics* to be a "middle" poem, it must have been social, not literary, assumptions that led Donne to think that its subject matter was only a little higher than the "seven foot of earth" that marks a grave (see ch. 3 above). So too, in Jonson's *Epicœne* (1609), Sir John Daw, a miserable poetaster who yet reflects accurately the assumptions about literature held by his kind, finds in the social infelicities of the *Georgics* a handy means for condemning Virgil's poetry: "*Homer*, an old tedious prolixe asse, talkes of curriers, and chines of beef. *Virgil*, of dunging of

---

[1] Joseph Addison, *Miscellaneous Works*, ed. A. C. Guthkelch, 2 vols. (London, 1914), 2:11; See ch. 1 above, and the studies of English georgic by Durling and Chalker cited there.

land, and bees. *Horace*, of I know not what" (2.3.62-66).[2]
That is a fictional critic speaking, but one may find much the
same attitude implied by *The Arte of English Poesie* (1589),
in which George Puttenham writes that according to tradition
the style of the *Georgics* "is counted meane" (i.e., middle),
yet also cannot resist pointing out elsewhere that all the pos-
sible protagonists of georgic, such as "the common artificer,
servingman, yeoman, groome, husbandman, day-labourer,"
are "base and low" (pp. 162, 164-65). Such attitudes were
well entrenched and required more than appeals to literary
theory to shift them. Although Spenser had begun the nec-
essary work, we have seen that the best of the succeeding
generation of poets did not immediately follow him up.

From the beginning of the seventeenth century, however,
another powerful force was also at work. The New Science,
which began eccentrically with the pronouncements of Bruno
and Dee, and more firmly in the writings of Francis Bacon,
significantly helped to dispel prevailing anti-georgic prejudices
among the English and to replace them with a wholly new
spirit. It is fair to say that in this task the New Scientists
helped Virgil, and that Virgil in turn helped the New Scientists.
For the scientific-technological movement harnessed the old
Virgilian vision, and this combination of pragmatic experi-
ment with literary insight proved remarkably fertile. Thomas
Sprat, in his *History of the Royal Society*, aptly remarks how
moderns might profitably make use of the ancient writers:

> [M]ethinks, that wisdom, which they fetch'd from the
> ashes of the dead, is something of the same nature, with
> Ashes themselves: which, if they are kept up in heaps
> together, will be useless: but if they are scattred upon
> Living ground, they will make it more fertile, in the bring-
> ing forth of various sorts of Fruits.[3]

---

[2] *Ben Jonson*, ed. Herford and Simpson, 5:185.
[3] Facs. ed. Jackson Cope and Harold Whitmore Jones (Saint Louis: Wash-
ington Univ. Studies, 1958), pp. 24-25.

The result of this fruitful combination of poetic vision and new science was what amounts to a georgic revolution in the seventeenth century, a revolution that preceded and was directly responsible for the well-known Agricultural Revolution of the eighteenth.

THE EIGHTEENTH CENTURY

When Dryden firmly established the fashion for rhymed couplets during the Augustan Age, he had more than a century's worth of such verse (imperfect, to be sure) with which to work. It has taken criticism some time to recognize the extent and importance of that earlier history. So too, when Dryden established the georgic as a popular mode and genre, his way had been made ready for him. Certainly one reason for the success that georgic was to enjoy in the eighteenth century was the coincidence of literary trends with social and economic changes. For it was in the eighteenth century that a long transformation in English agriculture finally reached its culmination in what was called the New Husbandry and, later, the Agricultural Revolution. Historians of agriculture have stressed the importance of certain mechanical inventions, such as the seed-drill and the horse-drawn hoe, which Jethro Tull developed just after 1700. Crop seeds, which had been hand-broadcast since the beginning of history, now could be planted in rows, producing a much greater yield per acre. But fifty years passed before these revolutionary devices came into common use. Arthur Young (the friend of Fanny Burney), who wrote extensively on agricultural theory, who became Secretary to the Board of Agriculture (1793), and who founded a periodical, *Annals of Agriculture* (1784-1809) in order to give farmers a place to record experiments, nevertheless wrote as late as 1770 that the new machines were worthless, since farm laborers might be expected to hitch them up and immediately bash them against a fencepost or a wall.

Nevertheless, Young, with his keenness for experimentation and innovation and his conviction that modern agriculture could enrich and transform the whole country, exemplifies the temper of his time. He urges the aristocracy and intellectual leaders to involve themselves in husbandry, to take an active part in directing the work—something that had only begun to be conceivable around 1700. What would once have been a gentleman's shame has, by the latter part of the eighteenth century, become his civic duty:

> It is the business of the nobility and gentry who practise agriculture, and of authors who practise and write on it, to help forward the age; to try experiments on newly introduced vegetables, and if they are found good, to spread the knowledge of them as much as possible; to endeavour to quicken the motions of the vast but un-wieldy body, the common farmers. But to omit this either in practice or in writing, is to reduce themselves to the level of those whom they ought to instruct; and to submit to that ignorance and backwardness, which left to them-selves, cloud any country, in an enlightened age, with the darkness of many preceding centuries. Common farmers love to grope in the dark: it is the business of superior minds, in every branch of philosophy, to start beyond the age, and shine forth to dissipate the night that involves them.[4]

There still is class feeling here in plenty. It is doubtful, too, whether Young does justice either to the necessity for any sensible farmer to conduct experiments cautiously or to the extent to which the new husbandry came from below, in the practice of farmers, rather than from above, in the theories of writers. Still, there has been an important change; now it is the gentleman's duty not to scorn but to lead his laborers in their civilizing work.

[4] *Rural Œconomy; or, Essays on the Practical Parts of Husbandry* (London: T. Becket, 1770), pp. 36-37. Among the earliest to plead that gentlemen involve themselves in agriculture are Timothy Nourse, in *Campania Fœlix* (1700, 1706, 1708), and Stephen Switzer (a defender of Virgil's husbandry against the aspersions of Jethro Tull) in *Ichnographia Rustica* ([early version 1715], 1718, 1742).

Indeed, to a large extent Young feels confident that he is preaching to the converted:

Perhaps we might, without any great impropriety, call farming the reigning taste of the present times. There is scarce a nobleman without his farm: most of the country gentlemen are farmers; and that in a much greater extent of the word, than when all the country business was left to the management of the stewards, who governed, in matters of wheat and barley, as absolutely as in covenants of leases, and the merit of tenants; for now the master oversees all the operations of his farm, dictates the management, and often delights in setting the country a staring at the novelties he introduces. The practice gives a turn to conversation, and husbandry usurps something on the territories of the stable and the kennel; an acquisition which I believe, with reasonable people, will be voted legal conquest.

But to speak in another strain: all parts of rural œconomics are, at present, much studied, and no less practised. It is impossible but this admirable spirit, which does so much honour to the present age, must be attended with great effects. For men of education and parts cannot apply to any thing without diffusing a light around them; much more so when they give their attention to a business that hitherto has occupied few besides the most contracted and most ignorant set of people in the world. And facts, as far as they have been discovered, warrant this opinion; for, I apprehend, no one will dispute there having been more experiments, more discoveries, and more general good sense displayed, within these ten years, in the walk of agriculture, than in an hundred preceding ones. If this noble spirit continues, we shall soon see husbandry in perfection, as well understood, and built upon as just and philosophic principles, as the art of medicine. (pp. 173-75)

Ten years is surely too short a time. Like some propagandists of the Renaissance, Young is insufficiently aware of the accomplishments of his predecessors. Yet there is no doubt that a revolution had taken place, in attitudes as well as agricultural practices.

By 1770, the English were well in the forefront of European agricultural progress; still, they continued to trade ideas with the Continent. Bound up with Young's essays is a newly translated tract by a Swiss agriculturalist entitled *The Rural Socrates*. The engaging author of this work proposes the formation of a new society with a significant name: "a Georgical Society of men of character, whose inflexible integrity, and complete knowledge of every thing relative to husbandry, might secure universal confidence and approbation." The members of this Georgical Society would travel the countryside and wake "a noble emulation" in the breasts of peasants, in order "to bring agriculture to a state of perfection." They would keep a journal of discoveries and summon the most worthy peasants, "in testimony of the public approbation, presenting them with the destined prize! I would choose to have it a medal, representing a labourer driving his plow; in the air the genius of agriculture, placing a crown on his head, composed of ears of corn and vine leaves interwoven, with this motto, 'For the best cultivator' " (pp. 475-76). Somewhat patronizing, we may feel; yet surely the thought that a peasant could be stirred to "noble emulation" would have seemed strange to most people in the early seventeenth century. Such a georgic ideal of heroism would have been almost inconceivable; noble emulation was for budding Aeneases, not for plowmen. Nevertheless, a student of the seventeenth century who reads about these Enlightenment projects of the Rural Socrates and of Arthur Young may well recognize several familiar notes in this unfamiliar context: experiment, trial, dirtying of hands, working cooperatively, publishing the results. All these progressive sentiments, including the awarding of honors to the contributors to, rather than the destroyers of, a fruitful society, go back to Francis Bacon.

Indeed, some of the innovative methods and programs that characterized the Agricultural Revolution may be traced back well beyond Bacon, to the economic transformations associated with the Tudor accession. The basis of efficient farming is improvement of the soil, and that can only be accomplished by crop rotation and, as Young insistently argues, by what he calls "proportion"—the division of a farm into pasture and arable, so the livestock may be fed in summer and kept over in winter and may in turn help work and fertilize the fields.[5] Such essential innovations as the practice of up-and-down husbandry (the shifting of fields from pasture to arable and back again at proper intervals), the draining of fens, the development of new fertilizers, and the floating of water-meadows, all came into common practice between 1550 and 1650.[6] Toward the end of the seventeenth century, new crops such as turnips, which were popularized as an efficient winter fodder by Charles, Viscount Townshend (known to posterity as Turnip Townshend), came into general use. In addition to these changes in agricultural technology, a second necessity was for the aristocracy as well as the rising middle class to change its views about what constitutes virtuous and public-spirited behavior—with the eventual literary consequence that at least some attention was shifted from the martial ideal that is proper to feudalism to the georgic ideal that is proper to a newly centralized and peaceful nation-state. A third necessity, or at least the only method available within the political pos-

[5] On soil husbandry, see Edward Hyams, *Soil and Civilization* (1952; New York: Harper & Row, 1976), esp. pp. 244-68.

[6] Differences of emphasis among recent agricultural historians are analogous to the familiar problem of whether there was a Renaissance or several renascences. R. H. Tawney, whose *The Agrarian Problem of the Sixteenth Century* (London: Longmans, Green, 1912), remains well known and influential if outdated in its evidence, is counterbalanced by Eric Kerridge, *Agrarian Problems in the Sixteenth Century and After* (London: George Allen & Unwin, 1969). Two recent studies I have found persuasive and useful are Eric Kerridge, *The Agricultural Revolution* (New York: Augustus M. Kelley, 1968), and *The Agrarian History of England and Wales*, ed. H.P.R. Finberg et al., in progress, esp. vol. 4 (Cambridge: Cambridge Univ. Press, 1967). Also useful is Mildred Campbell, *The English Yeoman in the Tudor and Early Stuart Age* (1942; New York: Augustus M. Kelley, 1968).

sibilities, was enclosure, the process of converting land from commons to private use, for that was the chief method that permitted the improvement of the soil by means of proportion, rotation, and fertilization.

Ironically, as feudal England was slowly and painfully transformed into a nation-state, the way to agricultural progress and general prosperity lay directly through social injustice and widespread rural suffering. Although the process took at least two centuries—and is reflected in literature from *Utopia* to *The Deserted Village*—the decade that seems decisively to have tipped the balance from a basically feudal to a basically modern system of land use was that of the 1650s. Expropriations, forced and voluntary sales, enclosures, and the expulsion of tenants so greatly accelerated as a result of the Civil War that the economic pressures practically forced land- and rent-holders to increase the efficiency of their operations in order to survive. Forests were cut down, fields were plowed up, rents were doubled and doubled again, and out of this chaos emerged the New Husbandry and the Augustan Age. It is no coincidence that remarkably similar historical processes underlay the composition of Virgil's *Georgics*: civil war, land expropriation, new capital formation, and the prospect of a period of national unity and peaceful prosperity somewhere just ahead.

Since the forces leading to change were well under way in the seventeenth century, one would expect to find in its literature more reflections of the georgic transformation than critics have spoken of. In any period the mass of writers may follow events, but ordinarily at least a few anticipate them. Indeed, such proves to have been the case. Although Thomas Tusser's *Five Hundreth Pointes of Good Husbandrie*, like other agricultural treatises of the sixteenth century, was conservative in orientation, we have noted that the riddle-poem "Husbandrie" anticipates later, more Virgilian attitudes. In *Observations touching Trade and Commerce with the Hollander, and other Nations; Presented to King James* (posthumously published), Sir Walter Ralegh tries to persuade the

124

king that his treasury would gain more by building up the
nation's prosperity than by pillaging it with taxes. "Then how
much more mighty things might we make," he asks the king,
"where so great abundance and variety of homebred com-
modities and rich materials grow for your people to work
upon, and other plentiful means to do that withal, which other
nations neither have nor cannot want, but of necessity must
be furnished from hence?"[7] But Ralegh, writing from the
Tower, had less luck even than Bacon in trying to persuade
King James to take the long-range, public-spirited view.

The agricultural historian G. E. Fussell has called the period
from 1600 to 1640 "the age of Markham."[8] During this time
Gervase Markham published a number of treatises on hus-
bandry—though he tended to reprint the same work under
different titles. An early title page suggests the sort of work
he is known for: *The English Husbandman. The First Part:
Contayning the Knowledge of the true Nature of every Soyle
within this Kingdome: how to Plow it; and the manner of the
Plough, and other Instruments belonging thereto. Together
with the Art of Planting, Grafting, and Gardening after our
latest and rarest fashion. A worke never written before by any
Author: and now newly compiled for the benefit of this King-
dome* (1613). Although the conclusion of his title hints at
altruistic patriotism, Markham was really a hack opportunist,
not an innovator. His works are chiefly significant as evidence
that there was a market for various do-it-yourself publica-
tions. His "Second Booke" of husbandry, which appeared in
1614, contained practical advice on kitchen-gardens and cattle
as well as angling and the breeding of fighting cocks. Ambi-
tious to be a Renaissance man of letters in his peculiar kind,
Markham published works on a variety of other practical

[7] *The Works of Sir Walter Raleigh, Kt.*, 8 vols. (1829; New York: Burt
Franklin, n.d.), 8:375.

[8] *The Old English Farming Books from Fitzherbert to Tull* (London:
Crosby Lockwood & Son, 1947), p. 21. Also useful is F.N.L. Poynter, *A
Bibliography of Gervase Markham* (Oxford: Oxford Bibliographical Society,
1962).

subjects: the breeding of race-horses, archery, how to get wealth, country contentments or the husbandman's recreations, the grammar of soldiership, and the essentials of veterinary practice. Other writers in the period published manuals on hunting, fishing, horsebreeding, dog training, and the like. For the most part these books are concerned more with the sporting than with the practical side of country life. As Young would put it, they address the stable and the kennel, which were the traditional concerns of the English gentry, rather than the barnyard. Moreover, they seem often to be addressed to amateurs, to would-be country gentlemen or to city-dwellers who dreamed of a change of occupation. Whatever pragmatic emphasis there may be is on traditional lore and on the recurrent theme of self-enrichment, usually couched in some variant of the perennial formula: Get rich quick! These writers show little interest in the sort of innovation and experimentation that characterize the treatises written by Worlidge and others after the Restoration. Moreover, however detailed and practical a given writer's advice may be, he is likely to reveal his adherence to old-fashioned views by portraying the country against which he sets his advice as a place for pleasant, essentially pastoral, relaxation—not for georgic improvement of the common good. The popularity of such treatises confirms that the pastoral mode still dominated the thinking not only of those who purchased books of poetry, but even of those with an interest in husbandry.

COWLEY, BACON, AND BRUNO

The one writer before Dryden whom recent historians of the English georgic cite is Abraham Cowley, though they commonly treat him as a kind of sport or exception, not as a connecting link to an earlier tradition. His *Several Discourses by Way of Essays* (1688) includes the century's fullest collection of verse translations from Virgil and Horace on husbandry and the country life.[9] Although Cowley's translations are skilled, they cannot be said to accomplish much more philosophically than to bring together in a crowning summary the fruits of a century-long practice of extracting happy-husbandman poems from the classics without offending the English taste for gentlemanly leisure.[10] Far more novel and significant is Cowley's introductory essay to the poems, "Of Agriculture." Cowley begins with an evocation of Virgil, perhaps in recognition that, while Horace had provided more country poems for imitation (as Cowley's translations confirm), Virgil was the more serious advocate of husbandry. "The first wish of *Virgil* (as you will find anon by his Verses) was to be a good Philosopher; the second, a good Husbandman." Of husbandry, Cowley argues that "There is no other sort of life that affords so many branches of praise to a Panegyrist: The Utility of it to a mans self: The Usefulness, or rather Necessity of it to all the rest of Mankind: The Innocence, the Pleasure, the Antiquity, the Dignity" (pp. 400-401).

Cowley remarks forcefully on that crucial difference between Roman and English attitudes toward husbandry, which had earlier given trouble to English teachers of the *Georgics:*

> [W]e have no men now fetcht from the Plow to be made Lords, as they were in *Rome* to be made Consuls and Dictators, the reason of which I conceive to be from an evil Custom, now grown as strong among us, as if it were a Law, which is, that no men put their Children to be bred up Apprentices in Agriculture, as in other Trades, but such who are so poor . . . [that they lack the means to farm efficiently]. Whilst they who are Proprietors of the Land, are either too proud, or, for want of that kind of Education, too ignorant to improve their Estates. (p. 401)

[9] Rpt. in *The English Writings of Abraham Cowley*, ed. A. R. Waller, 2 vols. (Cambridge: Cambridge Univ. Press, 1905-06), 1:409-28.

[10] For an overview of happy-husbandman poetry, see Maren-Sofie Røstvig, *The Happy Man* (Oslo: Akademisk Forlag, 1954), pp. 71-116.

Cowley's words reveal that he knows very well that, though he may personally think that agriculture is the best of subjects for praise, his age did not. Even this late in the seventeenth century, panegyric chose for its commonest subject not farming but war.

Yet agriculture, Cowley goes on to argue, is the one necessary art, to which all others may be said to be "like Figures and Tropes of Speech which serve only to adorn it." The chief stumbling-block to a recognition of this fact, and to a consequent acceptance of agricultural reform, is the deeply ingrained contempt, first for agriculture and second for manual labor—and, therefore, a double contempt for the combination. As Cowley ironically argues, the wrong accomplishments are valued and therefore honored by English society:

> Behold the Original and Primitive Nobility of all those great Persons, who are too proud now, not onely to till the Ground, but almost to tread upon it. We may talke what we please of Lilies, and Lions Rampant, and Spread-Eagles in Fields d'Or, or d'Argent; but if Heraldry were guided by Reason, a Plough in a Field Arable, would be the most Noble and Antient Armes. . . .
>
> And yet, who is there among our Gentry, that does not entertain a Dancing Master for his Children as soon as they are able to walk? But, Did ever any Father provide a Tutor for his Son to instruct him betimes in the Nature and Improvements of that Land which he intended to leave him? (p. 404)

To remedy this unreasonable state of affairs, Cowley proposes the foundation of an agricultural college in each of the universities. Four professors would preside over a body of scholars and fellows, and it is surely no coincidence that the four fields that those professors would take for their specialties correspond almost exactly to the four books of Virgil's *Georgics*. "First, *Aration*. . . . Secondly, *Pasturage*. Thirdly, *Gardens, Orchards, Vineyards* and *Woods*. Fourthly . . . the Government of *Bees* . . . (p. 405). Cowley departs from Virgil only

128

by assigning to the fourth professor activities that Virgil had omitted, such as the care of swine and poultry, the study of decoys and ponds, and even the science of field sports, "which ought to be looked upon not onely as Pleasures, but as parts of Housekeeping." This last proposal is an amusing reversal of earlier writers on husbandry, who had continually endeavored to portray the practical side of husbandry as if it were a pleasurable sport.

Although Virgil might appropriately be denominated honorary founder of Cowley's proposed agricultural college, still Cowley insists that there must be nothing backward-looking or theoretical about the projected course of study. For that reason he insists, somewhat disingenuously, that his professors are not to read "Pompous and Superficial Lectures out of *Virgils Georgickes, Pliny, Varro* or *Columella*," but should oversee the development of a practical training program—so practical, indeed, as serendipitously to pay all the college's expenses out of resultant income. Cowley's caution almost certainly reveals that he was aware of complaints that the first holders of chairs in science and mathematics at the universities had disappointed their founders' hopes by their unenterprising pedantry.[11]

If we look forward in time, we may recognize in Cowley's project the typical voice of the eighteenth-century agriculturalists and, beyond them, the eventual foundation of land-grant and agricultural colleges, whose aims and programs are not very different from what Cowley suggests. If we look back, we may recognize the voice of the man whom Cowley, in his ode "To the Royal Society," calls the Moses of the scientific movement: Francis Bacon, with his emphasis on practice, experiment, and concern for the common welfare. The place of Bacon in Cowley's thinking about agriculture is even more

[11] The truth of the charge is much debated, but the existence of such criticism is undoubted. See Christopher Hill, *Intellectual Origins of the English Revolution* (1965; London: Panther Books, 1972), pp. 14-84; Barbara Shapiro, *John Wilkins 1614-1672* (Berkeley: Univ. of California Press, 1969), pp. 118-47; and further works cited by Shapiro, p. 253n.

evident in an earlier treatise on the founding of an all-purpose scientific college, *A Proposition For the Advancement of Experimental Philosophy*, which Cowley published in 1661, the year before the Royal Society received its charter. Among the facilities of the college is to be a "Garden, containing all sorts of Plants that our Soil will bear." Another garden is "destined only to the tryal of all manner of Experiments concerning Plants, as their Melioration, Acceleration, Retardation, Conservation, Composition, Transmutation, Coloration, or whatsoever else can be produced by Art either for use or curiosity" (p. 251). One of the sixteen resident professors of this earlier and more ambitious college will take agriculture for his specialty. Concerned that his project should not appear too visionary to be put into practice, Cowley once again misleadingly dissociates it from its obvious progenitor: "[W]e do not design this after the Model of *Solomons* House in my Lord *Bacon* (which is a Project for Experiments that can never be Experimented) but propose it within such bounds of Expence as have often been exceeded by the Buildings of private Citizens" (p. 251). At this point we may fairly say that Cowley is speaking more as a fund-raiser than as a scientific historian.

Among the wonders of Solomon's House to which Cowley refers, doubtless he remembered Bacon's "large and various orchards and gardens, wherein we do not so much respect beauty, as variety of ground and soil."[12] There the fellows of the House practice experiments in grafting and innoculation. "And we make (by art) in the same orchards and gardens, trees and flowers to come earlier or later than their seasons; and to come up and bear more speedily than by their natural course they do. We make them also by art greater much than their nature; and their fruit greater and sweeter and of differing taste, smell, colour, and figure, from their nature. And many of them we so order, as they become of medicinal use" (3:158). Some of Bacon's more spectacular mechanical pre-

[12] *The Works of Francis Bacon*, ed. James Spedding, Robert Leslie Ellis, and Douglas Denon Heath, 14 vols. (London: Longmans, 1857-74), 3:158.

dictions have overshadowed these agricultural projects in later commentary, yet history has borne out his instinct that agricultural experimentation would play a part in the general advancement of science and technology.

Like Cowley, Bacon tries to redirect panegyric impulses from their usual subjects, such as war and conquest, to activities he considers to be more useful: innovation and invention. He is taken by the idea of raising statues not to kings or generals but to inventors and similar benefactors of mankind. In Solomon's House are two long galleries: one a museum of notable discoveries, the other for statues of "all principal inventors." "For upon every invention of value, we erect a statua of the inventor, and give him a liberal and honourable reward" (3:165-66). Taking note in *The Proficience and Advancement of Learning* (1605) that "men have despised to be conversant in ordinary and common matters" (3:418), Bacon assures his readers that much glory can be gained through the innovations he proposes. Using the example of Virgil, he draws a significant analogy between the *Aeneid* and traditional philosophy on one side and the *Georgics* and his own philosophy on the other, arguing somewhat disingenuously that "Virgil promised himself, (and indeed obtained,) . . . as much glory of eloquence, wit, and learning in the expressing of the observations of husbandry, as of the heroical acts of Æneas" (3:419). Bacon might rather have said that Virgil deserved as much glory for his middle poem but that as yet too few readers were ready to grant it to him. Should Bacon's campaign of transvaluation succeed, however, soon there would be many more such understanding readers. Such is the context of a seminal passage that Stanley Fish has given prominence by using it as epigraph and chapter title in *Self-Consuming Artifacts*:[13] "And surely if the purpose be in good earnest not to write at leisure that which men may read at leisure, but really to instruct and suborn action and active life, these Georgics of the mind, concerning the husbandry and tillage thereof,

---

[13] (Berkeley: University of California Press, 1972), p. 78.

are no less worthy than the heroical descriptions of Virtue, Duty, and Felicity" (3:419). In context, "Georgics of the mind" refers not to a tendency of Bacon's philosophy to consume itself (although the husbandman plows and harrows his field before he seeds it), but rather to a strenuous program of training the mind to appreciate the civilizing endeavors of the georgic vision.

In support of his effort to redirect human priorities, Bacon ransacks history and literature for time-honored precedents. He points out in *The Advancement of Learning* that, according to Dionysius the Areopagite, the highest orders of angels represent love and knowledge, but that power and ministry are assigned to the lower orders—which is as much as to say that the scientist and scholar should have priority over the administrator and soldier. Similarly the Bible frequently honors invention and intellectual innovation. By taking a euhemeristic approach to the classics, Bacon is also able to argue that even those militant heroes so often honored by humanity who performed the most constructive deeds, "founders and uniters of states and cities, lawgivers, extirpers of tyrants, fathers of the people, and other eminent persons in civil merit," could rise no higher than to the rank of demigod. "[O]n the other side," Bacon asserts, "such as were inventors and authors of new arts, endowments, and commodities towards man's life were ever consecrated amongst the gods themselves; as was Ceres, Bacchus, Mercurius, Apollo." At least two of these four gods were agricultural benefactors. They are rightly called gods, Bacon explains, because they benefited not the inhabitants of a single place or time, but all humanity, and because their deeds were not violent but have "the true character of divine presence, coming in *aura leni*,[14] without noise or agitation" (3:301-302). By these criteria Aristæus, the hero of *Georgics* 4 who invented a method for

---

[14] Bacon's "*aura leni*" or "gentle breeze" is from the Vulgate, 3 Kings 19:12, which corresponds to the "still small voice" of the Authorized Version, 1 Kings 19:12.

bringing back bees from the dead, would rank higher than Aeneas, who founded Rome after endless killing.

In his efforts to overturn habitual attitudes, Bacon recognizes that the inherently different values of an aristocracy whose origins are feudal might impede his reforms. In his essay "Of Nobility" (*Essayes*, 1625), he observes an important reactionary dynamic: "Nobility of birth commonly abateth industry; and he that is not industrious, envieth him that is" (6:406). In "Of the True Greatness of Kingdoms and Estates," he writes:

> Let states that aim at greatness, take heed how their nobility and gentlemen do multiply too fast. For that maketh the common subject grow to be a peasant and base swain, driven out of heart, and in effect but the gentleman's labourer. (6:446)

Roman moralists of Virgil's time and after frequently make the same point. That is the negative side of Bacon's view; when he comes to positive advice, he echoes the Romans and expands on what Ralegh also was trying to explain to King James:

> And herein the device of king Henry the Seventh (whereof I have spoken largely in the history of his life) was profound and admirable; in making farms and houses of husbandry of a standard; that is, maintained with such a proportion of land unto them, as may breed a subject to live in convenient plenty and no servile condition; and to keep the plough in the hands of the owners, and not mere hirelings. And thus indeed you shall attain to Virgil's character which he gives to ancient Italy:
>
> *Terra potens armis atque ubere glebæ.*[15]
> (6:447)

The very basis of a nation, economically and culturally (including its ability to wage any war that should be necessary), rests on the character and quality of its agriculture.

[15] *Aeneid* 1.531: "A land strong in arms and in fertility of soil."

The convergence of Bacon's views with Ralegh's is evident in several of Bacon's other remarks in the *Essayes*. In "Of Plantations," Bacon recommends that a leader should choose, as the best sort of colonists, "gardeners, ploughmen, labourers, smiths, carpenters, joiners, fishermen, fowlers, with some few apothecaries, surgeons, cooks, and bakers" (6:457). Proper use of the soil is essential, and the colonists should develop such natural resources as timber, salt, soap, silkworms if the climate allows, pitch and tar from evergreens, drugs from plants, and the like. "But moil not too much under ground," he warns, "for the hope of mines is very uncertain, and useth to make the planters lazy in other things" (6:458). In Bacon's opinion, England should not seek too rapid enrichment (doubtless he has in mind the example of Spain, as well, perhaps, as the sad projects of Elizabeth and Ralegh), but should instead seek wealth that is more genuine, lasting, and beneficial to humanity. In "Of Riches," he argues that "The improvement of the ground is the most natural obtaining of riches; for it is our great mother's blessing, the earth's; but it is slow" (6:461). Still, it must be admitted that even the clear-sighted Bacon is not always prepared, in the *Essayes* at least, to put the georgic vision of peaceful national prosperity first. In the passage quoted earlier from "Of the True Greatness of Kingdoms and Estates," which recommends the creation of a strong yeoman class in England, it will have been noticed that Bacon quotes not from the *Georgics* but from the *Aeneid* a line in which fertility of soil is balanced equally with strength of arms. In fact, that particular turn in the argument, that a king should support small land ownership for military reasons, has a venerable history. So we need not be too surprised when Bacon concludes his discussion of how a nation's economic and social fabric may be strengthened by the pursuit of georgic values with an appeal to the epic sensibility of his audience:

But above all, for empire and greatness, it importeth most, that a nation do profess arms as their principal honour,

study, and occupation. For the things which we formerly
have spoken of are but habilitations towards arms; and
what is habilitation without intention and act? (6:449)

Civil wars, Bacon subsequently remarks, are like a fever, but
a good foreign war is like exercise; it warms and invigorates
the body politic.

In order better to understand Bacon's attitude toward labor,
however, it is helpful to turn for a moment to the work of a
man who preceded him in the field by a few years. Benjamin
Farrington credits Giordano Bruno with having brought to
England and to Bacon's attention "a revolutionary conception
of science as power."[16] Farrington illustrates his thesis with
a significant quotation from Bruno's *Lo Spaccio della Bestia
Trionfante*, or "Expulsion of the Triumphant Beast." Bruno,
who visited Oxford in 1583 and then spent the next two years
in London, made a considerable acquaintance among the ad-
vanced English thinkers of his time. In 1584 he published *Lo
Spaccio*, which he dedicated to Sir Philip Sidney. At the end
of the Second Dialogue and the beginning of the Third, Bruno
introduces an important figure whom he variously names Dil-
igence, Solicitude, and Labor. Leisure, the opponent of Labor,
tells a little story about her:

> To the first father of men, when he was a good man, and
> to the first mother of women, when she was a good
> woman, Jove granted me [that is, Leisure] as a compan-
> ion. But when the latter and the former became wicked,
> Jove ordained that the first father should seize her so that
> she would be his mate and that he might cause [his fore-
> head to sweat and her belly to ache]. . . . [T]he conclusion
> . . . depends on the fact that I was declared the companion
> of Innocence and she [Labor], the companion of Sin.[17]

[16] *The Philosophy of Francis Bacon* (Chicago: Univ. of Chicago Press,
1966), p. 27.

[17] Bruno, *The Expulsion of the Triumphant Beast*, trans. and ed. Arthur
D. Imerti (New Brunswick: Rutgers, 1964), p. 204. I use this text for the
English; the Italian cited below is from *Lo Spaccio della Bestia Trionfante*,

Leisure is, of course, retelling the story of the garden of Eden, the fall, and the respective curses of labor and of childbirth that were pronounced upon Adam and Eve and their descendants. According to tradition, one of the earliest results of the fall was that the easy life of Eden was taken away, and that from then on humanity was obliged to work, and to work hard and long, in order to survive. In Genesis 3:17-19, and in many later interpretations, the curse of labor is conjoined with sin and suffering and with the curse of death, and both are closely involved with the new and perpetual necessity of tilling the soil in order to earn one's daily bread. The same verse that condemns Adam to eat his bread in the sweat of his face also reminds him that he is made of dust and shall return to the ground at his death.

Thus Bruno's character Leisure may be said to speak for the traditional view of things. Work is a curse that belongs to the fallen world; leisure is a happy state that humanity possessed before it fell from original innocence. Bruno, however, who ended his career at the stake, was scarcely a traditionalist; his sympathies in the dialogue are clearly with Work and not with Leisure. To agree with Leisure would mean to throw up one's hands and accept things as they are; but to agree with Work means to set one's hands and mind to the hard labor of changing and improving the world. Bruno has introduced Leisure's views, which are traditional though not usually expressed in so unbalanced a manner, mainly in order to refute them. He subsequently gives to Sophia or Wisdom, who cites Jove himself as her authority, another and quite different story about origins:

> And [Jove] added that the gods had given intellect and hands to man and had made him similar to them, giving him power over the other animals. This consists in his being able not only to operate according to his nature,

---

ed. Antimo Negri (Milano: Marzorati, 1970), p. 132. Since addle-pated Leisure confuses the curses on Adam and Eve, I substitute in square brackets the correction provided by another speaker, Saul.

. . . but also to operate outside the laws of that nature, in order that by forming or being able to form other natures, other paths, other categories, with his intelligence, by means of that liberty without which he would not have the above-mentioned similarity, he would succeed in preserving himself as god of the earth. That nature certainly when it becomes idle will be frustrative and vain, just as are useless the eye that does not see and the hand that does not grasp. And for this reason Providence has determined that he be occupied in action by means of his hands, and in contemplation by means of his intellect, so that he will not contemplate without action and will not act without contemplation.

In the Golden Age then, men were not because of Leisure more virtuous than beasts have hitherto been, but they were perhaps more stupid than many of the beasts. Now that difficulties have been born and needs have arisen among them, because of their emulation of divine acts and the adaption to inspired affects, their minds have become sharpened, industries have been invented, skills have been discovered, and always, through necessity, from day to day new and marvelous inventions are summoned forth from the depth of the human intellect. Whence, always removing themselves more and more from their bestial being by means of their solicitous and urgent occupations, they more closely approach divine being. (205-206)

Bruno has reversed his earlier story, and for the myth of devolution from original innocence has substituted a myth of human progress or evolution from ignorant bestiality.[18]

Bruno calls the force that drives evolution need or necessity,

[18] On primitive invention of arts and sciences, see Arthur O. Lovejoy and George Boas, *Primitivism and Related Ideas in Antiquity* (Baltimore: Johns Hopkins Press, 1935); and Erwin Panofsky, "The Early History of Man in Two Cycles of Painting by Piero de Cosimo," *Studies in Iconology* (1939; New York: Harper & Row, 1972), pp. 33-68.

in the original *difficultadi* and *necessitadi*. In a key phrase, which introduces the whole idea of man's perpetual inventiveness, he begins: "e sempre di giorno in giorno, per mezzo de l'egestade"; that is to say, "and always from day to day, driven by need [egestade]," man proceeds to invent new arts and industries. In this passage, Bruno is resorting to something that had become almost habitual in his time; he is bringing together and synthesizing the classical myth of the Golden Age with the biblical myth of Eden. There are several sources for the story of the Golden Age, including especially Hesiod's *Works and Days* and Ovid's *Metamorphoses*, but there is only one classical source for the view that the loss of the Golden Age might not be a disaster but actually a good thing: that source is Virgil's *Georgics*. If, as seems obvious, the *Georgics* is a poem about work, then its heart is that often-quoted passage, perhaps the most famous in the poem, known as the Jupiter Theodicy. It will easily be seen that the Jupiter Theodicy has more than a passing relationship to Sophia's version of man's origins—which she attributes (perhaps on Virgilian authority) to Jupiter himself. In Virgil's version of origins (*Georgics* 1.121-46), Jupiter removes the easy life of the Golden Age—the honey that drips from oaks, the wine that runs in rivers—in order to force mankind to turn to agriculture, labor, invention, and at length to civilization. Virgil sums up the force Jupiter employs to bring about these results in the final lines of the passage: "labor omnia vicit / improbus et duris urgens in rebus egestas," "Labor conquers all things, wicked labor, and driving need when life is hard." *Labor improbus*, a phrase difficult to translate, incorporates Virgil's recognition that labor is still a painful curse even though it leads at the same time to many good things. *Urgens egestas*, driving need, necessity, want, or even hunger, is the underlying, the motivating force behind the whole divinely ordained process; obviously it corresponds with Bruno's *egestade*, which he names as the driving force behind scientific and technological progress. For nostalgia for a past Golden Age, Virgil substitutes the vision of cooperative effort to bring about a Golden Age in the future, and that is precisely the shift in attitude and the call for new effort that Bruno and Bacon were urging on their readers.

What Virgil provided Bruno, and others of his time who were beginning to think along similar lines about these matters, was another way of interpreting Genesis 3:19, the primary text that defined both the nature of labor and the position of man in a fallen world. Not for nothing did Bacon sometimes present his goal of advancing science under the metaphor of a journey back into Eden; but that return could be accomplished not by longing for the past, but by journeying resolutely into the future, not by passively waiting on events, but by setting human hands and minds to the control of history. Between conflicting conservative and modernist interpretations of Genesis, the value of agriculture and of labor in general stood in the balance. John Donne, for example, abruptly concludes his bleak tour through history in "The Progresse of the Soule" with a harsh and conventional reminder:

> Who ere thou beest that read'st this sullen Writ,
> Which just so much courts thee, as thou dost it,
> Let me arrest thy thoughts; wonder with mee,
> Why plowing, building, ruling and the rest,
> Or most of those arts, whence our lives are blest,
> By cursed *Cains* race invented be,
> And blest *Seth* vext us with Astronomie.[19]

Not only did agriculture arise from the fall, but the first farmer ("*Caine* that first did plow") was the first murderer. Out of such materials, little could be built.

For Bacon, however, the fall was less a permanent curse than an opportunity: a chance for man, with God's help and approval, to take matters into his own hands and by his labors to regain the control over nature that he lost in the garden of

---

[19] *The Satires, Epigrams and Verse Letters of John Donne*, ed. W. Milgate (Oxford: Clarendon Press, 1967), p. 46.

Eden. Bacon concludes the "Plan" of the *Magna Instauratio* with a prayer that is virtually a distillation of all his aspirations:

> Therefore do thou, O Father, who gavest the visible light as the first fruits of creation, and didst breathe into the face of man the intellectual light as the crown and consummation thereof, guard and protect this work, which coming from thy goodness returneth to thy glory. Thou when thou turnedst to look upon the works which thy hands had made, sawest that all was very good, and didst rest from thy labours. But man, when he turned to look upon the work which his hands had made, saw that all was vanity and vexation of spirit, and could find no rest therein. Wherefore if we labour in thy works with the sweat of our brows thou wilt make us partakers of thy vision and thy sabbath. Humbly we pray that this mind may be steadfast in us, and that through these our hands, and the hands of others to whom thou shalt give the same spirit, thou wilt vouchsafe to endow the human family with new mercies. (4:33)

Later in this same work, Bacon ends the second book of the *Novum Organum* with a similar hope:

> [C]reation was not by the curse made altogether and for ever a rebel, but in virtue of that charter "In the sweat of thy face shalt thou eat bread," it is now by various labours (not certainly by disputations or idle magical ceremonies, but by various labours) at length and in some measure subdued to the supplying of man with bread; that is, to the uses of human life. (4:248)

The phrase that Spedding translates "in virtue of that charter" reads, in the original, "in virtute illius diplomatis." Bacon has taken the same step as Bruno; he has reconstituted the primal curse in the spirit of Virgil's georgic theodicy and called it not a curse but a *diploma*: that is, a government document conferring privileges on the persons addressed, a grant of human liberty, a promise, should men fulfill the terms, of future prosperity and the return of Eden.

Taking into account the whole body of Bacon's writings, not just those moments when he talks specifically about agriculture, it is clear that his philosophy could not have been better calculated to lead the nation toward a georgic vision of its greatness. It is Bacon above all who was responsible for the tone of the eighteenth-century agricultural treatises. He emphasized hard practical work and experimentation, insisted that humanity (under God's benevolent eye) take its destiny into its own hands, stressed the material benefits and the fruitfulness of all useful endeavors, praised invention and discovery, and popularized an optimistic view of history that encouraged people to plan for the long term and to cooperate with one another for the material benefit of humanity. Bacon supports these broad goals with relevant imagery, which includes recurrent georgic images of building, of path-cutting, of sea voyages and discovery, of planting and nourishing, and of bringing to fruition.[20] In *The Advancement of Learning*, Bacon poises the wisdom of Solomon against that of Virgil, one pessimistic and the other optimistic, one condemning idleness and the other urging effort. The two quotations tellingly complement one another: *"Dicit piger, Leo est in via,"* "The lazy man says there is a lion in the path" (Prov. 22:13); and *"Possunt quia posse videntur"* (3:329), "They can because they think they can" (*Aeneid* 5.231).

Although the farmers and agricultural laborers of the early seventeenth century have not recorded their opinions about Genesis 3:19, it would have been only natural for them, as well as their intellectual leaders, to remember the curse when they considered their occupations. As Edward Hyams argues, such thoughts lingered in men's consciousness as late as the end of the nineteenth century, when American pioneers were settling the Oklahoma territory. Those farmers, Hyams writes,

---

[20] See Brian Vickers, *Francis Bacon and Renaissance Prose* (Cambridge: Cambridge Univ. Press, 1968), pp. 174-201.

"were simple and honourable men with a worthy purpose, that of keeping their families in bread and independence by the sweat of their faces—of religiously fulfilling the terms of the curse laid upon Adam and Eve."[21] What Bacon did was to reconsider the nature of that curse and to start a long process that would put work in a different perspective: difficult and painful still, even wicked, but carrying in itself great promise for human advancement and peaceful prosperity. Thus labor was transformed from its shameful place at the bottom of the social ladder to a new pioneering role as the shaper of history and the benefactor of humanity. Of course, great time and effort were necessary to bring about such a sweeping social and psychological transformation, and the shift in perspective could never be universal.

Hartlib and Worlidge

If Bacon was the originating, he was not the proximate, source of Cowley's enthusiasm for reformed agriculture. That honor belongs to such men as Boyle, Wilkins, and Hartlib, who were active during the critical period between Bacon's death in 1626 and the founding of the Royal Society in 1662. Of these intermediate figures, perhaps Hartlib was the most representative, because of his fondness for corresponding and working with other innovators. In "Of Agriculture," Cowley describes the sort of professor he wants for his proposed college and reveals, perhaps unintentionally, something about the intellectual tradition to which he is indebted. His model professors "should be men not chosen for Ostentation of Critical Literature, but for solid and experimental Knowledge of the things they teach . . . ; so industrious and publick-spirited as I conceive Mr. *Hartlib* to be, if the Gentleman be yet alive" (p. 405; Hartlib died in 1662).

Samuel Hartlib, Milton's compeer in the reform of education, represents the convergence in the middle seventeenth

[21] Hyams, *Soil and Civilization*, p. 140.

century of all those intellectual attitudes that were eventually to contribute to an English version of the georgic point of view on life, and thus at length to prepare a social nexus sufficiently firm to ensure an enthusiastic response to georgic poetry. In Hartlib were combined an almost messianic commitment to religious reform, to educational reform, and to the advancement of science along Baconian lines for the benefit of humanity. Hartlib's "Experimental Academy," which opened briefly in 1630, took Bacon as its prime authority for a program that proposed to discard "emptie and barren Generalities, being but the very husks and shales of sciences,"[22] in favor of humanistic studies and training in various practical affairs. Among Hartlib's unpublished papers are notes on how much it might cost to found a "College of Tradesmen" such as one proposed by William Petty, and elsewhere there are suggestions for training students in such "mechanical" employments as navigation, surveying, and husbandry (pp. 45, 51).

Hartlib was also involved with writing prefaces for, encouraging, publishing, and sometimes begetting, during the crucial decade of the 1650s, a number of books on husbandry—books whose spirit contrasts sharply with Gervase Markham's. Hartlib transcribed and published Cressy Dymock's *An Essay for Advancement of Husbandry-Learning. Or Propositions for the Erecting a Colledge of Husbandry* (1651). The plan was to apprentice students for seven years to a society of fellows, who were to perform agricultural experiments and to spread the knowledge and practice of good husbandry throughout the country (pp. 63, 96). Hartlib also directed to the Council of State a prefatory Epistle to Sir Richard Weston's *A discours of Husbandrie used in Brabant and Flanders* (1650), a book which proposed that the English might profitably imitate the Dutch and improve their land on

---

[22] G. H. Turnbull, *Hartlib, Dury, and Comenius* (London: Hodder & Stoughton, 1947), p. 37. Further quotations from Hartlib's unpublished writings (except the letters to Boyle) are from this work.

a national scale. William Du-Gard, the publisher, was active at that time in the publication of state proclamations and other official tracts. New editions appeared in 1652 and 1654. Still other treatises published between 1651 and 1655 in which Hartlib had a hand concerned farming, gardening, raising silkworms, and the natural history of Ireland, mentioned earlier, "*with the several way[s] of Manuring and improoving the same.*" Another tract outlines a scheme for draining the fens and improving the wastes of England; still another discourses on the grafting of fruit trees.

The cooperative spirit in which many of these treatises were conceived and written is suggested by one of Hartlib's notes, which refers to "The promised Observations of the Husbandry of Clover from Mr. Tho. Mackworth's friend" (p. 98). A similar group spirit is suggested by Hartlib's letter to Robert Boyle, in which Hartlib reports that he has "received a special commission from Sir Charles Culpepper" entreating Hartlib "most passionately to put you [Boyle] in mind of the promise you were pleased to make unto him, about the new invented plough of Dr. *Wilkins*."[23] In 1657, Hartlib again wrote Boyle, and some names well known in connection with the Civil War turn up among this circle of georgical correspondents:

Here you have a vindication of the decaying clover-grass [a method of fertilization with which Hartlib was perennially preoccupied], written and sent unto me by Mr. *Wood* from *Dublin*. . . . I suppose you remember the great expectations I have of the Quaker of *Durham, Anthony Pierson*, his promises of husbandry. I have not yet obtained any thing from his hands; but major general *Lilburne* pretends to know his universal compost; and a friend of his was pleased to entrust me with it. . . . [Here Hartlib describes the application of the compost in detail and concludes:] A greater quantity of lime, or laid in any other manner on the land, burns out the vegetable salt and spoils it, as is experienced in the West by colonel

[23] Shapiro, *John Wilkins*, p. 134.

144

Monck. . . . Thus I have discovered unto you, that magnet of husbandry without any reserves.[24]

Hartlib's "universal compost" is the agricultural equivalent of the alchemist's *elixir vitae*; though it might never be found, nevertheless the pursuit of it led questing scientists to one genuine discovery after another. And, unlike some earlier alchemists, Hartlib offers in the spirit of Bacon and the New Science freely to share the secret of this "magnet of husbandry" with his correspondent.

On November 27, 1655, John Evelyn visited Hartlib at Charing Cross. He notes that the "honest and learned Mr. *Hartlib*" has "propagated many Useful things and Arts," and reports him to be "Master of innumerable Curiosities, and very communicative."[25] Evelyn also took an interest in agricultural reform; he reports that on the afternoon of April 11, 1656, a group that included Wilkins, Boyle, Lord George Berkeley, and Evelyn himself, called on Colonel Thomas Blount after dinner, in order to have a look at his "new invented Plows" (3:169-70). After the Reformation, John Wilkins, of Wadham College, Oxford, who has turned up twice in these notices, became a member of the third most popular committee of the Royal Society (after Mechanical and Trade): the aptly named "Georgical" Committee. Other familiar figures on that committee included Aubrey, Boyle, Evelyn, Oldenburg, and Waller.[26]

[24] *The Works of the Honourable Robert Boyle*, ed. Thomas Birch, 6 vols. (London: W. Johnston et al., 1772; facs. Hildesheim: Georg Olms, 1965-66), 6:92-93. Although educational historians commonly think of Hartlib as a follower of Comenius, he took the lead in agriculture, a subject in which Comenius appears not to have shared his interest.

[25] John Evelyn, *Diary*, ed. E. S. de Beer, 6 vols. (Oxford: Clarendon Press, 1955), 3:162-63.

[26] Thomas Birch, *The History of the Royal Society of London*, 4 vols. (London, 1756-57; facs. New York: Johnson Reprints, 1968), 1:406-407. The committees and their memberships were: Mechanical (67), Astronomical and Optical (15), Anatomical (3 named), Chemical (7 named), Georgical (31), Histories of Trade (35), collecting phenomena of nature and experiments (21), and Correspondence (20).

Clearly there were growing circles of people in England who shared Hartlib's interest in a Baconian reform of agriculture; one of his main achievements was to inspire others with the reforming fervor and to persuade them to publish in a similarly Baconian spirit of cooperation. The best-known result of this intellectual ferment (leaving aside the question of whether Hartlib had a significant part in the founding of the Royal Society) is Milton's open letter to Hartlib, *Of Education*. Milton, of course, was no man's follower; he represents another powerful center for the development of the georgic spirit during the period. Still, he presumably knew that Hartlib would approve when he urged that students be encouraged and taught how "to improve the tillage of their Country, to recover the bad Soil, and to remedy the waste that is made of good," or when he suggested that such men as "Hunters, Fowlers, Fishermen, Shepherds, Gardeners," be brought in to give a practical dimension to the teaching and to help clarify "the rural part of *Virgil*."[27]

The title of a treatise that Hartlib published in 1652 summarizes the optimism, even the apocalyptic fervor, with which he was promoting various experiments in husbandry: *Cornu Copia. A Miscellaneum of lucriferous and most fructiferous Experiments, Observations, and Discoveries, immethodically distributed; to be really demonstrated and communicated in all sincerity*. The proliferation of scientific and propagandistic treatises on agriculture between 1650 and 1655, quite different in tone from those of Markham and earlier writers, again reveals—as the negative responses of such Royalists as Walton and Vaughan also reveal—that at the midpoint of the Interregnum fundamental changes in the way people viewed and practiced agriculture were well under way. Movements to enclose and rationalize land, to drain fens and float watermeadows, to marl the fields or sweeten them with chalk and lime were already well established. Important new crops were

[27] *The Works of John Milton*, ed. Frank A. Patterson et al., 18 vols. (New York: Columbia Univ. Press, 1931-40), 4:282, 284.

first introduced on a large scale: carrots, turnips used to winter cattle, red and white seed clover.[28] Some of these improvements had been developed over the course of a century, but they now found new support from the urge to put the Baconian agenda "really" and "in all sincerity" into practice. At the same time, the perception of the propagandists that the great majority of the English still resisted the new georgic vision accounts for the many proposals in the 1650s to found reformed schools and colleges which would teach such practical arts as scientific husbandry.

From the beginning, the New Science went hand in hand with religious reform, which in England (though not everywhere on the Continent) meant Protestant reform. The Puritan Revolution seemed, therefore, to be a heaven-sent opportunity for those with the right views to put their ideas about agriculture into practice, and thus to develop still further ideas by experiment. It might at first seem odd that people wanted to publish and to read about farming in the midst of the turmoil of the second civil war, or that such men as Lilburne and Moncke should concern themselves with fertilizer when they would seem to have had more important matters in hand; but in point of fact, agricultural unrest—as Gerrard Winstanley certainly knew—was close to the heart of the whole revolutionary movement. Though things did not always work out as the visionaries would have wished, the furthering of the agricultural revolution was one of the most concrete results of the Civil War. In the 1650s, while private gain was scarcely forgotten, still there was a new and seemingly genuine sense that agriculture could be a civic and a public-spirited activity, and that its improvement might benefit the whole nation and at length all of humanity.

The title to a sequel to *A discours of Husbandrie* further

[28] See Kerridge, *The Agricultural Revolution*; fen drainage, pp. 222-39; marling and liming, pp. 240-50; floating water-meadows, pp. 251-67; carrots, pp. 268-69; turnips, pp. 270-76 (with a denial of the importance of Turnip Townshend); clover, pp. 280-88. On the introduction of sainfoin and lucerne in 1645, mentioned in Worlidge's poem below, see pp. 278, 288.

reveals the new spirit: *Samuel Hartlib his Legacie: or An Enlargement of the Discourse of Husbandry used in Brabant and Flanders; wherin are bequeathed to the Common-Wealth of England more Outlandish and Domestick Experiments and Secrets in reference to Universall Husbandry* (1651; also 1652, 1655). The same spirit persisted through the Restoration; in a petition to Parliament, Hartlib claims to have benefited his adopted country with "The best experiments of industry practised in husbandry and manufactures and in other inventions and accomodations tending to the good . . . of this age and posterity" (p. 88). In 1646 the government had granted Hartlib a pension of £100 a year in recognition of his services to the country, although by 1660 the payments were £700 in arrears.[29] Cowley, whose interest in agriculture went back at least to 1661, was one of the beneficiaries of Hartlib's "legacy"; and the audience for his essays had been well prepared by the agricultural reform movement of the 1650s, which Bacon did so much to inspire and over which Hartlib informally presided as coordinator and publicist.

It is generally agreed that Francis Bacon, hard as he tried, was not a successful experimenter. But before new inventions or new ways of doing things can come into general use, it is necessary to change people's minds. At that task, Bacon was the master, and Hartlib and Cowley were among his more notable successors. The work of shifting the consciousness of a whole society is also, as Shelley says, the responsibility of poets. When, at the very beginning of the georgic revolution, Spenser defied his time and spoke of himself as the plowman-poet of *The Faerie Queene*, he placed himself at the forefront of the new movement. When Jonson insisted, against the conventions of aristocratic *sprezzatura*, that he who would "write a living line, must sweat," he revealed his capability of forwarding that movement; but he drew back. Subsequently other poets, most notably Milton, would take up the task, and, at about the time of the Restoration and the founding

[29] See Fussell, *The Old English Farming Books*, p. 48.

of the Royal Society, letters would converge for a time with science in praise of the New Husbandry. That convergence may be seen in the work of those men who had feet in both camps: Aubrey, Evelyn, Cowley, and Dryden.

The impact of science on the poetic perception of landscape and society is evident in what may be the earliest specimen of an entirely georgic landscape poem—georgic, that is, in genre as well as in mode and spirit. John Worlidge, in his *Systema Agriculturæ: Being The Mystery of Husbandry Discovered* (1669; 2d edn. 1687), includes as its frontispiece an engraved landscape, which shows all the various classes of agricultural activity discussed in the book (see fig. 1). Opposite that engraving Worlidge prints a poem, the title of which indicates its practical function: "The Explanation of the Frontispiece." The poem, an "Epitomy" of the book, almost a table of contents, is nevertheless capably written in the plain style suitable for georgic and favored by the Royal Society. During the course of the century, landscape poets had learned to organize their poems visually, like painters;[30] Worlidge, presumably aided by the engraving, has succeeded in painting a harmonious and even a lovely scene, in which useful georgic activities and crops replace the customary pastoral details. Harmony, variety, and beauty emerge from the practicalities of New Husbandry. I reproduce the poem in full, since I believe it has not been reprinted or mentioned in previous criticism.

> FIrst cast your eye upon a *Rustick Seat,*
> Built strong and plain, yet well contriv'd and neat,
> And scituated on a healthy Soyl,
> Yielding much Wealth with little cost, or toyl.
> Near by it stand the *Barns* fram'd to contain
> Enriching stores of *Hay, Pulse, Corn,* and *Grain;*
> With *Bartons* large, and places where to feed
> Your *Oxen, Cows, Swine, Poultrey,* with their breed.

[30] On the evolution of landscape poetry see James Turner, *The Politics of Landscape* (Cambridge, Mass.: Harvard Univ. Press, 1979), esp. pp. 8-35.

On th' other side hard by the House, you see
The *Api'ary* for th' industrious *Bee*.
Walk on a little farther, and behold
A pleasant *Garden* from high Windes and Cold
Defended (by a spreading, fruitful *Wall*
With Rows of *Lime*, and *Fir-trees* streight and tall,)
Full fraught with necessary *Flow'res* and *Fruits*,
And Natures choicest sorts of *Plants*, and *Roots*.
Beyond the same are Crops of *Beans* and *Pease*,
Saffron, and Liquorice, or such as these;
Then *Orchards* so enrich'd with fruitful store,
Nature could give (nor they receive) no more,
Each *Tree* stands bending with the weight it bears
Of *Cherries* some, of *Apples*, *Plums*, and *Pears*:
Not far from thence see other *Walks* and *Rows*
Of *Cyder fruits*, near unto which there flows
A *Gliding Stream*; the next place you discover
Is where *St. Foyn*, *La Lucern*, *Hops*, and *Clover*
Are propagated: Near unto those *Fields*,
Stands a large *Wood*, *Mast*, *Fewel*, *Timber* yields.
In yonder Vale hard by the *River* stands
A *Water-Engine*, which the Winde commands
To fertilize the *Meads*, on th' other side
A *Persian Wheel* is plac't both large and wide
To'th same intent; Then do the *Fields* appear
Cloathed with *Corn*, and *Grain*, for th'ensuing Year.
The *Pastures* stockt with *Beasts*, the *Downs* with *Sheep*,
The *Cart*, the *Plough*, and all, good order keep;
Plenty unto the *Husbandman*, and Gains
Are his Rewards for's Industry and Pains.
    Peruse the Book for here you onely see
    Th' following subject in Epitomy.

The latest in crops appear in this poem, in harmonious balance
intended to enrich the soil as well as the scene. Two windmills,
one of which is evidently a water-engine, may be seen on the
print, as well as the Persian wheel with its irrigation canal
and the network of ditches used to float the water-meadow.

As Kerridge notes, the technique of floating the meadow would result both in richer crops and in the extension of the season, so that corn and grain could be readied early "for th'ensuing Year." "The two great functions of the floated water-meadow were to produce an abundance of grass in April and provide hay to last right through until then." Lucerne, one of the crops that the poem assigns to the other side of the stream, was still experimental; it was fed green to horses. Sainfoin was introduced from France about 1645 by Sir Richard Weston, who was also the first in England to experiment with seed clover, to which the poem also refers.[31] Altogether, such details show that the author of the poem, presumably Worlidge himself, was familiar with the latest methods in farming. It is also clear, I think, that the poet took esthetic interest as well as moral and economic satisfaction from contemplating such a georgic scene. Even as late as 1669, Worlidge felt obliged to apologize in his preface (perhaps with some irony) for publishing a book on "so mean and *Rustick* a *Subject* . . . when every *Shop* and *Library* is replete with the *Fruits* and *Labors* of the most *Acute Wits.*" Yet he also knows that the time for his book has come; that ambitious and public-spirited readers are ready to put their hands to the plow, "not onely for the benefit of your *Selves* and *Posterity*, but the *Kingdom* in general" (B2ʳ).

The moral argument, now familiar to Worlidge's readers, that hard work and a commitment to the new husbandry will produce material benefits for society as a whole as well as the individual, may be traced back to the 1650s and the pamphlet war between two ministers, Joseph Lee and John Moore, on the subject of enclosure. To Moore's traditional charge that the new husbandry makes "chaffer and merchandize" of the rural laborer for the owner's "gain and profit," Lee answers:

The advancement of private persons will be the advantage of the publick. . . . [I]f men by good husbandry, trenching,

---

[31] Kerridge, *The Agricultural Revolution*, p. 257; on new crops, see note 29 above.

manuring their Land, etc. do better their Land, is not the Common-wealth inriched thereby?[32]

Thus moral theory was beginning to put the improvement of the land into a new light.[33] In an earlier stage of the enclosure movement, which came to a peak in the 1550s amid a flurry of sermons and broadsides, those who opposed enclosure had been unable to prevent it, yet they had at least won a moral and in some respects a legal victory. They were able to convince most readers that enclosure was purely a matter of selfishness and greed. When the issue gained new urgency in the 1650s, however, the moral rights and wrongs were less clear, because the New Husbandry added potentially beneficial to selfish reasons for change. As early as 1641, an anonymous Utopian tract, *A description of the famous Kingdome of Macaria*, which Turnbull associates with Hartlib (p. 88), applied Thomas More's arguments justifying a colonial agriculture that improved yields (see ch. 5 below) to a fictional kingdom representing the home country. Anyone in Macaria who held his land without improving it "would be banished by the Council of Husbandry."[34] By the 1650s, this new Utopian principle was finding practical application.

One thing about Worlidge's poem that may trouble a discriminating reader is its lack of tension or complex feeling. The darker side of Virgilian labor—sweat, pain, harshness, individual defeat—so evident in Spenser's poetry and in Mil-

[32] Moore, *A Scripture-word Against Inclosure* (1656), p. 6; Lee, *A Vindication of a Regulated Inclosure* (1656), pp. 22-23. See also Moore's *The Crying Sin of England, of not Caring for the Poor* (1653) and Lee's *Considerations Concerning Common Fields and Inclosures* (1654).

[33] For discussion of this process from an economic viewpoint, see Joyce Oldham Appleby, *Economic Thought and Ideology in Seventeenth-Century England* (Princeton: Princeton Univ. Press, 1978), esp. pp. 1-72, 84-87, 101, 132-33, 245. I would differ from her interpretation only in arguing that the new economics that accompanied the new husbandry was as much a "moral economy" as its predecessor, and also that the process of change was not without early Medieval precedents, although in the seventeenth-century agricultural and economic revolution the process was (as she notes) secularized.

[34] Appleby, *Economic Thought and Ideology*, p. 86.

ton's, has entirely vanished. Here is georgic made easy: in Worlidge's phrase, "Yielding much Wealth with little cost, or toyl." Worlidge's optimistic emphasis is not really surprising, since his poem is intended, presumably, as an advertisement for the volume; nonetheless his tone is instructive, because it reminds us that on the whole, the early proponents of scientific georgic, to whose works the poem serves as something of a coda, also regularly stress the easy and optimistic side of husbandry. From a typical tract of Hartlib's, for example, the reader gathers that all one need do to effect a tenfold or better gain in productivity is to plant this or that crop, or to manure the fields with a universal compost. Indeed, it appears that since 1550 there had been something like a fourfold increase in agricultural yields, but that result was not achieved so simply or so easily as most of the farming manuals imply. Except for Boyle, all the chief figures whom we have been considering—Bruno, Bacon, and Cowley as well as Hartlib—were not so much technologists as propagandists, whose significance should not be underestimated, yet an important part of whose work was simply to persuade people that technological advancement would be fairly easy and therefore worth pursuing. It would not have served the turn of these writers to have called too much attention to the inevitable difficulties lying in the way of progress. True, Virgil, Spenser, and Milton were, in their fashions, also propagandists, in the sense that they wanted to persuade their readers to change their thinking and to take certain courses of action; but they were poets, too, who appreciated the complexity of history and the difficulty of accomplishing the tasks to which they had set their hands.

Another factor was that the georgic scientists aimed at goals which, while large, were nonetheless more limited than those of the poets. If science and technology could be reformed, they often assumed, then human nature and politics would somehow follow. (So, in the *New Atlantis*, scientific enlightenment eliminates prostitution.) Spenser and Milton, and Virgil too, had broader goals, therefore goals more difficult to achieve.

Added to those differences in aims was a final factor: time. When Worlidge wrote, the technological georgic battle was, in effect, as good as won. Over the course of the century, new crops had been planted and the soil had been well drained and manured; attitudes had begun to come around on a large scale; it was necessary for Worlidge, and later for Dryden, only to reap the poetic harvest. Those changes in the agricultural background help explain why Worlidge's poem has more in common, in style and in tone, with the easy georgic of the eighteenth century than with the strenuous, pioneering georgic of the sixteenth and seventeenth centuries.

FIVE

Georgic and Christian Reform

COMMON OPINION has it that the cultural factors underlying the technological revolution in agriculture and industry were closely connected to the rise of Protestantism. The phrase that is often attached to these cultural factors is "Protestant work ethic." The term would not have come into such general use if there were not something in it, and enough has been written on the subject by such diverse historians as Max Weber, R. H. Tawney, Christopher Hill, and Perry Miller to demonstrate an undeniable rapprochement between Protestantism, especially in its more Calvinist forms, and modern industrial capitalism. Yet in the field of English literature there is a striking discrepancy between fact and theory. Protestantism came forcefully into the English cultural mainstream during the sixteenth century, yet not until the late seventeenth century did more than a few pioneering writers espouse anything much resembling a "work ethic." Either other factors were operating or, as it would seem, the influence of the Reformation cut both ways. If we look at the earlier history of the Christian West, and especially at labor in the Middle Ages, then the puzzle only grows deeper.

Whatever cultural force it was that energized the georgic revolution in English consciousness and literature, it had to be something more than the working of sheer self-interest. Greed, ambition, and the profit motive, as exemplified in the writings of Thomas Tusser or, more ambitiously, in the productions of Gervase Markham, are insufficient in themselves to account for the remarkably innovative and creative aspects of the transformation that took place, even if these motives wove themselves into the story in their usual fashion. The theory I would propose is that not the Reformation itself, but rather the impulse toward reform—not always just the same thing—led to the eventual success of the georgic revolution. In order to understand better what happened in the sixteenth and seventeenth centuries, however, it will be useful to consider briefly what happened earlier: in particular, to consider what were the traditional Christian interpretations of the theme of work as it is found in the Bible and also what attitudes toward work were common in the Middle Ages. Although most students of the English Renaissance know the danger in taking that period at its own valuation, the habit is sometimes hard to break. Still, the passage of time should allow us greater objectivity.

Biblical Georgic and Its Interpreters

At the source of human history, just after Adam and Eve fell from the eternal spring of the garden of Eden into humanity's long pilgrimage through time toward the final consummation of the Second Coming, stands the triple curse: the curse on the Serpent, the curse on Eve, and the curse on Adam, which is the curse of labor. "[C]ursed is the ground for thy sake; in sorrow shalt thou eat of it all the days of thy life; Thorns also and thistles shall it bring forth to thee; and thou shalt eat the herb of the field; In the sweat of thy face shalt thou eat bread, till thou return unto the ground; for out of it wast thou taken: for dust thou art, and unto dust shalt thou return" (Gen. 3:17-19). It is a harsh and apparently a pessimistic text, yet from a Christian perspective one not without hope. Labor is, from the beginning, the opposite of lost paradisal ease, from which Adam and Eve are barred by the angel with the flaming sword; yet what the first Adam destroyed, the second Adam can repair. St. Paul writes: "For we know that the whole creation groaneth and travaileth in pain together *until now*" (Rom. 8:22, italics added). In *Paradise Lost*, Milton makes much of the tradition that the first protevangelium, the promise of the warfare between Christ and Satan that will work our salvation, is concealed in the curse on the Serpent. Concealed in the other two curses, as in the fall in general, are the promise of the Second Eve, who will bring forth the chosen seed, and that of the Second Adam, who will redeem the world—and labor in the world—as well as humanity.

Christianity, as Chesterton enjoyed remarking, is a paradoxical religion. Among the longest-running of its paradoxes is its insistence that the true Christian must commit himself to act in the world for the sake of charity as well as of self-preservation: to feed the hungry, clothe the naked, visit prisoners and the sick (Matt. 25:34-46). At the same time, true Christians must also despise the world and lay up treasures in heaven (Matt. 6:19-21). The slight but significant disparity between what Matthew and Luke report concerning what Christ said in his Sermon on the Mount, whether it was "blessed are the poor in spirit" (Matt. 5:3) or just "blessed be ye poor" (Luke 6:20), has been characteristically resolved by orthodox Christians in the same way that they construct gospel harmonies: by addition. Though the Christian Church has oscillated over the centuries between the poles of other-worldly spirituality and commitment to social justice in this world, in general it has tried to adhere to the spirit of both pronouncements. When it has failed to do so, reformers have arisen.

Insofar as Christianity is an otherworldly religion, it has always condemned worldly activities. From that side of the picture, labor in the world becomes sinful or, at best, meaningless. The *De Contemptu Mundi* of Pope Innocent III, whose title sums up this strain in Christian thought, makes the case against labor, invention, and the whole georgic approach to life, citing for its proof-texts what had become a traditional source for this attitude, Ecclesiastes:

[A]lthough the investigator ought both to sweat at his many vigils and to spend wakeful nights in labor and sweat, yet there is scarcely anything so low, so easy, that a man can wholly understand it. . . . Hear what Solomon thinks about this, "All things are full of labor; man cannot utter it" [*Eccl.*, i, 8]. . . . "Because though a man labor to seek it out, yet shall he not find it" [*Eccl.*, viii, 17].[1]

What applies to intellectual labors applies to all the arts and sciences, by means of which humanity has constructed its all too ephemeral civilizations:

> Men scurry about through hedges and by-ways, they climb mountains, cross hills, leap over rocks, dart through crags, scramble out of pits, penetrate caverns, tear up the bowels of the earth, the depths of the sea, secret rivers, forest shades, trackless solitudes. . . . They hammer and fuse metals, they carve and polish stones, cut and hew wood, spin yarn and weave garments, rip and sew, build houses, plant gardens, cultivate their fields, tend vineyards, heat ovens, build mills, fish, hunt, and go fowling. . . . If you do not believe me, let Solomon be believed who said, "I made me great works; I builded me houses; I planted me vineyards; I made me gardens and orchards . . . also I had great possessions of great and small cattle above all that were in Jerusalem before me. . . . I withheld not my heart from any joy; for my heart rejoiced in all my labor: and this was my portion of all my labor. Then I looked on all the works that my hands had wrought, and on the labor that I had labored to do: and, behold, all was vanity and vexation of spirit, and there was no profit under the sun" [*Eccl.*, ii, 4-11]. (p. 128)

Yet from an early period there was opposition to such Christian otherworldliness. Through Philo Judaeus, the classical Roman "gospel of work" entered biblical exegesis to join traditional Jewish respect for labor, as in his *De sacrificiis*

---

[1] Quoted from George Boas, *Essays on Primitivism and Related Ideas in the Middle Ages* (Baltimore: Johns Hopkins Press, 1948), p. 127 (see *Patrologia Latina*, 217:707).

Abelis et Caini, which, like the *Georgics,* was written in the first century B.C.:

> [T]oil is the enemy of leisure, the first and greatest good, waging unheralded war against pleasure. For ... God has appointed toil for men as the source of all good and of all virtue, apart from which you will find nothing fair established for the human race. ... [T]he eye of the soul cannot apprehend virtuous practices unless it makes use of toil, like light, as a co-worker. ... Prudence and courage and justice are all beautiful and perfect goods, but not in leisure are these things found. One must be content if they have been won over by continuous care.[2]

To the curse on Adam ("God has appointed toil") Philo assigns a meaning of which Cato himself would not have disapproved.

At the time of Constantine the Great, Lactantius wrote that God fashioned man "mortal and frail" so that "He might set virtue before man, that is, the endurance of evils and labors, through which he might be able to gain the reward of immortality." Thus work is given a part in the redemptive process. Two lives, Lactantius says, are given to man, temporal and spiritual. "The former we receive through birth, the latter we acquire through labor—so that, as we said before, immortality might not be possessed by man without any difficulty."[3] Lactantius takes an eschatological view, in which man's entry into heaven is of primary importance, yet God has so arranged things that that goal must be attained in part by human labors in the world. Far more extreme is the position taken by Origen, in his tract written against Celsus, a proto-ecologist who apparently had argued that God favors animals over men, since he does not require them to work for their food. According to Origen, Celsus had complained that "We, laboring and perishing in our labor, are fed in scarcity and

---

[2] Boas, *Primitivism,* pp. 12-13.
[3] Boas, *Primitivism,* p. 40 (*Pat. Lat.,* 6:750).

with toil. But for them all things are grown unsown and un-ploughed." What Celsus had failed to understand, Origen argues, is precisely the point that Virgil makes in his Jupiter theodicy: "that God, wishing to exercise the human under-standing in every respect, that it might not remain fallow and ignorant of the arts, created man in want, so that by his very want he might be forced to invent arts, some for food, others for shelter." What had seemed at first to be an evil—God's imposition on man of want and the need to work for food and shelter—may thus be seen from another perspective to be a significant good:

> The lack of necessities of life at any rate was the foun-dation not only of the art of agriculture but also of vin-iculture, of horticulture, as well as of carpentry and metal-working. . . . The lack of shelter was the incentive to weaving, wool-carding, and spinning, as well as of house-building. And thus the understanding rose to the general principles of art. The lack of utilities also caused things produced in foreign parts to be conveyed by the arts of navigation and piloting. . . . For the irrational [animals] have their food all ready for them, but they have not even an impulse towards the arts. And they have also natural covering. For they have hair or feathers. . . . [L]et this be our defense against . . . Celsus.[4]

Even St. Augustine, who will hardly be suspected either of facile optimism or of Pelagianism, can be eloquent on the subject of humanity's industrious inventiveness:

> It is He, then, who has given to the human soul a mind. . . . What wonderful—one might say stupefying—ad-vances has human industry made in the arts of weaving and building, of agriculture and navigation! With what endless variety are designs in pottery, painting, and sculp-

[4] Boas, *Primitivism*, p. 194.

ture produced. . . . How skilful the contrivances for catching, killing, or taming wild beasts.[5]

Bruno might easily have found matter to feed his optimism in this chapter of *The City of God*—but only by ignoring what Augustine says elsewhere. The citizens of the heavenly city can hope for little more than an occasional truce with the city of the world in which they find themselves living. If they are lucky enough to live in the right time and place, still they can be no more than *peregrinatores* in the earthly city—a term often translated as "pilgrims" but one that means something more like foreigners or aliens who are permitted to dwell within the city walls but who have no rights of citizenship. Such people owe it to their neighbors to labor in the building, but their hearts must be elsewhere.

Other passages in the Bible that were amenable to georgic interpretation, or that could be incorporated into the georgic mode when poets were so minded, in the same way that they adapted Psalm 23 and the parable of the Good Shepherd to the pastoral mode, include the concept of Israel as the promised land and that of Israel as the vineyard of the Lord. Both images are basic and recurrent.[6] Before the Jews under Joshua had even finished conquering Palestine, they celebrated their newly georgic status at the anniversary of the Passover: "And they did eat of the old corn of the land on the morrow after the passover, unleavened cakes, and parched corn in the selfsame day. And the manna ceased on the morrow after they had eaten of the old corn of the land; neither had the children of Israel manna any more; but they did eat of the fruit of the land of Canaan that year" (Joshua 5:11-12).

Several parables portray man as a worker in God's vineyard

[5] *The City of God* (XXIV.22), trans. Marcus Dods (New York: Random House, 1950), pp. 851-52.

[6] On Israel as the promised land, see esp. Gen. 12:1-3, 13:14-18, 17:1-8, Exodus, and the many recapitulations of Exodus throughout the Bible. On Israel as a vineyard, see esp. Ps. 80:8, Isa. 5:1, Jer. 2:21, Hos. 14:7, John 15:1.

or in his fields, including especially Matthew 20, which begins with the familiar comparison of the Kingdom of Heaven to "an householder, which went out early in the morning to hire labourers into his vineyard." The implied meaning of the parable, that people must earn their way into heaven by working hard under the divine taskmaster (but that his grace may recompense equally those who begin at the eleventh hour) is precisely equivalent to Lactantius' view of the role of labor with respect to eternal salvation. Other parables display man in a less active role, with God or his ministers as the husbandman and humanity as the field or the plant to be tended. Such is the parable of the barren fig tree, which the divine landowner determines to cut down after three fruitless years. The dresser, however, pleads for one more chance: "Lord, let it alone this year also, till I shall dig about it, and dung it: And if it bear fruit, well: and if not, then after that thou shalt cut it down" (Luke 13: 8-9). Such sources would allow later writers to picture the clergy not only as pastors but also as husbandmen or even as plowmen.

Other biblical episodes with georgic relevance include the story of Ruth, who gained a husband and a secure place in Israel by laboring in the fields. From that labor, as Isaiah prophesied, the chosen seed was to emerge in the course of time. "And there shall come forth a rod out of the stem of Jesse, and a Branch shall grow out of his roots" (11:1). Second only in prominence to the reconstituted city of Jerusalem as a symbol for apocalyptic renewal is the promise that, after the "Day of the Lord," each inhabitant of the renewed Israel would live in peace once more "every man under his vine and under his fig tree."[7] And, in what may be thought the most universal georgic image of all, the Bible views humanity as a crop to be harvested, as in Christ's parables of the seeds and of the wheat and tares. Therefore, in a recurrent extension of that image, human history, which began with the fall of man into labor, would end with a universal harvest. "Put ye in the

[7] 1 Kings 4:25; and see Jer. 8:13, Joel 1:7, 1:12, 2:22, and esp. Mic. 4:4 and Zech. 3:10.

sickle, for the harvest is ripe: come, get you down; for the press is full, the vats overflow" (Joel 3:13). Like so many other biblical images, this one receives its last transformation in Revelation:

> [B]ehold a white cloud, and upon the cloud one sat like unto the Son of man, having on his head a golden crown, and in his hand a sharp sickle. And another angel came out of the temple, crying with a loud voice to him that sat on the cloud, Thrust in thy sickle, and reap: ... for the harvest of the earth is ripe. (14:14-15)[8]

In the same tradition, Jesus, after viewing the multitudes in the familiar pastoral image as "sheep having no shepherd," adds a georgic equivalent: "Then saith he unto his disciples, The harvest truly is plenteous, but the labourers are few; Pray ye therefore the Lord of the harvest, that he will send forth labourers into his harvest" (Matt. 9:36-38).

A favorite text of seventeenth-century reformers who wanted to abolish the institution of tithes for the support of the ministry was St. Paul's Second Epistle to the Thessalonians:

> Neither did we eat any man's bread for nought; but wrought with labour and travail night and day, that we might not be chargeable to any of you: Not because we have not power, but to make ourselves an ensample unto you to follow us. For even when we were with you, this we commanded you, that if any would not work, neither should he eat. (3:8-10)

So familiar was this text that when Guigo the Carthusian cited it in a letter to the monks of Mons Dei (early twelfth century), he did not even trouble to quote the best-known part directly.[9]

---

[8] See also Gen. 8:22, Isa. 17:11, Jer. 5:24, 8:20, 51:33, Hos. 6:11, Joel 3:13, Amos 4:7, Matt. 13:39, Mark 4:29, Luke 10:2, John 4:35.

[9] Boas, *Primitivism*, pp. 119-21 (*Pat. Lat.*, 174:332-33). For an earlier citation, see St. Athanasius' *Life of Saint Anthony* (Westminster: Newman, 1950), pp. 21, 65. St. Paul's advocacy of labor is further reflected in Acts 18:1-3, describing his work as a tentmaker, and in Acts 20:34, 1 Cor. 4:12,

Parasitical behavior, especially on the part of the clergy, came to be known as living off the sweat of other men's faces. St. Bernard employs a typical variation of Genesis 3:19 to make the point: "The clergy fatten on the sweat of others, they devour the fruits of the earth without charge."[10]

A number of other texts on the value of labor have been conveniently gathered together by Milton in his *Christian Doctrine*:

> INDUSTRY is that by which we honestly provide for ourselves the means of comfortable living. Gen.ii.15. "to dress it and to keep it." iii.19. "in the sweat of thy face thou shalt eat bread." Prov. x.4. "he becometh poor that dealeth with a slack hand." v.5. "he that gathereth in summer is a wise son." xii.11. "he that tilleth his land shall be satisfied with bread." xiv.23. "in all labor there is profit." xxi.5. "the thoughts of the diligent tend only to plenteousness, but of every one that is hasty only to want." xxii.29. "seest thou a man diligent in his business? he shall stand before kings." 1 Thess. iv.11,12. "work with your own hands, as we commanded you; that ye may walk honestly toward them that are without, and that ye may lack of nothing." 2 Thess. iii.12. "we exhort by our Lord Jesus Christ, that with quietness they work, and eat their own bread."[11]

Thus it is clear that, for those who were so disposed, there were more than a sufficiency of biblical texts to support a georgic view of life.

Georgic imagery frequently appears in the Bible in a context

Eph. 4:28, and 1 Thess. 4:11. See also *The Didache*, trans. James A. Kleist (Westminster: Newman, 1948), p. 23, cited by J. L. Illanes, *On the Theology of Work* (Dublin: Four Courts Press, 1982), pp. 19-20.

[10] Letter 158 to Pope Innocent II, in *The Letters of St. Bernard of Clairvaux*, trans. Bruno Scott James (London: Burns & Oates, 1953), p. 228.

[11] *The Works of John Milton*, ed. Frank Allen Patterson et al., 18 vols. (New York: Columbia Univ. Press, 1931-40), 17:230-33. The first of these texts provided Milton with authority for the work Adam and Eve perform before the fall (see ch. 7 below).

of reform: vats overflow, fields are ripe for harvesting, grass is taken off and burnt, barren trees are cut down, and out of sin and suffering comes renewal. So it is not surprising that Guigo and Bernard resort to georgic imagery to rebuke luxury and to stress the power of labor to renovate the soul and to atone for social injustice. When St. Bernard wrote in 1124 to rebuke Abbot Arnold for abandoning his post at a moment critical to the establishment of the Cistercian reform, he turned naturally to biblical georgic in order to reinforce his point:

> Alas! what will happen to those new plantations of Christ set by your own hand in "the wilderness and fearful desert places"? Who will be there to dig them about and dung them? Who will build a hedge round about them and prune away their untoward growth? Either these still tender saplings will be easily uprooted by the first storms of trouble, or else for lack of anyone to clean the ground about them they will be choked by the weeds that grow up with them, so that they will bear no fruit. (Letter 4; pp. 21-22)

At this stage in the Cistercian movement, when it had all the typical marks of Christian reform, there was no great distance between farmwork and spiritual cultivation. The return to what was conceived to be the original spirit of Benedict's Rule meant the sanctification of labor and its tools (Rule, chs. 31-32), and, as in biblical times, it demanded a concerted effort that was both literally and figuratively georgic to clear the ground and to nourish and prune the plants.

Therefore, when Milton turned to georgic imagery in his campaign against the prelacy, he was working in a long-established tradition of georgic reform that went back to the biblical prophets. In *Animadversions*, Milton tells a parable so biblical in spirit, so representative of the reforming impulse of his time, and so typical of his own views, that it deserves substantial quotation:

> A certaine man of large possessions, had a faire Garden, and kept therein an honest and laborious servant, whose

skill and profession was to set or sow all wholesome herbs
. . . and what ever else was to be done in a well-husbanded
nursery of plants and fruits; now, when the time was
come that he should cut his hedges, prune his trees, looke
to his tender slips, and pluck up the weeds that hinder'd
their growth, he gets him up by breake of day . . . and
who would thinke that any other should know better
than he how the dayes work was to be spent? Yet for all
this there comes another strange Gardener that never
knew the soyle, never handl'd a Dibble or Spade to set
the least pot-herbe that grew there, much lesse had en-
dur'd an houres sweat or chilnesse, and yet challenges
his right the binding or unbinding of every flower, the
clipping of every bush, the weeding and worming of every
bed both in that, and all other Gardens thereabout; the
honest Gardener, that ever since the day-peepe, till now
the Sunne was growne somewhat ranke, had wrought
painfully about his bankes and seede-plots at this com-
manding voyce, turnes suddenly about with some won-
der, and . . . modestly refus'd him, telling him . . . that
he had already perform'd himselfe. No, said the stranger,
this is neither for you nor your fellowes to meddle with,
but for me onely that am for this purpose in dignity farre
above you, and the provision which the Lord of the soyle
allowes me in this office is, and that with good reason,
ten fold your wages; the Gardener smil'd and shooke his
head, but what was determin'd I cannot tell you till the
end of this Parliament.[12]

The ease with which Milton weaves the imagery of biblical
georgic and the assumptions of a long line of commentary
into a current political-religious dispute is typical, of him and
of his time.

Later in *Animadversions*, Milton calls on the same stock of
imagery once more, when he gives his definition of a "true
Pastor," who "for greatest labours . . . requires either nothing

[12] *Works*, 3:158-59.

... or a very common and reasonable supply." God "can easily send labourers into his Harvest, that shall not cry, Give, give." And georgic imagery appears again when Milton criticizes the gentry who put their sons into the clergy for the sake of fat benefices: "God has no neede of such, they have no part or lot in his Vineyard, they may as well sue for Nunneries, that they may have some convenient stowage for their wither'd daughters, because they cannot give them portions answerable to the pride and vanity they have bred them in" (3:160-63). Milton's position on tithes, which was extreme for the time, was to prove almost as unpalatable to Parliament and Cromwell as it was to the bishops. But the general sentiment, and the texts and images in which it was couched, had been familiar to reformers for a millennium and a half, and were only too familiar to Milton's opponents. What is notable about Milton's position on tithes is that it is based not only on liberty of conscience and freedom of the individual to cultivate his own soul, but on the dignity of labor and the need for each man to work for himself. The alternative is to condone the grave injustice that results when, contrary to the injunction in Genesis, one man supports another in the sweat of his face, or to allow into God's harvest hireling laborers and humanly appointed supervisors, no more committed to God's work than are the hireling shepherds of "Lycidas."

WORK IN THE MIDDLE AGES

With his cutting reference to nunneries, Milton was employing a familiar rhetorical device of associating something he disliked—in this case use of the Church to maintain younger sons at the expense of parishioners—with the customs and institutions of the Catholic Church, to which he knew his readers would respond with loathing. The nunnery was especially apt for Milton's argument, because, during the century following the dissolution, the English had grown accustomed to think of convents and monasteries as hotbeds of vice, and especially of laziness and economic parasitism. When new sects or forms of religions arise, they often define themselves partly by attacks on their predecessors. In particular, they are apt to argue that failures and abuses in older institutions not only result from corruption but are basic to their nature. Thus St. Paul argued that Christianity differs from Judaism as the living spirit differs from the dead letter, even though Isaiah, for one, indicates both that such abuses existed and that they were unacceptable to Judaism as defined by the prophets. Thus, in similar fashion, Protestants routinely accused Roman Catholics of worshiping sticks and stones and of holding stubbornly to the Pelagian doctrine of the efficacy of works—charges that were certainly not true, yet that gained a certain credibility because widespread abuses had arisen during the disastrous fourteenth century and had grown worse under corrupt Renaissance popes. In England at the dissolution, many smaller foundations still had not recovered, materially or spiritually, from the Black Death, civil war, and economic depression, whereas many of the great foundations had grown too prosperous for their own good.[13] Abuses were common enough to make Thomas Cromwell's propaganda plausible and widely popular.

One motive of the dissolution was to bring the monastic lands into the secular world and put them to more efficient use. Marvell's "Upon Appleton House" accuses the Cistercian nuns not only of hidden corruption, but of too much fondness for "holy leisure" (97).[14] Because the nuns are idle, the only "Fruit their Gardens yield" is a harvest of secret vice (219), and, when Sir William Fairfax rescues Isabel Thwaites from the clutches of the nuns, he rescues the conventual lands for better and more patriotic uses.

> Thenceforth (as when th'Inchantment ends
> The Castle vanishes or rends)

---

[13] David Knowles, *The Religious Orders in England*, 3 vols. (Cambridge: Cambridge Univ. Press, 1950-59); *The Monastic Order in England*, 2d edn. (Cambridge: Cambridge Univ. Press, 1963).

[14] *The Poems and Letters of Andrew Marvell*, ed. H. M. Margoliouth, 2d edn., 2 vols. (Oxford: Clarendon Press, 1967).

The wasting Cloister with the rest
Was in one instant dispossest.
. . . .
And what both *Nuns* and *Founders* will'd
'Tis likely better thus fulfill'd.
(269-76)

On this point Marvell is not especially sectarian; almost any Englishman of his time would have agreed that the "wasting Cloister" had been a nonproductive burden better cleared away like the barren fig tree.

Probably the Tudor monasteries were inefficient in part because they were content to farm in the old ways and to refrain from racking up rents beyond what was needed to feed the monks and the statutory number of travelers and poor— or to pay the increasing exactions imposed by Cardinal Woolsey and Cromwell on behalf of their royal master.[15] Contrary to common opinion, the monastic lands were not given to favorites but were sold off at market value by the crown over the whole course of the sixteenth century, as the Tudor monarchs paid for wars and other extravagances out of capital— a policy disastrous to the Stuart exchequer but beneficial to the nation in the long run. It was customary to determine land prices as a multiple of yearly rents, and the rise in purchase prices for monastic lands from twenty to more than thirty times annual rents over the course of the century[16] is a good indicator not of royal greed (since few purchasers would pay more than fair market price) but of increasing land value, which was beginning to result from improved methods of

---

[15] See Knowles, *Religious Orders in England*, 3:241-59; and Joyce Youings, *The Dissolution of the Monasteries* (London: George Allen & Unwin, 1971). For royal taxation of monasteries in earlier periods, see Lawrence A. Desmond, "The Statute of Carlisle and the Cistercians 1298-1369," and William J. Talesca, "The Cistercian Dilemma at the Close of the Middle Ages: Gallicanism or Rome," both in *Studies in Medieval Cistercian History Presented to Jeremiah F. O'Sullivan* (Spencer, Mass.: Cistercian Publications, 1971), 138-62, 163-85.

[16] Knowles, *Religious Orders in England*, 3:393-96.

husbandry. That in turn would allow increases in rents to compensate for the higher purchase price. If this reading of the situation is accurate, it is also ironic, since in an earlier period it was the monasteries that were in the forefront of technological evolution and increased agricultural efficiency.[17]

Recent studies demonstrate that the Middle Ages were not so backward as Renaissance scientists were accustomed to depict them. Agricultural and industrial revolutions nearly as significant as those of the modern period took place during the early Middle Ages and underlay the great cultural and artistic accomplishments of the twelfth and thirteenth centuries. Such essential labor-saving devices as the horse-collar, the moldboard plow, and the iron horseshoe all were Medieval developments unknown to the ancient world.[18] Slavery, still very common in the ninth century, had virtually disappeared by the thirteenth, although the institution lingered longer in England than elsewhere.[19] The development in the early Middle Ages of the water mill, which Roman engineers rarely put to practical use, had an importance equivalent to that of the steam engine, since it produced enormous savings of human and animal energy as well as providing a new means for the accumulation of capital. The Domesday survey of 1086 in England counted 9,250 manors, populated by 287,045 tenant families, and on those desmesnes were a total of 5,624 water mills.[20] The commonest use of these basic power sources was

---

[17] A common opinion, true of periods of reform and expansion, I should think, although some recent studies question the monastic contribution to Medieval agriculture. See Georges Duby, *Rural Economy and Country Life in the Medieval West*, trans. Cynthia Postan (1962; Columbia: Univ. of South Carolina Press, 1968); B. H. Slicher van Bath, *The Agrarian History of Western Europe, A.D. 500-1850*, trans. Olive Ordish (London: Edward Arnold, 1963); Nigel Harvey, *The Industrial Archaeology of Farming in England and Wales* (London: B. T. Batsford, 1980).

[18] See Duby, *Rural Economy*, and Jean Gimpel, *The Medieval Machine* (London: Book Club Associates, 1977).

[19] Duby, *Rural Economy*, pp. 33, 37-41, 48-54, 154, 191-96, 221-22, 229, 279.

[20] Gimpel, *The Medieval Machine*, pp. 11-12.

to grind grain for flour, but they were also connected to mechanical pounders and used extensively for fulling cloth, and as early as the eleventh century some were even harnessed to stamp iron ore and to forge iron by means of mechanical triphammers.[21] Flemish and Florentine clothmakers developed mass-production methods, which the Flemish emigrants introduced into England. When Richard Coeur de Lion went on crusade, the metalworkers in the Forest of Dean were able to fill his order for 50,000 horseshoes.[22]

Recent studies have argued that the mechanical clock, under whose auspices humanity moved from natural and ecclesiastical time to industrial time, probably was first developed and put to public use during the Middle Ages. Other inventions included the button and the stern-hinged rudder.[23] As is well known, the introduction of the stirrup revolutionized cavalry warfare. Finally, all three of the discoveries that the Renaissance loved to celebrate as proofs of its ability to outdo the accomplishments of the ancient world were introduced during the Middle Ages: the compass in the thirteenth century, the cannon in the fourteenth, and printing in the fifteenth, before the Renaissance reached Mainz. Caxton set up the first English press in 1477 at Westminister, then a Benedictine abbey.

The monasteries, which from the first emphasized the value and the importance of work, were in the forefront of technological development, and they also developed the economic and managerial skills needed to put that technology into practice. According to the Benedictine Rule, although a monk's first duty is the *opus Dei* or celebration of the communal offices, he is also to engage in both manual and intellectual labor. "Idleness is the enemy of the soul. The brethren, there-

---

[21] Gimpel, *The Medieval Machine*, pp. 13, 66-67; see also R. J. Forbes, "Metallurgy," in *A History of Technology*, ed. C. S. Singer et al. (Oxford: Clarendon Press, 1956), p. 75; and *The Cambridge Economic History of Europe*, vol. 2 (Cambridge: Cambridge Univ. Press, 1952).

[22] Gimpel, *The Medieval Machine*, p. 64.

[23] Lynn White, Jr., *Machina Ex Deo* (Cambridge, Mass.: MIT Press, 1968), pp. 129-30, 160-61.

fore, must be occupied at stated hours in manual labour, and again at other hours in sacred reading" (ch. 48).[24] In the early days of the order, the monks evidently did at least some field work themselves. Passages in the Rule imply that such labors were not unusual, though also not inevitable: "[I]f the circumstances of the place or their poverty require them to gather the harvest themselves, let them not be discontented; for then are they truly monks when they live by the labour of their hands, like our fathers and the apostles" (ch. 48). In England, over the course of the centuries, the monks became, in effect, landowners and managers rather than farm laborers; under their direction the Benedictine abbeys dominated the country's agriculture and accomplished a good deal in the way of land clearance and drainage.

From the Rule it may also be deduced that, from the first, the monks were engaged in other kinds of manual labor: "If there be craftsmen in the monastery, let them practise their crafts with all humility, provided the abbot give permission" (ch. 57). "The monastery should, if possible, be so arranged that all necessary things, such as water, mill, garden, and various crafts may be within the enclosure, so that the monks may not be compelled to wander outside it, for that is not at all expedient for their souls" (ch. 66). Often a monastery grew so rich, and so well supplied with servants, that the monks had little need or opportunity for more than a token performance of manual labor. Yet recurrently the pressures of Christian and monastic humility led to reform, as is indicated, for example, by the *decreta* of the synod of Aachen (816): "That monks shall work with their own hands in the kitchens, in the bakery, and in other workshops, and shall wash their robes on due occasion" (ch. 4).[25] When the English mystic Augustine Baker joined the reformed Benedictine monastery of St. Jus-

---

[24] *The Rule of Saint Benedict*, ed. Abbot Justin McCann (London: Burns Oates, 1952), p. 111.

[25] *Corpus Consuetudinem Monasticorum*, ed. K. Hallinger, 2 vols., 1 (Siegburg, 1963), 451.

tina's in Padua in 1605, he had to be taught how to wash his linen, "with which point of laundry he was unacquainted."[26]

Reform could also take the form of the foundation of new orders. Beginning in the twelfth century, the most important centers for technological innovation and application were the Cistercian abbeys. Typifying the shifting balance between conservatism and reform is the coincidence that St. Bernard was giving new life to Cîteaux and Clairvaux at about the same time that Peter the Venerable was finishing Cluny III, the immense Parkinsonian headquarters of a reform movement that now ruled 1,500 abbeys and priories and had grown sclerotic through sheer size, wealth, and political success. As some recent studies have argued, the abbeys could take from society as well as contribute to it, by the accretion of gifts of already-developed lands and of secular wealth.[27] Cluny appears to have reached that condition by the twelfth century, as many of the monasteries in England may have in the sixteenth. The quarrel between Bernard and Peter,[28] between the austere labors and prayers of the Cistercians and the total emphasis on liturgical celebration of the Cluniacs, may be said to have begun when Bernard's young cousin Robert was persuaded to leave Clairvaux for Cluny. The Cluniac Grand Prior who persuaded him, as St. Bernard describes him in a letter to his cousin, has the typical aristocrat's attitude toward manual labor, since the Church as well as the world may harbor the aristocratic spirit:

> He called voluntary poverty wretched and poured scorn upon fasts, vigils, silence, and manual labour. ... "When," he asked, "was God pleased with our sufferings;

[26] *Memorials of Father Augustine Baker and Other Documents Relating to the English Benedictines*, ed. Dom Justin McCann and Dom Hugh Connolly, Catholic Record Society, 33 (London, 1933), 85.

[27] Georges Duby, *The Early Growth of the European Economy*, trans. Howard B. Clarke (Ithaca: Cornell Univ. Press, 1974).

[28] On this quarrel, see *Letters of St. Bernard* and David Knowles, *Cistercians and Cluniacs* (London: Oxford Univ. Press, 1955).

... what sort of religion is it to dig the soil, clear forests, and cart muck?" (Letter 1; p. 4)

Although at any time the Church or the monastic orders might entertain a complacent and economically parasitic spirit of this kind, since it is in the nature of all human institutions to decay, the impulse to Christian reform kept pulling in the other direction. The Benedictine order reformed itself many times. But perhaps the clearest instance of Medieval monastic reform is represented by the Cistercian order in the first century after its foundation. The first regulation set down by the General Chapter of 1134 was that "None of our monasteries is to be constructed in towns, castles or villages, but in places remote from human intercourse."[29] The consequences that resulted from general obedience to this rule in the early period of the order were economic as well as spiritual. Citeaux began as a remote clearing in a wood. Clairvaux was founded on poor and undeveloped land, and the early accounts are full of stories of toil and near starvation.[30] When St. Bernard set out in formal procession from Citeaux to found Clairvaux, he carried a cross at the head of a file of twelve men who bore equipment for the celebration of Mass and the offices, a supply of food, and a variety of agricultural and building tools. At times the monks sustained themselves on beech leaves, roots, and nuts from the surrounding forest, while they cleared the fields and built the monastery in stages.

When the first monastery at Clairvaux had been completed, it soon proved too small. Bernard, who summoned a chapter for advice, was reluctant to throw away the work already done: "See how the buildings have already been built in stone with great sweat and at great expense." But at length he acceded to the construction of Clairvaux II, which was to

[29] *Analecta Divionensia*, ed. Ph. Guignard (Dijon, 1878), cited by Wolfgang Braunfels, *Monasteries of Western Europe* (Princeton: Princeton Univ. Press, 1972), p. 243.

[30] See Geoffrey Webb and Adrian Walker, *St. Bernard of Clairvaux* (Westminster, Md.: Newman Press, 1960).

become the architectural model for Cistercian monasteries all over Europe. From the first, one might see how hard manual labor was connected with an enthusiasm for technological development:

> Resources flowed, workmen were swiftly assembled, and the brethren too threw themselves into the work in every way. Some felled trees, some dressed stone, others built walls, and others again parted the river from its scattered channels and diverted the flow of its waters to a mill. But fullers too, and bakers, tanners, smiths and other craftsmen all organized their respective machinery for their work so that the babbling brook, carried hither and yon by buried conduits to every building, gushed and welled up wherever there was occasion for it; then, having fulfilled their appointed tasks through all the workshops, and the monastery having been cleansed [of its sewage], the waters, which were split up, returned to the main river bed.[31]

In England, as the Middle Ages progressed, the Cistercians specialized in raising sheep and were responsible in large part for developing the wool trade. The early foundations, such as Fountains (1135), were essentially similar to those on the Continent. All were built near running water, which was diverted for drinking, washing, and sewage disposal, but also for running what amounted to a series of compact factories within the enclosure. At Clairvaux there was a mill to crush olives for oil, another to grind corn and mechanically sift the flour from the bran. The water went to a brewery and a fuller's mill, where it worked mechanical wooden pestles by an arrangement of cams. From there it ran to the tannery and the reredorter or *necessarium*. Not until Queen Elizabeth installed her famous jakes at Richmond Palace did Renaissance England see anything approaching this sort of plumbing. Concerning the many mills at Clairvaux, the author of a twelfth-

---

[31] Braunfels, *Monasteries of Western Europe*, p. 244.

century report marvels: "How many horses would be worn out, how many men would have weary arms if this graceful river, to whom we owe our clothes and food, did not labour for us."[32] According to Jean Gimpel, the plant at Clairvaux was typical:

> Monasteries built in countries separated by thousands of miles—Portugal, Sweden, Scotland, Hungary—all had very similar waterpowered systems within almost universally similar plans for the monasteries themselves. It has been said that a blind Cistercian monk moving into any of the monasteries would instantly have known where he was. In certain ways the discipline imposed by Saint Bernard on his monks—the rigid timetable, the impossibility of deviating from the Rule without facing punishment—brings to mind the work regulations that Henry Ford imposed on his assembly lines.[33]

One curious impetus to all this technological activity was probably, as Duby suggests, the desire of the monks to live exactly according to the Benedictine Rule, and therefore to eat like modest Romans of the sixth century: to eat bread, drink wine, and cook their food in olive oil, a diet better suited to Italy than to northern Europe.[34] As a result fields had to be cleared, vines coaxed to grow where they had never been before, and olives brought north by ship or cart. Another impetus, at least in the early years, would seem to have been the desire to give and not to take: to feed the hungry, clothe the naked, and lift some of the burden of labor from the ordinary worker and even the draft animal.

The activities and the state of mind represented by the Medieval Cistercian "factories" involve two aspects of work:

---

[32] David Luckhurst, "Monastic Watermills," Society for the Protection of Ancient Buildings, no. 8 (London, n.d.), p. 6; cited by Gimpel, *The Medieval Machine*, p. 6.

[33] Gimpel, *The Medieval Machine*, p. 5; and for architectural plans and discussion, see Braunfels, *Monasteries of Western Europe*, pp. 67-110.

[34] Duby, *Early Growth of the European Economy*, esp. p. 18.

First, manual work, *labor*, is seen to be important and beneficial to humanity. Second, organization and mechanization are seen as equally important, in order to remove from labor as much brute sweat as possible. Man must carry Adam's inevitable burden, but charity to one's fellows demands that it be lightened as far as may be. Even those at the base of the work pyramid, the bound peasants, could be saved many hours of labor, since they could bring their grain to the abbey mills, which in essence took the place of the individual mortars and pestles of the ancient world. The slave grinding flour in a back room was replaced by a public mill that did the work for a moderate charge. Possibly there are tensions and contradictions between the ideals of *labor* and of τέχνη, yet during the years when the monasteries were in proper working order they valued both. Virgil incorporates the same combination into the *Georgics*, whose essential spirit includes both the terrible effort implied by "nudus ara, sere nudus" (1.299), "Strip to plow, strip to sow," and the naming of the Pleiades and the Hyades as civilization flowers under the twin pressures of labor and need.

In the fourteenth century, a series of catastrophes swept through Europe. Weather changes, crop failures, the appearance of the great plague in 1348, and the widespread destruction of the Hundred Years' War came together to bring the Medieval agricultural and industrial revolutions to an end. For a century and a half, populations declined, buildings and fields decayed, and there was a great diminishment in the spirit of initiative that was needed to reverse the decline and rebuild. Historians, accustomed in recent times to argue that the drives toward religion and secular advancement are distinct or opposed, often account for the almost total disappearance of interest in technology and invention as a turning away from the world toward "mysticism."[35] Such a theory, however, will hardly hold up when we consider that the same St. Bernard who presided over the building of Clairvaux and its daughter

[35] E. g. Gimpel, *The Medieval Machine*, pp. 199-204.

177

abbeys was the greatest mystic of his time, and that he was engaged in preaching his great commentary on the Song of Songs during precisely those years that the abbey buildings were going up and the mills and conduits were being installed. A more likely theory is that two things are required to begin a technological revolution. First is a spirit of optimism, of confidence that one's efforts will bring forth some reasonably predictable fruit. Religion, as the early chronicles reveal, gave Bernard and his monks that optimism, and events confirmed it. What happened to people during the fourteenth century, however, was enough to destroy almost anyone's confidence, since whatever they built was likely to be immediately swept away. The second requirement, history repeatedly suggests, is desire for reform, a desire often born from religious idealism and almost inevitably pitted against conservative, aristocratic attitudes that combine scorn for labor with the drive to accumulate wealth and honor and then sit on them. In the Middle Ages as in the seventeenth century, an aristocrat might be found in religion as well as in the world. How opposing attitudes might operate within the Church is well exemplified by the enmity between Clairvaux and Cluny.

Chaucer and Langland

What a reform-minded monk in Medieval England might have thought about labor is suggested by a passage in *Our Daily Work*, a treatise thought to have been written by Richard Rolle, the Hermit of Hampole: "Idleship wastes goods that are won by goods, and therefore S. John says that nothing is worse than idleness, and not only because he wins nought, but because he wastes those that are won."[36] This certainly is a succinct statement of the economic principle by which it can be judged whether a monk, a monastery, or a whole religious order is contributing materially as well as spiritually

[36] Geraldine Hodgson, ed., *Rolle and "Our Daily Work"* (London: Faith Press, 1929), p. 37.

to society, from which it can rarely dissociate itself altogether. Again it illustrates that mystics are not necessarily impractical or uninterested in matters of social welfare. Rolle goes on to give his theoretical reasons for the importance of labor:

> For Job says: *Homo enim ad laborem natus est*; that is to say, "Man is born to travail." And therefore, the man that travails not, he lives not as a man.
>
> To travail was man bound after he had sinned, through God's bidding, Who thus said to him: *In sudore vultus tui vesceris pane tuo, donec revertaris in terram de qua assumptus es* . . . that is thou shalt travail stalwartly and not faintly, for He bids thee travail "with sweat of thy face"—he that travails, that sweats heartily, he that swinks: and so thou shouldest . . . all thy life thou (shalt) travail, that thou lose no time. . . . [T]herefore speaks the Psalm writer where he thus says:—*Manus habent et non palpabunt* . . . "They have hands," he says, "but they work not." (pp. 37-39)

The manner in which Rolle transforms Job's bitter complaint into a condition for being fully human is breathtaking, and typical of how Christian paradox can turn shame and weakness into strength. In a similar spirit, Dame Julian of Norwich portrays Christ in the image of a ragged peasant eager to "delve and dyke, toil and sweat, and turn the earth upside-down" for the sake of suffering humanity.[37] The reformed Franciscans were actively spreading similar views about the poor worker. Only by accepting his implication in the consequences of the fall can man begin to do something about his sorrowful state and thus take some part in constructing a civilizing bulwark against the negative forces of history.

The decay of the monastic ideal in England is well exemplified by Chaucer's monk. Harry Bailey, who recognizes his

---

[37] *Revelations of Divine Love* (14:51), cited by Beatrice White, "Poet and Peasant," in *The Reign of Richard II*, ed. F.R.H. Du Boulay and Caroline M. Barron (London: Athlone Press, 1971), pp. 58-59.

aristocratic pretensions, repeatedly addresses him as "My Lord, the Monk" (7.1924-29), and the General Prologue tells us that "He was a lord ful fat and in good poynt" (1.200). Here is a monk who loves to dress richly and (against the rules of his order) to hunt. Naturally his aristocratic pride leads him to have a low opinion of work:

> What sholde he studie and make hymselven wood,
> Upon a book in cloystre alwey to poure,
> Or swynken with his handes, and laboure,
> As Austyn bit? How shal the world be served?
> Lat Austyn have his swynk to hym reserved!
> (1.184-88)[38]

Although interpretations of Chaucer vary widely, still it seems clear enough that Chaucer intends his Monk to serve as a negative exemplum, an instance of everything a monk ought not, ideally, to be.

With respect to labor, the Monk's opposite is the Plowman, who is the brother of Chaucer's Christlike Parson. It is true that Chaucer invites us to like many of his characters, including not a few of his rogues; still, the two brothers belong to quite a small group of wholly admirable characters. In his portrait of the Plowman, it is instructive to note how closely Chaucer associates manual labor with the basic Christian virtues, including humility, peacefulness, and obedience to the two great commandments that include all the rest: love of God and love of neighbor.

> With hym [the Parson] ther was a Plowman, was his brother,
> That hadde ylad of dong ful many a fother;
> A trewe swynkere and a good was he,
> Lyvynge in pees and parfit charitee.

[38] *The Works of Geoffrey Chaucer*, ed. F. N. Robinson, 2d edn. (Boston: Houghton Mifflin, 1957); parenthetical refs. are to Robinson's "fragment" and line numbers. Robinson suggests (p. 656) that Chaucer's "Austyn" refers to Augustine's Epistle 211 (*Pat. Lat.*, 33:958) and *De Opere Monachorum* (40:547ff.).

God loved he best with all his hoole herte
At alle tymes, thogh him gamed or smerte,
And thanne his neighebor right as hymselve.
He wolde thresshe, and therto dyke and delve,
For Cristes sake, for every povre wight,
Withouten hire, if it lay in his myght.
His tithes payde he ful faire and wel,
Bothe of his propre swynk and his catel.
(1.529-40)

One suspects Chaucer of playing one of his typical games with his reader here, since he persistently puts the Plowman's worst foot forward and then forces the reader to swallow the resultant social scorn by following up these base images with the unexceptionable axioms of Christian love. First come the cartloads of dung, then the Plowman's peaceable behavior and his perfect charity; next come the threshing, the diking, and the delving, then the information that he performs these menial chores out of constant love for Christ and the poor. When we remember the circumstances in which the poem was produced, as a work read to a circle of courtiers, then we may think that Chaucer was attempting on a small scale something very similar to what Spenser later undertook: to persuade his aristocratic audience that a plowman might, in his own humble way, be as admirable as a "verray, parfit gentil knyght."

In Chaucer's time, both orthodox reformers and Lollards put a high value on manual labor. They shared a reforming impulse but differed on the essential question: What is to be done? As his willing payment of tithes indicates, the Plowman belongs to those who respect the social order; therefore he (and probably Chaucer as well) represents reform by good example and good works rather than by revolution. Not long before Chaucer wrote the General Prologue, John Ball and Wat Tyler had given voice to another sentiment, as expressed by the popular refrain:

When Adam delved, and Eve span,
Who then was the gentleman?

At that time, and for a long time afterward, such a question went beyond the permissible bounds. To give up one's possessions and place in society and turn to manual labor was one thing; to require that society be leveled by universal equality in the performance of labor was quite another. Yet doubtless injustice, and especially the imposition of arbitrary fines and taxes and abuses in the Church, often led to both these responses. Jean Gimpel recounts an instructive tale of how the water mill, originally a technological boon to the rural laborer, might become a means of oppression. In 1331, Abbot Richard of St. Albans, anxious to preserve his monopoly on the grinding of grain, had all the farmhouses in the neighborhood searched for unauthorized millstones. He brought the stones to the abbey and, in a symbolic gesture, paved a courtyard with them. Fifty years later, during the Peasant Revolt, countrymen burst into the monastery and tore up the stones, which still represented their humiliation and economic subjection.[39]

Against the recurrent impulse to overturn society by force was poised the alternative reformist impulse to embrace work in the spirit of Rolle or of Chaucer's Plowman precisely because it is shameful. Such a response accorded well with the principle of Christian humility, with the biblical ideal of the Suffering Servant, with Christ's dictum that the first shall be last and the last first, and even with the Pauline mystery that Christ saved humanity by becoming "a curse for us" (Gal. 3:13). These principles often operated in the Middle Ages and continued to have some force in later periods. Donne, attached as he was to all the aristocratic objections to manual labor, nevertheless was moved to appeal to this tradition several years after his ordination, in "To Mr. Tilman after he had taken orders." As Helen Gardner notes, the particular scruples Donne raises in this poem were not mentioned by Tilman in his earlier poem, but "Men tend to ascribe to others the same motives as have influenced them themselves."[40] As was the

---

[39] Gimpel, *The Medieval Machine*, pp. 16, 219.

[40] *The Divine Poems of John Donne*, ed. Helen Gardner, 2d edn. (Oxford:

case in the verse letter to Woodward, Donne is able to associate himself with husbandry and labor in a spiritual context; but the Tilman poem reveals more clearly the conflict between aristocratic embarrassment and priestly self-denial:

> Thou, whose diviner soule hath caus'd thee now
> To put thy hand unto the holy Plough,
> Making Lay-scornings of the Ministry,
> Not an impediment, but victory;
> What bringst thou home with thee? how is thy mind
> Affected in the vintage? . . .
> Why doth the foolish world scorne that profession,
> Whose joyes passe speech? Why do they think unfit
> That Gentry should joyne families with it[?]
> (1-6, 26-28)

Donne had once been very much part of that world he now condemns, so it is not surprising if he feels somewhat strange to find his own hands on the plow—or if he feels relief in sharing that strangeness with someone in the same predicament. Yet a gentlemen might find, Donne's poem argues, intenser joy in the very acceptance of social debasement. Neither the situation nor the metaphor was new; both are rooted in the Bible and both have lengthy pedigrees, literary and social. For example, St. Bernard reminded two of his correspondents of the bibilical text on which Donne's metaphor is based: "Learn from the Gospels that no one who has put his hand to the plough may look back."[41]

Probably the fullest, and certainly the most familiar, Medieval argument for the importance of manual labor and farmwork is found in *Piers Plowman*. That poem, which has obvious affiliations with peasant discontent and with the popular tradition that associated reform with the figure of the plow-

---

Clarendon Press, 1978), p. 129. For Tilman's poem see H. Harvey Wood, "A Seventeenth-Century Manuscript of Poems by Donne and Others," *Essays and Studies by Members of the English Assn.*, 16 (1930), 184-86.

[41] Letter 2, p. 13; see also Letter 1, p. 6; and Luke 9:62: "And Jesus said unto him, No man, having put his hand to the plough, and looking back, is fit for the kingdom of God."

man, nevertheless brings its indignation against social injustice into conformity with traditional teachings. Of its several spokesmen, including Holy Church, Conscience, Reason, and Kind Wit, the figure of Piers himself is the most fascinating and powerful. In the Prologue, with its "fair feeld ful of folk" (17), the poet reveals the problem that his poem will confront: a world full of social and moral injustice.[42] From the first, he makes a connection between the spiritual and the economic orders that is so close as to be virtually indistinguishable. Some evildoers betray their trust out of avarice for wealth (later, Lady Mede):

> Persons and parisshe preestes pleyned hem to þe Bisshop
> That hire Parisshe were pouere siþ þe pestilence tyme,
> To haue a licence and leue at London to dwelle,
> To syngen for symonie for siluer is swete.
> (Prologue.83-86)

The other great class of evildoers are the wasters:

> Heremytes on an heep with hoked staues
> Wenten to walsyngham, and hire wenches after;
> Grete lobies and longe þat loþe were to swynke
> Cloþed hem in copes to ben knowen from oþere;
> Shopen hem heremytes hire ese to haue.
> (Prologue.53-57)

Others labor to rebuild what is being destroyed, only to see what they have gained wasted once more:

> Some putten hem to plouȝ, pleiden ful selde,
> In settynge and sowynge swonken ful harde;
> Wonnen þat þise wastours with glotonye destruyeþ.
> (Prologue.20-23)

When Lady Mede argues before the king that such is and ought to be the way of the world, Conscience opposes to this

---

[42] *Piers Plowman: The B Version*, ed. George Kane and E. Talbot Donaldson (London: Athlone Press, 1975). Parenthetical citations are to *passus* and lines in this edn.; I have silently removed brackets, italics, and other editorial apparatus.

aristocratic scheme of things a visionary society out of biblical georgic:

> Ac kynde loue shal come ȝit and Conscience togideres
> And make of lawe a laborer; swich loue shal arise. . . .
> Alle þat beren baselard, brood swerd or launce,
> Ax ouþer hachet or any wepene ellis,
> Shal be demed to þe deeþ but if he do it smyþye
> Into sikel or to be siþe, to Shaar or to kultour:
> *Conflabunt gladios suos in vomeres &c.*
> Ech man to pleye with a plow, Pykoise or spade,
> Spynne or sprede donge or spille hymself with sleuþe.
> (3.299-310)

When the military ideal, on which aristocracy is based, is replaced by an ideal of labor, then the georgic image of beating the implements of war into those of farming naturally arises.[43] Equally striking, in a class with the lion lying down with the lamb, is the hope to "make of law a laborer"; that is, to convert that privileged group of men who drain the Church and prey on society into honest and humble contributors to the common good. That is what Conscience demands of the king, but this spokesman of an absolute vision is unlikely to get his way on this side of the Apocalypse. His is the great and demanding vision of the end, of that final goal toward which humanity should strive, but which it can never hope to reach in this life.

In the meantime, Piers Plowman suddenly pokes his head into the poem to suggest a more workable solution. Those who would repudiate injustice and flee the Seven Deadly Sins, which bring damnation in their train, must find and follow Truth; and the way to find Truth, Piers tells us repeatedly, is not by pilgrimage to Rome or Jerusalem but by the spiritual "pilgrimage" of honest labor.

> I wol worshipe þerwiþ truþe by my lyue,
> And ben his pilgrym atte plow for pouere mennes sake.

---

[43] In addition to Isa. 2:4, the most familiar locus, see Micah 4:3 and also Joel 3:10 and its close analogue in *Georgics* 1.508.

My plowpote shal be my pik and putte at þe rotes,
And helpe my cultour to kerue and close þe furwes.
(6.101-104)

"To be a pilgrim at the plow, for the sake of the poor"; it is
the same idea that is represented by Chaucer's Plowman, who
dikes and delves for his poorer neighbors. In the latter part
of the poem (before the poet turns to Do-Well, Do-Better,
and Do-Best), the world of men is represented as a "half acre,"
which must be cooperatively worked for the good of all.
Clearly this image derives both from the historical situation
and from familiarity with the basic imagery of biblical georgic:

Now is Perkyn and þe pilgrimes to þe plow faren.
To erie þis half acre holpen hym manye;
Dikeres and Delueres digged vp þe balkes;
Therwiþ was Perkyn apayed and preised hem yerne.
Oþere werkmen þer were þat wroȝten ful faste,
Ech man in his manere made hymself to doone,
And somme to plese Perkyn piked vp þe wedes.
(6.105-11)

The connections among true Christian morality, economic
well-being, and manual labor are close and inseparable. To
sin against one's neighbors and the social system is synony-
mous with a refusal to work; and the penalty is similar to
that suffered by the lazy farmer in Virgil's *Georgics*: "Truth
shall teach you to drive his team, or you shall eat barley bread
and drink of the brook" (6.134-35). Even the hermits must
take up their spades if they wish to drive away hunger (6.183-
90).

The seeds of the Protestant Reformation and the dissolution
of the monasteries may be seen in *Piers Plowman*, but its
author actually says nothing that might not have been spoken
by St. Bernard or any of a number of monastic reformers. It
is primarily reform rather than overthrowing of institutions to
which the poem calls its readers. But the warning should have
been clear: if institutions are generally perceived as wasters
rather than winners, then they will lack support in time of

crisis. Over the following two centuries, Piers became a kind of subversive underground spokesman for religious radicals. In 1550, when the religion of England hung in the balance, Robert Crowley published three editions of the poem. As John N. King explains, the reformist Crowley "kidnapped this orthodox medieval [poem] . . . , converting it, through his preface and marginal notes, into a powerful revolutionary attack against monasticism and the Roman Catholic hierarchy."[44] A fourth printing appeared in 1551; then, having done its work, the poem went out of print for another two centuries. Piers had proved to be a useful lever against the Roman Catholic establishment, but was less useful after an Anglican establishment had triumphed.

Still, *Piers Plowman* reminds us how appealing, in reform-minded times, are the ideas of a general return to the basics of manual labor and of working together in a spirit of cooperation for the benefit of society as a whole. Indeed, the ideal has survived the general disappearance of aristocracy from the stage of Western government, while its constant opponent—which between the ninth and the seventeenth centuries we have identified with aristocratic ideals, but which a Christian might have thought to have some connection with original sin—has also survived in altered forms. So, in *The Revolt of the Masses*, Ortega y Gasset complains that "The world is a civilised one, its inhabitant is not. . . . The new man wants his motor-car, and enjoys it, but he believes that it is the spontaneous fruit of an Edenic tree." Similarly Freud, puzzled by the general nostalgia for primitive or pastoral ways of life, asked a question more perennial than he may have realized: "How has it come about that so many people have adopted this strange attitude of hostility to civilization?"[45] The twentieth-century version of antipathy to work, which

[44] King, *English Reformation Literature* (Princeton: Princeton Univ. Press, 1982), p. 322; see pp. 319-39.

[45] Ortega (London: G. Allen & Unwin, 1932), .p. 89; Freud, *Civilization and Its Discontents*, trans. Joan Riviere (London: Hogarth Press, 1930), p. 44; I owe the collocation of these observations to Leo Marx, *The Machine in the Garden* (London: Oxford Univ. Press, 1964), pp. 7-9.

contemporary European economists call the "English disease," is no longer a monopoly of aristocrats, but is shared by the managerial classes and the labor unions as well—and seems to have its well-rooted counterpart even in the Union of Soviet Socialist Republics. But in the seventeenth century, as in the Middle Ages, only the gentry or those with pretensions to the gentry had sufficient leisure to entertain such attitudes. Others worked, willingly or grudgingly, and for their pains earned the contempt of all but reformist visionaries and a few charitable Christians.

SKELTON, MORE, AND LATIMER

At the beginnings of the humanist movement in the English court, John Skelton seems to have been more outraged by the appearance of upstart aristocrats in the Church than anything else:

> With pryde inordynate,
> Sodaynly upstarte
> From the donge carte,
> The mattocke and the shovll,
> To reygne and to rule.
> (*Collyn Clout*, 643-47)[46]

But if the note of reform in *Collyn Clout* (c. 1523) seems at times to be mixed with personal envy and not a little aristocratic pride on the part of the poet as well as his victims, still the familiar refrain may be heard:

> A preest without a letter,
> Without his vertue be greatter,
> Doutlesse were moche better
> Uppon hym for to take

---

[46] *Poems*, ed. Robert S. Kinsman (Oxford: Clarendon Press, 1969), p. 114; see also *Agaynst a Comely Coystrowne*, poem 4 (pp. 5-6): "For Jak wol be a Jentylman, that late was a grome" (l. 42).

A mattocke or a rake.
. . . .
Theyr styrops of myxt golde begared,
There may no cost be spared;
Theyr moyles [mules] golde dothe eate,
Theyr neyghbours dye for meate.
(270-74, 317-20)

When Skelton gets well started, he is a difficult poet to stop. Although he hits out at Lutherans and Wycliffites (540-56) and at Cardinal Woolsey's dispossession of convents (387-401), and he has some of the pride of a humanist priest in an age of widespread clerical illiteracy (270), still he has heard and gives voice to the complaints of the common people.

In reaction to modern historians' habitual neglect of the Medieval work ethic and the remarkable technology it brought into use, some recent historians of science have blamed the decay of that technology in the late Middle Ages and early Renaissance on the humanist revival of the Classics.

> [M]anual labor was extolled for seven hundred years by monks, especially the Benedictines, as being not merely expedient but spiritually valuable as well. With the late medieval revival of Greek and Roman attitudes, however, the classical contempt for manual labor reasserted itself.[47]

This judgment, one might suppose, holds true for many humanists, yet it oversimplifies the matter to blame the decay of technology on humanism alone. Another factor is surely the perpetual tendency of all human accomplishments, however energetically they come into being, to decay. Thus, as we have seen, the water mill, which began as a welcome conserver of human sweat and probably played a large part in the disappearance of slavery from Europe, might, if wrongly used, become an instrument for economic repression. Many monasteries, before they were dissolved—good and bad alike—had become net drains on the economic well-being of the people,

[47] White, *Machina Ex Deo*, p. 104.

to whose welfare they once contributed so much. An abusive transformation of the spirit governing the use of monastic technology, and therefore of how the laity viewed that technology, is revealed (among the usual accusations of spendthrift ways and of "wanton lasses" brought into the enclosures) by Collyn Clout's unexpected charge that this ancient technological component of the monastic way was somehow a wicked innovation:

> How ye breke the dedes wylles,
> Turne monasteries into water mylles,
> Of an abbey ye make a graunge—
> Your workes, they say, are straunge—
> So that theyr founders soules
> Have lost theyr bedde-roules.
>
> (417-22)

No one had turned the monasteries into water mills and granges; that is one of the things they had been for many centuries. But such, evidently, was the common perception. So in *Rede me and be nott wrothe* (Strasbourg, 1528), the Reformers William Roy and Jerome Barlow have a fictional monk complain not only that his order's brothels are closed and their bastards dispersed, but that "Oure wynning mill hath lost her gryndinge / Which we supposed never to decaye" (45-46). The same charge that Marvell was to voice, and that was to become a Protestant commonplace—that the monks violated the founders' wills (in both senses of that word) and too often turned from prayer to profit—is exemplified by Skelton's water mill. The image suggests that Abbot Richard's method of running a mill had become standard, and that physical plants which had been built to support the spiritual life and to feed and clothe the poor had become ends in themselves. The centuries of progress had drawn to a close during the years of plague and famine, and institutions that once had pioneered now merely conserved.

If some humanists disdained the work of hands, it was probably because they already had well-developed aristocratic tastes that needed little reinforcement from the works of Greek or Roman aristocrats. Those so inclined, although they responded sympathetically to the pastoral and the military epic, were perfectly capable (as we have seen in one instance) of reading Cato, Varro, or Virgil's *Georgics* with an eye to the didactic details while still remaining untouched by the underlying spirit of labor. To the contrary, Thomas More, in the most notable work of English humanism, comes down squarely and forcefully on the georgic side of the debate. However one interprets his *Utopia*, and many critics have found it to be a puzzle, More is unambiguous on this point at least, since he enforces it with respect to both England and Utopia. In Utopia, the fifty-four cities are laid out so that none is within twenty-four miles of its neighbors, yet travelers can walk from one to another in a day. The chief reason for this scheme is to allow each city a sufficiency of agricultural land. "Everywhere in the rural districts they have, at suitable distances from one another, farmhouses well equipped with agricultural implements. They are inhabited by citizens who come in succession to live there."[48] In the cities, behind the blocks of houses, lie "broad" communal gardens, where the citizens vie with one another to raise the best "vines, fruits, herbs, flowers" (p. 65).

As in England, the chief occupation in Utopia is agriculture; but unlike the English all the citizens of Utopia take part in the work freely, as a condition of citizenship:

> Agriculture is the one pursuit which is common to all, both men and women, without exception. They are all instructed in it from childhood, partly by principles taught in school, partly by field trips to the farms. (p. 68)

In addition to agriculture, the citizens practice various manual crafts:

> Besides agriculture (which is, as I said, common to all), each is taught one particular craft as his own. This is generally either wool-working or linen-making or ma-

[48] St. Thomas More, *Utopia*, ed. Edward J. Surtz (New Haven: Yale Univ. Press, 1964), p. 61.

sonry or metal-working or carpentry. There is no other pursuit which occupies any number worth mentioning. (pp. 68-69)

Since labor is not an end in itself, however, no one works harder than he or she must. As a result of the efficient, equitable, and universal distribution of manual labor, no one is "wearied like a beast of burden with constant toil from early morning till late at night." The working day is six hours (pp. 69-70). Work clothes, which are sturdy and simple, are designed to last for seven years. Buildings, too, are built of stone and designed to "last very long" (p. 74). No one is kept against his will at "superfluous labor," since the end of labor is to allow the citizens leisure to withdraw "from the service of the body" and to devote themselves "to the freedom and culture of the mind. It is in the latter that they deem the happiness of life to consist" (p. 75).

Utopians compensate for population growth by planting colonies and improving the soil. They prefer to make common cause with the natives, by introducing new agricultural "procedures" that "make the land sufficient for both, which previously seemed poor and barren." Therefore it is "a most just cause for war" if a people does not "use its soil but keeps it idle and waste" yet forbids its use to others "who by the rule of nature ought to be maintained by it" (p. 76). Since the Utopians have no standing army or military class, they prefer bribes to the use of force (p. 84). Like many humanists of More's time, they regard war "with utter loathing," as an activity "fit only for beasts and yet practiced by no kind of beast." Nevertheless, "men and women alike," they prepare themselves to fight with constant exercises (p. 118). Thus, while Hythloday says little about the Utopians' literary taste, clearly they would have small sympathy for either pastoral or epic. For them, war is not a glorious occupation but an unpleasant necessity, to which they resort only "to protect their own territory or to drive an invading enemy out of their friends' lands or . . . to deliver them by force of arms from the yoke and slavery of the tyrant" but (unlike Henry, Charles, or Francis) not to gain glory or renown (p. 118).

The social injustices of England, Hythloday remarks, which commonly drive men to vagabondage, theft, and then to the gallows, are due almost entirely to mistaken agricultural policies. Enclosure is one problem. According to common report, the sheep are "so greedy and wild that they devour human beings themselves and devastate and depopulate fields, houses, and towns." But, of course, those truly responsible for these evils are the leaders of "idle and sumptuous" lives, namely "noblemen, gentlemen, and even some abbots."

> They leave no ground to be tilled; they enclose every bit
> of land for pasture; they pull down houses and destroy
> towns, leaving only the church to pen the sheep in. And,
> as if enough English land were not wasted on ranges and
> preserves of game, those good fellows turn all human
> habitations and all cultivated land into a wilderness. (pp.
> 24-25)

If the georgic spirit leads men to turn wilderness into fields and thus to build up their nation and civilization, the act of transforming cultivated land into wilderness is quintessentially anti-georgic and anti-civilized. More's protests against enclosure are familiar, yet they bear repetition in order to emphasize how he attributes enclosure to the usual aristocratic failings: idleness, greed, pride, contempt for the worker.

Indeed, More pursues that point relentlessly through Hythloday, mounting a general attack on the whole aristocratic way of life and on war, its chief raison d'être:

> Now there is a great number of noblemen who not only
> live idle themselves like drones on the labors of others,
> as for instance the tenants of their estates whom they
> fleece to the utmost by increasing the returns (for that is
> the only economy they know ...) but who also carry
> about with them a huge crowd of idle attendents who
> have never learned a trade for a livelihood. As soon as

193

their master dies or they themselves fall sick, these men are turned out at once, for the idle are maintained more readily than the sick. (pp. 21-22)

Aristocrats and their aristocratic servants are good for little else than fighting and thieving:

[A] man who has been softly brought up in idleness and luxury and has been wont in sword and buckler to look down with a swaggering face on the whole neighborhood and to think himself far above everybody will hardly be fit to render honest service to a poor man with spade and hoe, for a scanty wage, and on frugal fare.

"But this," Hythloday's tablemate urges, "is just the sort of man we ought to encourage most," because, being of "loftier and nobler spirit than craftsmen and farmers," such men make the best soldiers. "Of course," replies Hythloday, "you might as well say that for the sake of war we must foster thieves." Indeed, he argues, princes often wage war only to keep such men occupied, and therefore "men's throats must be cut without cause lest, to use Sallust's witty saying, 'the hand or the mind through lack of practice become dulled' " (pp. 22-23).

In More's *Utopia* we see the humanist grounds for a debate between what are usually thought to be middle-class and upper-class values, between work and war, building and conquering, georgic and epic, a debate that was to find its fullest literary statement in the works of Milton. Though the instincts of some humanists were conservative, others, such as Erasmus and More, combined their humanism with a powerful drive toward Christian reform. Underlying More's vision of Utopia, perhaps even more basic than his emphasis on communal ownership of goods, is the economic and moral principle that no man or woman should earn his bread in the sweat of another's face. For that is the problem in England; too many are idle and wasteful, while others work like slaves from morning until night; too many live "like drones on the labors of others," while they swagger about the neighborhood thinking themselves "far above" those who support them. The flowers of civilization—peace, material well-being, health, happiness, and leisure for mental activities—must grow not from the labors of the few but the equal and cooperative labors of all. If Hythloday and "More" can be said to disagree about these issues, their disagreement is not whether such a reform of abuses is desirable, but whether and in what manner such a reform might be achieved. Hytholoday, like Langland's Conscience, wants all or nothing; "More" is willing to compromise himself by working with princes in order to see at least some progress in the direction of his ideals.

The sixteenth century saw a decisive shift in the ancient struggle within a Christian society between conservatism and reform. This time reform did not simply purify but overturned whole institutions. In England, the Reformation put an end not just to monastic abuses but to monasteries. At the same time, the tenuous balance between Church and State, embodied in the long contest between emperors and popes and between such leaders as Henry II and Thomas à Becket, was also decisively altered. Secular power gained a permanent ascendancy, both theoretical and actual, over religious power. Thus Phineas Fletcher speaks for the dominant English tradition when he deplores the triumph of Alexander III (pope from 1159 to 1181) over Frederick Barbarossa, calling him "that monstrous Prelate, who / Trampled great Fredericks necke with his proud durty shooe." Equally infamous was the victory of "famous Hildebrand" (Gregory VII, 1072-85), "Who forc't brave Henry with bare feet to stand, / And beg for entrance."[49] These events, though acted out long before between princes and prelates who were equally Roman Catholics, were still significant because of their bearing on the doctrine of Royal Supremacy. Of course, not all English Protestants supported the Establishment's Erastian views, yet the dissenting enemies of the royal supremacy, in spite of military

---

[49] *The Locusts, or Apollyonists* (3.34-35), in *The English Spenserians*, ed. William B. Hunter, Jr. (Salt Lake City: Univ. of Utah Press, 1977), p. 355.

successes, were unable to enforce an alternative. Eventually the balance was righted not by restoring the power of religion but by diminishing that of the monarchy.

One unforeseen result of the Reformation was therefore the enhancement of secular power and secular ideals. Those institutions which, by means of earlier reforms, had recurrently embodied the ideals of humility through manual labor were abolished. As a result, one hears almost nothing about the value of manual labor as an ideal in the early stages of the Reformation in England, apart from aristocratic calls on the peasants to do their duty. As we have seen, only in the 1590s does a reformist ideal of labor begin to re-emerge, and, although such men as Spenser and Bacon certainly were moved in varying degrees by religious idealism, nevertheless the models they proposed for the cooperative sharing of labor were secular, not religious. Spenser hoped for a band of chivalrous knights, who would not be afraid to sweat or to dirty their hands in the service of their country and religion. Bacon hoped for a brotherhood of scientific technologists, who would leave matters of theology and ethics to others while they concentrated on enhancing the material knowledge and well-being of the people. Bacon's vision, the more purely secular of the two, proved more successful. Yet both these writers drew on the long tradition of Christian reform for their ideas and energies. Indeed, it might be said that, just as many of the colleges at Oxford and Cambridge had once been religious foundations that were secularized, so the ultimate models for Salomon's House in the *New Atlantis* were Monte Cassino, Clairvaux, Canterbury, and Fountains—also secularized.

One prelate of the Reformed Church who preached the value of work was Hugh Latimer, but he seems to have been something of a special case. Although he was one of those who helped bring the Reformation into England, he was born on a farm and educated in the last days of Medieval Catholicism. In his first sermon to King Edward VI (March 8, 1549), he spoke out against the "exorcioners, violent oppressers, ingrossers of tenamentes and landes, thoroughe whose covetousnes, villages decaye and fall downe." "For wher as have bene a great meany of householders and inhabitaunce, ther is nowe but a shepherd and his dogge."[50] Latimer was especially conscious of the oppression of the rural poor because, as he tells the young King, he is a countryman himself:

My father was a yeoman, and had no landes of his owne, onlye he had a farme of iii or iiii pound by yere at the utter most, and here upon, he tilled so much as kepte halfe a dosen men. He had walke for a hundred shepe, and my mother mylked xxx kyne.

But those were the days before the recent increases in rents, when the land still supported its occupants in prosperity:

He kept hospitaliti for his pore neighbours. And sum almesse he gave to the poore, and all thys did he of the sayd farme. Wher he that now hath it, paieth xvi pounde by yere or more, and is not able to do any thing for his Prynce, for himselfe, nor for his children, or geve a cup of drincke to the pore. ([Dv-vi])

No wonder if Latimer spoke out on a subject about which many of his colleagues kept silence.

In his famous "Sermon of the Plough," preached to the citizens of London outside St. Paul's (January 18, 1548), Latimer cites two texts in support of what he recognizes to be an unusual metaphor. One is, "He that soweth, the husbanman, the plowghman wente furth to sowe his seede" (apparently an adaptation of Matt. 13:3), and the other is the text cited earlier in connection with St. Bernard: "No man that putteth his hand to the plough and loketh backe, is apte for the kingdom of god."[51] Significantly, Latimer tells his auditors

[50] *The fyrste Sermon of Mayster Hughe Latimer, whiche he preached before the Kynges Majest. wythin his graces palayce at Westmynster MDXLIX the viii of Marche* (1549), Ciii^v, Diiii.

[51] *A notable Sermon of the reverende father Maister Hughe Latemer, whiche he preached in the Shrouds at paules churche in London, on the xviii. daye of January* (1548), Aii^v. This and the foregoing sermon both are repro-

that he learned the latter text from the monks, who were accustomed to "rack" it against those who left the monasteries, precisely the context in which St. Bernard had once applied it. But in Bernard's day the text applied literally as well as figuratively; now no longer. Now, Latimer says, he has learned the true application: to "diligente preachyng of the worde of God" (Aiii).

Latimer recognizes that the metaphor may upset his audience:

> For preachyng of the Gospel is one of Goddes plough workes, and the preacher is one of Goddes plough men. Ye may not be offended wyth my similitude: in that I compare preachynge to the laboure and worke of ploughinge, and the preacher to a ploughman. Ye maye not be offended wyth thys my similitude, for I have ben sclaundred of some personnes for suche thynges. It hath bene saied of me. Oh Latimer, nay, as for him I wil never beleve hym whyle I lyve, nor never trust him, for he lykened our blessed Ladye to a saffrone bagge. . . .
>
> For as the ploughman first setteth furth his plough, and then tilleth hys lande, and breaketh it in furroughes, and sometyme ridgeth it up agayne. And at an other tyme harroweth it, and clotteth it, and sometyme doungeth it, and hedgeth it, diggeth it, and weedeth it, pourgeth and maketh it cleane: So the prelate, the preacher hath many divers offices to do. (Aiii, [v])

The more Latimer senses that part of his audience may resist his metaphor, the more he relishes its details. For their resistance helps him to make his point.

At the center of the sermon Latimer evokes the very conflict we have seen so many times, between the workers and the gentry:

> Oh London London, repente repente, for I thynke God is more dyspleased with London, then ever he was with

---

duced (with minor substantive errors) in Hugh Latimer, *Sermons*, Everyman Edition (London: J. M. Dent, 1906).

the citie of Nebo. . . . And ye that be prelates loke well to your offyce, for right prelatynge is buisye labouryng and not lordyng. Therefore preache and teache, and let your ploughe be doyng. . . . [L]et your ploughe therfore be going and not cease, that the ground maye brynge foorth fruite. But nowe me thynketh I heare one saye unto me, wotte you what you say? It is a worke? It is a labour? how then hath it happened, that we have had so manye hundred yeres, so many unpreachynge prelates, lordyng loyterers and idle ministers? . . . But this muche I dare saye, that sence lordyng and loiteryng hath come up, preaching hathe come downe. . . . For ever sence the Prelates were made Lordes and nobles, the ploughe stand-eth, there is no work done, the people sterve. Thei hauke, they hunt, thei card, they dyce, they pastyme in their prelacies with gallaunte gentlemen, with theyr daunsyng minyons, and with their freshe companions, so that ploughyng is sette a syde. And by the lordyng and loy-trynge, preachyng and ploughyng is cleane gone. (Bii^v-iiii)

Latimer's emphasis on preaching is Protestant; otherwise his argument sounds like nothing so much as a Medieval sermon. His audience may, if they like, think he is speaking about the past, about those "many hundred years" when the Church was Catholic; still he makes notable use of the present tense. It is no wonder if his fellow Protestant ministers were often uncomfortable with him, until martyrdom had made him safe for the cause.

Literary and religious metaphors require some link with the world of daily activity if they are to retain their full force. The Bible's georgic metaphors grew out of farming practice, and so were understood. As English agriculture lost esteem, and came to be practiced only for the profits it brought to the landowners, it was natural that georgic metaphors in poetry or sermons should also lose their effect. Latimer was unusual for his time because his georgic images were rooted in his experience and observation:

And as dilygentlye as the husbande man plougheth for the sustentacion of the bodie: so dilygentlye muste the prelates and ministers labour for the feedynge of the soule: bothe the ploughes muste styll be doynge, as moost necessarye for man.

Both plows were not doing, however:

But nowe for defaulte of unpreachynge Prelates me thynke I coulde gesse what myghte be sayed for excusyng of theym. They are soo troubeled wyth lordlye livinge, they be so placed in palacies, couched in courtes, ruffelyng in their rentes, dauncyng in their dominions, burdened with ambassages, pamperyng of their paunches leke a Monke that maketh his Jubilie, mounchynge in their maungers, and moilyng in their gay manoures and man-syons, and so troubeled wyth loyterynge in theyr Lorde-shyppes: that they canne not attende it. ([Bvi^v-vii])

As the century progressed, however, loitering in lordships, as Latimer so well puts it, rose to the state of an art; and that art was enshrined in pastoral poetry. Bernard, against considerable opposition from the establishment of his time, founded (in effect) a new order. Thomas More, defender of the old faith, and Hugh Latimer, proponent of the new, both were executed. Tit for tat, a modern reader may say: what led to both tragedies was religious fanaticism. Yet many Catholics and Protestants survived those troubling times. What More and Latimer had in common was a habit of affronting royal power by daring to give, or to represent in their persons, uncomfortable advice. Thus the reforming spirit twice encountered a newly untrammeled secular pride, and was twice broken.

WITHER AND WINSTANLEY

The attitude of the Establishment, of the newly intertwined Church and State, toward manual labor at the beginning of the seventeenth century is probably represented at its most typical by Donne, and at its most charitable by Herbert. It was necessary that laborers should labor, so they could keep themselves from idleness and pay their tithes and rents, but there was no real virtue in the labor. The gentleman might well look down on rural farmers and workmen as his inferiors, worthy of his contempt and ridicule but perhaps best simply ignored. The pastor might recognize even the poorest laborer as his brother in Christ, yet it was his duty to teach that laborer proper Christian contempt for all the works of this sinful world. Man is condemned by God's curse to labor and to sweat, and because of his universal and absolute sinfulness his labors can achieve no spiritual value. (Yet even Herbert is quick to argue the virtue of tithes. Evidently what has no spiritual value must be pursued, *faute de mieux*, for its material value.) In effect, the aristocratic valuation of manual work, which had always been present in Western society in one form or another since at least Classical times, achieved a theoretical as well as a practical dominance in England during the first stages of the Renaissance and Reformation. Having acceded to the abolition of the monasteries and accepted a theology that allowed no merit in works, whether of the mind or the hands, the Church no longer was in a position to offer a working alternative. Thus, whereas reform of these aristocratic attitudes in most cases retained a strong Christian component, that reform often had to come from outside the dominant Christian consensus.

Those who would break the consensus, although history might judge them right in the end, were often eccentric, peculiar, and even somewhat mad. Such seems to have been the case with George Wither, on whose peculiarities many literary historians have remarked. Douglas Bush notes that although Wither was "a zealous champion of righteousness, liberty, and moderation," he supported those good ends "in his own egoistic and irritating way."[52] Joan Grundy, referring especially to the poetry written after 1641, calls Wither a "religious

---

[52] *English Literature in the Earlier Seventeenth Century, 1600-1660*, 2d edn. (Oxford: Clarendon Press, 1962), p. 82.

maniac."[53] Yet perhaps something of the maniacal was necessary for someone who went against the stream as often as Wither did and who lacked the extraordinary combination of genius and sanity that enabled Spenser and Milton to advocate innovation as if it were the most natural thing in the world.

We noted earlier Wither's effort, in 1613, to make his peace with the establishment by assuming a pastoral guise. But he seems to have been unable to hold his muse to the security afforded by that convention for long. Even while he was languishing in prison, he severely bent the pastoral mode in his lively and eccentric work, *The Shepheards Hunting*. Under the name of Philarete (i.e. lover of excellence) he participates in a shepherdly colloquy to the music not of birds or lambs, but of "ratling Shackles, Gyves, and Boults, and Chaines" (3.233).[54] His stoic protestations grow tedious, yet there is nothing tedious about his inventive description of how he assembled a pack of beagles—that is, satirical poems—in order to hunt down the wolves and evil creatures who were threatening to prey on his flock:

> My eager Dogges and I to Wood are gon.
> Where, beating through the *Coverts*, every Hound
> A severall *Game* had in a moment found:
> I rated them, but they pursu'd their pray,
> And as it fell (by hap) tooke all one way.
> Then I began with quicker speed to follow,
> And teaz'd them on, with a more chearefull hallow:
> That soone we passed many weary miles,
> Tracing the subtile game through all their wiles. . . .
> Nor crost we onely Ditches, Hedges, Furrowes,
> But Hamlets, Tithings, Parishes, and Burrowes:
> They followed where so ev'r the game did go,
> Through Kitchin, Parlor, Hall, and Chamber to.
> And, as they past the *City*, and the *Court*,
> My *Prince* look'd out, and daign'd to view my sport.
> (3.37-57)

---

[53] *The Spenserian Poets* (London: Edward Arnold, 1969), p. 161.
[54] Hunter, *The English Spenserians*.

The violations of decorum, which begin when the shepherd's watchdogs are inexplicably transformed into a pack of hunting beagles, and which grow as the pack leads its master through kitchens and chambers in pursuit of its prey, are symptoms of a mind forced only half-unwillingly into rebellion by political constraints that would imprison the poet not only in the Marshalsea but in the pastoral mode as well. As the prince looks out of his palace window at this strange sight, this rural invasion of city and court, he might be wise to view it more as a portent than a compliment.

In 1635, Wither published *A Collection of Emblems*. On the surface, nothing could have been more derivative and conventional. Still, in at least one respect Wither's collection is highly original. No other English emblematist had treated the theme of labor as Wither treats it. Although Geffrey Whitney (1586) had used a number of potentially georgic plates,[55] and took for his motto "Victoria ex labore, honesta, et utilis," "Victory, achieved by Labour, honourable and useful," only one of his emblems may be said to be georgic in spirit. The plate illustrating "In utrumque paratus" (p. 66) shows two hands emerging from a cloud, one holding a sword and the other a mason's trowel, and the accompanying poem urges the reader to be prepared to undertake either epic or georgic activities:

> That to defende, our countrie deare from harme,
> For warre, or worke, wee eyther hande should arme.

Other poems, however, either ignore the potentially georgic content of their plates, or else turn them to the most courtly use:

> Let maidens sowe; let schollers: plie the schooles.
> Give PALINURE: his compasse, and his carde.
> Let MARS, have armes: let VULCANE, use his tooles.
> Give CORYDON, the ploughe, and harrowe harde.

---

[55] *A Choice of Emblemes, and Other Devises* (Leyden: Christopher Plantyn, 1586), facs. ed. Henry Green (London, 1866; New York: Benjamin Blom, 1967), pp. 23, 64, 66, 88, 138.

Give PAN, the pipe: give bilbowe blade, to swashe.
Let Grimme have coales: and lobbe his whippe to lashe.

(p. 145)

These gentlemanly sentiments, as a marginal note indicates, are owed to Horace (*Ep.* 2.1. 114-17). Another poem, beneath a plate that shows a man chopping at a tree with an ax, reveals the theology that prevents labor from having any value in itself:

Here, man with axe doth cut the boughe in twaine,
And without him, the axe, coulde nothing doe[.]
Within the toole, there doth no force remaine;
But man it is, that mighte doth put thereto.
    Like to this axe, is man, in all his deeds;
      Who hath no strength, but what from GOD proceeds.

(p. 228)

Similarly, Henry Peacham (1612) uses several georgic wood-cuts, but in each case his poem quickly moves on from a georgic beginning to pursue other interests.[56]

George Wither proceeds quite otherwise. As many as fourteen of his emblems have to do with labor, and his poems fully reinforce the georgic implications of his plates. Thus in one plate a snake twists about an upright spade and crowns it with a laurel wreath, against a background that shows the labors of learning and of plowing.

True *Glory*, none did ever purchase, yet,
Till, to be *Vertuous* they could first attaine,
Nor shall those men faire *Vertues* favour get,
Who *labour* not, such *Dignities* to gaine.
And, this *Impresa* doth inferre no lesse:
For, by the *Spade*, is *Labour* here implide . . .
    For, where a vertuous *Industry* is found,
      She, shall with Wreaths of *Glory*, thus be crown'd.

(p. 5)[57]

---

[56] *Minnerva Britanna* (facs. Leeds: Scolar Press, 1966), pp. 61, 117, 157, 179, 192.

[57] *A Collection of Emblems* (1635; facs. Columbia: Univ. of South Carolina

Another plate shows the sun shining on two shocks of grain while the harvesters work in the background. The gist of the poem is to urge perseverance:

> And, from this *Emblem*, let each *Lab'ring-Swaine*
> (In whatsoever course of life it be)
> Take heart, and hope, amidst his daily paine,
> That, of his *Travailes*, he good fruits shall see.
>
> (p. 44)

A third plate shows an upright spade above a globe of the world, circled by a laurel wreath and the serpent of eternity (see fig. 2). The poem argues that true glory is gained not by aristocratic parentage, but by laborious deeds:

> True *Glory*, doth on *Labour*, still attend;
> But, without *Labour, Glory* we have none.
> *She*, crownes good *Workmen*, when their Works have end;
> And, *Shame*, gives payment, where is nothing done.
>
> (p. 92)

It is clear that Wither (like Spenser) is simply reversing the usual priorities here; few other poets of his time can be found who do so as plainly as this. In the old dispute between the merit of blood and deeds, poets might argue that the two should have equal weight, but the sort of deeds they customarily praised had little to do with the spade. Thus a treatise on nobility published in 1595 argues that if true nobility can be earned by merit, it can also be squandered by ignoble behavior. "[W]hen as the noble born doth exercise some craft, or handiworke, that is vile and derogating from nobilitie. . . . [M]anie descending of a high linage, giving themselves to some vile exercise, have darckned, and wholly lost their nobilitie. . . . You may see then, howe corporall and base exercise, doth bring contempt unto the nobility of bloud, and convert it into his contrarie."[58]

Press, 1975). In addition to poems discussed or mentioned in the text, see pp. 29, 48, 143, 148, 250.

[58] *Nennio, or A Treatise of Nobilitie* [by Giovanni Battista Nenna], trans.

In another of Wither's plates, Hope wields still another spade while in the background a husbandman sows a field (see fig. 3). In the poem Wither dissociates himself from those sects who act as if they "stood in feare / That, with *Good-works* their *God* offended were," as well as those who put all their trust in works without grace. Worst of all, however, are those who are strict Supralapsarians. "So *worke*," Wither concludes, "that thy *believing* may approve / Thou wrought'st not for thy *Wages*; but, for *love*" (p. 141). Probably Wither's position may best be characterized as a moderate left-wing Arminianism—a position he shares with Milton.[59] Another poem (see fig. 4) shows the same balance between works and grace, as Wither varies his metaphor and makes God, not the individual, the active husbandman:

> Before the *Plowman* hopefull can be made,
> His untill'd earth good Hay or Corne will yeeld,
> He breakes the hillocks downe, with *Plough* or *Spade*;
> And, harrowes over, all the cloddie Field. . . .
>   Our *craggie Nature* must be tilled, thus,
> Before it will, for *Herbes of Grace*, be fit. . . .
>   Oh *Lord*, thou know'st the nature of my *minde*;
> Thou know'st my *bodyes* tempers what they are;
> And, by what meanes, they shall be best inclin'de
> Such *Fruits* to yeeld, as they were made to beare.
> My barren *Soule*, therefore, *manure* thou so;

[Sir] William Jones (1595), fol. 77. Ironically, prefatory poems by Spenser, Daniel, and Chapman praise the translator (then a gentleman and subsequently a knight) for his meritorious labors.

[59] See Maurice Kelly, ed., [*Christian Doctrine,*] *Complete Prose Works of John Milton*, 8 vols. (New Haven: Yale Univ. Press, 1953-82), 6:74-86; Dennis Richard Danielson, *Milton's Good God* (Cambridge: Cambridge Univ. Press, 1982); and on the distinction, sometimes blurred by Calvinist attacks, between Arminianism and Erastianism, see William M. Lamont, *Godly Rule: Politics and Religion 1603-40* (London: Macmillan, 1969). Briefly, Arminians differed from Calvinists and many moderate Anglicans of the period on the five points condemned by the Synod of Dort, which included universality of grace, resistibility of grace, and therefore freedom of will (enabled by grace).

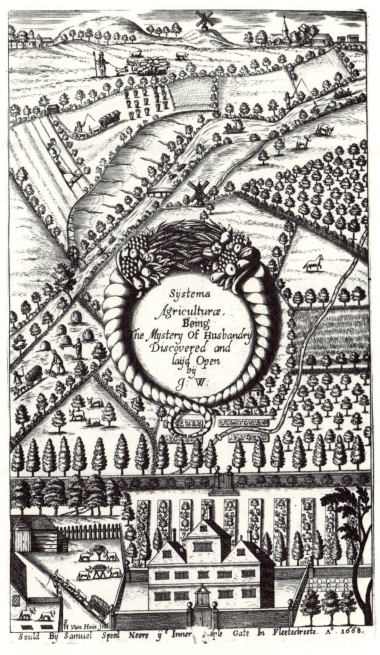

Sijstema
Agriculturæ.
Being
The Mystery Of Husbandry
Discovered and
laijd Open
bij
J: W:

H. Van Hove Jnu

Sould By Samuel Speed Neere ye Inner Temple Gate In Fleetestreete. Aº. 1668.

1. Frontispiece: John Worlidge, *Systema Agriculturæ* (1669).

Where, Labour, wisely, is imploy'd,
Deserved Glory, is injoy'd.

ILLVSTR. XXX.

Book. 2

If thou thy Duties truely doe,
Of thy Reward, behopefull too.

ILLVSTR. VII.

Book. 3

2. (left) p. 92; 3. (right) p. 141: George Wither, A Collection of Emblems (1635).

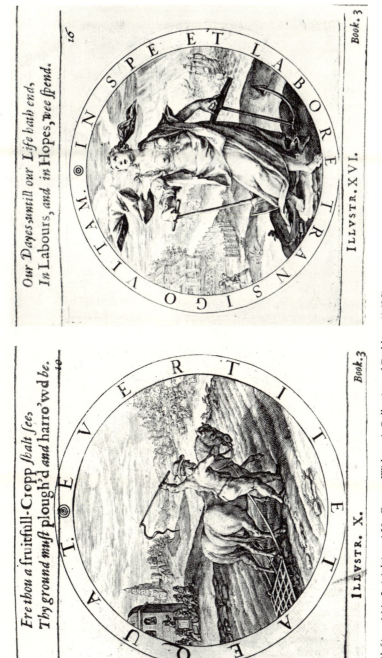

Ere thou a fruitfull-Cropp shalt see,
Thy ground must plough'd and harro'wd be.

Our Dayes, untill our Life hath end,
In Labours, and in Hopes, wee spend.

ILLVSTR. X.

ILLVSTR. XVI.

Book. 3

Book. 3

4. (*left*) p. 144; 5. (*right*) p. 150: George Wither, *A Collection of Emblems* (1635).

A DIALOGVE

BETWIXT
A HORSE of WARRE,
and a MILL-HORSE;

Wherein the content and safety of an humble and painfull life,
is preferred above all the *Noyse*, the *Tumults*,
and *Trophies* of the *Warre*.

Full of harmelesse Mirth, and variety.

LONDON,
Printed by *Bernard Alsop*, And published according to Order, 1645.

6. Title page: *A Dialogue Betwixt a Horse of Warre, and a Mill-horse* (1644).

210

So, *harrow* it; so *emptie*, and so *fill*;
So *raise* it *up*, and bring it *downe*, so *low*
As best may lay it *levell* to thy *Will*.
                                        (p. 144)

Space does not allow discussion of a number of other relevant poems, such as the one that describes the cooperative efforts of Hope and the husbandman (p. 106) or the one that recommends the ox as the emblem of what slow but persevering toil can accomplish (p. 173). We may fittingly conclude the discussion by citing an emblem of particular importance, which shows the figure of Hope holding a spade in one hand and an anchor in the other (see fig. 5). In the background on one side a man digs his field; on the other a ship sails out to sea. Wither's poem approaches its theme by way of the same topic with which we began this chapter, Adam's fall and punishment, and, on account of his peculiar interests and (for his time) unusual theological beliefs, he treats it as few of his countrymen were prepared to do:

As soone as our *first Parents* disobey'd,
Forthwith a *Curse*, for their offence, was layd,
Inforcing them, and their succeeding race,
To get their Food, with sweatings of the Face.

But afterward, "this *Doome* to mitigate," "*God* gave them Hope."

By *Sinne*, the *Labour* is on us intail'd;
By *Grace*, it is, that *Hoping* hath not fail'd;
And, if in *Hope*, our Labours wee attend,
That *Curse* will prove a *Blessing*, in the end.
                                        (p. 150)

Although Wither has more than once been accused of a tedious moral didacticism, he is often far more original than he may seem to a modern reader—in part because his heresies have become our outworn commonplaces. It was not easy for an Englishman of 1635 to revive this Virgilian and Medieval attitude toward the curse of labor. Perhaps by a happy coincidence (since one never knows precisely how a plate and a poem may have come together) the engraving too is Virgilian in spirit, showing the laborer with his spade on one side, for *labor*, and on the other side a ship setting forth in the spirit of hope and exploration, for *techne*.

In 1641, Wither published *Haleluiah, Or, Britans Second Remembrancer*.[60] This collection of hymns for various occasions includes several on the theme of labor, and several intended specifically for the use of laborers. Unlike Donne or Herbert, Wither was capable of feeling real empathy for the laborer, of putting himself in the laborer's place, and the moral advice implicit in these hymns is no different from what he would have applied to himself. The hymns are intended to be sung to various popular psalm and hymn tunes, and are competent in that kind. "Hymn VIII" of Part I, "Before we begin our Work," begins in a spirit that typifies a series of three hymns for working:

> Since thou hast LORD, appointed so,
> That Man by labour must be fed;
> Loe, with a chearefull mind I go
> To labour for my daily-bread.
>
> (p. 13)

In "Hymn IX," Wither recognizes the hardships suffered by the laborer but argues that if he accepts them patiently he will be happier than the rich idler. Again he offers a positive interpretation of Genesis 3:19:

> Or, wherefore, by a murm'ring Tongue,
> Should I augment my Care,
> Because I am not rang'd among
> Those *Drones* that Idlers are?

[60] Text as rpt. by Spenser Society, no. 26 (1879; New York: Burt Franklin, 1967). In addition to the hymns discussed, see "After our Worke is done" (pp. 39-40), "A Hymn at Seed-time" (pp. 64-66), "For a Sheep-shearing" (pp. 68-70), "For a Labourer" (pp. 434-36), "For a Shepherd" (pp. 436-38), "For a Handicraftsman" (pp. 438-40); all page numbers refer to the replicated text.

For, *Labour* yeelds me true content,
    (Though few the same doe see)
And, when my toyling houres are spent,
    My Sleeps the sweeter be.

Though *Labour* was enjoin'd at first,
    To be a Curse for Sin,
Yet Man, by being so accurst,
    May skrew a *Blessing* in.
And, He that with a patient minde,
    This pennance doth sustaine,
Shall by his paines true pleasures finde,
    And many comforts gaine.
           (p. 14)

This hymn is to be sung "*as the* 14. *or* 15. *Psalmes.*" Although Wither urges the laborer to accept his lot patiently, the homely violence with which he also urges him to "skrew" the curse of labor into a blessing probably arises from the knowledge that such advice would be thought heterodox.

"Hymn XLI. When *Harvest* is come home" pictures the happy moment when the year's toil reaches its fruition:

The *Fruits*, for which we delv'd and plough'd,
    And, toyled long, with care;
In Barnes and Stacks, are hous'd and mow'd;
    Of which right glad we are.
When Winds, and Frosts, and Rains, and Snows,
    Make barren Grove and Field;
When naught on hill, or valley grows,
    Which, food for man, doth yeeld:
We, to relieve our wants, have hope,
    By thy free Bounty, Lord.
           (p. 67)

In the preface to another hymn, "For a husbandman," Wither explains that "Upon the Husbandmans labour the temporall wellfare of all Common-weales depends: this *Hymn* therefore, teacheth him to sanctifie his endeavours by prayer, and thanksgiving." The hymn begins with a prayer that the laborer's pains may avert the curse of Adam, and that, although (because of the curse) "*thornes* and *bryers*" are "*natives* of our fields," God may bless those fields and make them yield abundant fruits. Prayer and grace have their parts in lifting the curse, but so, obviously, does labor:

> Let not thy Love permit
> My cost, my time, or pain,
> In digging, and in dressing it,
> To be employ'd in vain.
> (p. 432)

Of course, Wither was not entirely alone in advocating the value of labor, but the ascendancy of Calvinist doctrine in the earlier seventeenth century made it rare for anyone to do much more than reiterate the customary injunctions against idleness. In this view, to work is better than to play, but neither activity has real merit.

Occasionally labor is treated positively in the genre of the resolve—by its nature an active form of devotion—although ordinarily the georgic note is strictly spiritual. Thus Bishop Hall writes: "I will be content to pant, and blow, and sweat, in climbing up to Heaven; as, contrarily, I will be warie of setting the first step downeward towards the pit" (*Meditations and Vowes*, 1.60 [1605]).[61] And the obscure young minister Arthur Warwick, who is known only by his single publication, *Spare-Minutes; or, Resolved Meditations and Premeditated Resolutions* (1634), exhibits distinctly Arminian sentiments in his call to georgic renovation of the soul:

> When I plant a choyse flower in a fertile soyle, I see nature presently to thrust up with it the stinging nettle, the stinking hemlocke, the drowzie poppie, and many such noysome weedes. . . . But if I weed out these at first, my

[61] Quoted from John L. Lievsay, ed., *The Seventeenth-Century Resolve* (Lexington: Univ. Press of Kentucky, 1980), p. 14.

flower thrives to its goodnesse and glory. This is also my case when I endevour to plant grace in the fertill soyle of a good wit. For luxurious nature thrusts up with it either stinging wrath, or stinking wantonnesse, or drowzie sloath or some other vices, which robb my plant of its desired flourishing. But these being first pluckt up, the good wit produceth in its time the faire flower of vertue. (2.28; Lievsay, p. 137)

"[W]hen I endevour to plant grace" is a formulation that exhibits remarkable theological naiveté, yet it points toward the secularization of spiritual georgic, which was to result from the changing views brought in with the Age of Reason.[62]

With the outbreak of the Civil War, political and religious radicalism began to break down the barriers of more orthodox Reformed theology. Land was a constant matter of dispute, as perusal of the Army Debates and Leveller manifestoes reveals.[63] There was growing feeling that the parliamentary victory had made the plight of the rural laborer and small farmer worse rather than better, and there were growing complaints about the injustices of the "Norman Yoke" of land ownership and taxation. The best-known and most remarkable exponent of this radical georgic ferment was Gerrard Winstanley, chief spokesman for the Diggers. In an earlier century, Winstanley might have founded a monastery or a community of Beghards. Among orthodox Anglicans, Presbyterians, Congregationalists, and other relatively respectable sects, however, there was no provision for a religious reform of that kind. As a result,

---

[62] See, e.g., Caleb Trenchfield, *Occasional Observations* (1664), 31; in Lievsay, *The Resolve*, p. 185. Trenchfield, observing the need for "good husbandry" in keeping an orchard, argues that the same labors are needed to develop the character. Good thoughts must be "fenced with circumspection, stak't with resolution, digged about with religious exercise, wed with caution, and watered with prayer."

[63] See Don M. Wolfe, ed., *Leveller Manifestoes of the Puritan Revolution* (1944; New York: Humanities Press, 1967); A.S.P. Woodhouse, *Puritanism and Liberty* (Chicago: Univ. of Chicago Press, 1951).

Winstanley and his followers seem quickly to have isolated themselves by the extremity of their theological positions, and the fact that their movement was peaceful did not save it from savage attacks. The reforming of Reformation, as Milton called it, was not easily to be accomplished, because the dominant parties already considered themselves to have been reformed. Lacking acceptable provision within the Church to accommodate the reforming drive, and to distinguish legitimate from illegitimate modes of reform, the reformist urge was driven either to the extremes of religious sectarianism or else toward secularization.

Winstanley's earliest surviving tract, *The Mysterie of God* (1648), begins with what sounds like an Arminian manifesto, that Christ died for all mankind, that the curse against Adam was temporary, and that God will destroy death and deliver the world from bondage; but it soon goes beyond Arminianism to a Pelagian doctrine of the efficacy of works and to the universalist theory that at the end of the world all mankind will be saved. None of the ideas for which Winstanley was to be best known appear in this tract, but its theological optimism (using that word in its common, non-technical sense) might be said to prepare the way for what followed. In *Truth Lifting Up Its Head Above Scandals* (1648) Winstanley introduces a significant theory: that the fall of man physically corrupted the earth:

> [H]e then dyed and corrupted, and fell into all venimous and stinking unrighteousnesse: and as his body went to the earth, he did still poyson and corrupt the earth, and caused it to bring forth poysonous Vipers, Todes and Serpents, and Thornes and Bryars.
>
> For the curse being first falen upon mankinde, through man it fell upon the other creatures, and the Earth was cursed for his sake; and the poyson of mans unrighteous body, dunging the Earth, filled the grasse and herbs with strong unsavory spirits, that flowed from him, whereby

the cattell feeding, comes to be made bitter spirited, and mad one against another.[64]

Curiously, as religious fervor approaches its most fervent and radical extremes it often verges into secularism, as it does in Winstanley's case. He seems to be feeling, here, for a naturalistic or scientific explanation of Genesis 3:19; within a year he will be proposing an essentially political or ideological exegesis.

In the key tracts, beginning with *The New Law of Righteousness* (1649), Winstanley locates the curse of Adam in the system of land ownership, a connection to which he was presumably led not only because complaints about landlords and their abuses were in the air but because the Bible revealed that God directed the primal curse not directly at Adam but at the soil for his sake. (As Milton's Adam remarks, "On mee the Curse aslope / Glanc'd on the ground" [*Paradise Lost*, 10.1053-54].) The curse, Winstanley argues, was not on some Adam of the distant past, but on the Adam within us (p. 211), for "the first *Adam* yet sits in the Chair, and corrupts the Creation by his unrighteous wisdome and power" (p. 200). The essence of the problem is private ownership of land by rich oppressors, whose titles come to them from the Norman conquest, and the acquiescence of those who keep the mighty in power by selling their labor. The land belongs to all in common; no one has a right to more land than he can work; and no man has a right to rule over another. Whether Winstanley thinks that the communistic distribution of the land will result in a divine miracle of a restored, prelapsarian earth, or whether his thinking was more practical and scientifically oriented is not always clear, and his interpreters have differed on this point. Yet it is clear enough that what began with religious fervor, with visions and voices, was in the end remarkably close, as far as its georgic component is concerned,

---

[64] Quoted from *The Works of Gerrard Winstanley*, ed. George H. Sabine (Ithaca: Cornell Univ. Press, 1941), pp. 113-14.

to the arguments being put forward by Samuel Hartlib at about the same time. One man was a half-crazed visionary, the other a New Scientist, but both thought that poverty and hunger could be averted and a new Golden Age brought in if only people could start to farm the common land and to make proper use of it.[65]

There is also a noticeable similarity to the main argument of *Piers Plowman*. The problem is oppression and greed, and the solution (though now unbounded by orthodox restraints) is manual labor:

> O you great *Adams* of the earth, that cals the earth yours, and looks upon others as servants and slaves to you, as if the earth were made only for you to live at ease and honour upon it, while others starved for want of bread at your feet. . . . Behold the King the Lord of Hosts hath sent his servants, to bid you let Israel goe free, that they may serve him together, in community of spirit, and in community of the earthly treasure. . . .
>
> But be it so, that some wil say, This is my Land, and cal such and such a parcel of Land his own interest; Then saith the Lord, let such an one labour that parcel of Land by his own hands, none helping him: for whosoever shal help that man to labour his proper earth, as he cals it for wages, the hand of the Lord shal be upon such labourers; for they lift up flesh above the spirit, by their labours, and so hold the Creation stil under bondage.
>
> Therefore if the rich wil stil hold fast this propriety of *Mine and thine*, let them labour their own Land with their own hands. And let the common-People, that are the gatherings together of Israel from under that bondage, and that say the earth is ours, not mine, let them labour together, and eat bread together upon the Commons, Mountains, and Hils. (pp. 195-96)

[65] On this resemblance, see Sabine, *Works of Winstanley*, p. 14.

In this central statement of the Digger creed, one may see the influence not only of Genesis 3 but also of Exodus and of biblical georgic in general. The model for Winstanley's rural communism is the Israelite community with its inheritance of a Promised Land. The poor will leave the Egypt of economic oppression and settle on the common and undeveloped lands of England, their Israel. As in *Piers Plowman*, the punishment of the rich will be that they must then either work for themselves or starve.

Like Milton, Winstanley saw tithing as an important part of the problem. So long as the clergy lived by the sweat of others, the Church would be corrupted by the curse of Adam. John Platt, the rector of West Horsley, was a principle opponent of the Digger colony, and protests against the injustice of tithing survive in the Diggers' songs:

> They neither plow nor sow,
> Nor do they reap or mow,
> Nor any seed do finde,
> But Priests the people grinde:
> The tenth of all things they do crave;
> And thus each man is made a slave.
> (from *The Diggers Mirth*, 1650)

The essence of Christian justice was still that each man should earn his own bread in the sweat of his own face; that he should dig, plow, sow, and reap for himself, not for others; and that no man should be allowed to make his bread by grinding the poor.

Still, although the Digger movement revived traditional themes belonging to Christian reform, it also incorporated new elements as well. It represented a revolution too radical for its own time, although over time its influence has increased. Even the Levellers hurried to dissociate themselves from the movement. In the end, the scientific rather than the religious reformers carried the day. Both the modern agricultural revolution and the prevalence of the georgic genre in eighteenth-century poetry, which reflects that revolution, owe much more to Bacon, Hartlib, and Cowley than to Winstanley and the experiment on St. George's Hill. Yet we may doubt whether, lacking the underlying impulse toward religious reform evident in Hartlib and also in Bacon, the georgic revolution of the seventeenth century could ever have taken place. Since the Anglican Church and the dominant sects were hostile to the works of hands, and therefore to the georgic ideal, the Agricultural Revolution (unlike the Medieval technological revolution) was inevitably secularized. Still, it drew great energy from the Bible and from the reforming fervor with which Christian charity and humility have recurrently risen against that perennial enemy of georgic, aristocratic pride.

SIX

Georgic and the Civil War

GRADUALLY, over the course of the seventeenth century, the almost unthinking aristocratic scorn for farm and other manual labor, which most writers shared at first, was displaced by increasing interest in, and eventually enthusiasm for, agricultural reform and improvement of the land for the benefit of the nation. A number of minor poets, as well as a few major ones, contributed to a georgic revolution of the mind, a far-reaching transformation in attitude among England's leaders. Reflected in and, in part, brought about by poetry, this georgic revolution prepared the way for widespread acceptance of the modern agricultural revolution during the eighteenth century and thus also helped lay the groundwork for the industrial revolution that followed. Poets began to propose and to hold up for their readers to admire and imitate new models for virtuous and heroic behavior. These models, instead of being based on the leisured, aristocratic *sprezzatura* of pastoral or the martial valor and energy of epic, involved laboring for the common good, just as Spenser had projected. As we have seen, much of the hard work of changing stubbornly held English prejudices against agriculture and labor was undertaken by religious reformers, New Scientists and their allies, and others working outside poetry. Yet poetry constituted the field in which a myriad minor shapers of opinion and such major revolutionaries as Spenser, Jonson, and Milton worked; there can be little doubt that it formed as well as reflected changing public opinion during this critical century.

Royalist Georgic

Such sweeping mental changes, though gratifying to those of an innovative turn of mind, were bound to be painful to those who were attached to things as they were—or as they had been in some imagined and idealized past. Therefore, other poets, nostalgic for what they recalled as a gentler, more pastoral existence that was being swept away by religious and political faction and by the Civil War, lashed out against georgic values, which they associated in their poetry with the rise of ignorant Puritan upstarts and "base Mechanicks."[1] As we have already seen, the prescient Donne aligned himself with this reaction at its earliest stage, even before there was a significant movement against which to react. Although the Civil War was to end with a restored king and a reconstituted court, nevertheless the courtly values of the earlier age never quite regained their old ascendency. In this regard, one may say that the Cavaliers fought a losing battle, for they were eventually displaced by Whig magnates and gentlemen farmers. Moreover, the alignment was never quite one of Puritan against Cavalier. Conservative Puritans—and there were many—were likely to oppose a georgic reformation; some Anglicans with reformist consciences supported it.

Thus in *Virgidemiarum. The three last Bookes. Of byting Satyres* (1598), Joseph Hall, later Bishop of Norwich and opponent of Milton and the Smectymnuans, hits out as savagely as any Puritan sectary could wish against the abuses of landlords. His sympathy is with the tenant in his impoverished cottage:

> Of one bayes breadth, God wot, a silly cote,
> Whose thatched spars are furr'd with sluttish soote
> A whole inch thick, shining like Black-moors brows

---

[1] I quote from Abraham Cowley, *The Civil War* (3.41), ed. Allan Pritchard (Toronto: Univ. of Toronto Press, 1973), p. 108; but the phrase was a stock canard of anti-Puritan polemic—see Thomas N. Corns, "Milton's Quest for Respectability," *Modern Language Review*, 77 (1982), 769-79.

Through smok that down the head-les barrel blows.
At his beds-feete feeden his stalled teme,
His swine beneath, his pullen ore the beame.
                              (5.1.59-62)[2]

The tenant lives badly because the landlord lives well, on "double trebles of his one yeares price" (58). Against Jonson's picture of grateful farmers streaming in to Penshurst, glad to present their rents in kind, we may set Hall's darker picture of a similar event:

> Yet must he haunt his greedy Land-lords hall,
> With often presents at ech Festivall;
> With crammed Capons every New-yeares morne,
> Or with greene-cheeses when his sheep are shorne
> Or many Maunds-full of his mellow fruite,
> To make some way to win his waighty suite. . . .
> The smiling Land-lord showes a sunshine face,
> Faining that he will grant him further grace. . . .
>   (73-78, 89-90)

But the story ends unhappily, with expulsion and enclosure:

> My old Tenant may be turned out of doore,
> Tho much he spent in th'rotten roofes repayre,
> In hope to have it left unto his heyre;
> Tho many a loade of Marle and Manure led,
> Reviv'd his barren leas, that earst lay dead.
> . . . .
> Would it not vexe thee where thy syres did keepe,
> To see the dunged foldes of dag-tayled sheepe,
> And ruined house where holy things were said,
> Whose free-stone wals the thatched roofe upbraid,
> Whose shril Saints-bell hangs on his loverie,
> While the rest are damned to the *Plumbery*?

---

[2] Rpt. in *The Collected Poems of Joseph Hall*, ed. A. Davenport (Liverpool: Univ. of Liverpool Press, 1949), p. 77.

According to popular story, the first thing Henry VIII did with the confiscated monasteries was to cart off the lead roofs and the bells to be melted down; Hall makes of such misappropriation a symbol for private greed.

John Collop, a Laudian Anglican and supporter of the king, creates his "Character of a Compleat Gentleman" (1656) mainly out of negatives, and thus he reveals that he too can condemn the abuses of landlords as roundly as any Puritan:

> Thou pluck'st no houses down, to rear thy own. . . .
> Thou not inclosest to fence out the poor,
> But an inclosure art to keep their store.
> Sheep eat no men, thy men thy sheep do eat;
> In tears of others wil'st not stew thy meat.
> To dogs the Childrens bread thou dost not give,
> Make thy dogs fat, scarce let thy servants live.
> Thy father gives thee dirt, thou mak'st it gold,
> Virtue refines it to a better mold.
>   (3, 9-16)[3]

The savage images in these lines, of man-eating sheep, tenants stewed in their own tears, and dogs grown plump while children starve, all are recognizable as belonging to the stuff of common complaint. Out of popular protest this royalist poet has made a powerful indictment of abuses by landlords and, almost in passing, has epitomized the georgic response to injustice: "Thy father gives thee dirt, thou mak'st it gold."

Henry Colman, who confessed his Laudian sympathies and his support of the king in "To the Church," nevertheless found no contradiction in taking a reformist view of labor in another poem of the same period, "On povertie" (1640):

> Shall I . . .
>
>   grind
> The poore, cozen the widdowes, and ne'r mind

---

[3] From *Poesis Rediviva*, in *The Poems of John Collop*, ed. Conrad Hilberry (Madison: Univ. of Wisconsin Press, 1962), pp. 71-72. See also William Chamberlayne, *Pharonnida* (4.3.49-106), 2 vols. in one (1659), 2:49-53.

The needy orphants clamours, shall I reape
The corne another sow'd [?]
(31, 33-36)[4]

The traditional protest against reaping another's corn looks back to biblical georgic as well as at current abuses; grinding the poor, too, is an image with georgic affiliations and possibly biblical origins.[5] Prophetic attacks against economic injustice easily fall into the language of Old-Testament georgic.

After the Civil War was well under way, Royalists found additional grounds for complaint, now against taxes, fines, and land expropriations. In "A Committee" (1656), Robert Fletcher compares the Puritan commissioners to a *"Raw-bon'd Herd* of *Pharoahs* Kine / Which eat up all your fatlings, yet look lean," and to "gleaners of the field, where, if a man / Escape the sword that milder frying pan, / He leaps into the fire" (9-10, 13-15). Wat, the farmworker, is "undone," as delinquent owners are "fleec'd and torn" (26-27). In "Another [Epigram on the People of *England*]," Fletcher reveals, in a parabolic tale based on the fall and England's equivalence to Eden, how Puritan ideology was being undermined by greed for land:

Brittain a lovely Orchard seem'd to be
Furnish'd with nature's choise varietie,
Temptatious golden fruit of every sort,
Th' *Hesperian Garden* fann'd from fein'd report,
Great boyes and smal together in we brake,
No matter what disdain'd *Priapus* spake,
Up, up we lift the great Boyes in the trees,
Hoping a common share to sympathize:
But they no sooner there neglected streight
The shoulders that so rais'd them to this height;
And fell to stuffing of their own bags first,

[4] Henry Colman, *Divine Meditations (1640)*, ed. Karen E. Steanson (New Haven: Yale Univ. Press, 1979), pp. 141-42.
[5] Isa. 3:14-15; Matt. 21:33-44; Luke 20:9-18.

And as their treasure grew, so did their thirst.
Whiles we in lean expectance gaping stand
For one shake from their charitable hand.
But all in vain the dropsie of desire
So scortch'd them, three Realms could not quench the fire.

$(1-16)^6$

As these self-appointed georgic laborers break the pastoral peace of England's orchard, the unexpected combination of archetypal biblical imagery with the mischief of a boyish prank adds poignance as well as comedy to this tale of human greed.

Not all High-Church writers gave religious georgic a political dimension. Richard Crashaw, a Laudian until his conversion to Roman Catholicism about 1646, brings georgic into the theological center in his epigram "Upon the Crowne of Thorns." This poem, first published in 1646, became entirely georgic when it was revised for *Carmen Deo Nostro* (1652) by the omission of two extraneous and ungeorgic lines:

KNow'st thou This, Souldier? 'Tis a much chang'd plant
    which yet
    Thy selfe didst sett.
O who so hard a Husbandman did ever find
    A soile so kind?
Is not the soile a kind one, which returnes
    Roses for Thornes?[7]

To "sett," of course, means to put a plant into the soil, and Crashaw's "hard" husbandman recalls both the familiar biblical metaphor of evil as hardness of heart and Virgil's favorite epithet for agricultural man in the *Georgics, durus.* Seldom has georgic's power to turn death into life, destruction into creation, by planting seeds in the ground been so succinctly

---

[6] From *Ex Otio Negotium* (1656), in *The Poems and Translations of Robert Fletcher*, ed. D. H. Woodward (Gainesville: Univ. of Florida Press, 1970), pp. 139, 200.

[7] *The Poems English, Latin and Greek of Richard Crashaw*, ed. L. C. Martin, 2nd edn. (Oxford: Clarendon Press, 1957), p. 290.

expressed. Underlying Crashaw's poem is the georgic paradigm of Christian salvation: "So is the kingdom of God, as if a man should cast seed into the ground . . . and the seed should spring and grow up, he knoweth not how. For the earth bringeth forth fruit of herself; first the blade, then the ear, after that the full corn in the ear" (Mark 4:26-28). At the same time, the image of thorns blossoming into roses succinctly expresses the power of Christ's blood to reverse the effects of the fall, undoing that act which gave both to roses and to earth their thorns. When sin has destroyed innocent pastoral, only hard georgic can restore it.

Crashaw again reminds us of the Christian affinity for georgic at the conclusion of "Sospeto d'Herode," when he turns to the enemy whom Herod fears as a rival, the Christ Child lying in the stable:

> What armour does he weare? A few thin clouts.
> His Trumpets? tender cryes, his men to dare
> So much? rude Shepheards. What his steeds? alas
> Poore Beasts! a slow Oxe, and a simple Asse.

The Virgilian conflict between two heroic ideals, martial and georgic, is here implied, in a Christian pattern that we have seen in *Utopia* and that Milton will make explicit in *Paradise Regained*. In his poetic dialogue with Cowley, "On Hope," Crashaw views the Christian's spiritual life under still another georgic metaphor:

> Thou [hope] art Loves Legacie under lock
> Of Faith: the steward of our growing stocke.
> Our Crown-lands lye above, yet each meale brings
> A seemly portion for the Sons of Kings.
> (31-35)

The association between hope and georgic in Wither's emblems and here in Crashaw's poem is appropriate, since it belongs to the georgic spirit to overcome difficulties and be optimistic. Since Crashaw was the least earth-bound and utilitarian of poets, his use of georgic argues how central the mode is wherever such theological principles as Christian humility and hope are taken seriously.

Unlike literal georgic, spiritual georgic does not always stress the significance of human labor. Thus in *Flowres of Sion* (1623) Drummond of Hawthornden englishes the parable of the seed with brilliant visualization, but he retains an emphasis on germination as a miraculous process:

> So a Small seede that in the Earth lies hidde
> And dies, reviving burstes her cloddie Side,
> Adorn'd with yellow Lockes, of new is borne,
> And doth become a Mother great with Corne;
> Of Graines brings hundreths with it, which when old
> Enrich the Furrowes with a Sea of Gold.
>
> ("[An Hymne of the Resurrection]," 41-46)[8]

Toward the end of this simile, "Furrowes" reminds us that a human husbandman has some part in this otherwise purely natural, though divinely inspired, process. Southwell lays similar stress on divine impulsion in "Seeke flowers of heaven," as well as in his meditation—similar to Crashaw's epigram on the crown of thorns—on "Christs bloody sweat":

> Fat soile, full spring, sweete olive, grape of blisse,
> That yeelds, that streams, that pours, that dost distil,
> Untild, undrawne, unstampt, untoucht of presse,
> Deare fruit, cleare brookes, faire oile, sweete wine at will:
> Thus Christ unforst prevents in shedding blood
> The whips, the thornes, the nailes, the speare, and roode.
>
> (1-6)[9]

The third line confirms even as it denies that Southwell is thinking in terms of divine husbandry. The final implication

[8] *The Poetical Works of William Drummond of Hawthornden*, ed. L. E. Kastner, 2 vols. (1913; rpt. New York: Haskell House, 1968), 2:19.

[9] *The Poems of Robert Southwell, S.J.*, ed. James H. McDonald and Nancy Pollard Brown (Oxford: Clarendon Press, 1967), pp. 18-19, 52.

is that the georgic acts of tilling, drawing, stamping, and pressing will be accomplished by the instruments of the crucifixion.

The recusant poet John Abbot (alias Rivers) thinks little of human husbandry in *Devout Rhapsodies* (1647):

> Fond men with the laborious Spider toile
> By day and night are troubled, keep a coile,
> To purchase Lands, and Titles, and all done,
> 'Tis but a silly Cobweb they have spun.
> ("Sermo nonus," p. 71)[10]

True georgic is divine georgic, whose ultimate fruits are not of this world:

> Our Scripture is a more Celestiall seed,
> Not Philosophik Darnell, or that weed
> That growes in one day, in the following fades;
> But planted by Gods hand, shootes forth, the blades
> Increases so, that in the branches rest
> Your towring Eagles, and make them their Nest.
> ("Sermo Primus," p. 5)

Without the pressures of religion to counterbalance their aristocratic assumptions, however, Royalist poets typically found it difficult to sympathize with the georgic mode. Charles Cotton, unlike most of his peers, made some effort to bring country laborers into his poetry, but he was not wholly successful. The cycle of poems on the hours and the seasons that he called "Quatrains" probably were written in the early 1650s, although they remained unpublished until 1689.[11] Cotton's models appear to include Hesiod, the Medieval books of hours, the divine offices, and the *Georgics*; his chief subject is the cycle of labor, through a day and through the seasons of the year, on a country estate. Yet as "Morning Quatrains"

---

[10] *Devout Rhapsodies* (1647).

[11] See *Poems of Charles Cotton*, ed. John Buxton, The Muses' Library (London: Routledge & Kegan Paul, 1958), pp. xxix-xxxiii, 261; I quote from this text, which is based on an early MS.

reveals, Cotton is seldom able to rise above the constraints of his social position to achieve a fully georgic tone:

> *Vulcan* now makes his Anvil ring,
> *Dick* whistles loud, and *Maud* doth sing,
> And *Silvio* with his Bugle Horn
> Winds an Imprime unto the Morn.
> . . . .
> *Hob* yokes his Oxen to the Team,
> The Angler goes unto the stream,
> The Wood-man to the Purlews hies,
> And lab'ring Bees to load their thighs.
> (41-44, 53-56)

Everything is too cheerful and effortless for georgic, and the very names are indicative of the social problem: Hob and Dick are patronizing conventions, Vulcan and Silvio are literary importations, and none of these human figures is observed any more closely than the bees that set forth to gather honey.

James Turner's suggestion, that most writers in the period would prefer to describe laborers quitting their work or on holiday rather than actually at their chores, is confirmed by the greater realism of Cotton's "Evening Quatrains":

> Each one has had his Supping Mess,
> The Cheese is put into the Press,
> The Pans and Bowls clean scalded all,
> Rear'd up against the Milk-house Wall.
>
> And now on Benches all are sat
> In the cool Air to sit and chat,
> Till *Phoebus*, dipping in the West,
> Shall lead the World the way to Rest.
> (33-40)

It is hard not to notice, however, that these stanzas describe things much more vividly than people. Moreover, such small moments of realism tend to break down under the weight of conventional stereotyping at precisely those points where the laborers are named as individuals, as in "Night Quatrains":

> The Fire's new rak't, and Hearth swept clean
> By *Madg*, the dirty Kitchin-Quean,
> The Safe is lock't, the Mouse-trap set,
> The Leaven laid, and Bucking wet.
>
> Now in false Floors and Roofs above,
> The lustful Cats make ill-tun'd Love,
> The Ban-dog on the Dunghil lies,
> And watchful Nurse sings Lullabies.
> (53-60)

Cotton is well aware that there is work going on all over the estate; he is rather sympathetic than otherwise to the workers; he has a sharp ear for country sounds and a sharp eye for the details of housekeeping; but he still cannot see a worker properly even when he is looking right at him.

Yet the pressures of the Civil War were beginning to do their work, even on Royalists. Meditative poetry, which since the beginning of the seventeenth century had seen the landscape only in pastoral or natural terms, began to make use of georgic details that earlier poets had managed to ignore. A striking example is that of Edward Benlowes, a Royalist who may have been brought up as a Roman Catholic. In 1652, Benlowes published *Theophila*, which he characterized on the title page as a "Divine Poem." The last—and (we may speculate) the latest written—of *Theophila*'s thirteen English cantos (there are Latin cantos interspersed) is "The Pleasure of Retirement," a startling anomaly for its time, for it is a religious meditation based on a landscape that is georgic as well as pastoral, a landscape that is populated by realistic workers. The speaker presents himself in rather conventional terms, as a gentleman onlooker, a stroller, an angler (10-12), a man appreciative of conventional pastoral sights (7-9, 13-24); yet amid green fields, golden sands, nibbling ewes, and shepherds

231

with oaten pipes appear almost casually a number of strikingly realistic georgic details:

STANZA I.

WHen lavish *Phoebus* pours out melted Gold;
And *Zephyrs* breath doth Spice unfold;
And we the blew-ey'd *Skie* in Tissue-Vest behold.

II.

Then, view the *Mower*, who with big-swoln Veins,
Wieldeth the crooked Sythe, and strains
To barb the flowrie Tresses of the verdant Plains.
. . . .

IX.

In neighbring *Meads*, with Ermin Mantles proud,
Our Eyes and Ears discern a Crowd
Of wide-horn'd Oxen, trampling Grass with Lowings loud.

X.

Next *Close* feeds many a strutting udder'd Cow;
Hard by, tir'd Cattle draw the Plough,
Whose galled Necks with Toil and Languishment do bow.

XI.

Neer which, in restlesse Stalks, wav'd *Grain*
promotes
The skipping Grasshoppers hoarse Notes;
While round the aery *Choristers* distend their Throats.

XII.

Dry Seas, with golden Surges, ebbe and flow;
The ripening *Ears* smile as we go,
With Boasts to crack the Barn, so numberless they show.

. . . .

XIV.

Soon as the Sultrie *Month* has mellow'd Corn,
Gnats shake their Spears, and winde their Horn;

The *Hindes* do sweat through both their Skins, and
　　Shopsters scorn.

XV.

Their *Orchards* with ripe *Fruit* impregned be,
　　Fruit that from Taste of Death is free,
And such as gives Delight with choice Varietie.

. . . .

XXIII.

This the *Spring-Garden* to spiritual Eyes,
　　Which fragrant Scent of Gums out-vies;
Three *Kings* had thence their triple mystick Sacrifice.

XXIV.

O, happier *Walks*, where CHRIST, and none beside
　　Is Journeies End, and Way, and Guide!
Where from the humble *Plains* are greatest *Heights*
　　descry'd.

XXV.

Heav'nward his *Gaze*.

The appearance of the edenic fruit, free of the "Taste of
Death," signifies that Benlowes' soul, with his imagination,
has left the ground to start its journey "Heav'nward." Yet
before he makes that leap, Benlowes fills his landscape with
closely observed details. The mower's "big-swoln Veins," the
"galled Necks" of the cattle, the hinds who sweat through
skin and through clothing that a shopman would scorn, are
permitted to be parts of the whole order of things. We may
wonder if Benlowes, who toured the Continent after he left
Cambridge in 1624, was influenced by genre painting, since
clearly he is thinking partly in terms of composing a poetic
landscape. When he returns from his devotions back down to
earth, it is once again to a partly georgic scene:

LXXXII.

But, hark, 'tis late; the *Whislers* knock from Plough;
　　The droyling *Swineheards* Drum beats now;
Maids have their *Cursies* made to th' spungy-teated Cow.

233

LXXXIII.

Larks roosted are, the folded *Flocks* are pent
In hurdled Grates, the tir'd *Ox* sent
In loose Trace home, now *Hesper* lights his Torch in's Tent.

LXXXIV.

See glimmering Light, the *Pharos* of our Cot;
By *Innocence* protected, not
By *Guards*, we thither tend, where *Ev'n-song*'s not forgot.[12]

Surviving evidence, of deeds, lawsuits and the like, reveals that Benlowes was a perfect case study of what happened to old-fashioned landlords in the 1650s.[13] He was caught up in large-scale political and economic events that by the end of the decade would result in a revolution in agricultural practices and in people's attitudes toward husbandry.[14] Either landowners learned new ways, or they were forced out. Benlowes, who was typical of the better class of Royalist landlords, did not trouble to raise his rents to their full potential. He was a bachelor, and he had plenty to live on. But he carelessly allowed himself to encumber his estates with debts, and he lost his manor house to a fire, which also burnt up much of the press-run of the recently published *Theophila*. In the late 1640s, the Parliamentarians sequestered his estates, and he was forced to compound for them. Then in the 1650s he was subjected to a Cromwellian tax against Royalist landowners, which was popularly and ominously known as "decimation." Forced at last to sell out to a London capitalist who had lent him funds, Benlowes tried desperately at the last hour to put his rents up to current levels. His motive was to receive a fair price for his lands, since that price would be determined, as was the custom, as a multiple of annual rents. Evidently

[12] *Theophila* (1652), pp. 236-39, 246-47.

[13] See Harold Jenkins, *Edward Benlowes* (Cambridge, Mass.: Harvard Univ. Press, 1952).

[14] See ch. 4 above, and Christopher Hill, "The Agrarian Legislation of the Revolution," *Puritanism & Revolution* (1958; New York: Schocken Books, 1964), pp. 153-96.

he was insufficiently forceful and hardhearted: his tenants refused to agree to the increases, and he subsequently lost most of the purchase price of his patrimony through lawsuits. The new owner, we may guess, succeeded better than Benlowes in racking up the rents. The end result, common in the 1650s, was that everyone concerned was either forced off the property or taught to farm a great deal more efficiently.

Thus economic forces and political turmoil forwarded the impulse to agricultural reform, and the attention of conservative landowners was drawn, willy-nilly, toward the practical details of farming. The last canto of Benlowes' poem suggests that he had begun to look about him rather sharply, but just a little too late. Later, in 1672, John Worlidge was to address his preface to *Systema Agriculturæ* explicitly to the survivors, those willing or able to adjust to the new scientific methods of husbandry: "[S]o many of your *Tenants* exercised in onely the *Vulgar Methods* of *Agriculture*, are forced to withdraw their hands from the *Plough*, and revert their *Tenements* into your own possessions, that you your selves may cultivate that which is your own; and you that continue in your *Farms* may by your *Industry* mannage them after the best and most advantagious Ways for the propagating of such things, that we are most deficient of, and that may most retaliate your *Cost* and *Industry*, and most improve your *Lands*, not onely for the benefit of your *Selves* and *Posterity*, but the *Kingdom* in general."[15] Worlidge uses the old biblical image of withdrawing the hand from the plow in a significantly new sense. St. Bernard had applied it to those who ran away from monastic labor and discipline; Hugh Latimer converted it to describe prelates who refused to preach. Now Worlidge gives the image a secular and a scientific turn. No man withdrawing his hand from the plow, Christ had warned, was fit for the kingdom of God. That kingdom has become the kingdom of scientific agriculture, personal profit, and national prosperity—or, more

---

[15] Sig. B2ʳ. Worlidge, who takes for his title-page epigraph Virgil's "O Fortunatos nimium, sua si bona Norint / Agricolas," evidently interpreted those famous words more practically than his predecessors, in terms more of income than of psychic satisfaction.

immediately, a georgic estate well laid out like the one pictured in Worlidge's frontispiece. Those who fail to keep up with or to understand this basic social transformation "are forced to withdraw their hands from the *Plough*," and are excluded from the new kingdom.[16] Benlowes lacked Worlidge's clear insight into the economic and scientific developments that were revolutionizing agriculture; although the georgic imagery in the latter part of *Theophila* may well reflect Benlowes' last-ditch efforts to investigate his estates in hopes of straightening them out, nevertheless they help the narrator toward the old-fashioned consolations of devotion, not the rapidly evolving remedies of agricultural reform.

GEORGIC IN THE REVOLUTION

With the exception of Milton and Marvell, the Puritan cause had few poets between 1640 and 1660 capable of matching the Royalists who published during that period. In the long run, of course, the exception turned out larger than the rule, but in the short run numbers (and quality, too) must count for something. Against Vaughan, Suckling, Lovelace, Herrick, Cleveland, and many a less well-known yet still skillful Cavalier propagandist, all of whom looked down their noses at rural labor, the Puritan cause was forced to rely, in poetry at least, mainly on such spokesman as the anonymous author of *Bishops, Judges, Monopolists* (1641). To a Cavalier, the country was, or should be, a place of pastoral ease; to a Puritan, it was beginning to appear as a place of georgic labor, and the gentlemen pastoralists as idle drones or caterpillars. Thus monopolists are like Egyptian locusts, and England is not a garden but an orchard, in which all right-thinking men ought to be sharing the work:

> HOw comes this swarme of Locusts to appeare
> More this, then any other Temperate yeere,

[16] In a similar vein, and typical of eighteenth-century thinking, Squire All-worthy's farm in *Tom Jones* becomes a garden of Eden, and its potential loss is equivalent to the fall.

This crew of moaths and cankers that bereaves
Our flourishing Orchard both of fruit and leaves?
Who do not onely vex us here about,
But pester all the Trees the Realme throughout?
I meane those Drones, that fly about in mists,
Divelish *Projectors*, damn'd *Monopolists*.
                              (1-8)[17]

Were it not for Thomason's indefatigable collecting of tracts, we would lack even this poor statement of Puritan opinion.

Another anonymous tract, *Five Strange and Wonderfull Prophecies*, hits out at Royalists and sectaries alike. One poem, "Scottish *Merlin* his Prophesies of Old England," hints obscurely at discontent with the Church and the poetic establishment:

False Prophets shall sow fancies for good seeds,
And men be pleased then with *Pans* rude reeds:
Apollo shall become a Shepherd Swaine,
And on the mountaines keep his flocks againe,
And men shall wade in bloud up to their chins,
And all this come upon them for their sins.
                              (A1ᵛ)[18]

Whether this is a protest against importation of the classics or the writing of pastoral poetry is uncertain. What is certain is that the writer sees chaos in the land, and that he fears it:

Then cork shall float, and Gentry downe shall sink,
And paper then much store of bloud shall drink:
Then Commons shall grow proud, but very bare,
And to be then enclos'd shall take great care.
                              (A2ʳ)

The common people, and especially the working people, will rise:

---

[17] *Bishops, Judges, Monopolists* [1641], p. 5. The one surviving copy (British Library, Thomason Tracts E 171[2]) has lost its title page; this is the inner title, and the date is Thomason's.

[18] Thomason, E 146(13), dated May 1642.

The Hammer and the Spade shall think that they
Could without King or Kesar the land sway.

(A2^r)

Though it seems that the author of the tract, who speaks with gnomic obscurity, disapproves of these rude upstarts, he still captures the enthusiasm that fills the working rebels, and probably he echoes their slogans.

The fullest statement of the reformist impulse toward a new model of behavior, which would replace the standards of epic by those of georgic, is an allegorical work of 1644, entitled *A Dialogue Betwixt a Horse of Warre, and a Mill-horse; Wherein the content and safety of an humble and painfull life, is preferred above all the Noyse, the Tumults, and Trophies of the Warre* (see fig. 6). As one might expect, the poetry is not great, but it is often competent and amusing; and the work gains in significance because it approaches rather closely, from its odd allegorical viewpoint, the ripest opinions of John Milton. The "Cavalliers Warre-Horse," as the inner title calls him, invites the Mill-horse to join him: "Come therefore to the Wars, and doe not still / Subject thy selfe to beare Sacks to the Mill." The Mill-horse, who speaks in old-fashioned black-letter, gives all the reasons why a georgic career should be preferred to a military one, hard and drudging as it may seem:

> Despise me not thou Cavalliers War-Horse
> For thouogh to live I take an idle course,
> Yet for the common-wealth I always stand,
> And am imploy'd for it, though I'm nam'd
> A *Mill-Horse*, I am free and seem not under
> Malignants that doe townes and houses plunder,
> Transported on thy back, while thou must be
> Halfe guilty of their wrong, and injurie.
> Done to their country, while without just cause,
> Thou fightest for the King against the Lawes. . . .
> What though upon my back I carry sacks?
> Thy meat is plunderd out of barnes and stacks;
> While thou dost feed on Stolen Oates and Hay

238

The *wronged Farmers* curse the strength away
Of all thy Diet, often wishing that
Diseases may consume thy ill-got fat.
                    (A1ᵛ)¹⁹

The War-horse replies scornfully:

                    such a poore thing art thou
Who Gentry scorne, beare till thy ribs doe bow
Burthens of corne or meale, while that Kings are
My Royall Masters both in Peace and Warre.
                    (A2ʳ)

When the war has ended the Cavalier Horse anticipates a more glorious and honorable career for himself than for his country cousin:

In time of Peace my blood shall not be spilt,
But like to *Noble Beere*, shall run *at Tilt*. . . .
I shall be made a *Bishop*, and grow fat . . .
But thou shalt weare thy selfe out, and be still
An everlasting Drudge unto some Mill.

The Mill-horse cannot deny this fate; but he finds in labor, not war, true glory and true service to country:

No matter, I wil spend my life and health,
Both for my Country and the common-wealth,
And it is *Prince-like* (if well understood)
To be ill-spoken off for doing good. . . .
Scorn is a burthen laid on good men still,
Which they must beare, as I do Sackes to Mill.
                    (A3ᵛ)

If we hear, in the Mill-horse's apologia, faint echoes of Samson at the Mill of Gaza, of Abdiel suffering the reproaches of Satan, of Milton wearing out his eyes in the service of liberty, or of Milton's preference for georgic over epic in *Paradise Regained*, it is because both the small poet and the great were caught up in the same large events and were attuned to the

---

¹⁹ Thomason, E 80(5), dated January 1643/44.

resultant moral transformations. Both had learned that, because it is creative and beneficial to the nation, obscure labor may be more honorable in the sight of eternity than ostentatious but destructive war. The Cavalier Horse, however, learns nothing; with comic realism the anonymous poet allows his parting words to end the poem with a revelation of invincible ignorance:

> If thou lik'st not my discourse very well,
> *Mill-horse* take up my taile, and so farwell.
>
> ([A4ᵛ])

The Mill-horse, who knows that those who are reviled will be blessed, and that the meek shall inherit the earth, will indeed remain to take up the tale (as well as the tail) after his nobler cousin has departed.

Because the Royalists wrote so much more poetry than the Puritans, however, the tale of the growth of georgic consciousness is told most dramatically by their resistance to it. We may begin the story with Drayton, whose *Poly-Olbion* (1613) initiated the vogue for loco-topographical poetry that was to reach into the eighteenth century and grow increasingly hospitable to the georgic vision. In *Poly-Olbion*, the most competent and realistic of early topographical poems, Drayton praises the various regions for their cheeses, their flocks, and their fields of grain. Yet all these commodities seem to flow with paradisal ease and naturalness from the British soil, as if Adam had never fallen and the intervention of human laborers—to plant, to herd, to harvest—were unnecessary. The "deare soyle" of Kent typically brings forth "Thy Conyes, Venson, Fruit; thy sorts of Fowle and Fish: / . . . thy Hay, thy Corne, thy Wood" as if no farmers were necessary. Kent's orchards are "golden Gardens" that "seeme th'*Hesperides* to mock." Finally a gardener appears, in what is probably the only truly georgic passage in the entire poem:

> Unto whose deare increase the Gardiner spends his life,
> With Percer, Wimble, Sawe, his Mallet, and his Knife;

Oft covereth, oft doth bare the dry and moystned root . . .
And kils the slimie Snayle, the Worme, and labouring Ant,
Which many times annoy the graft and tender Plant:
Or else maintaines the plot much starved with the wet,
Wherein his daintiest fruits in kernels he doth set:
Or scrapeth off the mosse, the Trees that oft annoy.

(18.657-97)[20]

So unusual is this description of the details of husbandry,
however, that Drayton feels obliged to apologize for it:

But, with these tryfling things why idly doe I toy,
Who any way the time intend not to prolong?

(18.698-99)

When Drayton recounts the earlier history of the land, he
allows laborers to make another brief appearance in a tale of
former wars:

For those Rebellions, Stirres, Commotions, Uprores, here
In *Richard Burdeaux* raigne, that long so usuall were;
As that the first by *Straw*, and *Tyler*, with their Rout
Of Rebels brought from *Kent*, most insolent and stout. . . .

(22.405-408)

What of these peasant rebels and their deeds? Nothing much.
Neither Drayton nor his intended audience has any interest
in the doings of such social nonentities:

Since they but Garboyles were, in a deformed masse,
Not ordered fitting warre, we lightly overpasse.

(22.423-24)

Drayton prefers to recount the doings of kings and barons,
who know how to behave epically; and, when he turns to the
natural scene, he admires utility yet constantly transforms it
into pastoral beauty, so that in his landscapes a reader will

[20] *The Works of Michael Drayton*, ed. J. William Hebel, 5 vols. (Oxford:
Shakespeare Head, 1931-41).

encounter many a lovely shepherdess but nothing like Benlowes' sweaty, big-veined workers.

The conversion of England into an Eden had become a patriotic reflex, and the colonies underwent an equivalent transformation. In "The Battel of the Summer Islands," Waller manages to convert even economic transactions into edenic manifestations, *negotium* into *otium*:

> Tobacco is their worst of things which they
> To English Land-lords as their Tribute pay:
> Such is the mould, that the blest Tenant feeds
> On pretious fruits, and payes his rent in weeds. . . .
> Heaven sure has kept this spot of earth uncurst
> To shew how all things were created first.
> (29-32, 46-47)[21]

Bermuda is the best known of such poet-created paradises, but the process extended to the Americas. Drayton's ode "To the Virginian Voyage" echoes the travel literature:

> VIRGINIA
> Earth's onely Paradise.
>
> Where Nature hath in store
> Fowle, Venison, and Fish,
>   And the fruitfull'st Soyle,
>   Without your Toyle,
> Three Harvests more,
> All greater then your Wish.
> (23-30)

Bacon and Ralegh were already beginning to realize that nothing could be better suited for plantation than a georgic spirit,[22] and few poetic vehicles are better fitted to the georgic mode than the English Horatian ode, with its patriotic energy. Yet the only georgic note that Drayton strikes, a brief concluding praise of "industrious Hakluyt" (68), seems quite anomalous

[21] Edmund Waller, *Poems* (1645), pp. 52-53.
[22] See, e.g., Bacon's "Of Plantations," *Essayes* (1625).

after all his assurances that the blissful mariners and settlers may drift "Without . . . Toyle" toward a new "Golden Age" (28, 37). Drayton may well have been the most capable among English poets of celebrating leisure with such energy—but the paradox belongs more to the time than to the man.

Even at the midpoint of the Interregnum many Royalist poets excluded georgic from their idealized visions of the countryside. The protagonist of John Chalkhill's "CORYDONS Song" (1651) is a plowman rather than the usual shepherd, but he proves to be that paradox, a gentleman-plowman, who has rejected the city and the court (a sacrifice few plowmen are called on to make), and his labors certainly do not deserve the Virgilian epithets *durus* or *improbus*:

> But oh the honest country man
> Speaks truly from his heart,
> > High trolollie lollie loe,
> > High trolollie lee,
> His pride is in his tillage,
> His horses and his cart:
> > *Then take care away,*
> > *And wend along with me.*
> > > (17-24)[23]

Patrick Cary's "Country Life" (1651) is more straightforward, in that its aristocratic countrymen pretend to be neither shepherds nor husbandmen, but simply gentlemen at their rural sports: dancing, bowling, fowling, angling, walking, and talking.[24] (Cary, excluded from his inheritance because his mother brought him up a Roman Catholic, offers a case study of how an English aristocrat of his time would rather beg incessantly than work.)

Even after the Restoration, the old aristocratic vision had its adherents. The countryman in Philip Ayres' "In Praise of

---

[23] The poem survives only as quoted by Izaak Walton. I quote from *The Compleat Angler* (1661), p. 85; refrains expanded.

[24] See *The Poems of Patrick Cary*, ed. Sister Veronica Delany (Oxford: Clarendon Press, 1978), pp. 23-26.

a Countrey Life" likes to rest in the shade, where "No Project [ominous word] spoils his Sleep" (14).[25] Like many earlier praisers of the country, he need never exert himself, because his food and amusements come to him where he rests:

> Fruit-Trees their loaded Boughs extend,
>   For him to take his Choise;
> His wholsome Drink the Fountains lend,
>   With pleasant purling Noise;
> In Notes untaught, Birds that like him are free,
> Strive which shall most delight him with their Harmony.
>   (25-30)

The scene and attitude are perennial, and could be traced down through the eighteenth century and the Romantic era into our own time; but no longer was it the only vision possible.

During the Civil War, some Cavalier poets began writing "bucolics," or pastoral georgics, which touch on georgic subjects in effortless and usually humorous fashion. Thus the heroine of Lovelace's "Amarantha. A Pastorall" begs for milk from a herd of passing cows, and, "Out of the Yeomanry oth' Heard,"

> A rev'rend Lady Cow drawes neare,
> Bids *Amarantha* welcome here;
> And from her privy purse lets fall
> A Pearle or two. . . .
>   (89, 91-94)[26]

Herrick too indulged in georgic humor, in two "bucolics" in which herdsmen replace shepherds. One is a parody of the traditional pastoral singing contest; the stakes are a heifer and a steer and the judge is "*Lallage* (with cow-like eyes)." The

---

[25] *Lyric Poems, Made in Imitation of the Italians* (1687), p. 133.

[26] *The Poems of Richard Lovelace*, ed. C. H. Wilkinson (1930; Oxford: Clarendon Press, 1963), p. 110.

other is a neat-herdess's lament for her lost steer, which has expired after being bitten by a mad dog.[27]

Cows are a good deal more resistant to gentrification than sheep, so the unsuitability of such georgic objects to the romantic pastoral makes them fertile sources for Cavalier comedy. In a similar vein, Suckling digs his reader in the ribs in "A Ballade. Upon a Wedding," when he has his rustic narrator remark that the festivities take place "At *Charing-Crosse*, hard by the way / Where we (thou know'st) do sell our Hay" (7-8).[28] In another instance, when Colonel John Jephson resorts to the modesty topos in the poem he contributed to Lovelace's *Lucasta*, he hits on the device, at once modest and comic, of posing as a rustic:

> But as the humble tenant that does bring
> A chicke or egges for's offering,
> Is tane into the buttry, and does fox
> Equall with him that gave a stalled oxe:
> So, (since the heart of ev'ry cheerful giver
> Makes pounds no more accepted then a stiver,)
> Though som thy prayse in rich stiles sing, I may
> In stiver stile write Love as well as they.
>   (5-12)[29]

---

[27] *The Poetical Works of Robert Herrick*, ed. L. C. Martin (1956; Oxford: Clarendon Press, 1963), pp. 243-44, 305-306; cf. Catullus 2.3; Ovid, *Am.* 2.6. Although it is generally interchangeable with "pastoral," Herrick uses "bucolic" in his poems about cowherds.

[28] *The Works of Sir John Suckling; The Non-Dramatic Works*, ed. Thomas Clayton (Oxford: Clarendon Press, 1971), p. 80.

[29] *Poems of Lovelace*, p. 4. In another commendatory poem, W. Rudyerd turns to georgic to compare Lovelace's verse to the "smoothnesse" of his mistress and contrast it with poetry too full of metaphors, "like those chickens hatcht in furnaces, / Produce one limbe more, or one limbe lesse, / Then nature bids" (p. 6).

For the custom of foxing in the buttery on quarter-days, see also Peter Hausted, *Ad Populum* (1644):

> Ye offer'd up a Capon-Sacrifice
> Upon his Worship at a New-yeares Tide:
> For which i'th Buttery having stuff'd your hide

Characteristically, Jephson converts the tenants' enforced rents into cheerful gifts of love comparable to his own poem, yet his good-humored joking probably gives us a glimpse into real country transactions.

But the husbandmen and other rude mechanics, who could be safely ridiculed earlier in the century while they remained in their places, are associated with much more biting and even fearful humor as the Civil War progresses, especially in the early 1650s when the countryside was being turned upside down. Early in the war, Cowley can treat these simple countrymen just as Virgil had in the *Georgics*, as the hapless victims of civil war:

> The'astonisht *Plowmen* the sad noyse did heare,
> Look'ed up in vaine, and left their worke for feare.
> (*The Civil War*, 2.15-16)

In *The Fable of Philo* (1645), John Abbot actually imitates the relevant passage in the *Georgics*:

> the Drum shall speak
> In every Village warre, the Rurall swaine
> Shall leave his tillage, Shepheards leave the plaine . . .
> the Glebe Land
> Shall unmanured and untilled stand.
> The plough shall be neglected.
> (pp. 13-14)

There is a clear echo of Virgil's "non ullus aratro / dignus honos, squalent abductis arva colonis" (1.506-507); "The plow is not duly honored; the lands, robbed of the tillers, lie waste." William Chamberlayne also turns to the *Georgics* in *Pharonnida* (1659), which was written later but recalls with

---

> With store of Drinke, as heartlesse as 'twas cold . . .
> Ye tooke your leave.
> (p. 5)

Although the Royalist Hausted is chiefly outraged by the readiness of the laborers to change masters, he scarcely gives an idyllic picture of life before the war.

remarkable sympathy the same early moment when peace
gives way to civil war:

> whilst, with such hast, as new
> Shorn Meadows, when approaching stormes are nigh,
> Tir'd Labourers huddle up; both parties try
> To levy Armies. The sad Scholar throws
> His Books aside, and now in practice shews
> His studied Theoricks; the stiff Labourer leaves
> Ith' half-shorn fields the uncollected sheaves,
> To female Taskers, and exchangd his hook
> Into a Sword.
>
> (2.2.62-70)

Especially effective is Chamberlayne's transference of Virgil's
epithet "stiff" (*rigidus*) from the sword to the unfortunate
laborer. Of course, much of the georgic that arose during the
period was simply native. An anonymous pamphlet of 1645,
which sees the countrymen as impartially the victims of both
sides, imitates and probably echoes popular complaint:

> Ich had zix oxen tother day,
> And them the Roundheads vecht away,
>   A mischief be their speed.
> And chad zix horses left me whole,
> And them the Cabballero's stole:
>   Chee voor men be agreed.[30]

The author of this tract does not indicate whether he inclined
toward king or Parliament.

Most poets, however, were more partisan. The extent to
which common laborers were obtruding themselves on the
attention of horrified Royalists is evident in the works of John
Taylor, the Water Poet. The title of his collection published

---

[30] *The western Husbandmans Lamentation* (1645) as quoted by Joseph
Frank in his bibliographic anthology, *Hobbled Pegasus* (Albuquerque: Univ.
of New Mexico Press, 1968), p. 116. Chamberlayne's *Pharonnida* is quoted
from the 1659 edn., 2 vols. in one, 1:104. See also John Quarles, *Fons
Lachrymorum* (1648): "Intruding *Mars* molests the active *plough*" (p. 98).

in 1641 is characteristic: *A Swarme of Sectaries, and Schis-matiques: Wherein is discovered the strange preaching (or prating) of such as are by their trades Coblers, Tinkers, Ped-lers, Weavers, Sow-gelders, and Chymney-Sweepers.* Again and again Taylor reverts indignantly to lists of base profes-sions that are getting above themselves:

> A Preachers work is not to gelde a Sowe,
> Unseemly 'tis a Judge should milke a Cowe:
> A Cobler to a Pulpit should not mount,
> Nor can an Asse cast up a true account.
>
> (p. 2)

But the unseemly has in fact occurred:

> THese kind of Vermin swarm like Caterpillars
> And hold Conventicles in Barnes and Sellars,
> Some preach (or prate) in woods, in fields, in stables,
> In hollow trees, in tubs, on tops of tables . . .
> These are the Rabshekaes that raile so bitter,
> (Like mungrill Whelpes of Hells infernall litter)
> Against that Church that hath baptiz'd and bred them,
> And like a loving mother, nurst and fed them.
>
> (p. 7)

In Mad Fashions, Od Fashions, All out of Fashions (1642), Taylor complains of a world turned upside down. Images of the country, of labor, and of trades appear and reappear in this phantasmagoric poem—clear indications of the sources of Taylor's anxiety:

> The Cony hunts the Dogge, the Rat the Cat,
> The Horse doth whip the Cart (I pray marke that)
> The Wheelbarrow doth drive the man (oh Base)
> And Eeles and Gudgeons flie a mighty pace. . . .
> For when many a worthy Lord and Knight,
> And good Esquire (for King and Countreys Right)
> Have spent so much time with Great Toyle, and Heede,
> All Englands Vicious garden how to weed,

So like a Wildernesse 'twas overrun,
That though much hath been done; All is not done.

(A2)

It is instructive that Taylor now commends the king's sup-
porters for their toil and heed, as georgic workers in the garden
of England, because that was scarcely a role that England's
leaders would have claimed a few years earlier. The Royalist
Thomas Jordan liked Taylor's frontispiece and poem well
enough to appropriate them for the pamphlet he entitled *The
World turn'd upside down* (1647).

Cowley wrote his unfinished *Civil War* when it was possible
for a Royalist to sympathize with the common farmers, be-
cause it looked as if the king might prevail. A little later,
Cleveland, reacting to the Westminster Assembly, strikes a
more troubled note, yet still speaks with a scornful and con-
fident superiority:

> Thus *Moses* Law is violated now,
> The Ox and Asse go yok'd in the same plough.
> ("The Mixt Assembly," 93-94)[31]

By 1647, the situation of the Royalists has considerably de-
teriorated. Thomas Jordan republishes Taylor's complaint:

> The felt-maker and sawcie stable Groome
> Will dare to pearch into the Preachers roome.[32]

In *Times Whirligig*, Humphrey Willis complains:

> Thus doe the froth of all the earth,
> A spawne sprung from a dunghill birth,
>   now prince it in our land:
> A people come the Lord knowes how,
> Both fame and nameless till just now,
>   must every one command.[33]

[31] *The Poems of John Cleveland*, ed. Brian Morris and Eleanor Withington
(Oxford: Clarendon Press, 1967), p. 28; see Deut. 22:10.
[32] Cited by Frank, *Hobbled Pegasus*, p. 146; cf. *Mad Fashions*, A3ᵛ.
[33] Frank, *Hobbled Pegasus*, p. 147.

And in 1649, Samuel Bold contributed a deeply pessimistic georgic elegy to the collection edited by Richard Brome in honor of the recently deceased Lord Hastings:

> WHat Soil is this, where nothing that is good,
> Nor Vertues branch, can live, nor Beauties bud? . . .
> A Soil that fosters Brambles, Shrubs, and Thorns;
> Slaughter's the Lamb, and sets up Beasts with Horns.
> A Soil, that nurses Briars, Weeds, and Rape;
> But starves the Olive, Fig-tree, and the Grape.[34]

England, so often compared to Eden by an earlier generation, now echoes with images of the fall and the apocalypse.

Lovelace too strikes a solemn note, in his well-known poem to Charles Cotton, "The Grasse-hopper" (1649). Don Cameron Allen's identification of the political element in that poem has been generally accepted. It seems significant, then, that the Royalist grasshopper lives a life of pastoral ease all through the summer, is fed without toil by nature and the heavens, and then is lost in a grim georgic harvest that echoes the Bible as well as Aesop:

> But ah the Sickle! Golden Eares are Cropt;
>   *Ceres* and *Bacchus* bid good night;
> Sharpe frosty fingers all your Flowr's have topt,
>   And what sithes spar'd, Winds shave off quite.
>   (13-16)[35]

The opposition which Lovelace implies between kingly or Royalist ease and the irresistible energy of the Puritan harvest reveals his perceptive insight into the attitudes of the two parties, conservative and progressive. His response, as a Royalist, is not to fight or to labor, but to poise a glass against the onslaught, therefore to retreat from the challenge into the

---

[34] *Lacrimae Musarum . . . upon the death of the most hopefull Henry Lord Hastings* . . . Collected by R. B. (1649), pp. 32-33.

[35] Allen, *Image and Meaning* (1960; Baltimore: Johns Hopkins Press, 1968), pp. 152-64; *Poems of Lovelace*, pp. 39, 192, 199.

inner world of personal friendship and stoic resignation. Thus he leaves the fields of England to their new masters.

In "The Ant," another Aesopian poem posthumously published in the second *Lucasta* (1659), Lovelace refers even more clearly to the social and political changes that the Civil War had brought to rural England:

> Forbear thou great good Husband, little Ant;
>   A little respite from thy flood of sweat;
> Thou, thine own Horse and Cart, under this Plant
>   Thy spacious tent, fan thy prodigious heat;
> Down with thy double load of that one grain;
> It is a Granarie for all thy Train.
>
> Cease large example of wise thrift a while,
>   (For thy example is become our Law)
> And teach thy frowns a seasonable smile:
>   So *Cato* sometimes the nak'd Florals saw.
> And thou almighty foe, lay by thy sting,
> Whilst thy unpay'd Musicians, Crickets, sing.

The ant should lay by his work because Lucasta "holy makes the day" (13-18).

> *Austere* and *Cynick*! not one hour t'allow,
>   To lose with pleasure what thou gotst with pain:
> But drive on sacred Festivals, thy Plow;
>   Tearing high-ways with thy ore charged Wain.
> Not all thy life time one poor Minute live,
> And thy o're labour'd Bulk with mirth relieve?
>   (1-12, 19-24)

A Roman devotion to work is now ascendant in England ("For thy example is become our Law"), and the ant's habit of driving its plow on "sacred Festivals" presumably refers to the Puritan abolition of religious holidays and Sunday play. The "unpay'd Musicians, Crickets," like the grasshopper of the earlier poem or Lovelace himself, are now out of fashion with their Royalist devotion to pastoral leisure.

Lovelace strikes an even more bitter anti-georgic note in a late satire, "On *Sanazar*'s being honoured with six hundred Duckets," also written during the 1650s and published in 1659. He begins by alluding to the georgic tale of Louis XI, who, after he came to the throne, rewarded a husbandman for his earlier hospitality:

'Twas a blith Prince exchang'd five hundred Crowns
For a fair Turnip; Dig, Dig on, O Clowns!
(1-2)

The precise reason for Lovelace's anger is not evident until much later in the satire, when he launches an attack on upstart, presumably Puritan poets, in terms mainly of agricultural labor:

There is not in my mind one sullen Fate
Of old, but is concentred in our state.
Vandall ore-runners, Goths in Literature,
Ploughmen that would *Parnassus* new manure . . .
No wonder if a Drawer Verses Rack,
If 'tis not his 't may be the Spir't of Sack;
Whilst the Fair Bar-maid stroaks the Muses teat,
For milk to make the Posset up compleat.
(206-209, 216-19)

The good-natured, superior scorn the Cavalier had once shown for his country inferiors no longer suffices to meet the situation. Increasing turmoil in the world of agriculture is one likely stimulus of Lovelace's use of these georgic metaphors (which embrace even the barmaid) as well as for the remarkable bitterness of his tone. Evidently Lovelace saw a reflection of these social and economic changes in poetry, and he gives us a perfect metaphor for what was happening: Parnassus, once the haunt of muses and gentlemen, an idyllic pastoral scene, is being ploughed up and manured by enterprising georgic poets. Nothing is safe from them any longer, not even the realm of poetic imagination.

Even well after the Restoration, the old aristocratic preference for war over labor persisted in some circles. Thus, in spite of his interest in country matters, Charles Cotton, in "On the Death of the Most Noble Thomas Earl of Ossory" (obit 1680), could ask his soldiers "Who now in Honour's path shall lead you on, / Since your beloved General is gon?":

> Hang your now useless Arms up in the Hall,
> There let them rust upon the sweating Wall;
> Go, till the Fields, and with inglorious Sweat,
> An honest, but a painful living get:
> Your old neglected Callings now renew,
> And bid to glorious War a long adieu.
> (31-32, 41-46)[36]

With the Restoration, still other poets could go back to pretending that nothing had happened, that the old order in society and poetry could be restored to just what it had been before the Civil War disordered England's values:

> The scholar doth look
> With joy on his book,
> Tom whistles and plows amain;
> Soldiers plunder no more,
> As they did heretofore,
> For the King enjoyes his sword again.[37]

---

[36] *Poems of Charles Cotton*, p. 132; and see Herbert of Cherbury's "Ditty in imitation of the Spanish," in which growing old is given a turn contemptuous of georgic:

> See but the bravest Horse, that prideth most,
>   Though he escape the Warr,
> Either from master to the man is lost,
>   Or turn'd unto the Carr,
> Or else must die with being ridden Post.
>   (16-20)

(Written before Herbert's death in 1648, and published in 1665.)

[37] *A Countrey Song, Intituled, the Restoration* (1661), in Frank, *Hobbled Pegasus*, p. 461. The song derives from Martin Parker's well-known interregnal ballad, "When the King enjoys his own again."

Tom had apparently been put back in his place. Yet accelerating changes in agricultural practices, brought on in part by the economic troubles of the 1650s, meant that Tom's place would never again be quite what it was before. Landlords no longer could afford simply to ignore their workers and their estates, and what necessity required of them they found ways to make palatable by changes in attitude and interest. What had been shameful was now respectable; the courtier was displaced in importance by the gentleman farmer; and minor poets came to pride themselves on the fashionable elegance of their georgic verses.

GEORGIC LOVE POETRY

Although a modern literary historian, asked for some typical examples of English pastoral, might first name *The Shepheardes Calender* or "Lycidas," the great majority of pastoral poems were love lyrics. Because it was assumed that love ought properly to be aristocratic in nature, the two modes went hand in hand. Thus the prospect of writing georgic love poetry would have seemed unnatural to a poet at the turn of the seventeenth century. We have already noticed that Donne saw an opposition between love and georgic, while as late as 1659 Lovelace's georgic ant commits an offense against love by neglecting to lay aside its work in honor of Lucasta. In one of his more cynical love lyrics, "Against Fruition [1]," published in *Fragmenta Aurea* (1646) but probably written between 1632 and 1637,[38] Suckling attacks the idealization of love by associating it with georgic instead of pastoral:

> Urge not 'tis necessary, alas! we know
> The homeliest thing which mankind does is so;
> The World is of a vast extent we see,
> And must be peopled; Children then must be;
> So must bread too; but since there are enough
> Born to the drudgery, what need we plough?
> (13-18)

[38] See Thomas Clayton, ed., *Works of Suckling*, pp. 37, 243.

Suckling associates the old sexual metaphor of plowing with the Cavalier's scorn for the laborer, as he glances also at the command to multiply in Genesis 1 and the curses on childbirth and work in Genesis 3; the result is a georgic metaphor for sexual disgust.

Suckling's extreme position called for an answer, and one was provided by Edmund Waller. Waller might disagree with Suckling on the subject of love, but not on the subject of agriculture, from which he carefully dissociates himself:

> I need not plough, since what the stooping Hine
> Gets of my pregnant Land, must all be mine;
> But in this nobler Tillage 'tis not so.[39]

Both sides of the dispute are thus couched in Cavalier terms, and no one questions that georgic activity is shameful. But the onset of the Civil War was subtly to effect even Royalist use of georgic in love poetry and eventually to give rise to a few specimens of a new sub-genre, georgic love poetry. In "Elinda's Glove," published in 1649, Lovelace wittily yokes his mistress's glove with some realistic details of rural economics:

> Thou snowy Farme with thy five Tenements!
> Tell thy white Mistris here was one
> That call'd to pay his dayly Rents:
> But she a gathering Flowr's and Hearts is gone,
> And thou left voyd to rude Possession.

> II.

> But grieve not pretty *Ermin* Cabinet,
> Thy Alablaster Lady will come home;
> If not, what Tenant can there fit
> The slender turnings of thy narrow Roome,
> But must ejected be by his owne dombe?

[39] Conveniently edited in *Works of Suckling*, p. 182, along with another response by Henry Bold (pp. 183-84).

III.

Then give me leave to leave my Rent with thee;
    Five kisses, one unto a place:
    For though the *Lute's* too high for me;
Yet Servants knowing Minikin nor Base,
Are still allow'd to fiddle with the Case.

Farms, rents, tenements left void to "rude Possession," narrow rooms, ejections, servants who know their places: a considerable freight of serious matter lies only a little beneath the surface of carefree persiflage. Feudal service, which for hundreds of years had provided love poetry with its dominant analogy, gives place to the laws of tenant farming and property rights. Presumably it is no coincidence that the poem was written at about the same time that Parliament was officially dispensing with some of the last vestiges of feudal obligation in the land laws and thus was recognizing an economic and social trend that was already well established. (The ordinance that abolished knight tenure in favor of free and common socage and thus recognized that land was held not by reason of feudal service but by private contract, bought and paid for, was passed in 1645; *Lucasta* was published in 1649.) Of course, Lovelace's tone is light and urbane, yet, often, so was the tone of the courtly or Petrarchan poet. Nonetheless, the political underpinnings of Lovelace's amusing lyric reveal that a radical transformation has taken place. In this respect, the social assumptions underlying the poem have more in common with the famous "proviso" scene in Congreve's *Way of the World* (1700) than with the lingering Petrarchan or even the anti-Petrarchan lyrics that some of Lovelace's contemporaries (but seldom Lovelace himself) were continuing to produce. We may add that Congreve's Augustan lovers inhabit a world in which property laws, as relating both to marriage and to land, are stable if potentially chafing to a high-spirited young couple, but that Elinda's lover inhabits an era of unpredictable change and turmoil in agricultural affairs, which is what Lovelace's images mostly suggest.

Rural troubles were just beginning to impose themselves on love poetry, as some nervous jokes in Andrew Marvell's dedicatory poem in the same volume also suggest:

> Some reading your *Lucasta*, will alledge
> You wrong'd in her the Houses Priviledge.
> Some that you under sequestration are,
> Because you write when going to the Warre.
>
> (27-30)

Between the licensing and publication of *Lucasta*, Lovelace, already twice jailed for his politics, was obliged to sell what was probably the last of his family estates, but his difficulties resulted from bail payments and debts rather than sequestration. Although sequestration was becoming a real threat, its full weight would not be felt for several more years. Robert Fletcher's "A Lenten Letany" (1656) speaks in quite a different tone:

> From a hunger-starv'd Sequestrators maw,
> From Revelations and Visions that never man saw,
> From Religion without either Gospel or Law,
> > *Libera nos, etc.*
>
> From the Nick and Froth of a penny pothouse,
> From the Fidle and Cross, and a great Scotch-Louse,
> From Committees that chop up a man like a Mouse.
> > *Libera nos, etc.*
>
> From broken shins and the bloud of a Martyr,
> From the titles of Lords and Knights of the Garter,
> From the teeth of Mad-dogs and a Countrymans quarter.
> > *Libera nos, etc.* (29-40)

There is no more half-hearted joking here; matters have gotten too far out of hand. The countryman, once the imagined repository of innocence or the safe butt of aristocratic wit, has become a mad dog, who offers his victims no quarter. Fletcher strikes a similar note in "An Elegy," when he questions God's ways to man: "Malignant Heaven! can there be envy there / Where never gall nor sequestration were?"[40]

Possibly the honor of publishing the first entirely georgic love lyric belongs to William Hammond, for his poem "Husbandry," which appeared in 1655. This curious work runs into difficulties, because Hammond seems not to have realized that he could not simply substitute georgic for pastoral without making some sort of adjustment. The result is so awful that it has a certain fascination:

> When I began my Love to sow,
>   Because with Venus' doves I plow'd,
> Fool that I was, I did not know
>   That frowns for furrows were allow'd.
>
> The broken heart to make clods torn
>   By the sharp arrows of Disdain,
> Crumbled by pressing rolls of Scorn,
>   Gives issue to the springing grain. . . .
>
> The harvest is not till we two
>   Shall into one contracted be;
> Love's crop alone doth richer grow,
>   Decreasing to identity.
>   (1-8, 13-16)[41]

It is odd that a poem that is in some respects so innovative should be such a crude and undigested mixture of Virgil, Petrarch, Shakespeare, and Donne. We may speculate that Hammond was unaware of what he was doing; husbandry was in the air, so he made use of it, but without quite knowing how to proceed.

Much more successful was a poem that appeared two years later. Unlike Hammond, Bishop Henry King, who may have written "Love's Harvest" as early as the 1630s, evidently re-

---

[40] *Poems and Translations*, pp. 134, 201.

[41] Rpt. in *Minor Poets of the Caroline Period*, ed. George Saintsbury, 3 vols. (Oxford: Clarendon Press, 1905-21), 2:490.

alized that something more was necessary than simply to sub-
stitute georgic for the usual pastoral. King's purpose is to
repudiate the too-common goal of love poetry, unwedded
bliss; as an effective means toward that end he hits on a witty,
tacit contrast between georgic fruition and what he considers
to be the fruitlessness of the conventional pastoral attitude
toward love:

> Love's Fruites are Legall use; and therefore may
> Be only taken on the Marriage day. . . .
>
> Then gather not those immature delights,
> Untill their riper Autumne thee invites.
> He that Abortive Corne cutts off his Ground,
> No Husband, but a Ravisher is found.
> > So those that reap their Love, before they Wed,
> > Do in effect but Cuckold their own Bed.
> > > (3-4, 7-12)[42]

Possibly King's may be the earliest georgic love lyric, since
Margaret Crum states that it is "Associated in MSS" with
another poem written in 1633. If so, we may speculate that
there may have been some connection with Suckling's
"Against Fruition," and the early date would attest all the
more to King's clever insight. The wittiness of the poem resides
chiefly in the reader's understanding that love poems are nor-
mally pastoral, not georgic. King not only uses georgic im-
agery, but he achieves a genuinely georgic spirit in this grave
jeu d'esprit, since he is arguing for such anti- or extra-pastoral
values as use, postponement of gratification for a later harvest,
and fruitfulness. The "husband" of the poem—Donne's pun
without the bitterness—husbands his happiness until it is ripe,
but the implicitly pastoral lover reaps "immature delights"
and is no better than a "ravisher" of his fields and of his
mistress. King successfully applies georgic motifs as the proper
tools with which to reform the love lyric; the resulting poem,

---

[42] *The Poems of Henry King*, ed. Margaret Crum (Oxford: Clarendon Press,
1965), p. 169.

unlike Hammond's, is sympathetic to its mode. That this poem should have been written by an Anglican bishop with Royalist sympathies demonstrates again that the urge to reform is at least as significant as religious affiliation per se in the movement from pastoral to georgic consciousness.

As the rise of the georgic spirit during the Civil War among political reformers elicited a corresponding Royalist backlash, so, presumably in response to that trend as well as to the Puritan redefinition of love,[43] a Royalist vogue for satirically georgic love poems appeared. This vogue mainly took the form of attacking unsuitable love in georgic terms. Thus, about 1645, Cleveland wrote "A young Man to an old Woman Courting him":

> Peace Beldam *Eve*: surcease thy suit,
> There's no temptation in such fruit.
> No rotten Medlers, whil'st there be
> Whole Orchards in Virginitie.
> Thy stock is too much out of date
> For tender plants t'inoculate.
>
> (1-6)

In the background is the suggestion that this unpleasant beldame is a landowner, who may have thought that land could be used to buy love: "Goe study Salve and Treacle, ply / Your Tenants leg, or his sore eye" (39-40). Another poem probably by Cleveland, "On an Alderman who married a very young wife," finds georgic imagery appropriate to depict the reverse situation:

> A Hayre or two is all the tithe
>   That from his bald pate you can gather
> Give him an houre glasse or a sithe
>   You'le stile him time or else Times father.
>
> (14-17)

---

[43] See, e.g., William and Malleville Haller, "The Puritan Art of Love," *Huntington Library Quarterly*, 5 (1942), 235-72; and William Haller, "Hail Wedded Love," *ELH*, 13 (1946), 79-97.

The opposition between love and land is even clearer in Robert Fletcher's bombastic and humorless "Degenerate Love and Choyce," which attacks the commercialization of love in georgic terms:

> But here yee groveling *Muck-worms*, yee that build
> Like *Ants* in Mole-hills; and tye field to field;
> Which varying God's decree, by joyning hands,
> Instead of marrying Children, wed your lands. . . .
> But the hog-trough worldings from these measures flirt,
> They love a great name though it's made of dirt. . . .
> Come *Worlding* let me undeceive thee now.
> If man's grand welfare hangs upon the plough . . .
> Then thou hast grasp'd to purpose. But if not,
> The end of wealth's mistaken in thy plot. . . .
> But there's a mean in judgment, a mid course,
> A difference betwixt a *Man* and's *Horse*. . . .
> Love never measur'd by the *Acre* stood,
> If we toll fairly, then the bargain's good.
>   (81-132)

There was nothing new in marrying for land; that had been the general practice for as long as land represented the principal form of wealth. But (with the notable and irreverent exception of popular drama) few Elizabethans would have thought the custom needed to be attacked or defended in poetry. Now in 1656, however, the pressures of social and economic change are enforcing a new consciousness, and poets are obliged to choose their sides.

With the Restoration, those who could not accept the rules of Worlidge's new kingdom became even more bitter than the Royalists who were victimized by the Civil War. Restoration drama is filled with heiresses and with tensions between love and land. But for the bitter extreme of georgic satire in love poetry, it would be hard to outdo Thomas Flatman's biting "Advice to an Old man of sixty three about to marry a Girle of sixteen" (dated 1671 in MS).[44] The old man's "crazy"

---

[44] For the date, see Saintsbury, *Minor Caroline Poets*, 2:490.

intention, Flatman complains, is as incongruous as if "he, when Harvest comes should plow / And when 'tis time to reap, go sowe" (7-8).[45] The poet epitomizes his contempt for the December lover in a second and even ruder georgic couplet:

> Nature did those design for Fools,
> That sue for work, yet have no tools.
>
> (11-12)

Where Bishop King valued the georgic spirit in a largely implicit contrast with pastoral, Flatman implies the opposite; his georgic imagery figures the total unsuitability of the prospective husband for his task. Flatman still can rely on his reader to realize that love poetry is ordinarily pastoral rather than georgic, so he can use pastoral as the unspoken norm of his satire. The elderly farmworker, with his total confusion about the proper season to plant and reap and his pitiful lack of tools, contrasts implicitly with a proper lover, who is certainly younger than he and probably a gentleman shepherd. In Flatman's opinion, there is no question that a man who turns up for work without his tools is a fool. His metaphor, based perhaps on his own firsthand experience as a landowner at Diss, can only refer to a propertyless farm laborer, who is imagined as presenting himself to the farmer in search of work at plowing or harvest time. He is peremptorily dismissed because he is so impoverished that he has sold or lost the necessary implements of his trade. Like old age, his poverty is equivalent to stupidity, and all the worse because it is rural and uncouth. In these aphoristic lines are epitomized the weight of a whole century's aristocratic contempt for georgic labor. The georgic battle was being won, yet opposition remained—and would continue to remain, for, as Spenser expected, the war would have to be fought again and again.

ROBERT HERRICK

Between about 1630 and 1660, the course of English history was such that those who had an interest in religious, political,

---

[45] Flatman, *Poems and Songs* (1674), pp. 65-66.

and scientific reform in the broad sense of the word either had to keep moving further and further to the left—which is what Milton did—or else they were likely to find themselves relegated to the conservative side of events and opinion. Earlier, Royalists such as Joseph Hall, John Collop, Henry Colman, and Henry King had been drawn to the georgic ideal. Francis Bacon, the founder of progressive scientific georgic in modern England, was closely associated with the monarchy throughout his career and was deposed by Parliament chiefly for that reason.[46] After the war began, however, the division between those who supported and those who opposed the rise of georgic was drawn more sharply than before. Many Royalists, already ideologically and esthetically opposed to the georgic ideal, were separated from their lands or were understandably reluctant to improve their estates under the threat of sequestration or an increase in levies and fines. Puritan landowners, to the contrary, could experiment with new agricultural techniques with some confidence in what the future might bring, and indeed with some satisfaction that they were helping to contribute to that future. By and large, therefore, Cavalier poets were inclined to see anything georgic as increasingly ugly, base, and threatening to what they valued, whereas Puritan poets treated georgic as fruitful, progressive, and beneficial to an emerging nation. Two poets who, aside from Milton, illustrate most subtly and imaginatively Royalist and Puritan attitudes toward georgic immediately before and during the Civil War are Herrick and Marvell. Marvell, of course, seldom commits himself fully on any issues and likes to consider both sides of a case. Yet his sympathy to the georgic spirit is often consonant with Puritan thought at its best during the Interregnum. Like most Royalists, Herrick was unwilling to commit himself to georgic in its fullest sense, yet, unlike other aristocratic poets, he is willing to explore the rising mode in considerable depth and to turn it to his own purposes.

[46] For another view of Bacon see Christopher Hill, "Francis Bacon and the Parliamentarians," *Intellectual Origins of the English Revolution* (1965; London: Panther Books, 1972), pp. 85-130.

By the time Herrick began writing *Hesperides* (probably in the early 1630s), English landscape poetry, under the influence of painting, had grasped a central point of the genre: that landscape must be unified by some organizing principle. The poet may simply choose to report what an eye would see as it sweeps across the scene. Yet the untrained or unprepared eye sees only a chaos of disparate objects. Various kinds of order are imposed on the landscape by the assumptions of the viewer. Not surprisingly, therefore, most of the early English landscape poems (unlike their Medieval predecessors) are formed by the presuppositions of the pastoral esthetic. Gradually, poets learn how to construct pleasing compositions, using mountains, valleys, meadows, streams, trees, flowers, sheep, nymphs, and shepherds, balancing one texture or color against another—air against water, mountain against meadow, flower against fruit—and thus creating a pleasing, easeful, and naturalistic whole. Even though most of the British countryside that a poet of that time was likely to encounter was man-shaped and man-dominated, the poet's instinct usually was, as we have seen, to ignore the worker and to assimilate any pasture or plowland into the untilled and (as we would now say) unspoiled natural scene. The growth of georgic consciousness immediately before and during the Civil War, however, made such acts of the censoring imagination more difficult. From then on, poets who wrote about the countryside would have either to celebrate or satirize farming—that is, descend to georgic. Otherwise, they would be obliged to retreat to the Lake District or the moors in order to seek out retreating nature in its wilder forms.

One may find interesting early reflections of these fundamental changes in the viewing of landscape in two of Herrick's poems. One is a brief epigram, "A good Husband," which begins by alluding to an epigram by that exponent of the gentlemanly georgic mode, Horace (*Ep*.1.6.48):

A MASTER of a house (as I have read)
Must be the first man up, and last in bed:

With the Sun rising he must walk his grounds;
See this, View that, and all the other bounds:
Shut every gate; mend every hedge that's torne,
Either with old, or plant therein new thorne:
Tread ore his gleab, but with such care, that where
He sets his foot, he leaves rich *compost* there.[47]

In this miniature celebration, the principle of organization is
walking the bounds, and to "View" "this" or "that" object
is to see it with a landlord's eye and to consider its condition
and utility. In keeping with his subject, Herrick stresses own-
ership and enclosure; these are "his" grounds and "his" glebe,
which are everywhere to be closed in by mending the hedges
and shutting the gates. Significantly, he ends by touching on
a topic that was soon to cause tremendous excitement among
new-georgic scientists and experimentalists of the time: "*com-
post.*" Perhaps word was already going around the neigh-
borhood. But Herrick is a conservative and a Royalist. His
compost is not decayed clover leaf; it has the qualities of an
aristocratic, not a scientific, magic; it appears wherever the
master sets his foot, precisely like those astonishing transfor-
mations that the king effected in the masque by virtue of his
mere presence. No labor, no actual work of fertilizing is in-
volved. Perhaps, if we were to look a little deeper into the
political implications, we might interpret Herrick's compost
as a metaphor for getting up as early as the workers and
supervising them more closely to be sure they never slacked—
though certainly he does not go so far as to say so. Perhaps
we might rather say, more generally, that for Herrick there is
a certain magic in the social system itself. A good master can
make his crops spring up more abundantly simply by the act
of attentive presence.

Probably "A good Husband" was written about the same
time as a much better known poem, "The Country life, to the
honoured M. *End[ymion] Porter*, Groome of the Bed-Cham-

---

[47] *Poetical Works*, ed. L. C. Martin, p. 259.

ber to His Maj[esty]," which Martin tentatively assigns to 1632 (p. xxxvii). The poem addressed to Porter is an expansion on the same georgic theme, with several close verbal echoes. Herrick begins with that stoic view of country life that praises its happy simplicity in contrast with city and court (1-4).[48] The wise man is happy because he limits his demands on life. Therefore, "Thou never Plow'st the Oceans foame / To seek, and bring rough Pepper home" (5-6). Herrick rules out trade and acquisition, activities very much in keeping with the spirit of Virgilian georgic, because his version of georgic is opposed to expansion, exploration, innovation, or exertion. His georgic hero conquers not the land but himself; for him, self-containment and self-sufficiency are primary virtues, essential to true peace of mind. Herrick's economic model is the self-sufficient farming villa of Martial and Horace:

> No, thy Ambition's Master-piece
> Flies no thought higher then a fleece:
> Or how to pay thy Hinds, and cleere
> All scores; and so to end the yeere.
>
> (11-14)

Yet what is admirable poetically about Herrick (if, for some, abominable politically) is his inclusion of normally forbidden details of the rural economy and social system. Here are workers demanding to be paid and debts demanding to be cleared. Although Porter is urged to limit his connections with the outer world, Herrick does not gloss over some of the real problems a landowner might encounter.

Yet there is tension in the very title of Herrick's poem. Endymion Porter is, in fact, a courtier, a Groom of His Maj-

---

[48] On which see Maren-Sofie Røstvig, *The Happy Man* (Oslo: Akademisk Forlag, 1954); Earl Miner, *The Cavalier Mode from Jonson to Cotton* (Princeton: Princeton Univ. Press, 1971); and James S. Tillman, "Herrick's Georgic Encomia," "*Trust to Good Verses*," ed. Roger B. Rollin and J. Max Patrick (Pittsburgh: Univ. of Pittsburgh Press, 1978), pp. 149-57.

esty's Bed Chamber, not a simple farmer. Therefore perhaps his estate is more a country retreat than a means of livelihood. Often it is the gentleman or the amateur, not the professional, who likes to think of his farm in terms of its economic self-sufficiency. The professional simply raises what will profit him most, and buys or trades for what he lacks on the market. Indeed, Herrick's landowner differs from Vaughan's idle stroller chiefly in that he is far more pragmatic and has a far sharper eye for rural details:

> When now the Cock (the Plow-mans Horne)
> Calls forth the lilly-wristed Morne;
> Then to thy corn-fields thou dost goe,
> Which though well-soyl'd, yet thou dost know,
> That the best compost for the Lands
> Is the wise Masters Feet, and Hands.
> (19-24)

Probably the hands of this master are his farmhands. It is clear enough who does the work and who the observing:

> There at the Plough thou find'st thy Teame,
> With a Hind whistling there to them:
> And cheer'st them up, by singing how
> The Kingdoms portion *is the Plow*.
> (25-28)

"[C]heer'st them up" certainly puts the best face on what Porter does—urge his workers to their labors. Evidently "them" includes the plowman and the two oxen, to whom Porter sings what was by then a proverbial theme: the importance of the plow in upholding the kingdom.

Even those parts of the estate that seem most pastoral are included within Herrick's georgic vision:

> This done, then to th'enameld Meads
> Thou go'st; and as thy foot there treads,

> Thou seest a present God-like Power
> Imprinted in each Herbe and Flower:
> And smell'st the breath of great-ey'd Kine,
> Sweet as the blossomes of the Vine.
> (29-34)

These cattle are more than just additions to the esthetic effect:

> Here thou behold'st thy large sleek Neat
> Unto the Dew-laps up in meat.
> (35-36)

Still, it is noticeable that Herrick minimizes the importance of labor. The cattle seem to grow from the rich soil of the meadow as naturally as the herbs and flowers on which they feed. The only other worker Porter encounters as he makes his rounds is a shepherd "piping on a hill" (evidently the pastoral convention was momentarily too strong to resist). The laborers enter the poem en masse only on holidays. Two or three phrases evoke them at their work; the last thirty lines describe their leisure and their festivities. Herrick concludes these festivities with Virgil's famous words: "O happy life! if that their good / The Husbandmen but understood!" (70-71). This is the voice of the landlord speaking, however, not that of a Virgilian philosopher, and it is a fine example of how the well-known words might be twisted to serve a purpose quite different from what Virgil intended. The husbandmen in question are the laborers, not the owner. Their happiness consists of holidays, rightly enjoyed. If only they knew how happy they were, they would certainly be content to stay in their places!

Since Herrick's poem breaks off at this point with a "*Caetera desunt*," we cannot tell how he proposed to reconcile the happiness of the landlord Endymion Porter and his workers'— or how he thought a realistic georgic contentment might be based on holidays alone. Perhaps "The Hock-cart," which concludes by reminding the workers that they are feasted not for their pleasure but in order to fatten them up for more labor, may indicate what Herrick's thinking was. On the whole, however, "The Hock-cart" is a far sterner poem. What primarily interests Herrick here is the owner's country happiness rather than his workers'. Watching the happy "young men and maids" (48) at their play is one of the pleasures of country living, but the pleasure is more one of observation than participation or real empathy. Moreover, as Herrick's pronouns repeatedly insist, since Porter is the owner, these are *his* holidays and *his* festivities.

In his humble way, Herrick belongs to the same social class as Porter. Concerning his several well-known poems on the theme of country contentment, Raymond Williams has remarked most clearly on their social and economic implications.[49] In "His content in the Country," for example, Herrick is able to rejoice that he is not condemned to be a mere laborer or tenant:

> Here, here I live with what my Board,
> Can with the smallest cost afford.
> Though ne'r so mean the Viands be,
> They well content my *Prew* and me. . . .
> Here we rejoyce, because no Rent
> We pay for our poore Tenement:
> Wherein we rest, and never feare
> The Landlord, or the Userer.
> The Quarter-day do's ne'r affright
> Our Peacefull slumbers in the night.
>
> (1-12)

True, Herrick also rejoices that he feeds "on no mans score" and that his flanks are not larded with "others meat" (14-16). He may have been generous in forgiving tithes, and his complaint against Much-more (see ch. 1 above) may only have

---

[49] Williams, *The Country and the City* (London: Chatto & Windus, 1973), pp. 33-34, 72-73.

been in jest. Still, it is hardly surprising that he does not fear the approach of Quarter Day, since, in effect, he sits on the collecting side of the table.

In other poems, Herrick looks at the farm laborer more closely; and all of them confirm that he was a more acute observer of rural labor than most other poets—especially Royalist poets—of his time. Yet he was not more notably sympathetic to what he observed. To Much-more, too hard pressed to pay his tithes, we may add Herrick's portrait of "wrie-nosed *Tooly*," who sells pheasant eggs. However hungry he may be, this country entrepreneur "ne'r so much as licks the speckled shells," unless an egg happens to be addled and therefore worthless for sale. Tooly feeds a "Cock and Hen," but he has never yet had the pleasure of picking so much as a bone of them. Herrick lays his behavior to superstition and observes him with wry irony. A more likely explanation, however, is that Tooly is a man on the verge of starvation, who cannot afford to eat the small merchandise on which he must rely for subsistence, tempting as it may sometimes be to him. As Richard Baxter was to note, in the *Poor Husbandman's Advocate to Rich Racking Landlords* (1691), independent husbandmen were even worse off than farm servants, since if "their hennes breed Chickens, they cannot afford to eate them, but must sell them to make their rent. They cannot afford to eate the egges that their hennes lay . . . but must make money of all."[50]

Suffering from similar problems is the wretched Nodes, who is evidently an itinerant laborer:

> Where ever *Nodes* do's in the Summer come,
> He prayes his Harvest may be well brought home.
> What store of Corn has carefull *Nodes*, thinke you,
> Whose Field his foot is, and whose Barn his shooe?

[50] Cited by G. E. Fussell, *The English Rural Laborer* (London: Batchworth, 1949), p. 28. I have not been able to verify this quotation, which seems to derive from the manuscript treatise.

Not even Herrick's editors have commented on this poem. Its broad meaning seems clear enough: here is a laborer who works for hire. He is possessionless, his only land being the dirt on his feet. Herrick's more specific meaning seems to be that this sly laborer works some of the grain he is hired to harvest into his shoes, and thus he ekes out his inadequate pay with a little extra that he can carry off and eat. The sharp-eyed Herrick has observed his trick, but he reveals no observable pity for the desperation that presumably lies behind it.

In "Upon *Chub*," Herrick turns his poet's eye on a small landlord or perhaps an independent tenant farmer:

> When *Chub* brings in his harvest, still he cries,
> Aha my boyes! heres wheat for Christmas Pies!
> Soone after, he for beere so scores his wheat,
> That at the tide, he has not bread to eate.

It may be, as J. Max Patrick suggests, that Chub sells his wheat in order to buy beer.[51] Another explanation is that he uses or sells the grain he harvests to brew beer. Several times when famine struck during the sixteenth and seventeenth centuries, for example in 1620, complaints were voiced and laws passed against brewing, because it was thought that the practice robbed the poor and the nation of necessary food for the sake of selfish gain.[52] In either case, however, Chub acts in typical landlordly fashion; he promises his workers a good feast at Christmastide, when generosity and good cheer were the traditional means of eking out low wages. Meanwhile, he has converted the grain to his own uses and pocketed or drunk

---

[51] *The Complete Poetry of Robert Herrick*, ed. Patrick (1963; New York: W. W. Norton, 1968), p. 432n.

[52] On laws against malting, see *The Agrarian History of England and Wales*, vol. 4, ed. Joan Thirsk (Cambridge: Cambridge Univ. Press, 1967), 581-86. Ordinarily, malt for brewing was made from barley, but sometimes oats or wheat were used (see Eric Kerridge, *The Agricultural Revolution* [New York: Augustus M. Kelly, 1968], p. 163); or Herrick may have been thinking of so-called "*wheat* barley" (Thirsk, p. 170).

the profits, so the men and their families can go hungry. It is likely enough that when Chub says he "has not bread to eate," what is really implied is that he has nothing to spare at festival time for the "boyes" he had jollied into working harder at the harvest.

Toward the labor, the hardships, and the abuses of the rural scene Herrick directs a keen but seldom an indignant eye. He observes everything; he is amused, and at times he may mildly disapprove of what he sees; still, he feels no urge to intervene or to promote any change in the order of rural society and agricultural practice. As for himself, his brother Thomas, and such friends as Endymion Porter, they are fortunate, if only they are wise enough to know their own happiness. "O fortunatos nimium," he rejoices, like many another Royalist of his time. Assuredly Herrick's is a Royalist or more broadly an aristocratic variation on the georgic mode. The central tenets of the philosophy embodied in his country poems might almost be summed up, not too unfairly, in what (*mutatis mutandis*) was to become the unofficial rallying cry of British labor: "I'm all right, Jack." Instead of commitment to political change and historical progress, instead of working to advance the general prosperity and greatness of the nation—which are among the most significant and characteristic aims of Virgilian and Spenserian georgic—Herrick employs his often startlingly real insights into the agricultural scene to commend tradition, to uphold the social hierarchy, and to assure the contentment of himself, his servant, and his circle of friends. Out of Horace and Martial, and out of the pastoralized seventeenth-century tradition of the "happy man," Herrick develops his own form of georgic.

In a sense, Herrick's georgic is simply a revised version of or a substitute for pastoral. The gentleman's farm still is a place where he can take his ease, retreat from the world, and recuperate from the strains of business or court life. Instead of playing his shepherd's pipes on a shady hillside, the owner can stroll about and supervise his workers. In addition to pastoral ease such georgic has the advantage that it will bring in better rents each quarter-day. At his most cynical or bitter, Herrick perceives the country as a place where one man exploits another, and where all struggle for advantage and survival. No wonder, then, if he took his leave of the countryside in "To *Dean-bourn*" by voicing savage complaints about the "warty incivility" of the country and its rural inhabitants. The Civil War only emphasized what he already knew. His parishioners are "A people currish; churlish as the seas; / And rude (almost) as rudest Salvages." When Herrick is in a better mood, however, more in control of his insight into the human predicament, he sees the country as a place where a well-governed man can be stoically self-sufficient. A small farm, a country vicarage, or (after his ouster) even a humble "cell" offers the ideal refuge from the ills of ambition and poverty alike. Where Donne retreated with a mistress or his God into the private microcosm from which he scoffed at all forms of georgic, Herrick chose rather to adapt georgic to his needs. In some respects georgic offered him, even better than pastoral, a mode that could be usefully adapted to the theme of Stoic retreat. By employing some of its conventions and rejecting others, he was enabled to depict himself with his maid Prue at Dean Prior, subsisting on beans and modest salads, escaping the storms of life by restricting his wants and his energies to a Stoic—yet still an Epicurean—minimum.

Herrick's georgic is significant not only because it is embodied in some of his finest poetry, but because it represents, at a surprisingly early period, some of the elements that would go into the georgic of the late Restoration and the eighteenth century. That georgic represents something of a compromise between Puritan enthusiasm for and Royalist rejection of the georgic mode—just as Whig politics represented something of a compromise between Puritan and Royalist ideologies. Not all the Augustan poets resemble Herrick in his rejection of the public component of Virgilian georgic—that is to say, Virgil's insistence that the husbandman's private and even obscure deeds will have an ultimate effect on the state and on society as a whole. But some of them clearly did, viewing georgic poetry as simply another opportunity to retreat from responsibility to others. Pope's juvenile but brilliant "Ode on Solitude" typifies the private use of georgic and his fourth *Moral Essay* (esp. lines 173-204) the public. Most Augustan georgic does, however, accept Herrick's attitude toward labor. Labor is something valuable, something necessary, but on the whole it is better to gloss over it quickly and leave it to others. It is quite proper for a landowner to take an interest in the workings of his estate, and for a poet to celebrate and encourage that interest; but no one would expect the owner to put his own hand to the plow. As the old feudal relationship between master and workers gives way to the new system of land ownership and labor for hire, it even becomes legitimate to speak in poetry about the economic details of husbandry. Yet always there is a strong pull to make georgic easy, gentlemanly, more like pastoral.

ANDREW MARVELL

That Marvell is among the most subtle of English pastoralists, most readers know and a host of distinguished commentaries testify. Among his recurrent themes are retreat from the world, resignment of ambition, enjoyment of rural ease and beauty, celebration of innocence and young love, and the quest for renewal of the Golden Age. In other poems, the pastoral mode supports religious devotion or provides a background for investigations into the pains and intricacies of being in love. Yet many critics have wondered why Marvell chose a mower rather than the usual shepherd as his spokesman in one group of poems generally thought to be pastoral.[53] That teasing question has been more often asked than answered. Abstruse the-

---

[53] On pastoral in Marvell's poetry and in support of the view that the Mower poems belong to that mode, see Frank Kermode, "Two Notes on Marvell," *N&Q*, 197 (1952), 136-37; J. B. Leishman, *The Art of Marvell's Poetry* (London: Hutchinson, 1966); Donald M. Friedman, *Marvell's Pastoral Art* (London: Routledge & Kegan Paul, 1970); Ann E. Berthoff, *The Resolved Soul* (Princeton: Princeton Univ. Press, 1970).

ory aside, however, pastoral may be defined as poetry that has to do with shepherds and sheep, as its name indicates— or, in its rougher Theocritan vein, with goatherds and their goats. The sheep may, of course, be dispensed with, for when a reader versed in the conventions comes across a love dialogue, say, between Damon and Clorinda, he will assume there is a flock somewhere in the background. Perhaps Damon has left his sheep to care for themselves while he attends to other affairs. Surely it is quite another matter, however, if the poet were to equip Damon with a plow or a scythe. When he does that, he does not simply assume a convention but violates it— or else reveals that he is observing some other convention entirely. English pastoral figures simply do not take up their scythes and labor until they pour with sweat under the midday sun. At most, they may pick up a lamb, fend off a threatening wolf with their crooks, or pipe their flocks back to the fold for the night. Usually they prefer to lie at ease on a shady hillside, where they sing, admire the landscape, make love, or lament their amatory difficulties.

Damon, of course, is not a shepherd but a farm laborer, and it is immediately evident that he is characterized by a number of qualities that are more georgic than pastoral. Marvell seems to base his novel figure on contemporary agricultural conditions as well as classical literary sources. As a mower, Damon is presumably an independent laborer who works for hire, and who presents himself to the farmers and bailiffs of the neighborhood at harvest time, when extra hands are wanted. A professional specialist, Damon owns his scythe and brings it with him when he reports for work. "*Damon the Mower*" has been compared to Virgil's second eclogue, which it resembles in some respects, but Damon is unlike Virgil's Corydon in being a laborer. Significantly, his rival is the shepherd. The love situation and the rivalry between professions are similar to those in Dyer's "*Coridon* to his *Phillis*," in which, it may be remembered, the protagonist loves a divine shepherdess and speaks of himself in terms of plowing.[54] Dyer's Coridon finds himself in a pastoral milieu—and somewhat out of place—because pastoral was the only mode available for fashionable love poetry in that earlier period. By the time Marvell wrote "*Damon* the Mower," however, opposition between georgic and pastoral ideals was more sharply defined, and georgic was far more prominent. Consequently, Marvell can portray a richer version of the conflict than Dyer, and he can put that conflict where it properly belongs, in a setting more georgic than pastoral.

As he swings his scythe, Damon confesses his love for the shepherdess Juliana and recounts how he has brought her presents emblematic of the Golden Age: defanged snakes and "Oak leaves tipt with hony due" (38).[55] What do his gifts imply? Several critics have suggested that Marvell is alluding to Virgil's "Messianic" Eclogue. In the Golden Age to come, Virgil there proclaims, the serpent will perish and the stubborn oak will distill honey (*Ec.* 4.24, 30). Yet the allusion is puzzling, since Damon is no messiah, even in an ironic sense, nor does Marvell's poem anticipate a Golden Age. A plausible alternative is that Marvell is alluding to Jupiter's edict in *Georgics* 1.121-46. Like God in Genesis 3, Jupiter removes the Golden Age into the irretrievable past and establishes georgic labor in its place. Damon would seem to have reasoned that, if Jupiter brought the Golden Age to an end by putting black poison into the serpent's tooth and shaking honey from the trees, he can undo that curse by pulling the teeth of a grass snake and dipping some oak leaves in honey. His immediate purpose in giving Juliana these pathetic gifts is to bridge the gap between himself, a farm laborer condemned by the curse, and Juliana, who enjoys an aristocratic substitute for that *otium* he has lost. His gifts announce that a mower is as good as a shepherd, although that shepherd shares with Juliana the

---

[54] In *Englands Helicon* (1600); see ch. 1 above.

[55] *The Poems and Letters of Andrew Marvell*, ed. H. M. Margoliouth, 2d edn., 2 vols. (Oxford: Clarendon Press, 1967), 1:42.

shepherdess a leisurely, golden, but artificial world from which poor mowers are excluded.

Juliana fails to ask the questions that might begin to close the gap: what do the gifts mean, and who is the giver. Still the rejected mower exults in his georgic role and boasts that he is as good as any shepherd:

> I am the Mower *Damon*, known
> Through all the Meadows I have mown.
> On me the Morn her dew distills
> Before her darling Daffadils.
> And, if at Noon my toil me heat,
> The Sun himself licks off my Sweat.
>
> (41-46)

Although the shepherd suitor is known for his great wealth, Damon is known for his great labors:

> What, though the piping Shepherd stock
> The plains with an unnum'red Flock,
> This Sithe of mine discovers wide
> More ground then all his Sheep do hide.
>
> (49-52)

To him, Damon boasts, belong also the "golden fleece" he shears from the closes and hay that is richer than any shepherd's wool.

Damon's wit conceals a difference; he does not really own the ground he uncovers, nor the golden fleece, nor the hay in which he claims to be "richer far" than his rival. Yet, as Traherne might have argued, Damon possesses these things in the most meaningful way. Because of his detachment from ownership, he "discovers" what the shepherd's possessions hide from him: the land. The grass, which is so much richer than wool, belongs to him because he is capable of rightly seeing and appreciating it. Moreover, the ground he uncovers, the grass he cuts, the meadows he has mown all over the region, testify that Damon is a laborious and skillful worker who belongs to a profession at once proud (from his point of view) and shameful (from Juliana's).

Had Juliana accepted Damon's gifts, which represent a way of imagining more than anything intrinsically valuable, and had she accepted his suit, he might have shown her some of those unexpected natural beauties that he possesses without owning:

> The deathless Fairyes take me oft
> To lead them in their Danses soft;
> And, when I tune my self to sing,
> About me they contract their Ring.
>
> (61-64)

Damon has proven himself capable of coming to terms with Adam's curse in the time-honored way: by accepting the labor to which he is condemned and performing it gladly and well. The usual hardships of the rural worker, who must rise with the dawn and work all day under a hot sun, Damon converts into sensuous pleasures, into baths of dew and gentle lickings of a sun happy to serve him. To the burden of Adam's curse, however, is added the burden of unrequited love, with which he is less capable of dealing. Therefore Damon has fallen from proud independence into inward suffering and despair:

> How happy might I still have mow'd,
> Had not Love here his Thistles sow'd!
> But now I all the day complain,
> Joyning my labour to my Paine;
> And with my Sythe cut down the Grass.
>
> (65-69)

So infected is Damon by love that even his mowing fails him, and his scythe, no longer firmly under control, cuts into his ankle and brings him down. For this second, individual fall, brought about by unhappy passion, there is no cure so long as the lover embraces his wounds and refuses to change. Damon the Mower expects to die, a victim, we might say, of cross-cultural ambitions and intermodal despair.

By portraying a figure who gains contentment through labor well-performed rather than through ease, clearly Marvell is working in a georgic mode. Because the other Mower poems present the Mower after hours or too overcome by love to work, they do not stress labor. Nevertheless they reinforce the theme that Damon appreciates natural beauty and is closely attuned with wild nature. By doing so, Marvell engineers something of a reversal on the usual contrast between pastoral and georgic. Although pastoral ordinarily stresses the natural landscape and georgic the human, in terms of literary so-phistication and social purpose pastoral is really the more artificial mode. So the protagonist moves against a back-ground of natural innocence in "The Mower to the Glo-Worms," and, in "The Mower against Gardens," Marvell adds to the recognized theme of nature against art the related theme of ownership against free appreciation. The garden is an enclosure, within which luxurious man has imposed his perverse fancies, thus committing a sin that arises in part from ownership of what should be wild and free. Because the Mower (like Marvell) owns no land, his is the freedom of nature herself. To him belongs the entire countryside: the "sweet Fields," the "wild and fragrant Innocence" of "willing Nature," the "*Fauns* and *Faryes*," even "The *Gods* them-selves." They belong to him because he does not try to hedge them about or own them.

This unpossessive enjoyment of the landscape has for a close parallel that passage of the *Georgics* so often converted to pastoral in the seventeenth century—the one beginning "O fortunatos nimium" (2.458-512). There Virgil contrasts the husbandman's happy lot with life in the city and at court, where men are burdened by their possessions, ambitions, and anxieties. His labors have earned him a richer reward than theirs, for he has broad domains: caves, lakes, valleys, a whole countryside he is free to enjoy, though he own but a small part of it. He hears the lowing cattle, he wanders in the woods, he is acquainted with Pan and Sylvanus. Still, Marvell's mower goes beyond Virgil in this direction; he is untouched even by a farmer's cares—or by his greed, to which Virgil freely admits. Damon the Mower has no wife, no children, not even an ox or a sheep; until he is brought down by his entanglement with Juliana he is free, solitary, uncommitted. Thus, by taking for his central figure not a small farmer or a gentleman landowner but an independent laborer, Marvell extends the georgic mode in a fashion that will rarely be seen again in English poetry until the time of Wordsworth.[56] While in Marvell's hands georgic proves as subtle a tool as pastoral for investigating mental states, it enables him to modify those private concerns and to give them a different social and political context.

"Upon Appleton House" (c. 1651) is generally assigned to the sub-genre of country-house poetry, a kind in which high quality makes up for small quantity.[57] Recent criticism recognizes that the country-house poem changed over the course of the century in response to evolving social and political conditions. The ideal that Jonson portrays in "To Penshurst" is no longer tenable as tensions increase and the Civil War breaks out. The pastoral paradise gives way to Carew's image of Saxham as an ark amid the flood or a warm shelter against outer cold and darkness. Herrick's Endymion Porter, though he works no harder than Sir Robert Sidney or Sir Robert Wroth, must keep an eye on his georgic assets, while they could spend their time hawking and hunting. Even as the century began, Jonson was looking backward with nostalgia, hoping, as Geoffrey Walton has argued, to persuade his aristocratic readers to behave more aristocratically and to renew

[56] As Raymond Williams points out (pp. 86-95), sympathetic but gloomy views of rural labor may be found in poems by George Crabbe and Stephen Duck—himself originally a thresher.

[57] See G. R. Hibbard's classic essay, "The Country House Poem of the Seventeenth Century," *Journal of the Warburg and Courtauld Institute*, 19 (1956), 159-74; and William Alexander McClung, *The Country House in English Renaissance Poetry* (Berkeley: Univ. of California Press, 1977). Mary Ann C. McGuire, "The Cavalier Country-House Poem: Mutations on a Jonsonian Tradition," *Studies in English Literature*, 19 (1979), 93-108, notes how social and political forces may relate to transformations in poetic vision.

a time when the English gentry lived on and governed their estates instead of flocking irresponsibly to court.[58] Jonson carefully disguises the origins of the Sidney fortunes as well as Sir Robert's current financial difficulties, which have more to do with Westminster than with Derbyshire. Jonson's economics are consciously old-fashioned: so far as possible, he portrays the estate workers and tenants as people on holiday and as happy members of an extended family in a fading feudal tradition. As it was for Martial and Horace, Jonson's highest ideal is economic self-sufficiency, in which fruits, fish, and game spring up naturally and flow with ease toward the manorial board, whence they are generously dispensed to servants and visiting poets. We are not encouraged to picture Sir Robert toting up his quarterly accounts or sending cartloads of produce to market in order to pay off his heavy debts.

Quite otherwise, as we have seen, is the state of affairs portrayed in Herrick's poetry. Marvell too gives us glimpses of another, more modern economic universe, in which laborers work for hire and the latest techniques of New Husbandry may be casually introduced into the landscape. Unlike Herrick, Marvell was receptive to such developments and generally casts an approving eye on them. Far from pretending that the Fairfaxes have always lived at Nun Appleton, for example—though their tenure was in fact much longer than the Sidneys' had been at Penshurst—Marvell boasts that they have lived there for what he makes seem a relatively short time, and that they have wrested the place from outdated and inefficient predecessors. The house itself has just been rebuilt. In this country-house poem, virtue resides less in tradition and continuity—represented at Penshurst by the oak planted at the birth of Sir Philip Sidney and by Gamage's Grove—than in continued progress toward a better state of things, represented by the transformative power of General Fairfax's deeds.

[58] "The Tone of Ben Jonson's Poetry," in his *Metaphysical to Augustan* (London: Bowes & Bowes, 1955), pp. 23-44. On Sidney's financial problems, see J.C.A. Rathmell, "Jonson, Lord Lisle, and Penshurst," *English Literary Renaissance*, 1 (1971), 250-60.

There is a Fairfacian oak too, but its future growth will be assured only by the performance of more resolute deeds of the kind that have built and maintained the estate—therefore, by the judicious marriage of Maria, as a new Isabel Thwaites, to a "Fairfax" of another line.

All three Virgilian modes have some part in this dynastic poem. The epic strain refers chiefly to the past and to the wished-for future, in which Fairfax's descendants will emerge once more to play an active role in shaping their world. The pastoral strain centers on the theme of Nun Appleton as a *locus amoenus*, a place of retreat from the cares of the world, to which Lord Fairfax has retired to plant his gardens. Here— and in a possibly monitory parallel, the poet's retreat into the woods—Marvell at once admires and mocks the theme of pastoral ease and psychological regression into privacy and self-concern. Fairfax has resigned his great responsibilities at the bidding of his conscience, exchanging military rule for "These five imaginary Forts" (349-50). It is a pleasant conceit to turn guns into flowers and soldiers into bees, yet, ominously, another, grimmer transformation is taking place in the outer world: "War all this doth overgrow: / We Ord'nance Plant and Powder sow" (343-44). Marvell cannot quite fault Fairfax for obeying his conscience, yet he reveals his subtle disapproval of a virtue that turns inward and refuses to act in the world. His ambivalent judgment is embodied in a complex and precise image of interior husbandry:

> For he did, with his utmost Skill,
> *Ambition* weed, but *Conscience* till.
> *Conscience*, that Heaven-nursed Plant,
> Which most our Earthly Gardens want.
> A prickling leaf it bears, and such
> As that which shrinks at ev'ry touch;
> But Flowrs eternal, and divine,
> That in the Crowns of Saints do shine.
> (353-60)

Given Marvell's position of complete dependence, it is hard to see how he can criticize his patron more directly; yet the way the plant of conscience "shrinks at ev'ry touch" seems excessive. Usually Protestants countenanced only temporary withdrawals from responsibility. To retire permanently into make-believe gardens, however innocent in themselves, is little different from the false leisure of the Cistercian nuns. That Fairfax's descendants may one day emerge to take his place is an odd excuse for a man of proven abilities in the prime of life to grow flowers when his country needs him.

In contrast to the diminutive pastoral played out among the flowery forts are the georgic scenes that follow. Echoes of the Exodus from Egypt and of civil turmoil in England—events that Puritans customarily linked—have often been noted. But what do they mean? Marvell presents the reader with a visual masque in four scenes. First we see the water-meadows below the hill; the grass is so tall and rich that men are lost in it like divers in a sea. Then, in a scenic transformation like those effected by Inigo Jones's "Engines strange," the "tawny Mowers enter" like Israelites into a "green Sea," which divides on either hand (385-92). Marvell combines suggestions of sacred purpose with images of brutality as he depicts the husbandmen at their work:

> With whistling Sithe, and Elbow strong,
> These Massacre the Grass along:
> While one, unknowing, carves the *Rail*
> Whose yet unfeather'd Quils her fail.
> The Edge all bloody from its Breast
> He draws, and does his stroke detest.
>
> (393-98)

Yet the harvest must continue and this conscience-stricken mower get on with his job. In the end, the field is "quilted ore with Bodies slain," and the women who pile up the mown grass are like pillagers (423-25). Yet, as the workers celebrate their deeds in triumphant dance, their victory turns back again to primal innocence; their sweat smells like Alexander's, and that of their women is "fragrant as the Mead / Which they in *Fairy Circles* tread" (429-30). If Fairfax is the poem's most important reader, Marvell seems to be telling him that he should pay more attention to business and less to idle pleasures. He should attend to the business of his estate as well as its gardens and also to that other business that should concern him most, war and government. If a blood price must be paid for getting in the harvest and completing the foundation of the new commonwealth, then it is even more important for the best workers not to shrink from the task because of overtender consciences.

Another change of scene brings in the grazing cattle, who thriftily consume the stubble and dung the soil. Marvell emphasizes the levelness of the ground after the covering grass has been cut:

> A levell'd space, as smooth and plain,
> As Clothes for *Lilly* stretcht to stain . . .
>   this naked equal Flat,
> Which *Levellers* take Pattern at.
>   (443-44, 449-50)

Perhaps Levellers might take their example from this scene not only because it is flat but because the "Villagers in common" (451) make use of their vested rights to graze the commons after the meadow grass has been harvested for Fairfax. Thus they assert a just degree of equality with their landlord, and a beneficial balance is struck between old rights and new, the best of old and more recent agricultural practices. What the modern reader may take for a natural scene, however, is as likely as not artificial. In *The English Improver* (1649), Walter Blith stresses the importance of leveling water-meadows that are to be "floated" (pp. 19-[36]). "A Labourer with a Spade upon this wrought Land, will doe abundance in a day; but be most Exact, and curious, in Levelling thy Land, it brings more Advantages then thou art aware of, or I have time to shew" (p. 34). When a meadow is floated, it is advantageous to let the water run over the submerged fields as long as possible, depositing silt and nutrients from the river; but, as experience showed, too great a depth of water would kill the grass (by depriving its roots of oxygen). Therefore a

flat, level meadow could be floated to much better effect than
an uneven one, and it was worth a landlord's while to make
it flat by plowing, harrowing, and spading it.

In the final scene of Marvell's georgic masque, "*Denton* sets
ope its *Cataracts*" (466). Denton is the name of a village
upstream, not of the river, and as Ann Berthoff argues, the
flooding is not a natural catastrophe but a deliberate act.[59]
The cataracts in question are floodgates, and it is precisely
such floating of the water-meadows in previous years that has
produced the deep, lush grass that Marvell shows us in his
opening scene. Later, as the water recedes, Marvell notes how
it leaves the blank canvas of the meadows "fresher dy'd." He
calls the river a "little *Nile*," not only because it floods but
because it brings fertility. It was customary to let in the waters
when they were richest with silt, a fact that Marvell also notes.
As it recedes, the stream is "yet muddy" before reverting to
its usual crystalline clarity (625-40). Kerridge shows that the
use of this particular agricultural technique had been devel-
oped in most regions of England only during the past gen-
eration or two, so it would still seem novel. Its revolutionary
effect on stabilizing and increasing food supplies has been
remarked on above in chapter 4.[60]

Then what does the flood signify? Berthoff rejects the usual
view that it is a natural catastrophe reflecting the disasters of
the Civil War, and finds no irony in Marvell's descriptive
phrase, "these pleasant Acts" (465). She passes off the par-
adoxical stanza that follows, in which boats sail over bridges,
eels bellow in the ox, and fish climb the stables, as no more
than a "fireworks display" of "fancifulness" to celebrate the
floating, which should amuse the reader (p. 178). Yet Mar-
vell's vivid picture of portentously unnatural events is too
similar to the frontispiece of Thomas Jordan's *The World
Turn'd Upside Down* (1647) for the resemblance to be co-
incidental. Like that work, it embodies a metaphor for the

---

[59] On Denton, see Margoliouth, pp. 231-32, Berthoff, p. 159.
[60] For Kerridge, see ch. 4, n. 28.

Civil War that was popular in Royalist and Neutralist circles. At the time he was tutoring Maria Fairfax, however, Marvell was neither a Royalist nor a Neutralist, and as recent work has shown perhaps he never was during the Interregnum.[61] Marvell himself gives us the essential clue, for he begins the stanza with a disclaimer: "Let others tell the *Paradox*" (473). In other words, let those who fail to understand the true nature of the Civil War or who object to floating water-meadows[62]— over which, after all, contrary to the wild imagery, the water is only a few inches deep—let them be scandalized or fearful. Marvell and Fairfax know better. Denton opened the gates and brought on the flood, presumably on Fairfax's orders, since he inherited the town from Isabella Thwaites. As the two of them watch the unfolding of these technological wonders, perhaps from a boat, such is the lesson that Marvell would teach, when he suggests that the flood is a message from Denton, which, "jealous of its *Lords* long stay, / . . . try's t'invite him thus away" (469-70).

We may speculate further. When Marvell retreats into the woods later in the poem—self-indulgently, some critics think—he does so only for a time. While he is there, he learns the Hewel's lesson: rotten and idle oaks are cut down. The summons from Denton might well be interpreted by Fairfax as a call to duty. The Puritan general shares with his daughter's tutor the knowledge that what seems to others sheer bloody confusion and natural disaster is, in fact, purposeful, providential, and ultimately beneficial, for he himself is a prime

---

[61] See esp. Nicholas Guild, "The Contexts of Marvell's Early 'Royalist' Poems," and Gerard Reedy, S.J., " 'An Horatian Ode' and 'Tom May's Death,' " both in *SEL*, 20 (1980), pp. 125-36, 137-51.

[62] See Blith's *English Improver*: "The second Prejudice is against that great Improvement by floating Lands, which exposeth the Improver to Suit of Law for Turning a Watercourse . . . Although the improvement be ten fold greater than the Prejudice can be, and the Advantage be as Publique and farre more than the others pretended losse can be" (A2ᵛ). Presumably Fairfax has reached an accommodation agreeable to the villagers who have grazing rights on the commons.

shaper of events. Against the wasting of time in pastoral gardens Marvell sets the energetic use of time in georgic meadows. Labor and skill are needed, and the determination to use the most efficient methods to raise and bring in the life-giving harvest. A mower, glancing down to find his scythe edged with innocent blood, may well blanch, but if he refuses to press on until he has won the victory, that bloodshed will have been in vain. The poem closes with the promise of Maria's future wedding, with the return of the salmon-fishers from their labors, and with the retirement of poet and reader under night's dark hemisphere. Appleton House still is "*Paradice's only Map*," but the rude world threatens and Fairfax ought to be defending, maintaining, and spreading his Eden, not sitting at leisure while he awaits the appearance of a hypothetical heir a generation hence.

In his poems to Cromwell, the man who replaced Fairfax as the army's leader, Marvell gives a central place to the georgic activities of planting and building. It was characteristic of the poet who wrote not only "The Mower against Gardens" but also "The Garden," however, that among those georgic-spirited poems Marvell produced a piece of sharply anti-georgic rhetoric. In "The Character of *Holland*" (c. 1653), Marvell makes full use of what he must have presumed to be his audience's conservative antipathy to what may be called bourgeois georgic:

> Not who first sees the *rising Sun* commands,
> But who could first discern the *rising Lands*.
> Who best could know to pump an Earth so leak
> Him they their *Lord* and *Country's Father* speak.
> To make a *Bank* was a great *Plot of State*;
> Invent a *Shov'l* and be a *Magistrate*.
> Hence some small *Dyke-grave* unperceiv'd invades
> The *Pow'r*, and grows as 'twere a *King of Spades*. . . .
> Nor can Civility there want for *Tillage*,
> Where wisely for their *Court* they chose a *Village*.

How fit a Title clothes their *Governours*,
Themselves the *Hogs* as all their Subjects *Bores*!
(43-50, 77-80)

Like Milton, Marvell was not averse to seizing on an issue that happened to be much dearer to his audience than to himself in order to strengthen the rhetorical force of his polemics. Here we see Marvell doing his worst in that direction. Still, for many thoughtful Englishmen there was something about the Dutch War that was troubling, because they knew they were fighting against Protestant brothers in the cause of commercial rivalry. They were fighting, indeed, against precisely what they themselves wished to be. The honors that Hollanders paid to agricultural improvement, at which Marvell invites his readers to scoff, were at that very moment inviting the admiration of Hartlib and the imitation of innovative English farmers. Those who were imbued with the spirit of Francis Bacon would have thought it no bad thing if their magistrates were to be chosen from among the inventors of shovels and the drainers of fens. In years to come, England would reject James for Dutch William and be perfectly content, if politely amused, to be ruled by a king known as Farmer George.

That Marvell was consciously making use of an old antigeorgic prejudice and was not simply its unthinking victim is suggested by the fact that he was already moving in the progressive circles to which Milton and Hartlib belonged (although his suit to become Milton's assistant was deferred that same year) and is confirmed in all three of the Cromwell poems. In "An *Horatian* Ode" (1650), Marvell depicts Cromwell as a warrior who has risen to his post of responsibility from a country estate, in the old Roman manner (29-32). His is the role of founder, architect, and builder as well as military protector of the state. By "industrious Valour" he has "cast the Kingdome old / Into another Mold" (35-36) and has assured, by the king's execution, that this new Roman Capitol will endure (65-72). As Cromwell returns victorious from Ire-

288

land, Marvell portrays him at his moment of triumph in a georgic guise:

> He to the *Commons Feet* presents
> A *Kingdome*, for his first years rents.
>
> (85-86)

Although Spenser depicted Queen Elizabeth as a warrior knight in *The Faerie Queene*, he would scarcely have dared portray her or her most important advisers as tenant farmers bringing in the rent. But times had changed, and Cromwell, we need not doubt, found Marvell's commercial image no more demeaning than the falcon simile that follows it, as an emblem of fierce dignity under self-restraint. A year earlier, after all, Milton had addressed Cromwell in Sonnet 16 as the hero who has "plough'd" his "glorious way" to eminence, and he too means no disrespect.

In "The First Anniversary" (1655), Marvell continues to speak of Cromwell as an architect and a builder. With miraculous efficiency, the Lord Protector can "rig a Navy" while his subjects are dressing themselves, "And ere we Dine, rase and rebuild their State" (351-52). The Commonwealth was like a pile of stubborn stones, each contending to rise to the "highest Place," and it was Cromwell who gave order to the building (75-86). Marvell emphasizes both the difficulty of the labor and Cromwell's metaphorical role as a builder with hands as well as prime architect:

> Choosing each Stone, and poysing every weight,
> Trying the Measures of the Bredth and Height;
> Here pulling down, and there erecting New,
> Founding a firm State by Proportions true.
>
> (243-48)

Such imagery is biblical as well as Classical, and the two strains were readily compatible.[63] But whereas some Puritans tended

---

[63] On the use of biblical building imagery, see Annabel Patterson, *Marvell and the Civic Crown* (Princeton: Princeton Univ. Press, 1978), pp. 76-77; and more generally, Stanley Fish, *The Living Temple: George Herbert and*

to draw from the Bible the lesson that the Temple must not be built with human hands, Marvell proposes the opposite lesson. Granted that Cromwell and his associate builders are the instruments of providence, nevertheless they are given an active and energetic role to perform in the transformation of the state. Marvell's is a God who permits men to participate in making history.

In "The First Anniversary" as in "Upon Appleton House," a flood appears as a transforming force with both political and agricultural implications. When divine providence sent the biblical flood, its effect was to renew the face of the earth and to usher in a new age of agricultural prosperity. Marvell alludes to such traditional readings of the Noah story when he shows the flood of civil war receding to leave Cromwell as the ruling "Husbandman" of a transformed England:

> Thou, and thine House, like *Noah's* Eight did rest,
> Left by the Wars Flood on the Mountains crest:
> And the large Vale lay subject to thy Will,
> Which thou but as an Husbandman wouldst Till.
>
> (283-86)

Thus Marvell shows Cromwell taking up that same georgic role which he had offered Fairfax four years earlier, and which Fairfax had declined. The passage captures in biblical imagery the moment of pause and transformation, as the epic warrior hero becomes a georgic hero. This anniversary celebration—

Catechizing (Berkeley: Univ. of California Press, 1978), pp. 54-89. As Fish shows, the Calvinist emphasis is on building the temple "without hands," while on the other side Royalists were more likely to stress the supervision than the actual building. Thus, in "Upon His *Majesties* repairing of *Pauls*" (1645), Waller reserves his praise for Charles I: "He like *Amphion* makes those quarries leap / Into fair figures from a confus'd heap: / For in his art of Regiment is found / A power like that of harmony in sound" (11-14). Such an "art of Regiment" is essentially a Royalist concept, analogous to the king's power when observing a masque or the landlord's power when treading his grounds. Waller simply ignores the difficulties of the labor and the parts played by the quarrymen, bargemen, stonecutters, hoist operators, and other workers whose hands actually shaped and conveyed the stones from the quarry to their places in the renovated cathedral.

written at the crest of Puritan interest in agricultural reform, as exemplified by the publications of the Hartlib circle—marks a high point in Marvell's hopes for a georgic reformation of England.

By the time of Cromwell's death, the planting and building had obviously come to a halt, and it must be that Marvell, like Milton, was discouraged by the failure of successive governments to put the ideals of the Good Old Cause into practice. In "A Poem upon the Death of O. C." (1658), Marvell seems to skirt the use of architectural imagery, comparing the dead hero not to Solomon, the Temple builder, but to David dancing before the Ark (242), and not to the builders of the Roman Capitol but to Mars breaking down the double gate of Janus (234). Otherwise he would presumably have been forced to admit that the stones of Cromwell's state had not been truly laid and were beginning to fall to the ground. But Marvell had briefly introduced another kind of georgic imagery into "The First Anniversary," comparing Cromwell to a laborer and to an olive tree (from Oliver) who has "anointed" the brambles with his "Oyl" (259-60), as well as to a vine-grower (287-88). In the "Death of O. C.," Marvell expands on this imagery. The state is like a vine, one of whose branches has been pruned "by an untimely knife":

> The Parent-Tree unto the Grief succeeds,
> And through the Wound its vital humour bleeds;
> Trickling in watry drops, whose flowing shape
> Weeps that it falls ere fix'd into a Grape.
> So the dry Stock, no more that spreading Vine,
> Frustrates the Autumn and the hopes of Wine.
>   (95-100)

We may think that the lines illustrate Marvell's political acumen as well as the conventional exaggerations of elegiac lament. The metaphor, especially when Marvell portrays the vine of state as a "shady tent" (91) beneath which men may sit, is biblical; but the death of the vine may well have been inspired by Virgil's *Georgics* and its warning not to set iron prematurely to the young shoots.

Cromwell's death is like the interruption of a harvest, as the sap drips to the ground, never to be transformed into wine. Marvell picks up that image when he compares the disorders of the state to a great georgic storm, which brings thunder and powerful winds that undo all of the farmers' careful work:

> Out of the Binders Hand the Sheaves they tore,
> And thrash'd the Harvest in the airy floore;
> Or of huge Trees, whose growth with his did rise,
> The deep foundations open'd to the Skyes.
>
> (117-20)

Here too Marvell's reference is both Virgilian and biblical. The apocalyptic harvest that such optimistic Puritans as Milton had seen ripening about them in the England of the 1640s had yet to produce its first real fruits. Now it appears that, owing to some "secret Cause" (101) that can be attributed only to the providential will, the entire effort of plowing, planting, and tending the fields of transplanted Israel may be aborted and brought to nothing. The proper georgic response (which Marvell was in fact to take) is to put aside discouragement and begin working all over again, taking providential setbacks not as final rebukes but as tests of the will. The poem concludes on the most favorable note possible: perhaps Richard Cromwell may finish the work his father started. Perceiving the heir's relative weakness, Marvell tries to make the best even of that in a concluding georgic metaphor:

> Cease now our griefs, calme peace succeeds a war,
> Rainbows to storms, Richard to Oliver.
> Tempt not his clemency to try his pow'r,
> He threats no deluge, yet foretells a showre.
>
> (321-24)

For the shattering storm that now represents Cromwell as well as the effects of his death, Richard substitutes the mild

292

showers of life-giving rain. If only the English can refrain from trying his weakness, there may yet be a harvest. But it cannot be said that the poet sounds very hopeful.

Although Marvell never wholly commits himself to the georgic mode nor dismisses the pastoral, nevertheless he effects some remarkable reversals of conventional practice. In the Mower poems he demonstrates that a working hero can be as sensitive to beauty or to the mind's inwardness as any hero of pastoral, while possessing an independence and an energy that most pastoral heroes lack. In "Upon Appleton House" he introduces a georgic masque in which farm laborers dance a peasant triumph and uphold a vision of the social norms quite unlike any masque performed before the Stuart kings. Theirs are the transformations not of royal magic but of human labor reinforced by the technical ingenuity of the New Husbandry. Finally, in Cromwell, Marvell portrays a hero who is unafraid of work. He is the founder, the architect, the builder with his own hands of a transformed state. At his death, the vine of the New Israel in England withers and the harvest is lost; yet it is not too late for other men to rebuild and replant. They need only read the meaning of events truly and bring to them the right georgic spirit.

With his typically Elizabethan interest in matters of utility, Drayton could not refrain from discoursing briefly on the subject of gardening tools in *Poly-Olbion*, yet he felt obliged to apologize afterward for that breach of his readers' sensibility. During the half-century that followed, georgic came a long way from such tentative beginnings. From the bitter complaints of Laudian satirists, through the energetic quarrels between Puritans and Cavaliers, to the subtle maturing of theme and technique in the poems of Herrick and Marvell, the mode developed as an instrument capable of increasing range, sensitivity, and power. Not only did poets grow more capable of understanding Virgil's middle poem as something very different from his eclogues; by ceasing to transform it unwittingly and repetitively into familiar pastoral patterns they became newly capable of transforming it consciously and vigorously into new georgic forms appropriate to the new age. At length, Milton would fulfill what Spenser first undertook, and bring English georgic to its fullest potential.

The Civil War polarized men's attitudes, so that we may say with some accuracy that for a time Puritans favored georgic and Cavaliers opposed it. Yet Lovelace and Benlowes wrote georgic poetry, Cotton tried to write it, and Herrick has as good a claim to stand in the central tradition of English georgic as Marvell.[64] None of them were Puritans. Nor do the alternative terms that political historians currently find useful, court and country, work any better. Because the georgic mode tended to attach itself to the New Husbandry and therefore to the social and economic consequences of that revolutionary development—which include the abolition of feudal obligations, the increase of labor for hire, and the expansion of the economic marketplace—reformers and progressive thinkers were among its foremost advocates. Most of those who were of a conservative cast of mind simply railed against it; others, more subtle and adaptable in their thinking, came to terms with georgic and proceeded to turn it in new directions more favorable to their beliefs and purposes. A lover views his lady's glove in terms of tenant law instead of feudal obligation; a country gentleman incorporates the mowers' varicose veins into his religious meditations; and a country vicar finds it as pleasant to walk the bounds as to play on a shepherd's pipes. Doubtless many Puritans were meanwhile going out to marl their fields, leaving the field of poetry to the Cavaliers. Yet even the violence of the Royalist attack on georgic probably helped spread its appeal among those unknown readers of poems published between 1640 and 1660. After all, as the Mill Horse observed, encouragement can be drawn from such onslaughts:

---

[64] Because Lovelace represents his time so well, I have distributed discussion of his poems into several sections; the reader may get some sense of his important contribution to georgic poetry by piecing together the fragments.

it is *Prince-like* (if well understood)
To be ill-spoken off for doing good. . . .
Scorn is a burthen laid on good men still,
Which they must beare, as I do Sackes to Mill.

In the transformation of Royalist attacks from good-humored contempt to shocked outrage and then to outright fear and loathing, we may read those large changes that were underway throughout the English countryside of the 1650s.

SEVEN

Milton and the Georgic Ideal

MILTON'S FAMILIARITY with the *Georgics* is confirmed by the seventy or so verbal allusions to it in his poetry, which about equal his allusions to the *Eclogues*. His life as well as his poetry embodied the Virgilian virtues of long labor, heroism involving painstaking daily care instead of decisive military battle, and unflagging dedication to one's people and civilization. Milton uses the word "labor" over and over in his works. In a direct echo of Virgil, he has Lancelot Andrewes find rest in heaven from "duro . . . labore" (Elegy 3.64). In "The Passion" Jesus is tried by "labours huge and hard" (13-14). The Lady of Sonnet 9 is encouraged to "labour up the Hill of heav'nly Truth." The prose writings too are full of the theme of labor. In Prolusion 5, Milton recognizes Roman preeminence in laboriousness:

> The Romans, once upon a time masters of the world, attained the highest reach of empire, such as neither Assyrian magnitude nor Macedonian valor were ever able to approach. . . . Jupiter himself . . . gave it reluctantly, accompanied by unceasing warfare [*assidua bella*] and by tedious toil [*longos labores*], seeking to find out, I believe, whether the Romans alone might appear worthy to perform the duties of great Jove among mortals. . . .
>
> You have wondered sufficiently, my listeners, why I have mentioned all these things: now give heed. As often as I call up these matters and run them over in my mind, so often do I contemplate how great are the forces engaged in the struggle to uphold Truth, how great the zeal of all, how great the watchfulness demanded.[1]

[1] *The Works of John Milton*, ed. Frank A. Patterson et al., 18 vols. (New

In Prolusion 7 Milton takes farming for his model:

> Nothing is more excellent than art, and nothing also requiring more labor: nothing more sluggish than we, nothing more negligent. We permit ourselves to be outstripped by laborers and farmers in nightly and early morning toil. They are more unwearied in humble matters for common nourishment, than we in most noble matters for an abounding life. (12:273-75)

A familiar passage in *Areopagitica* couples labor and warfare in characteristically Virgilian and Miltonic fashion:

> When a man hath bin labouring the hardest labour in the deep mines of knowledge, hath furnisht out his findings in all their equipage, drawn forth his reasons as it were a battell raung'd, scatter'd and defeated all objections in his way, calls out his adversary into the plain, offers him the advantage of wind and sun, if he please; only that he may try the matter by dint of argument, for his opponents then to sculk, to lay ambushments, to keep a narrow bridge of licensing ... though it be valour anough in shouldiership, is but weaknes and cowardise in the wars of Truth. (4:347-48)

Valor is very well, though it did not get the Macedonians as far as laboriousness got the Romans; but for Milton true valor in matters of mind and spirit must consist less in sudden and surprising action than in long preparation and incessant application to the task at hand. (An associative connection with Virgil is suggested when, in his next sentence, Milton alludes to the *Georgics*.)

Milton appreciated the value of literal georgic activity in improving one's people and nation. He writes in *Of Education*, which he addresses to Hartlib, chief propagator at that time of the ideal in England: "[H]ere will be an occasion of

---

York: Columbia Univ. Press, 1931-40), 12:191-95. Unless otherwise indicated, all Milton's works are quoted from this edition; poetry is cited by (book and) line number, prose by volume and page number.

inciting and inabling them hereafter to improve the tillage of their Country, to recover the bad Soil, and to remedy the waste that is made of good: for this was one of *Hercules* praises." Speaking like a good Baconian and citing many of the very professions mentioned in Virgil's Jupiter theodicy, Milton also recommends calling on the "helpful experiences of Hunters, Fowlers, Fishermen, Shepherds, Gardeners, . . . Architects, Engineers, Mariners, Anatomists." Such practical studies will make "facil and pleasant" "those Poets which are now counted most hard," including "the rural part of *Virgil*" (4:282-84). That Milton should mention Virgil at this point is not surprising, since his plan to train the nation's future leaders in nation-building activities reflects the very essence of the georgic spirit.

Just once in his life, Milton took an anti-georgic stance—goaded, apparently, into an uncharacteristic position by resentment or amusement at his college nickname, "the Lady of Christ's":

> But why do I seem to those fellows insufficiently masculine? . . . Doubtless it was because I was never able to gulp down huge bumpers in pancratic fashion; or because my hand has not become calloused by holding the plowhandle; or because I never lay down on my back under the sun at mid-day, like a seven-year ox-driver; perhaps in fine, because I never proved myself a man in the same manner as these gluttons. (12:241)[2]

More characteristic is his determination, stated in Prolusion 7, "to strive earnestly after that true reputation by long and severe toil, rather than to snatch a false reputation by a hurried and premature mode of expression" (12:249). Of course, it may be argued that literary labor is not the same thing as

---

[2] We should not underestimate the comedy as well as the possible resentment in these insults, since Milton had been elected to preside at an undergraduate lark; see Roslyn Richeck, "Thomas Randolph's *Salting* (1627), Its Text, and John Milton's Sixth Prolusion as Another Salting," *English Literary Renaissance*, 12 (1982), 103-131.

manual labor. Milton recognized the distinction and confronted it in a manner that has more to do with Christian dedication than with aristocratic pride: "[E]ase and leisure was given thee for thy retired thoughts," he reminds himself in *The Reason of Church-government* (1641), "out of the sweat of other men" (3:232). Therefore he laid aside his cherished poetic plans for twenty years in order to join "the unwearied labours" of the Church's true servants and repay the moral debt.

In *An Apology for Smectymnuus* (1642), Milton reminds his readers that he has already told them why "I thought not my selfe exempted from associating with good men in their labours toward the Churches wellfare." He is indignant not only at his opponent's charge that he is a haunter of theaters and bordellos but also that he is lazy. To the contrary, he is "up, and stirring, in winter often ere the sound of any bell awake men to labour," and he strongly believes that "usefull and generous labours" strengthen the body and make for a healthy balance of body and mind (3:289, 298-99). In *Areopagitica* (1644), he speaks of his long preparations to be a poet as "the industry of a life wholly dedicated to studious labours" (4:296). One reason for rejecting censorship is that it would be intolerable for a licenser "who never knew the labour of book-writing" to condemn at one "hasty view" the work of "years," produced with great "industry," "midnight watchings," and "expence of *Palladian* oyl" (4:324-25). In the *Second Defense* (1654), Milton feels called on once more to explain why he has dedicated his life to labors of the mind: "For, if I avoided the toils and the perils of war, it was only that I might earnestly toil for my fellow-citizens in another way, with much greater utility, and with no less peril" (8:9). His friend Henry Oldenburg, the agent for Bremen, apparently questioned whether the *Second Defense* was worth the great effort Milton expended on it. In a letter of July 6, 1654, Milton replied that there is no labor more noble than "the vindication of Liberty." "An idle ease has never had charms for me," he goes on: "I am far from thinking that I have spent my toil

... on matters of inferior consequence" (12:65). Although Milton sometimes indicates that he finds writing polemical prose more irksome and trivial than writing poetry, he nowhere suggests that hard work is not needed for both. Particularly in *Areopagitica* but elsewhere as well, he speaks about a lifetime of dedicated labor. Unlike prose, poetry might flow with unpremeditated ease, yet in Milton's view to be a true poet obviously required the most lengthy and strenuous effort of all. First came the laborious task of preparation; then, God willing, inspiration might follow.

Just as he emphasizes the "labour of book-writing," Milton also insists on the connection between labor and political freedom. *Of Reformation* (1641) argues that "every wise Nation" knows that "their Liberty consists in manly and honest labours ... and when people slacken, and fall to loosenes, and riot, then doe they as much as if they laid downe their necks for some wily Tyrant to get up and ride" (3:53). In *Areopagitica*, Milton insists that good and evil are so closely "interwoven" in this fallen world that, like "those confused seeds which were impos'd on *Psyche*," it takes "incessant labour" to distinguish them (4:310). When the shortly-expected reign of Christ begins in England, it will be brought in by human effort as well as divine providence:

> What could a man require more from a Nation so pliant and so prone to seek after knowledge. What wants there to such a towardly and pregnant soile, but wise and faithfull labourers, to make a knowing people, a Nation of Prophets, of Sages, and of Worthies. We reck'n more then five months yet to harvest; there need not be five weeks, had we but eyes to lift up, the fields are white already. (4:341)

As we have already seen in chapter 5, Milton based his views on tithes—which were the economic support of traditional church government—largely on his conviction that each man should earn his own bread in the sweat of his own face. Therefore it is not surprising that he often turns to georgic imagery in order to emphasize the importance of a working priesthood. In *Animadversions* (1641), he opposes the practice of lay patronage with images that he derives from biblical georgic.[3] What the Church needs, he argues, is not sycophantic prelates who are indebted to their patrons, but "faithfull labourers in Gods harvest, that may incessantly warn the posterity of *Dives*" (3:143). According to *The Reason of Church-government*, a contemporary priest may learn from the Apostles that "laborious teaching is the most honourable Prelaty that one Minister can have above another." Milton prophesies that, with the removal of the dead hand of prelacy, a georgic spring will come to the English Church: "[W]hen the gentle west winds shall open the fruitfull bosome of the earth thus over-girded by your imprisonment, then the flowers put forth and spring, and then the Sunne shall scatter the mists, and the manuring hand of the Tiller shall root up all that burdens the soile without thank to your bondage" (3:198, 214). Referring to St. Anselm of Canterbury's defense of the prelacy against William Rufus, Milton remarks: "He little dreamt then that the weeding-hook of reformation would after two ages pluck up his glorious poppy from insulting over the good corne" (3:208). In his enthusiasm for a georgic reformation, Milton has not only "improved" but actually reversed his primary biblical text (Matt. 13:30), which indicates that wheat and weeds will not be separated until after the harvest.[4] But there are other passages in scripture as well as in Virgil that Milton might have cited in support of his enthusiastic image.

Like Hugh Latimer, Milton complains in *An Apology* that the English bishops, as soon as they are preferred to high

---

[3] On problems of lay patronage in the English Church, see Guy Fitch Lytle, "Religion and the Lay Patron in Reformation England," in *Patronage in the Renaissance*, ed. Lytle and Stephen Orgel (Princeton: Princeton Univ. Press, 1981), pp. 65-114.

[4] On Milton's habit of "improving" biblical images in his earlier tracts, see Thomas N. Corns, *The Development of Milton's Prose Style* (Oxford: Clarendon Press, 1982), esp. p. 62.

office, usually "change the teaching labour of the word, into the unteaching ease of Lordship over consciences, and purses" (3:362). Labor is exchanged for lordship, service for rule, humility for aristocratic pride; Milton's is the familiar and by now ancient complaint of the georgic reformer. In his latest protest against tithes, *Considerations . . . to remove Hirelings out of the church* (1659), Milton returns once more to the fundamental principle: it is "infirme and absurd, that he should reap from me, who sows not to me" (6:74).

According to Milton and many of his fellow Puritans, the original sin that brought lay patronage and tithing into the Church was the infamous Donation of Constantine. Against that unhappy precedent he cites not only theologians but poets, including Dante, Petrarch, and Ariosto. Oddly, the final authority on Milton's list is "*Chaucer's* Plowman" (3:28, 44). He was relying on an apocryphal *Plowman's Tale*, thought at the time to have been written by Chaucer.[5] Milton seldom supports an argument by appealing to a fictional character; presumably he recognized in the figure of the Plowman an ancient and widely popular spokesman for social reform. When he set down his outlines for tragedies in the Trinity College Manuscript, he considered just one British story that did not have a king for its hero: "Haie the plowman who with his two sons that were at plow running to the battell that was between the Scots and Danes in the next feild staid the flight of his countrymen, renew'd the battell, and caus'd the victorie" (18:245).

The religious and political implications of Milton's interest in georgic patterns of behavior is clear. Matching Marvell's Cromwell poems is Milton's admonition in the *Second Defense*, urging the Lord Protector to lead "the people from corrupt institutions to a better plan of life and discipline . . . to watch, to foresee, to cavil at no toil [*nullum laborem re-*

---

[5] See the *Complete Prose Works of John Milton*, ed. Don M. Wolfe et al., 8 vols. (New Haven: Yale Univ. Press, 1953-82), 1:579, n.30.

cusare] ... these are those arduous things, in comparison of which war is a playgame [*hæc sunt illa ardua, præ quibus bellum ludus est*]" (8:228-29). Earlier, writing to Leonard Philaras on his efforts to bring freedom to the Greeks (June 1652), a task resembling Milton's among the English, Milton concludes: "There is, however, something else besides to be tried, and in my judgment far the most important: namely that some one should, if possible, arouse and rekindle in the minds of the Greeks ... the old Greek valour itself, the old industry, the old patience of labour [*virtutem, industriam, laborum tolerantiam*]" (12:58-59). This advice reflects Milton's priorities better than it does the virtues of Periclean Athens, which fell for want of just such steadiness as Virgil found in Hesiod.

Not all of Milton's georgic references are metaphorical. As we have noted earlier, the power of a metaphorical system depends in part on the familiarity of writer and reader with the activity on which it is based. Like Virgil, Thomas More, and Spenser, Milton recognized that farming is at the very foundation of civilization and that cultivation is fundamental to culture. That is one reason why he thought it important for students at his ideal academy to learn how to improve their country's soil and make wastelands fertile. In the *History of Britain* (1670; begun c. 1648), he associates barbarism with the failure to cultivate the land: "For it seems through lack of tillage, the Northern parts were then, as *Ireland* is at this day; and the inhabitants in like manner wonted to retire, and defend themselves in such watrie places half naked" (10:85).

Milton subscribed to the usual views of the English at his time concerning the Irish. In behalf of Cromwell's government, he wrote a series of Observations on Ormond's *Articles of Peace* (1649), which followed a period of insurrection. The twenty-second article demanded that the English repeal laws that prevented the Irish from following certain agricultural customs, which included hitching their plows to their horses' tails. In Milton's vitriolic reply we may recognize his assumption (with More and Spenser) that it is the colonizer's duty to teach the colonized civilization and improved agricultural methods, which in effect are one and the same thing:

> [A]nough if nothing else, to declare in them a disposition not onely sottish but indocible and averse from all Civility and amendment, and what hopes they give for the future, who rejecting the ingenuity of all other Nations to improve and waxe more civill by a civilizing Conquest . . . preferre their own absurd and savage Customes before the most convincing evidence of reason and demonstration: a testimony of their true Barbarisme and obdurate wilfulnesse to be expected no lesse in other matters of greatest moment. (6:245)[6]

That the Irish wish to revert to hitching their plows to their horses' tails is, Milton recognizes, trivial in itself; yet he considers their adherence to such a custom symptomatic of their lack of civilization. It is almost like the refusal of Spenser's Brigants to plow their fields, which is at the root of all their other crimes. The supposed ineptitude of the Irish in agricultural methods seems to have stuck in Milton's mind. Later in the same work he employs a curious georgic image to criticize Ormond's appeal to the Covenant: "No man well in his wits endeavoring to root up weeds out of his ground, instead of using the spade will take a Mallet or a Beetle" (6:262). Perhaps, Milton implies, an Irishman or a Scot might be ignorantly guilty of just such a practice.

For Milton, labor was the dominant mode in the life of any dedicated man or nation. From his earliest youth when, as he tells his readers in the *Second Defense*, he often stayed up until midnight reading and studying, he was by nature an admirer of the georgic ideal. Although he was raised a gentleman, he gloried in work. Yet from his earliest days he also recognized the value of leisure, not as a permanent state but as a necessary respite from labor. In the first prolusion, he

---

[6] See also *Complete Prose*, 3:303-304.

praises God for the gift of sleep, in which "we refresh and renew ... our bodies, worn and fatigued by daily labors" (12:145). In Prolusion 6, the Vacation Exercise, he argues that "the alternation of labor and pleasure is wont to banish the weariness of satiety and to bring it to pass that things neglected for a while are taken up again more eagerly" (12:205). What is true for the individual is true for nations; therefore Milton argues in *The Reason of Church-government* in behalf of a public theater: "[B]ecause the spirit of man cannot demean it selfe lively in this body without some recreating intermission of labour, and serious things, it were happy for the Common wealth, if our Magistrates, as in those famous governments of old, would take into their care, not only the deciding of our contentious Law cases and brauls, but the managing of our publick sports, and festival pastimes" (3:239). In the same spirit he finds the need for occasional relaxation an important argument for marital compatibility in *Tetrachordon* (1645):

> No mortall nature can endure either in the actions of Religion, or study of wisdome, without somtime slackning the cords of intense thought and labour: which lest we should think faulty, God himself conceals us not his own recreations before the world was built; *I was*, saith the eternall wisdome, *dayly his delight, playing alwayes before him*. ... [N]o worthy enterprise can be don by us without continuall plodding and wearisomnes to our faint and sensitive abilities. We cannot therefore alwayes be contemplative, or pragmaticall abroad, but have need of som delightfull intermissions, wherin the enlarg'd soul may leav off a while her severe schooling; and like a glad youth in wandring vacancy, may keep her hollidaies to joy and harmles pastime. (4:85-86)

Leisure is not a grudging concession to human weakness; it has divine sanction and should be enjoyed to the full in its proper time. Yet even in these humane passages Milton reveals the intensity of his dedication to labor. In this fallen world, man cannot rest in leisure forever; his primary duty is to work with all his heart, strength, and patience at whatever occupation or task God sets before him.

THE EARLY POEMS

One reason for the greatness of Milton's poetry lies in his ability to combine labor with ease and learning with grace, in a manner that other poets sometimes spoke about but seldom accomplished. Especially notable, in view of the social context, is his possession of an easy *sprezzatura* without the aristocratic contempt that normally accompanied that virtue. He had one of the sharpest tongues of his age and has often been accused of elitism. Like Shakespeare, he learned to despise the fickleness of the common people, yet he shows little prejudice anywhere in his poetry against the laborer or "mechanick." Like Marvell, Milton was not above playing on his readers' prejudices in his polemical tracts; yet his fundamental position is to favor a Pauline democracy:

> This was the breeding of S. *Paul*, though born of no mean parents, a free citizen of the Roman Empire: so little did his trade debase him, that it rather enabld him to use that magnanimitie of preaching the gospel through *Asia* and *Europe* at his own charges: thus those preachers among the poor *Waldenses*, the ancient stock of our reformation . . . bred up themselves in trades . . . that they might be no burden to the church. . . . But our ministers think scorn to use a trade, and count it the reproach of this age, that tradesmen preach the gospel. It were to be wishd that they were all tradesmen; they would not then so many of them, for want of another trade, make trade of thir preaching: and yet they clamor that tradesmen preach; and yet they preach, while they themselves are the worst tradesmen of all. (*Hirelings*; 6:80-81)

What most Church of England ministers thought about mechanic preachers we have seen in the writings of John Taylor, the Water Poet. But Milton, like Spenser, thinks no "scorn" of trade or honest work. The real shame is to debase one's office by refusing to work, trading ecclesiastical livings and relying on the labors of others. Milton himself was fortunate; but no one can say that he abused his position in life by refusing to work.

Even when Milton celebrates leisure, play, and pastoral beauty in his early poetry, he finds a place for georgic elements that most of his contemporaries would have found jarring. Milton's celebration of the morning in "L'Allegro" includes a barnyard cock and hens, the plowman, milkmaid, and the mower whetting his scythe, as well as the usual shepherds. When "neat-handed *Phillis*" has finished making dinner, she leaves in haste with Thestylis "to bind the Sheaves" (86-88). The "drudging *Goblin*" of country legend sweats at his clumsy work:

> When in one night, ere glimps of morn,
> His shadowy Flale hath thresh'd the Corn,
> That ten day-labourers could not end.
> (105-109)

There is not even a hint that Milton is patronizing these simple country storytellers and their sense of wonder at this gigantic deed; his is an imaginative and sympathetic tact for the common worker that is rare outside of satire and radical invective. Perhaps only the crazed mind of George Wither or the capacious imagination of Shakespeare could produce anything much resembling Milton's attitude here. As heirs of the eighteenth and nineteenth centuries, it is hard for modern readers to realize just how unusual—and in this respect how modern—these unobtrusive and seemingly effortless passages really are.

In Milton's masque, Comus begins a lovely pastoral description with some georgic details:

> Two such I saw, what time the labour'd Oxe
> In his loose traces from the furrow came,
> And the swink't hedger at his Supper sate.
> (290-92)

True, the aristocratic Comus describes these laborers after their work is done, in the usual fashion; yet how many poets of 1634 would have thought to include a hedger in a noble celebration? A similar note is struck by the ditcher (*fossor*) who shoots the sparrow in *Epitaphium Damonis* (101-105).

Lycidas is a pastoral elegy, but it too is uncharacteristic of its time. Its narrator wonders whether it is worth his while "with uncessant care / To tend the homely slighted Shepherds trade" (64-65), hardly a typical pastoral formulation. He is determined to "scorn delights, and live laborious dayes," and he is conscious that his behavior is quite out of the ordinary in his social milieu:

> Were it not better don as others use,
> To sport with *Amaryllis* in the shade,
> Or with the tangles of *Neæra's* hair?
> (67-72)

Certainly nine out of ten early seventeenth-century pastorals were more likely to toy with an Amaryllis than to "scorn delights and live laborious dayes." The same views are evident in St. Peter's diatribe. The false shepherds care only for a selfish pastoral *otium*: to "scramble at the shearers feast" and play "flashy songs" on their "scrannel Pipes of wretched straw." They are completely uninterested in working at their trade:

> Blind mouthes! that scarce themselves know how to hold
> A Sheep-hook, or have learn'd ought els the least
> That to the faithfull Herdmans art belongs!
> (117-24)

Pastoral in *Lycidas* is a high calling, an "art" that allows moments of leisure and of piercing beauty but requires of its shepherds a strict and laborious devotion to duty.

Epitaphium Damonis is another pastoral elegy with a considerable admixture of the georgic spirit. Thyrsis, the narrator, has been interrupted in his pursuit of a career by his friend's death; his hard task is to rededicate himself to his profession.[7] When he thinks of his friend during his Italian journey, he remembers georgic details: "Nunc canit, aut lepori nunc tendit retia Damon, / Vimina nunc texit, varios sibi quod sit in usus" (143-44); "Now Damon sings, now he sets snares for rabbits, now he intertwines osiers to serve his various needs."[8] Thyrsis, like the spokesmen in several of Virgil's eclogues, is not simply a shepherd; his activities include the georgic as well as the pastoral:

> Heu quam culta mihi priùs arva procacibus herbis
> Involvuntur, et ipsa situ seges alta fatiscit!
> Innuba neglecto marcescit et uva racemo,
> Nec myrteta juvant; ovium quoque tædet, at illæ
> Mœrent, inque suum convertunt ora magistrum.
>
> (63-67)

"Ah, how my tilth-lands, once plowed, are tangled in shameful weeds, and the tall grain gapes open with rot. The unwedded grapes wither on their neglected vine, and the myrtle groves no longer please me. The sheep too disgust me; they mope and turn their faces toward their master." Thyrsis has simply abandoned his duties under the weight of his sorrow. His has proven to be a georgic world, where men are a hard race, "durum genus" (106; see *Georgics* 1.63), where crops wither and rot if not tended, and where animals pine away and die if they are not constantly cared for. As critics have recognized, neglect is evident in the refrain—"Go home, my lambs, your master has no time for you"—but it disappears at the conclusion as Thyrsis prepares to resume his life's work.

In Sonnet 9 (1645), Milton praises an unknown young lady for shunning "the broad way and the green" in order to join

---

[7] See Janet Leslie Knedlik, "High Pastoral Art in Milton's *Epitaphium Damonis*," in *Urbane Milton: The Latin Poetry*, ed. James A. Freeman and Anthony Low, *Milton Studies*, 19 (Pittsburgh: Univ. of Pittsburgh Press, 1984), 149-63.

[8] Translations of Milton's Latin poetry are mine.

the "few" who "labour up the Hill of heav'nly Truth." She has chosen the "better part," not only with the contemplative Mary but also with the georgic Ruth. Her "care is fixt," and she zealously attends the coming of the Bridegroom with "Hope that reaps not shame." The georgic virtues Milton praises in this sonnet are precisely the ones that he strove so hard to realize in his own conduct. The moments of innocent leisure that he recommends to Lawrence and Skinner in Sonnets 20 and 21 (1655) are, we should remember, the welcome rewards of hard labor and "deep thoughts." In Sonnet 22, Milton pictures himself not as a warrior but as a steady steersman; he does not fight in behalf of liberty but labors at a "noble task." In 1655, when Milton wrote these words—a few years after he had given his remaining sight (as he thought) for the defense of England, and a few years before he was to commence work at last on the epic version of *Paradise Lost*—a Royalist poet would have considered Milton's phrase oxymoronic. To speak of a "noble task" was much the same as speaking about a "Courtly Stable."⁹ But Spenser would have judged differently.

Paradise Lost

Under the overarching epic framework of *Paradise Lost*, there is a broad movement from pastoral to georgic. The early scenes in the Garden of Eden portray Adam and Eve enjoying the true pastoral *otium*, about which the Greek and Roman poets could only dream and fable.¹⁰ The fall transforms their state. Michael's mission is to take Adam and Eve out of the garden and set them in the subjected world, where Adam's sentence is to eat bread in the sweat of his face (10.205) and "to till / The ground whence thou wast tak'n, fitter Soile" (11.261-62). As in the *Georgics*, the new order will offer

---

⁹ On the ignoble etymology and connotations of "task" see *OED*.

¹⁰ On pastoral in *Paradise Lost* (and the *Aeneid*), see John R. Knott, *Milton's Pastoral Vision* (Chicago: Univ. of Chicago Press, 1971).

compensations, such as the invention of arts, fire, and tools (11.556-73), but these will be mixed blessings. After the flood, God gives man a new covenant, not perpetual spring but the yearly round of country life:

> Day and Night,
> Seed time and Harvest, Heat and hoary Frost
> Shall hold thir course, till fire purge all things new,
> Both Heav'n and Earth, wherein the just shall dwell.
>
> (11.898-901)

Until the Last Judgment, it is man's fate to live in the world of Hesiod's *Works and Days* and Virgil's *Georgics*. Even as the angel leads Adam and Eve from the garden at the conclusion of the epic, a last simile adumbrates man's condition in history:

> as Ev'ning Mist
> Ris'n from a River o're the marish glides,
> And gathers ground fast at the Labourers heel
> Homeward returning.
>
> (12.629-32)

Milton evokes a timeless picture of georgic man in a bleak evening landscape, but he complicates the sorrow by introducing a return home from labor. For labor ends at nightfall, at death, and finally, as the covenant of the flood reminds us, at the end of time, when man will return to paradise once more.

The pattern on earth is duplicated above. Before the War in Heaven, the angels enjoy all the varied delights of pastoral life. Along with internecine strife, Satan introduces technological change to heaven through his inventions of gunpowder and the cannon. Appropriately, they both involve the immediate violation of heaven's pastoral soil in a parody of georgic activity:

> to the work they flew,
> None arguing stood, innumerable hands

Were ready, in a moment up they turnd
Wide the Celestial soile.
(6.507-510)

This initial violation of the free-bearing soil by Satan's eager
Stakhanovite followers spreads further as the war escalates
on the second day. Milton introduces a scene of transcendent
violence with two brief but poignant lines of pastoral, which
claim that the delights of country *otium*, even in prelapsarian
Eden, are only shadows of a heavenly original:

Thir Arms away they threw, and to the Hills
(For Earth hath this variety from Heav'n
Of pleasure situate in Hill and Dale) . . .
From thir foundations loosning to and fro
They pluckt the seated Hills with all thir load,
Rocks, Waters, Woods, and by the shaggie tops
Up lifting bore them in thir hands.
(6.639-46)

Homer provided Milton with the original model for this pas-
sage (*Odyssey* 2.315-16), but Milton's context is a good deal
closer to Virgil's imitation of Homer in the *Georgics* (1.276-
83). This one day's damage to the hills of heaven portends
the permanent destruction of the Mount of Paradise by the
flood (11.829-35). Merritt Y. Hughes suggests that Milton
took the phrase "horned floud" in that passage from Virgil's
description of the Po (*Georgics* 4.371);[11] I would add that
perhaps the whole passage was suggested in part by the great
storm of 1.311-34, in which flood waters carry away the
farmer's dykes and crops, while "the Father himself" dashes
down mountains with his blazing bolts.

"God Almighty," Bacon assures us, "first planted a Gar-
den."[12] It is fitting that Milton's Son, following a Virgilian
pattern, pauses for a miraculous georgic moment to repair the
damaged landscape before proceeding to his epic warfare:

[11] John Milton, *Complete Poems and Major Prose*, ed. Hughes (New York:
Odyssey Press, 1957), p. 452.
[12] *Essayes* (1625), Essay 46.

312

At his command the uprooted Hills retir'd
Each to his place, they heard his voice and went
Obsequious, Heav'n his wonted face renewd,
And with fresh Flourets Hill and Valley smil'd.
This saw his hapless Foes but stood obdur'd.

(6.781-85)

The inanimate hills obey the Son as sheep obey their shepherd, but Satan's army, rooted in false admiration of "epic" heroism and insatiable of glory, cannot appreciate true creativity when they see it. For "to create / Is greater then created to destroy," as the angelic host proclaims when the Son returns "unwearied" from the greatest of his georgic labors, his "Six days work, a World" (7.606-607, 552, 568). Satan and his earthly followers have the illusion that warfare is more glorious than farming, gardening, or herding, activities accounted low and shameful. The Old-Testament Hebrews and the early Romans were not ashamed of such labors, and Virgil like Spenser tried to recall his audience to a similar attitude. "Be not ashamed," he prefaces some of his more mundane instructions, which he and Mæcenas reputedly read to Octavius himself during a four-day recitation of the *Georgics*. Milton again points the contrast between creating and destroying, georgic labor and military prowess, during his diatribe in Book 11 against wars fought for the sake of glory or booty:

Where Cattle pastur'd late, now scatterd lies
With Carcasses and Arms th' ensanguind Field
Deserted.

(11.653-55)

The passage turns on "Field," where military struggle and country labor both take place, and where (as in the Roman civil wars) the worse has driven out the better.

As we have seen, Milton did not believe that a fallen world precludes all enjoyment of pastoral *otium*. His poems contain more leisure and more play than those of most of his contemporaries, and his is a leisure almost untouched by "eating Cares" and anxiety about *tempus edax rerum*. Milton can delight in leisure because he has worked for it, because he is content to seek it not as a permanent state but as a well-earned respite from labor. He describes how students should relax from their work in *Of Education*:

> The interim of unsweating themselves regularly, and convenient rest before meat may both with profit and delight be taken up in recreating and composing their travail'd spirits with the solemn and divine harmonies of Musick heard or learnt. . . . [This relaxation will] send their minds back to study in good tune and satisfaction. (4:288-89)

Milton grew up in a musical household and took his organ with him as he moved from house to house throughout his life. A similar alternation between work and leisure appears in the sonnets to Lawrence and Skinner, in Apollo's occasional holidays from hard labor under King Admetus in *Mansus*, and even in the forced retirement of Elegy 1. Although the pleasure is genuine, these are at best leisured respites, which, like Apollo's song in *Mansus*, can be expected to do no more than soothe the hard labors of exile in this world: "Exilii duros lenibat voce labores" (64).

Milton qualifies the broad movement from pastoral to georgic, however, refining and modifying what was, after all, a fairly traditional view of the transition from prehistory to history. As he uses Satan and his followers to warn his readers against the false glitter of epic, so he also uses him to warn against a false pursuit of imperial georgic. For Satan is a laborer as well as a warrior, who understands full well that an empire cannot be built without sweat and toil. In his best-known description of his historical purpose, he declares:

> If then his Providence
> Out of our evil seek to bring forth good,
> Our labour must be to pervert that end.
> (1.162-64).

His work starts with the building of Pandemonium. As the devils rush to begin, Milton employs a combination of military and georgic imagery:

> Thither wing'd with speed
> A numerous Brigad hasten'd. As when Bands
> Of Pioners with Spade and Pickax arm'd
> Forerun the Royal Camp, to trench a Field,
> Or cast a Rampart.
>
> (1.674-78)

Mulciber's technological inventiveness, however, makes the work easy, so that what "incessant toyle / And hands innumerable [could] scarce perform," these "Spirits reprobate" accomplish "in an hour" (1.697-99).

Mammon's advice at the Great Consult is partly voted down; yet what he has to say about labor accurately describes one aspect of the final, anti-providential plan to which the devils agree:

> Our greatness will appeer
> Then most conspicuous, when great things of small,
> Useful of hurtful, prosperous of adverse
> We can create, and in what place so e're
> Thrive under evil, and work ease out of pain
> Through labour and indurance.
>
> (2.257-62)

Like Mammon's preference for "Hard liberty before the easie yoke / Of servile Pomp" (2.256-57), his determination to face his present sufferings with "labour and indurance" is a close parody of what man must do after his fall, "by small / Accomplishing great things" as Michael will advise Adam just before his exile (12.566-67). Certainly Satan gains his ends as a laborer as well as a warrior. He crosses the ghastly abyss of Chaos "with difficulty and labour hard / . . . with difficulty and labour hee" (2.1021-22). On his triumphant return to Hell, he emphasizes how his Virgilian sufferings have gained an empire of ease and leisure; he has "Toild out [his] uncouth passage," and as a result he has won for his followers a world without "hazard, labour, or allarme" (10.475, 491). Clearly Milton intends a parody not only of Aeneas and Odysseus, but of Christ, who by his sufferings will earn a new paradisal

315

land into which he will lead his followers at the end of time. As Milton qualifies his approval of postlapsarian georgic in order to exclude the imperial labors of Satan and his followers, so he also qualifies the prelapsarian pastoral enjoyed by Adam and Eve in the garden of Eden. In recent years, Miltonists have increasingly recognized the importance of work in Milton's Eden.[13] Before the fall, work is easy, various, and pleasant, and it may be put aside whenever it is appropriate. So we first glimpse Adam and Eve sitting down,

> after no more toil
> Of thir sweet Gardning labour then suffic'd
> To recommend coole *Zephyr*, and made ease
> More easie, wholsom thirst and appetite
> More grateful.
>
> (4.327-31)

We recognize the same pattern that Milton recommended for postlapsarian man: ease giving refreshment after labor, and labor giving ease a greater pleasure. So Adam tells Eve, as he

---

[13] See esp. Mary Ann Radzinowicz, "Man as a Probationer of Immortality," in *Approaches to* Paradise Lost, ed. C. A. Patrides (London: Edward Arnold, 1968), 31-51; Barbara Kiefer Lewalski, "Innocence and Experience in Milton's Eden," in *New Essays on* Paradise Lost, ed. Thomas Kranidas (Berkeley: Univ. of California Press, 1969), pp. 86-117; and—a work that appeared after I finished this book—Diane Kelsey McColley, *Milton's Eve* (Urbana: Univ. of Illinois Press, 1983). McColley shows that Milton took the authorizing text, Genesis 2:15, that God put Adam into the garden "to dress it and to keep it," far more seriously and positively than most Protestant commentators took it; they usually speak of prelapsarian labor only briefly and negatively as an antidote to idleness rather than as something valuable in itself (McColley, pp. 121-23). Of such a character is Herbert's passing comment in *The Country Parson* (*Works*, ed. Hutchinson, p. 174). A notable exception is Donne, who four times cites the text in Genesis 2:15 (*Sermons*, ed. Potter and Simpson, 3:67, 4:149, 7:424, 10:219) and who views prelapsarian labor in a highly favorable light. Unlike Milton, however, Donne distinguishes sharply between work before the fall, which is good, and work after the fall, which is thoroughly contaminated by the curse. Therefore he reveals no interest in the possibility that humanity might once again approach the condition of Eden through its labors.

explains why day and night both have their purposes in the divine scheme:

> God hath set
> Labour and rest, as day and night to men
> Successive, and the timely dew of sleep
> Now falling with soft slumbrous weight inclines
> Our eye-lids; other Creatures all day long
> Rove idle unimploid, and less need rest;
> Man hath his daily work of body or mind
> Appointed, which declares his Dignitie.
>   (4.612-19)

Theirs is a pleasant, agricultural labor: reforming the "Allies green," lopping the branches off luxuriant shrubs that grow without need of human "manuring," picking up the "Blossoms" and "Gumms" that fall and bestrew the ground "unsightly and unsmooth" (4.625-32). Unlike other commentators or hexameral poets, Milton seriously weighs God's prelapsarian injunction to dress and to keep the garden of Eden (Gen. 2:15; *PL*, 8.320, 9.205-207).

Milton conceives of Eden not only as a "garden" but as a "field," where crops grow without need of human tillage. In the morning, Adam calls Eve to work in the "fresh field," and after they have resolved the problem of her evil dream the two of them hasten off to work in the "Field" (5.20, 136). As Raphael descends from heaven, he passes the glittering tents of the angelic guard "and now is come / Into the blissful field" (5.292). Milton seems to envisage something like what one may see in some paintings and engravings of the period: a scene as agricultural in appearance as pastoral, except that the plants, shrubs, and fruit trees grow in divinely planted order and abundance. From the moment of creation there are "Fields" and "Meddowes" in which the herds and flocks begin "Pasturing at once" (7.460-62). No plowing, tilling, planting, manuring, weeding, or irrigating are needed in Milton's Eden (7.333-37), but the field plants require some tending (5.22).

Certainly, Milton's paradise is a long way from a Virgilian

farm, where even the happy husbandman must endure far longer and harder labors than he might wish. Yet there is no denying that Milton's pastoral Eden has at least some of the elements of georgic—those that are most satisfying, and that define humanity as more dignified than the idle beasts. And, of course, the Edenic georgic includes the most significant labor of all, that of knowing oneself, the world, and God—those intellectual labors about which Adam speaks to Eve. Thus, just as postlapsarian georgic allows each man to play his small but essential part in determining the course of history, so the georgic element in prelapsarian pastoral allows Adam and Eve to find their own freely chosen path toward fulfillment of the perfections with which they have been created but which at first are largely potential rather than actual.

Milton introduces several significant georgic similes into the Edenic books. When Satan is discovered at the ear of Eve and suddenly confronts the angelic guard in his full size, their "ported Spears" gather around him

> as thick as when a field
> Of *Ceres* ripe for harvest waving bends
> Her bearded Grove of ears, which way the wind
> Swayes them; the careful Plowman doubting stands
> Least on the threshing floore his hopeful sheaves
> Prove chaff.
>
> (4.980-85)

Like most of the epic similes in the poem, this one is proleptic; it looks ominously forward toward the crisis-point when man will prosper or be defeated, reaping a harvest of grain or of chaff. Another well-known simile compares Satan's approach to Eden to the relief a city-dweller feels as he visits the country—not a pastoral but a georgic country:

> to breathe
> Among the pleasant Villages and Farmes
> Adjoynd, from each thing met conceaves delight,

> The smell of Grain, or tedded Grass, or Kine,
> Or Dairie, each rural sight, each rural sound.
> (9.447-51)

The imagery would be revolutionary for its time in any context but is especially so because it implicitly attributes to Eden pleasures of a farming country hardly imaginable since the time of Virgil. Similarly, when poor Adam waits for Eve to return from her morning of solitary gardening, Milton creates not a pastoral but a georgic image once again:

> Adam the while
> Waiting desirous her return, had wove
> Of choicest Flours a Garland to adorne
> Her Tresses, and her rural labours crown,
> As Reapers oft are wont thir Harvest Queen.
> (9.838-42)

Even the well-known connections that Milton implies between Eve, Proserpina, Ceres, and Pomona take on new significance when one realizes their georgic implications.

What is perhaps most significant about Milton's addition of a georgic element to the usual prelapsarian pastoral is that it diminishes the distance between Eden and what fallen humanity may still hope to attain, aided by grace. As Patricia Johnston has persuasively argued, there is a considerable difference between the ideal that Virgil proposes in his "Messianic" Eclogue and the maturer ideal of his *Georgics*.[14] In the later work, the Golden Age is seen as lying not merely in the past, but also in the attainable future. It may be brought back into existence in historical time, if enough men labor to achieve it. Obviously as the world now is constituted one can feel only nostalgia and a sense of irreparable loss for a purely idle, pastoral Eden; but a partly georgic Eden might in some measure be within practical reach. That consideration would

[14] Patricia A. Johnston, *Vergil's Agricultural Golden Age* (Leiden: E. J. Brill, 1980).

naturally be important to a poet like Spenser or Milton, who wants his readers to take action—political, religious, historical action—to transform the real world.

Significantly, a quarrel about work initiates the train of events that leads to the fall. Adam and Eve are both free agents; from what Milton says, both are capable of resisting temptation and standing alone; yet given their circumstances they should never have parted. Human beings are not called on to stand alone when they can freely help one another, especially when they are married—that is what a helpmate is for. Eve misinterprets the nature of the work she and Adam have to do, and Adam allows her to have her way, although he knows better; so both share the fault (though not yet a sin) of parting. The essence of Eve's misinterpretation is utilitarian: the work must be done, at whatever cost, in the most efficient way. Adam argues that there are more important priorities. God has not imposed labor "so strictly" that it should transcend reason and love, "For not to irksom toile, but to delight / He made us, and delight to Reason joyn'd" (9.235-47). Neither idleness nor too much labor is consonant with true human dignity.

After the fall, of course, labor becomes man's hard lot, both his punishment and, if transformed by grace, a means for his redemption. Each son of Adam must sweat to earn his keep, and even intellectual labor is apt to encounter not a pleasant garden but, as Milton complains in *Of Education*, an "asinine feast of sowthistles and brambles" (4:280). Under a prelatical regime, university scholars are "unfortunately fed with nothing else, but the scragged and thorny lectures of monkish and miserable sophistry," and sent home "with such a scholastical burre in their throats, as hath stopt and hinderd all true and generous philosophy from entring, crackt their voices for ever with metaphysical gargarisms" (*Church-government*; 3:273). But if reformation can pull up these various weeds, there is hope yet for the future. As Virgil's readers can take hope from the example of the Sabine farmers, Milton's can take hope

from the generations before the coming of Nimrod, the first
tyrant, simple men who

> Shall lead thir lives, and multiplie apace,
> Labouring the soile, and reaping plenteous crop,
> Corn wine and oyle . . .
> Shal spend thir dayes in joy unblam'd, and dwell
> Long time in peace by Families and Tribes.
>
> (12.17-23)

What puts an end to this relatively idyllic estate is the advent
of kingship and war, which displace georgic with other values.
Men learn to prefer idle pleasures and epic manslaughter be-
fore humble labors, to the general detriment of humanity.

Milton leaves the matter of postlapsarian labor in *Paradise
Lost* as ambivalent as his complex close, and in doing so he
makes use of both of the two interpretive traditions of Genesis
3:19, the pessimistic and the optimistic. Labor is an unpleasant
and unavoidable curse. Adam wakes from a sleepless night to
say to Eve: "the Field / To labour calls us now with sweat
impos'd," to which Eve replies: "let us forth . . . / Wherere
our days work lies, though now enjoind / Laborious, till day
droop" (11.171-78). Yet already Adam sees cause for hope:
"with labour I must earne / My bread; what harm? Idleness
had bin worse" (10.1054-55). He hopes in the end to "earne
rest from labour won, / If so I may attain" (11.375-76). No
longer will human beings be blessed with the gift of just so
much labor as to make their leisure more pleasurable, even
in those rare times when they achieve an ideal society; yet
labor and the suffering it brings with it are evils that may,
when rightly used, be turned to good. The formula that Mam-
mon had parodically proposed in Hell lacked only the spirit
of obedience to divine providence to make it work. That for-
mula is the georgic spirit, the willing acceptance of long labor
in the daily cycle of ordinary existence. "[B]e lowlie wise: /
Think only what concernes thee and thy being," Raphael
tells unfallen Adam, who acknowledges that "to know / That

which before us lies in daily life, / Is the prime Wisdom"
(8.173-74, 192-94). After the fall, the lesson is all the more
applicable. Even on fallen earth there is a "paradise within,"
but that paradise must be earned and kept by constant labor
in a pattern exemplified by the Son himself, whose mortal
labors must now be tedious and hard:

> by small
> Accomplishing great things, by things deemd weak
> Subverting worldly strong, and worldly wise
> By simply meek; that suffering for Truths sake
> Is fortitude to highest victorie,
> And to the faithful Death the Gate of Life;
> Taught this by his example whom I now
> Acknowledge my Redeemer ever blest.
> (12.566-73)

To suggest continuous and difficult effort, Milton uses pres-
ent-participial constructions, run-on lines, and strong cae-
suras. Christ's passion and crucifixion, like death to the faith-
ful, are the climactic model, but (as so often elsewhere) Milton
dwells less on that unique climax than on the day-to-day
struggle in which each individual choice and moment of suf-
fering reflects the passion in miniature.

Paradise Regained

As *Paradise Lost* shows how humanity fell from an Edenic
pastoral into the long tale of historical georgic, which in the
first ages of the world was broken only by wicked digressions
into false, luxurious leisure or by the cruelties of epic ambition
and vainglorious warfare, so *Paradise Regained* depicts the
moment when, for the first time in history, georgic takes on
a new and more hopeful significance, as the georgic spirit is
given the power to bring Eden back within human reach.
Under Michael's tutelage, Adam foresaw the happy transfor-
mation of the curse of labor; the georgic agent of that trans-
formation is the hero of *Paradise Regained*. Milton's Christ

does not lift the burden of labor from human shoulders altogether, but he sanctifies labor and thus allows humanity the opportunity to assist in the divine work of planting and harvesting, giving to his followers the grace that will allow them to find a paradise within and even make it possible for them to achieve a just society on earth.

With characteristic reticence, Milton subtitled *Paradise Regained* "A / POEM. / In IV *BOOKS*," leaving to his later interpreters the task of sorting out just what kind of poem it is. Critics have proposed various models—brief epic, debate, Socratic dialogue, and even pastoral—though Northrop Frye calls the poem an "experiment . . . practically *sui generis*."[15] Majority opinion has recently favored brief epic; yet, as Walter MacKellar, who supports the brief-epic theory, notes, the poem is "nearly devoid of the usual epic machinery." Moreover, he adds, "Among numerous Italian and French Biblical poems of the 16th and 17th centuries, I have found none which even remotely resembles *Paradise Regained*."[16] With the possible exception of the *Christiad*, few or none of the Renaissance biblical epics belong to the kind of great tradition within which Milton liked to work. In his opening lines, Milton challenges not Vida—still less Jacobus Strasburgus—but his old friend and rival Virgil. Among other things, he implies that *Paradise Regained* will overgo the *Aeneid*. To be sure, thirty years before Milton published *Paradise Regained*, he considered writing a poem in imitation of the Book of Job, which he referred to in *The Reason of Church-government* as a "brief model" of the "Epick form" (3:237). Like *Samson Agonistes, Paradise Regained* often echoes Job and shares with

[15] See Barbara K. Lewalski, *Milton's Brief Epic* (Providence: Brown Univ. Press, 1966); Elaine B. Safer, "The Socratic Dialogue and 'Knowledge in the Making' in *Paradise Regained*," *Milton Studies*, 6 (1974), 215-26; Stewart A. Baker, "Sannazaro and Milton's Brief Epic," *Comparative Literature*, 20 (1968), 116-32; Northrop Frye, "The Typology of *Paradise Regained*," *Modern Philology*, 53 (1956), 227-38.

[16] MacKellar, ed., *Paradise Regained*, vol. 4 of *A Variorum Commentary on the Poems of John Milton* (New York: Columbia Univ. Press, 1975), 17, 10.

it a concern for trial, suffering, and patience. There is little to indicate, however, that Milton continued to think of Job as epic, or as an apt generic as opposed to typological model, at this late stage of his career. He says nothing about biblical genre in *The Christian Doctrine*, and in *Paradise Regained* itself, whereas Satan mentions four Greek genres, Jesus speaks only of Hebrew "Hymns," "Psalms," and "Songs" (4.254-65, 334-47).[17] In any case, Job has as good a claim to be called georgic as epic. Job is a farmer; his book begins and ends with descriptions of his georgic possessions, it subjects him to the georgic tests of storm, disease, and crop failure, and it reduces him to sitting on his dunghill. Such is the patient and humble hero, without military pretensions, whom Milton evokes in *Paradise Regained*.

The chief dissenting voice to the brief-epic theory is that of Louis L. Martz, who argues that the basic model for *Paradise Regained* is Virgil's *Georgics*.[18] He notes that the two works are about the same length and that each is divided into four books, a division to which Milton calls attention in his subtitle. That similarity may seem trivial until we remember that, as L. P. Wilkinson points out, the four-book structure of the *Georgics* was almost "unique" in its time.[19] Martz also argues that both poems are in a "middle style": not a flat level but

---

[17] Milton is alluding to Eph. 5:18-19; on the importance of this Pauline formulation see Anthony Low, "The Unity of Milton's *Elegia Sexta*," *English Literary Renaissance*, 11 (1981), 213-23.

[18] For the fullest and latest statement of Martz's position, see his *Poet of Exile* (New Haven: Yale Univ. Press, 1980), pp. 247-71, 293-304. Martz was briefly anticipated by E.M.W. Tillyard, *Milton* (1930; London: Chatto & Windus, 1966), p. 273, and is supported by Richard Neuse, "Milton and Spenser: The Virgilian Triad Revisited," *ELH*, 45 (1978), 606-32. Except for Ellwood, early commentators say little about the poem; most echo Phillips' casual remark that it is "heroic" but unsuccessfully so. Dunster, however, in his edition of 1795, observes that the "design and conduct" of *Paradise Regained* are as different from *Paradise Lost* "as that of the *Georgics* from the *Aeneid*" (p. 267).

[19] *The Georgics of Virgil* (Cambridge: Cambridge Univ. Press, 1969), p. 67n. I qualify Wilkinson's "unique" since he evidently overlooked the *Argonautica*, in four books but roughly double the length of *Paradise Regained* and the *Georgics*.

a style that allows for "frequent oscillations upward and downward from a middle way" (p. 293). Virgil scholars have often noted such a mixture of styles in the *Georgics* and have pointed to its abrupt transitions from low to high and back again. Another of Martz's arguments, that the poems are similar in spirit because both are didactic, is less persuasive. Everything Milton wrote is didactic to a degree, but there is little in *Paradise Regained* that resembles the detailed enumerations and instructions or the prosaic subject matter of the *Georgics*. Virgil's point is that every smallest action, from the spreading of dung on exhausted fields (1.80-81) to the extermination of mice in the granary floor (1.176-86), plays a necessary part in the husbandman's work, and therefore that no action is too trivial or shameful to be included. Milton would agree with that view in spirit but does not attempt to imitate it in his literal poetic practice.

Like Milton's other works, *Paradise Regained* incorporates within itself a number of subsidiary genres, including epic, pastoral, and hymn. A good case can be made, however, for its dominant mode's being georgic. Its four books, its middle style, and, as we shall see, its georgic hero and preoccupation with the georgic spirit in every book all point in that direction. Of course the poem is not literally a georgic, but neither is it literally an epic. Jesus wields neither a plow nor a sword. What we are looking for is a dominant structural pattern, style, and spirit. Twice in the *Art of Logic* Milton speaks admiringly of the four-book structure of the *Georgics*. Speaking of "division" or "method," which we would call structure, Milton remarks: "Thus in the *Georgics* Vergil distributes the matter before him into four parts, as was said above" (11:255, 481). Why Milton chose to distribute three temptations over four books has considerably exercised the critics; one reason may have been to confirm his georgic intentions and acknowledge the debt to his predecessor.

If the dominant mode of *Paradise Regained* is georgic, yet there are several difficulties to a theory that its dominant genre is also georgic. For one thing, whereas the *Georgics* is largely a narrated poem, *Paradise Regained*, like *Paradise Lost*, belongs to a mixed species of narrative and drama combined, in which a narrator speaks in his own voice and characters also speak in theirs. Epic, epyllion, and romance are all "mixed" in this sense, as are gospel, parable, and history. Still, Milton had a possible model for his poem within the *Georgics* itself, since much of Virgil's fourth book consists of the Aristæus episode, in which the characters speak at length in their own voices. Virgil's inner story has georgic details and spirit (Aristæus is a husbandman), yet it rises to a higher mood without ever touching on the militant brand of heroism normal to the epic. Although Aristæus is quite a different sort of character from Milton's Son, Milton might nevertheless have found many suggestive details in Aristæus' story: a son seeks advice from his mother about how to bring his dead bees back to life; he is sent into the wilderness to wrestle with the monstrous shape-changer Proteus; he learns that a curse was put on his hives because he was responsible for the deaths of Orpheus and Euridyce; he appeases the gods by sacrifice and learns how to become the georgic inventor of a way to restore bees to life. The *Georgics* ends with an apparently proleptic incident: the rebirth of Aristæus' bees. Many of Virgil's Christian readers interpreted the episode as a parable of sin and atonement, death and resurrection, as well as a story about invention, under the pressure of suffering and loss, for the benefit of humanity. The higher level of Virgil's last book might also have been a precedent for the elevation of Milton's Book 4.

A second difficulty is that, as both early commentators and modern critics remark, *Paradise Regained* is clearly a heroic poem of some sort. The son is an exemplary hero, Satan an exemplary antagonist, and the action in which they confront one another is mainly characterized by agonistic struggle, verbal or spiritual. These facts would ordinarily suggest that the poem is epic, since "heroic" and "epic" are frequently (although by no means always) synonymous terms in Renaissance critical parlance. Yet Milton is not known to be a writer who followed the crowds. What I think he did in *Paradise Regained* is to discover an essentially new genre (Northrop

Frye's "*sui generis*") or a combination of genres: one that is heroic in form but dominantly georgic in mode, spirit, and in many individual images and other details. In other words, *Paradise Regained* is a heroic georgic poem. The obvious model would be the Aristæus episode. Milton might also have been influenced by the analogous examples of various pastoral heroes, such as Paris in George Peele's play, *The Arraignment of Paris* (1584), or even the fictionalized figure of King James that Jonson brings into several of his masques as a heroic establisher of peace in the pastoral mode. Indeed, in Jonson's *Oberon* Prince Henry plays a guardedly georgic role, not of course as a plowman but as a civilizer of his father's initially rustic and culturally naive subjects. As the masque proceeds from the country to the court, he raises them up from savagery to civilization. I propose none of these particular works (except the *Georgics*) as a source for Milton, but rather as illustrations of some of the available models on which he might have drawn for a kind of heroism that was neither epic nor military. As we shall see, other possible models from the biblical and Roman worlds are suggested by Jesus in the poem, and include David, Gideon, Cincinnatus, and Curius (as well as Job). As I shall argue in the balance of this section, georgic, not epic, is the one mode that persists in every book of *Paradise Regained*, and, moreover, although the poem is a protracted *agon* between Christ and Satan, Milton may properly be said to portray that struggle more as a moment-by-moment labor than as a single, decisive, military battle.

The first indication that *Paradise Regained* is dominantly georgic in mode is found in its opening and closing frames. As critics have long noted, Milton's opening alludes to Virgil's declaration, in the discarded beginning of the *Aeneid*, that Virgil is the man who, having composed eclogues and georgics, is now about to sing of Mars:

> I who e're while the happy Garden sung,
> By one mans disobedience lost, now sing
> Recover'd Paradise to all mankind,
> By one mans firm obedience fully tri'd

Through all temptation, and the Tempter foil'd
In all his wiles, defeated and repuls't,
And *Eden* rais'd in the wast Wilderness.

(1.1-7)

Milton could assume that his readers would recognize his allusion to the Virgilian *rota*.[20] Yet there is something extraordinary about Milton's appeal here to Virgil's words. If Milton now views *Paradise Lost* as a mere pastoral, even as an apprentice work, then he seems also to be saying that *Paradise Regained* belongs to a higher genre than epic. Indeed, he seems to promise as much when he pledges "to tell of deeds / Above Heroic" (1.14-15). After all, his hero is by definition the greatest of all heroes. Yet little in the style or subject suggests that Milton was attempting anything like a hypothetical super-epic. There is also the matter of length: Why should Milton choose brief epic as an appropriate genre in which to outdo in its own terms the eminently successful full epic he had just written? He would simply be repeating himself in miniature. But if he wants his readers to view *Paradise Lost* for the moment as a pastoral, having to do with Eden and its loss, perhaps he is suggesting that *Paradise Regained* represents the next step: georgic.

That Milton keeps military terminology to a noticeable minimum in his opening lines is not surprising when we recall what Michael told Adam near the close of *Paradise Lost*:

Dream not of thir fight,
As of a Duel, or the local wounds
Of head or heel: not therefore joynes the Son
Manhood to God-head, with more strength to foil
Thy enemie.

(12.386-90)

Instead of predominant military imagery, we find the language of patient persistence: "*firm* obedience *fully* tri'd / Through *all* temptation, and the Tempter foil'd / In *all* his wiles." We also find that, since the first Adam has lost the garden, Jesus

---

[20] On the *rota*, see Introduction.

is to go out into the desert to *recover* paradise and that his victory over Satan in this opening paradigm of the action culminates in a georgic image: "*Eden* rais'd in the wast Wilderness." Even the next lines may be georgic, as Milton evokes the Spirit "who ledst this glorious Eremite / Into the Desert, his Victorious Field" (8-9). Milton played on "field" in just such a way in *Paradise Lost*. Such a pitting of the military and the agricultural against each other—which Milton employed to good effect in the Cromwell sonnet—occurs often in the classics and the Bible. Yet a central locus is the *Georgics*, which constantly opposes war and farming. Especially memorable is the passage (echoed, as we have seen, by several poets who deplored the English Civil War) with which Virgil ends Book 1:

> ergo inter sese paribus concurrere telis
> Romanas acies iterum videre Philippi;
> nec fuit indignum superis, bis sanguine nostro
> Emathiam et latos Haemi pinguiscere campos.
> scilicet et tempus veniet, cum finibus illis
> agricola incurvo terram molitus aratro
> exesa inveniet scabra robigine pila,
> aut gravibus rastris galeas pulsabit inanis,
> grandiaque effossis mirabitur ossa sepulcris.
> . . . non ullus aratro
> dignus honos, squalent abductis arva colonis
> et curvae rigidum falces conflantur in ensem.
>   (1.489-508)

"Therefore once more Philippi saw Roman battle lines clash against one another with equal weapons, nor did the gods think it unfitting to stain Emathia and the broad fields of Haemus a second time with our blood. Surely a time shall come in these lands when, as the farmer toils at the soil with his heavy hoes, he shall strike empty helmets and marvel at giant bones in their upturned graves. . . . The plow is not duly honored; the lands, robbed of the farmers, lie waste; curved pruning hooks are forged into stiff swords."

At the height of the Parthian temptation, preeminently a

temptation to epic military heroism, Milton returns to this war-and-farming topos with still another variation:

> The field all iron cast a gleaming brown,
> Nor wanted clouds of foot . . .
>   nor of labouring Pioners
> A multitude with Spades and Axes arm'd
> To lay hills plain, fell woods, or valleys fill,
> Or where plain was raise hill, or over-lay
> With bridges rivers proud, as with a yoke.
>   (3.326-34)

The scene recalls the war in heaven, the battle of the mountains, the building of Pandemonium and digging up of gold in Hell. The filling of valleys parodies Isaiah's prophecy of the last days, echoed by John at the baptism (Isa. 40:1-5, Luke 3:4-6). The raising of the hills recalls Babel and the Gigantomachia, and the bridging of rivers (as editors note) recalls Xerxes and his impious attempt to span the Hellespont on his way to conquer Greece. Above all, the strangely beautiful trompe-l'oeil field, of gleaming armor that mimics nature while masses of soldiers drift by like clouds, evokes the perversity with which war can turn creation into destruction, as epic aspirations destroy the pastoral landscape with a Satanic parody of georgic energy. Just so, we watch Satan's followers energetically rush to tear up the soil of heaven for gunpowder, while in a precisely opposite action the Son restores the wounded hills and valleys and fills them with living flowers.

The opening paradigm foretells the basic pattern that *Paradise Regained* enacts. After God's voice at the baptizing has initiated the action, Satan, remembering the prophecy in Eden that the Seed of the Woman will bruise his head, calls an infernal council, because he expects a renewal of open warfare at any moment. In other words, he expects to play an epic part. But Milton's hero, instead of calling up followers and taking to arms, retreats alone into the desert to meditate on his vocation. There, tempted by Satan, he fights and labors—Milton uses both metaphors—strenuously and continually.

The debate is so intricately interwoven that to remove any speech from its context is difficult. Almost the entire poem elaborates this lengthy verbal and spiritual struggle, which culminates in a curiously underemphasized climax. Then Jesus emerges from the desert for an angelic banquet before he quietly returns home to his mother.

The setting of the victory banquet—private, not in a palace but "in a flowry valley . . . / On a green bank" (4.586-87)—suggests that Jesus' triumph has not been of the epic kind. Having by his strenuous efforts recreated a spiritual garden or paradise, Jesus is given a moment of pastoral relaxation, in a familiar Miltonic alternation of effort with ease. While Jesus rests and refreshes himself, the angelic choir celebrates and interprets his deeds, providing the action with a closing frame. In a formal biblical hymn or anthem (4.594), the angels reveal that at the close of the action Milton views Christ's victory not as a battle won—an idea Milton explicitly rejects—but as an essentially georgic accomplishment. The angels celebrate the fulfillment of just that promise with which the poem opened: the second Adam, fully tried through all temptations (including that of epic heroism), by means of strenuous effort has raised an Eden in the waste wilderness and refounded paradise. The hymn contains frequent military elements, but they are either associated with Satan—eager as always to win glory in war and, as always, frustrated—or else they look to the beginning and end of providential history, not to the present time of the action. As the hymn progresses, it moves away from these muted epic notes toward georgic:

> True Image of the Father whether thron'd
> In the bosom of bliss, and light of light
> Conceiving, or remote from Heaven, enshrin'd
> In fleshly Tabernacle, and human form,
> Wandring the Wilderness, whatever place,
> Habit, or state, or motion, still expressing
> The Son of God.
>
> (4.596-602)

The verse points to perpetual activity of all kinds and in all places, minute by minute, rather than to a single decisive action:

> with Godlike force indu'd
> Against th' Attempter of thy Fathers Throne,
> And Thief of Paradise; him long of old
> Thou did'st debel, and down from Heav'n cast
> With all his Army.
> (4.602-606)

If "debel" echoes Virgil's famous "debellare superbos" (*Aeneid* 6.853), then it reminds us that Satan was once expelled after a war—but a war that even in *Paradise Lost* collapsed in its last stages, so that the rebellious angels dropped their weapons from slack hands and were driven over the precipice like goats.

Milton continues:

> now thou hast aveng'd
> Supplanted *Adam*, and by vanquishing
> Temptation, hast regain'd lost Paradise,
> And frustrated the conquest fraudulent:
> He never more henceforth will dare set foot
> In Paradise to tempt; his snares are broke:
> For though that seat of earthly bliss be fail'd,
> A fairer Paradise is founded now
> For *Adam* and his chosen Sons, whom thou
> A Saviour art come down to re-install.
> (4.606-615)

Phrases often begin with military terms but turn aside. For example, Jesus has "regain'd lost Paradise"; he has vanquished not armies but temptations; he has not counterattacked but "frustrated" Satan's "conquest fraudulent"; he is a breaker of snares; he is not a military victor but the *founder* of a new paradisal garden, into which he will lead his people. The passage turns on thrice-repeated "Paradise." Where *Paradise Lost* played a descending descant on "fall," "faild," "fell" (3.95-102), *Paradise Regained* marks a reversal with "fail'd," "fairer," "founded." A battle will be fought, in which Satan will drop from the skies "like an Autumnal Star / Or Lightning," to be "trod down" underfoot and receive his "last and deadliest wound" (4.619-22). But that warfare is yet to come; *Paradise Regained* has laid the foundations.

Milton disposes of Satan in a last brilliant image from the Gospels, which firmly removes from him the remaining vestiges of epic pretensions. The Son is unarmed, and though Satan is accorded his favorite military imagery it is now more ludicrously out of place than ever:

> hereafter learn with awe
> To dread the Son of God: he all unarm'd
> Shall chase thee with the terror of his voice
> From thy Demoniac holds, possession foul,
> Thee and thy Legions, yelling they shall flye,
> And beg to hide them in a herd of Swine.
> (4.625-30)

What seems for a moment to be an epic event is suddenly reduced, as the reader realizes that the legions and strongholds are nothing more than demons in possession of a sick man's body. As the poem begins with georgic, so it ends. Of course, the divine georgic need be laborious only when the Son clothes himself with weakness. Otherwise his voice or his look suffices to send the hills to their places like obedient sheep, or to dismiss Satan's army like a flock of timorous goats, or to send the demonic legions from their stronghold in a herd of swine.

The georgic images that frame *Paradise Regained* are reinforced by recurrent georgic themes throughout the poem. One important theme concerns vocation. Milton had touched on vocation throughout his career, from Elegy 6 and Sonnet 7 through *Samson Agonistes*;[21] he examines the subject most thoroughly in *Paradise Regained*. In part the examination

---

[21] See John Spencer Hill, *John Milton: Poet, Priest, and Prophet* (London: Macmillan, 1979).

deals with Christ's triple offices of prophet, king, and priest; and a chief concern of Satan, Jesus, and the poem itself is to define Christ's role in life. In religious terms, what does it mean to be the Messiah? In poetic terms, what does it mean to be the preeminent hero? The vocation of either the poet or his hero may determine genre. A poet who drinks wine will write elegiac; one who drinks water will write divine or heroic. A hero who relaxes is a pastoral hero; one who fights, an epic hero; and one who labors and builds, a georgic hero. Therefore, insofar as *Paradise Regained* is concerned with defining the role or mission of Jesus in the world, it is concerned with defining its own genre. To complicate matters, the two main characters have different ideas about the nature of their contest and so in a sense about the genre of the poem that tells their story. Satan wants to bring matters to a head, to fight or to win by sudden sleights of hand; Jesus, however, labors, waits, and stands.

After the georgic invocation and the baptism, Satan calls a council of his chief followers. Clearly he hopes to play an epic role, and therefore he introduces an epic convention into the poem. He recognizes that God works slowly, "for longest time to him is short," and he knows that the long cycles of time have at last brought Jesus "to youths full flowr" (1.55, 67). Yet his recognition teaches him little, since he immediately proposes to his followers that they anticipate the time *with something sudden*:

> Ye see our danger on the utmost edge
> Of hazard, which admits no long debate,
> But must with something sudden be oppos'd,
> Not force, but well couch't fraud, well woven snares,
> E're in the head of Nations he appear
> Their King, their Leader, and Supream on Earth.
> (1.94-99)

As ever, Satan attributes to his enemies his own drives; if he were Messiah, this is how he would act—as an all-conquering military hero. Milton's Satan views history, which is the outcome of contending intentions and deeds, more as a military struggle than a georgic labor. When his followers take up spades, it is characteristically as "Pioners" rather than as farmers. Consequently the council over which he presides ends on an urgent military note, with the devils, like a Roman Senate, acclaiming Satan as their Sulla: "Unanimous they all commit the care / And management of this main enterprize / To him their great Dictator," who earlier had "led thir march" from Hell and conquered Earth on their behalf (1.111-18).

The heavenly council uses no such language. Meeting without fuss or pomp, it is not an epic but a biblical council such as the one that opens the Book of Job. Indeed, the Father takes pains to puncture Satan's assumptions as well as to redefine the events about to take place:

> he might have learnt
> Less over-weening, since he fail'd in *Job*,
> Whose *constant perseverance* overcame
> Whate're his cruel malice could invent.
> He now shall know I can produce a man
> Of female Seed, far abler to *resist*
> *All* his sollicitations, and *at length*
> *All* his vast force, and drive him back to Hell,
> Winning by Conquest what the first man lost
> By fallacy surpriz'd. *But first I mean*
> *To exercise him in the Wilderness,*
> *There* he shall *first lay down the rudiments*
> *Of his great warfare*, e're I send him forth
> To conquer Sin and Death the two grand foes,
> *By Humiliation and strong Sufferance*:
> His weakness shall o'recome Satanic strength . . .
> To *earn* Salvation for the Sons of men.

To which the angels sing:

> Victory and Triumph to the Son of God
> *Now entring* his great duel, *not of arms*,
> But to vanquish by wisdom hellish wiles.
>   (1.146-61, 167, 173-75; italics added)

The Father emphasizes constancy, perseverance, and hard work over a long period: the Son will "earn," not win, salvation; he will lay down the rudiments and gradually prepare himself for battle. The military language refers always to the future and to a war that will be won not by arms but "By Humiliation and strong Sufferance."

When the poem returns to Earth, we find the Son "Musing and *much revolving* in his brest, / How best the mighty *work* he might *begin* / Of Saviour to mankind" (1.185-87; italics added). Characteristically, his entry into the desert is not sudden or hasty: "Thought following thought, and step by step led on" (1.192). We learn that from his youth Jesus has pondered the question of his vocation. Sometimes he considered an epic role: "victorious deeds / Flam'd in my heart, heroic acts . . . / To subdue and quell o're all the earth / Brute violence and proud Tyrannick pow'r" (1.215-19). But that alternative, which Satan might partly understand, he rejected before the poem opens. Instead, he

> held it more humane, more heavenly first
> By winning words to conquer willing hearts,
> And make perswasion do the work of fear.
> (1.221-23)

Milton had long preferred inward persuasion to the use of force. Yet he chooses here to echo the conclusion of the *Georgics*, in which Virgil distinguishes the ascendancy of Octavius over willing nations from the mere violence of war and thus marks the longed-for convergence between georgic and heroic (4.559-62).

"[H]igh are thy thoughts," Jesus' mother has told him, "but *nourish* them" (1.229-30; italics added). Job too was known for suffering and patience; what he typifies Jesus fulfills even in youth, as he recognizes that "my way must lie / *Through many a hard assay* even to the death" (1.263-64). Death will bring victory and the "promis'd Kingdom" (265), yet first come a slow nourishing and constant hard effort. *Kairos*, the due or the ripe time, is a concept the farmer must learn as he follows the circling constellations and observes the phases of the moon for tilling, planting, and harvesting.[22] That ripeness is all is often a theme of tragedy and epic, but it necessarily pervades georgic.

Following the angelic hymn, Satan enters to begin the temptations. These have a triple structure, suggested by the three gospel temptations and, as scholars note, corresponding to Christ's triple offices of prophet, priest, and king as well as to the traditional division of evil into flesh, world, and devil. Taking that structure for granted, since it has been thoroughly investigated, I want to suggest that the temptations have another, simultaneous structure that complicates and enriches their significance. This second structure is fourfold and congruent with the four books. By expanding the three biblical temptations to ten and distributing them one to the first book, two to the second, three to the third, and four to the fourth and (as we shall see) by linking the temptations within each book modally or generically, Milton superimposes a fourfold structure on his threefold original.[23] As a result, the structure of *Paradise Regained* is at once biblical and georgic.

The single temptation of the first book is to turn stones into bread. As Satan enters, he wears a disguise that would not be out of place in epic (Odysseus, Archimago) or masque (Comus). Yet his appearance, described in unusually realistic detail that has no parallel in the possible sources, hints at a vividly georgic milieu:[24]

[22] For other points of view on *kairos*, see Sister M. Christopher Pecheux, "Milton and *Kairos*," *Milton Studies*, 12 (1979), 197-211; Edward W. Tayler, *Milton's Poetry: Its Development in Time* (Pittsburgh: Duquesne Univ. Press, 1979).

[23] On triple structure, see Lewalski, *Milton's Brief Epic*; Elizabeth M. Pope, Paradise Regained: *The Tradition and the Poem* (Baltimore: Johns Hopkins Press, 1947); and Patrick Cullen, *Infernal Triad* (Princeton: Princeton Univ. Press, 1974). On the 1-2-3-4 pattern see Richard Douglas Jordan, "*Paradise Regained* and the Second Adam," *Milton Studies*, 9 (1976), 261-76. Combination of the divine number 3 with the mortal number 4 (standard in Renaissance numerology) may relate to the Son's role as son of both God and man or as Messiah and georgic hero.

[24] The only literary precedent critics have suggested for Milton's realistic portrayal is Giles Fletcher, *Christs Victorie and Triumph* (1610), 2.15.1; but except in that one stanza Fletcher's Satan is a conventional papistical hermit.

But now an aged man in Rural weeds,
Following, as seem'd, the quest of some stray Ewe,
Or wither'd sticks to gather; which might serve
Against a Winters day when winds blow keen,
To warm him wet return'd from field at Eve,
He saw approach.

(1.314-19)

Seeking to tempt the Son to mistake his vocation, Satan significantly assumes a georgic appearance especially calculated to appeal to a social reformer. Moreover, he speaks a georgic part. He offers the biblical temptation, of course, but he couches it in such terms that it becomes at root an attempt to undo the whole georgic theodicy of labor—or, in equivalent Christian terms, to undo the doom of Adam:

By Miracle he may, reply'd the Swain,
What other way I see not, for we here
Live on tough roots and stubs, to thirst inur'd
More then the Camel, and to drink go far,
Men to much misery and hardship born;
But if thou be the Son of God, Command
That out of these hard stones be made thee bread;
So shalt thou save thy self and us relieve
With Food, whereof we wretched seldom taste.

(1.337-45)

Satan's insistence that there is no escaping from the desert except by a miracle introduces the temptation to dispense with the hard labor of earning bread by a similar miracle. As the Son's reply confirms, the temptation is to mistrust God, to doubt not only that the Father will send the Son timely food but also that the whole system of life is fair and providentially governed. Doubt is extended to include the whole condition of humanity struggling under the curse of *labor improbus* and *urgens egestas*. Appealing to false pity, Satan urges the Son to lift all the hardships from life. But, as Virgil says, "pater ipse colendi / haud facilem esse viam voluit," "The father of agriculture himself did not want the way to be easy" (1.121-22). The georgic condition of fallen Adam is precisely what the Son has come to remedy but scarcely in such a sudden and easy fashion as Satan proposes. Instead of removing the curse of labor, Jesus himself is to undergo it, and thus to ennoble and transform it. He brings to humanity not free bread but the freedom of the inward Word. He will teach his followers not so much to escape the wasteland as to convert it into fruitful soil.

In Book 1, Milton balances the military urgency of Satan's council in midair with a relaxed heavenly council that stresses patience and repudiates military methods. Book 2 opens with what amounts to an even more informal and unpretentious council: a group of mostly nameless fishermen who gather "Close in a Cottage low" to consider the same question that so troubles Satan. These men, "new baptiz'd" (2.1) but not yet formally called as disciples, are filled with doubt because their Messiah, just announced, has apparently abandoned them:

> Then on the bank of *Jordan*, by a Creek:
> Where winds with Reeds and Osiers whisp'ring play
> Plain Fishermen, no greater men them call,
> Close in a Cottage low together got
> Thir unexpected loss and plaints out breath'd.
> (2.25-29)

Critics looking for epic councils have not noticed this humble georgic gathering. The disciples-to-be consider but immediately reject, as the young Jesus did, the concept of a military messiah: "arise and vindicate / Thy glory, free thy people from thir yoke, / But let us wait" (2.47-49). Their decision to wait and do nothing until the proper time is precisely right. Theirs is the rural patience of those who work with nature and not against it. Mary too meditates on the event: "But I to wait with patience am inur'd; / My heart hath been a store-house long of things / And sayings laid up." We leave her, "Meekly compos'd await[ing] the fulfilling" (2.102-104, 108), for a brief glimpse of Jesus, also weighing, meditating, "How to begin, how to accomplish best / His end" (2.113-14).

Into this humble and lowly world of honest workers bursts the incongruous Satan in his usual pomp. One council is not enough for him, so he calls a second. Naturally his language is swollen with military pride and urgency:

> Princes, Heavens antient Sons, Æthereal Thrones,
> Demonian Spirits now . . .
> such an Enemy
> Is ris'n to invade us, who no less
> Threat'ns then our expulsion down to Hell.
> (2.121-28)

Satan rejects Belial's suggestion to "Set women in his eye" (2.153) because Satan expects the Messiah to be the kind of hero he would like to be, an Alexander or a Scipio Africanus (2.196-200), someone determined to alter history and win fame by the use of epic force:

> Therefore with manlier objects we must try
> His constancy, with such as have more shew
> Of worth, of honour, glory, and popular praise;
> Rocks whereon greatest men have oftest wreck'd.
> (2.225-28)

Not the narrator but Satan introduces these shows of heroism into a book that was simple and rural up to this point. Even Satan recognizes the need to breach the Son's "constancy"; yet he cannot help thinking of heroic action in terms of honor, glory, and popular praise—rewards he himself craves—because they constitute his definition of "greatest." For him, to be "Above Heroic" must mean to win more applause than Alexander won. Such is the role Satan wants to play, and his followers sustain his illusions for a time: "He ceas'd, and heard thir grant in loud acclaim" (2.235).

Meanwhile the Son, after briefly meditating on hunger and endurance, seeks shelter for the night: "then laid him down / Under the hospitable covert nigh / Of Trees thick interwoven"

(2.261-63). The lines echo Virgil's description of how a husbandman ought to set out trees in order to give shelter to the newborn kings of the bees (as queens were then thought to be) as they lead their youthful followers from the hive to revel in freedom (*Georgics* 4.20-24). Virgil's mood of spring freshness, hopefulness, and freedom, as well as of youth and kingship, enriches the allusion. When Jesus wakes, Satan appears with new stage effects and begins the two temptations of Book 2, the banquet and wealth. These temptations have in common the easy pleasures of kingship, of succumbing to one's lower instincts and to material perquisites. Christ suggests as much when he concludes that "he who reigns within himself, and rules / Passions, Desires, and Fears, is more a King," while the scepter Satan offers is "better miss't" (2.466-67, 486).

Although the banquet owes something to the Roman satirists, Milton's imagery associates it mainly with epyllion and medieval romance. At the table are simulacra of Ganymede and Hylas, naiads, and "Fairy Damsels met in Forest wide / By Knights of *Logres*, or of *Lyones*" (2.350-65). The sudden appearance among the trees of a miraculous table and a suave host (289-301), tales of wandering in the wilderness (306-314), and the *Tempest*-like magical dissolution of the scene (401-403) all play on traditional romance themes. Jesus too remarks that he could by a miracle "Command a Table in this Wilderness" (2.384); but he refrains, for it is not his way or his genre. He refuses not only the obvious lures of gluttony and luxury, but also the subtler effort to involve him in the easy solution of difficulties that characterizes the romance mode.

· Wealth, the second temptation, is a pragmatic reversal on the ideals of romance. That Satan offers it, ostensibly, as a means to achieve "high designs, / High actions" (2.410-11) might seem to hint at epic goals; but in even the crudest and most militaristic epic, wealth is a dishonorable means to no more than a facade of honor. Satan's exemplars speak for themselves: "*Antipater* the *Edomite*, / And his son *Herod*" (2.423-24), men who bought their offices from Rome and became known to after times for parricide and the slaughter of innocents. With these figures we move from the illusions of romance to the materialistic "realism" that characterizes the corrupt historical world portrayed by Josephus and Suetonius. As alternative exemplars to both temptations, Jesus proposes a group of georgic heroes, with careers as fantastic as romance but as real as history. Farmers and shepherds, they come from two traditions, Hebrew and Roman: "*Gideon* and *Jephthah*, and the Shepherd lad, / Whose off-spring on the Throne of *Juda* sat . . . / *Quintius, Fabricius, Curius, Regulus*" (2.439-40, 446). David, we remember, was out herding sheep when the prophet Samuel chose him to be Israel's king. Gideon began his career in similar circumstances: "And there came an angel of the Lord, and sat under an oak . . . that pertained unto Joash the Abiezrite: and his son Gideon threshed wheat by the winepress, to hide it from the Midianites" (Judg. 6:11). Jephthah, the son of a harlot, began life as an outcast. Fabricius and Regulus embody the republican ideal of leaders who live simply. Quintius is that Cincinnatus who left his plow to lead Rome to victory; Curius gave the booty he won in war to the state and returned "to end his days in simple frugality on his farm."[25] Thus Jesus rejects Satan's proffer of luxurious romance heroism and the alternative of corrupt historical realism for the georgic simplicity foreshadowed by plain fishermen who met in a cottage. Satan's attempt to "raise" the style and transform the genre of the poem and its hero fails.

In Book 3, two subsidiary temptations, the gaining of glory and the conquest of David's throne, lead up to the main temptation, which is represented by the Kingdom of Parthia. Unremitting emphasis on military heroism and epic heroism, themes previously associated only with Satan, now pervade the debate and unite the book. The earlier temptations have taught Satan, he pretends, that Jesus is "good, wise, just." Since Jesus has rejected material rewards, he must crave the

[25] MacKellar, *Variorum Commentary*, 4:139.

true rewards of heroism, "fame and glory," which excite "to high attempts the flame / Of most erected Spirits" (3.11, 25-27). Satan's exemplars are all military heroes—Alexander, Scipio, Pompey, and Julius Caesar

> whom now all the world admires
> The more he grew in years, the more inflam'd
> With glory, wept that he had liv'd so long
> Inglorious: but thou yet art not too late.
> (3.39-42)

Jesus picks up Satan's image only to reveal that glory is ephemeral as well as sudden: "what is glory but the blaze of fame[?]" True glory is found in the approbation of God; such was Job's: "Famous he was in Heaven, on Earth less known" (3.47, 60-68). In response to Satan's arguments the Son sharply denounces the whole idea of martial heroism:

> They err who count it glorious to subdue
> By Conquest far and wide, to over-run
> Large Countries, and in field great Battels win,
> Great Cities by assault: what do these Worthies,
> But rob and spoil, burn, slaughter, and enslave
> Peaceable Nations[?]
> (3.71-76)

Similar diatribes appear in *Paradise Lost*, but there they are voiced by the narrator or his angelic spokesmen as part of a central generic strategy of subverting the epic, a theme that runs through the entire poem. In *Paradise Regained* the effect is more local. Jesus repudiates the kind of thinking that leads to the Parthian temptation; his criticism, aimed at Satan and his military epic values, does not attempt to criticize Milton's hypothetical epic predecessors, as the narrator had in *Paradise Lost*. Jesus proposes to replace martial glory with peace, wisdom, patience, and temperance. His exemplar is "still" patient Job (3.92), and Socrates is the pagan equivalent. Satan tries to attribute a desire for glory to the Father himself, but as in *Paradise Lost* Satan is simply projecting his own desires and so exposing himself, "for he himself / Insatiable of glory had lost all" (3.147-48).

Satan then proposes a second martial temptation: that Jesus gain David's throne by military victory against Rome. He introduces a biblical exemplar, one of the nine worthies, Judas Maccabæus. Jesus ignores this model of a heroism—which Milton probably thought righteous in its own context but irrelevant to the immediate situation—and, having already denounced military deeds, argues the necessity of patience and long preparation. "What if he hath decreed that I shall first / Be try'd in humble state, and things adverse, / . . . quietly expecting / Without distrust or doubt[?]" (3.188-93).

Having failed to persuade Jesus with the preparatory temptations to martial glory, Satan takes him up to a high mountain for the first formal temptation of the kingdoms of the world. Here "thou behold'st," he says, a grand roll of glorious cities and their empires: Assyria, Nineveh, Babylon, Persepolis, Ecbatana, Seleucia (3.267-93). But what Milton shows us before Satan redirects our attention is entirely different: a prospect not of man's empires but of the earth's natural abundance, quite like one of Virgil's welcome excursions through the world's great agricultural regions in the *Georgics* (e.g., 2.109-176):

> It was a Mountain at whose verdant feet
> A spatious plain out stretch't in circuit wide
> Lay pleasant; from his side two rivers flow'd,
> Th' one winding, the other strait and left between
> Fair Champain with less rivers interveind,
> Then meeting joyn'd thir tribute to the Sea:
> Fertil of corn the glebe, of oyl and wine,
> With herds the pastures throng'd, with flocks the hills,
> Huge Cities and high towr'd, that well might seem
> The seats of mightiest Monarchs, and so large
> The Prospect was, that here and there was room
> For barren desert fountainless and dry.
>   (3.253-64)

Thus we see peaceful cities in a natural landscape, set amid georgic fields and pastures. From this distance, sin and labor are both invisible, and realistic georgic verges on idyllic pastoral as it does in similar scenes depicted by Virgil. Into this panorama Satan introduces the Parthian army, with its almost lovely maneuvers and its mockery of living fields. He offers Jesus the Parthian command, and with it chivalric heroism, military conquest, and a kingdom won by glorious deeds. It is the epic temptation at its purest and broadest. Jesus refuses:

> Much ostentation vain of fleshly arm,
> And fragile arms, much instrument of war
> Long in preparing, soon to nothing brought,
> Before mine eyes thou hast set . . .
> Luggage of war there shewn me, argument
> Of human weakness rather then of strength.
> (3.387-402)

If anything can liberate Israel from Roman captivity, Jesus continues, it will be the growth of freedom among its people. Called by the Father's voice to repentance and sincerity, they will be saved not by military conquest but by a second (and spiritual) exodus to "their native land" (3.427-40). If all of *Paradise Regained* were given to such anti-epic argument, we might call it a revisionary epic like *Paradise Lost*. But only Book 3 focuses on the issue, while georgic alternatives to Satan's temptations appear in every book. Milton concludes the military temptations abruptly, with a flat dismissal of Satan's epic ideal: "So fares it when with truth falshood contends" (3.443).

Book 4 contains the temptations of Rome and Athens, the storm, and the pinnacle. Leaving the storm aside for the moment, we may call this the book of the three great cities. Nineveh and Babylon are, Satan knows, names to conjure with; but Rome, Athens, and Jerusalem represent the three preeminent cultures in the tale of Western civilization; and, as Satan mockingly suggests, Jerusalem is the crown of all: "I to thy Fathers house / Have brought thee, and highest plac't, highest is best" (4.552-53).

"Perplex'd and troubl'd at his bad success" (4.1) in the epic temptations, Satan returns to the attack, almost as stubborn as his adversary is patient:

> But as a man who had been matchless held
> In cunning, over-reach't where least he thought,
> To salve his credit, and for very spight
> Still will be tempting him who foyls him still,
> And never cease, though to his shame the more;
> Or as a swarm of flies in vintage time,
> About the wine-press where sweet moust is powr'd,
> Beat off, returns as oft with humming sound;
> Or surging waves against a solid rock,
> Though all to shivers dash't, the assault renew,
> Vain battry, and in froth or bubbles end;
> So Satan.
>
> (4.10-21)

This first extended simile in the poem is scarcely heroic. As the *Georgics* bears witness (2.279-87, 3.235-41, 4.511-15), not all extended similes belong to epic, and this one has a georgic tone and provenance. Most epic similes magnify; it progressively diminishes. Satan is reduced from a "matchless" hero and combatant to swarming flies at vintage time to the froth of waves dashing against the biblical rock. In this country metaphor, Satan as a swarm of flies (long associated with the devil under the name of Beelzebub) becomes no more than a predatory nuisance, and Jesus is seen as the husbandman at the winepress, summoning up a central image of biblical georgic.

Taking Jesus to the western side of the mountain, Satan shows him the "Imperial City," Rome, "With Towers and Temples proudly elevate / On seven small Hills" (4.33-35). If (as some editors think) there is an echo of Virgil's description of Rome in *Georgics* 2.535, it is ironic, since Virgil is praising the upright Rome of the early husbandmen: "Such a life the

ancient Sabines once lived, such Remus and his brother . . .
while yet none had heard the trumpet blare, and none the
swordblade ring upon the hard anvil" (2.532-40). But Mil-
ton's is the corrupt Rome of Tiberius, long past the critical
turning-point when Virgil could hope that Augustus might
bring back the ancient virtues. Unexpectedly, Milton does not
stress the military in connection with Rome; instead, he pre-
sents Rome as the embodiment of power, wealth, and luxury.
Parthia embodies the gaining of empire by glorious arms;
Rome is a great empire already won and beginning to rot. Its
bloodthirsty people, once victors, are now "Deservedly made
vassal" (4.133). Rome represents what Satan wants most:
power and the semblance of glory. But against the Satanic
vision of Rome, original of the Beast of Revelation, Jesus
poises still more country images of natural growth and im-
movable solidity:

> Know therefore when my season comes to sit
> On *David*'s Throne, it shall be like a tree
> Spreading and over-shadowing all the Earth,
> Or as a stone that shall to pieces dash
> All Monarchies besides throughout the world,
> And of my Kingdom there shall be no end.
> (4.146-51)

Satan behaves as though he does not even hear this re-
sponse; its georgic-apocalyptic vision is beyond his under-
standing. With Rome he has reached the limits of his ambition
in earthly terms: "I shall no more / Advise thee" (4.210-11).
Yet, having spied on Jesus' visit to the Temple, Satan suspects
that, unlike himself, Jesus prefers an empire of the mind. So
he proceeds to the temptation of Athens. Though seeming to
appreciate a point of view other than his own for once, he
introduces characteristic distortions. "Be famous then / By
wisdom" (4.221-22), he inauspiciously begins. If Jesus wants
intellectual empire over the pagans, he must learn their ways:
"Error by his own arms is best evinc't" (4.235). In Athens
Jesus may learn the "secret power" of poetry (4.254). He may

learn "resistless eloquence," which "Wielded at will that fierce Democratie, / Shook the Arsenal and fulmin'd over *Greece*, / To *Macedon*, and *Artaxerxes* Throne" (4.268-71). (Satan's mind tends ever in the same direction.) Or Jesus may learn philosophy to prepare himself for a kingdom (4.282). There is no disputing the attractiveness of Athens; much in the temptation approaches Milton's ideals. Yet Satan distorts even the kingdom of the mind, presenting it as error wrestling with error, poetry that wields secret power, rhetoric that operates like an army. Even the "low-rooft house / Of *Socrates*" (4.273-74)—equivalent to the fishermen's cottage—becomes a place in which to prepare for empire. Jesus naturally responds (as Socrates might to a Sophist) that the quest for knowledge is empty if not guided by "True wisdom"; it is like "Children gathering pibles on the shore" (4.319, 330). Besides, Israel can match Greece in poetry, in true rhetoric, and in knowledge of what makes nations good and happy (4.329-64).

Again Satan is "Quite at a loss, for all his darts were spent" (4.366). Having failed at persuasion and misdirection, he now tries force and fear. The storm scene has many sources, including the deep-rooted tree of *Georgics* 2.290-92. The larger pattern, however, beginning with Satan's prediction by the stars, followed by the storm, and then by birdsong, is much like the pattern of *Georgics* 1, in which the astronomical weather signs (276-315) are followed by the great storm (316-34) and then by the appearance of birds to signal a change to fair weather (393-414). Certainly the storm is a quintessentially georgic test. Satan tries hard to weight it with portentous epic significance (4.452-83), but Jesus dismisses the whole incident with wonderfully brief georgic realism: "Mee worse then wet thou find'st not" (4.486).

Although Satan has pretended that the thrones of Parthia and Rome are worth more than leadership of a small subjected nation caught between great powers, his storm speech reveals that he is aware that the highest priority is to gain "*David*'s Throne" and, as he cynically puts it, "get fast hold" of "*Israel*'s Scepter" (4.471, 480). From a worldly point of view this objective makes little sense, but Satan knows full well that he and Jesus are struggling for more than worldly stakes. Israel is a special people; David's throne has a divine sanction; Jesus' destiny is to be Messiah as well as king. "[S]woln with rage" (4.499) when his efforts to tempt and divert Jesus fail, Satan makes a last-ditch attempt; in effect, he offers Jesus Jerusalem and the Messiahship on Satan's own twisted terms. "Son of God to me is yet in doubt," he begins, "Of the Messiah I have heard foretold / By all the Prophets" (4. 501-503). Since Jesus has proved himself "To the utmost of meer man" (4.535), Satan will see if he is more. So he bears him up to the highest pinnacle of the Temple. "There stand, if thou wilt stand . . . if not to stand, / Cast thyself down; safely if Son of God" (4.551-55).

Satan employs force yet still uses fraud. By placing Jesus on the pinnacle of the Temple he implicitly offers him Jerusalem and a political Messiahship. Catholic and Protestant commentators agree that this episode is a temptation to presumption, vainglory, and the desire to win popular approbation by showing off in front of the Temple crowds. John Udall (1589) paraphrases Satan:

[I]f thou be certaine that thou art the verie sonne of God, of such Majestie and power: it is meete . . . that thou make it knowne unto the world, by some notable and singuler miracle . . . to throw thy selfe downe . . . which when the men of Jerusalem do behold, they cannot choose but confesse thee to be the onely, and very sonne of the everlasting God, and receive thee with a common applause . . . and so advaunce thee among them unto great honour.[26]

---

[26] *The Combate betweene Christ, and the Devill. Foure Sermons on the Temptations of Christ* (1589), E7; cited by Pope, pp. 80-81, who also cites similar comments by William Perkins, Daniel Dyke, Richard Ward, and others. See also Thomas Aquinas, *Summa Theologica*, who approvingly quotes Chrysostom's Homily 5 on Matthew, *Patrologiae Graecae*, vol. 57, cols. 212-13: "As Chrysostom says . . . 'The devil set Him (on a pinnacle of the Temple) that he might be seen of all' " (Pt. 3, q. 41, art. 4).

Should Jesus fall to his death, as Satan half expects, a threat will be eliminated. After all, to Satan's earlier satisfaction, God let the whole world go to the devil over the eating of an apple (*Paradise Lost*, 10. 485-90). Should the angels bear Jesus up, the Son will be propelled into public leadership before his time and on Satan's terms—as a popular hero and politico-religious leader against the armies of Rome.

Unexpectedly, Jesus, never willing to accept heroism on Satan's terms, takes a third course:

> To whom thus Jesus: also it is written,
> Tempt not the Lord thy God, he said and stood.
>
> (4.560-61)

This climactic utterance has at least a double meaning: Jesus refuses to tempt God by throwing himself down, and he rebukes Satan for playing the tempter. Thus Satan learns to his sorrow the answer he has sought and like Oedipus brings doom upon himself. His reaction leaves little doubt that he experiences something like a full revelation: "But Satan smitten with amazement fell" (4.562). Jesus has withheld himself from public recognition to the end: "hee unoberv'd / Home to his Mothers house private return'd" (4.638-39).

A tragic or an epic hero is by definition public. A pastoral hero, to the contrary, withdraws from public cares into privacy. But a georgic hero stands between the private and the public. He continues to work in obscurity, yet his deeds have momentous public results. In *Paradise Regained*, Milton fulfills his promise "to tell of deeds / Above Heroic, though in secret done, / And unrecorded left through many an Age" (1.14-16). Unlike such predecessors as Vida, who treated Christ as a conquering hero, Milton chose for his subject that portion of Jesus' career that balances between private life (which ends at the baptism) and public ministry (which has yet to begin). Peter and Andrew are among the crowd at the Jordan, and (as in John's Gospel) they have visited with Jesus; but he is yet to call them officially. Such a balance between the private and the public is precisely what Virgil repeatedly strikes in the *Georgics*. Like the *Georgics*, *Paradise Regained* does not describe a pastoral retreat from responsibility but instead dwells on small, recurrent actions, often trivial or inglorious in themselves, that nevertheless converge toward a turning-point in the world's history that will prove to be truly apocalyptic. As the *Georgics* has for its actual present climax (as opposed to its projected future climax) the rebirth of bees from the corpse of an ox, *Paradise Regained* crests on the simple words "he said and stood." Both these actions, though unobserved, reach far beyond their apparent simplicity. For like the *Georgics*, but on a larger scale, *Paradise Regained* looks forward to a future when heroic deeds will be done and celebrated and the world will be changed.

Unlike Virgil, Milton chose in effect to write his *Aeneid* first and then his *Georgics*, and thereby to reverse the usual priorities. It is hard to conceive of any of his predecessors or immediate contemporaries taking such a step. When Puttenham indicated in *The Arte of English Poesie* that although the style of the *Georgics* is accounted "meane" or middle, its subject matter is "base and low" (pp. 162, 164-65), he spoke for his time. As we have seen, his was the usual judgment. By 1671, however, when *Paradise Regained* was published, reformist views of labor and of agriculture were a great deal more prevalent than they had been. Still it would be a long time before such poets as Gray and Wordsworth would be prepared to offer models of georgic heroism at all comparable morally to Milton's Christ. Milton, who never had the aristocrat's contempt for honest work, was not a man to be ashamed of the georgic ideal, and in that he was ahead of his time. Probably in the process of transforming Virgilian epic in *Paradise Lost* he confirmed views that he had long held about the dignity of labor and learned that one may "by small" accomplish great things. After all, he learned that it is better to build than to destroy. As *Paradise Lost* already implied, Milton found a different solution to the issues that sufficiently troubled Virgil—whether greater value should be placed on heroic warfare or long labor, on the destruction of evil or the building of good, on the attainment of fame or hidden, patient toil for the common welfare. By distributing his poem's radical subject matter into four books, Milton acknowledged his debt to his predecessor.

Paradise Regained contains neither swords nor pruning hooks, and so it is literally neither georgic nor epic. But its four-book structure, its style and spirit, as well as much of its imagery, are georgic. Predominantly georgic in mode, heroically georgic in theme, it fittingly crowns the most arduous period of the georgic revolution, presenting to its readers the example of a new kind of hero: one who, in preparation for the climactic acts of his redemptive death and resurrection, labors and builds, lays the groundwork for a new civilization, and raises a spiritual Eden in the waste wilderness of human history. Although we have no conventional term to describe such a poem, heroic georgic seems appropriate.

Conclusion

IT IS GENERALLY recognized that during the sixteenth and seventeenth centuries England witnessed an unusual degree of socioeconomic change. At the upper levels of society, with which history has traditionally dealt, new men and their families rose to the top by their success as courtiers or their ability to manipulate the various patronage networks that controlled the government, the Church, and the schools and universities. At the lower levels of society, which historians have only recently begun to study in much depth, bondmen became free men, free men became gentlemen, and gentlemen became esquires and knights. Probably the greater number started their climb up the ladder of wealth and precedence by means of hard manual labor, or by utilizing special skills that they brought to newly unfolding opportunities for economic advancement. Manufacturing and trade offered many new men their primary means for advancement, but agriculture remained England's basic occupation, and possession and exploitation of land was by far the commonest and most acceptable means of getting ahead. Over the years, laborers or their sons became husbandmen, husbandmen became yeomen, and yeomen at last became gentlemen by knowing what crops to plant, what fertilizers to use, and where the best markets were.[1] In the course of their upward rise, they did not shrink from putting their hands to the plow. Yet, paradoxically, once they reached a certain level of prominence they discovered that manual work was from then on forbidden to them. Society was prepared to extend the title of gentleman to scholars, lawyers, and divines, whatever their family origins, as well as

---

[1] On social mobility in agriculture, see especially Mildred Campbell, *The English Yeoman Under Elizabeth and the Early Stuarts* (New York: Augustus M. Kelley, 1968); and, for a comic portrayal of the process, see Richard Brome's *Sparagus Garden* (1635).

to successful yeomen and tenant farmers; but, as Barnabe Rich noted in *Roome for a Gentleman* (1609), the two ineluctable requirements which those who aspired to gentility had to satisfy were, first, a sufficient income to keep up appearances according to their station and, second, a style of life that allowed them to "live without manuell labour" (p. 13). Even too much interest in or too close supervision of the labors of others were matters to be concealed and limited to business hours. Labor as a means of private wealth was *infra dignitatem*; labor as an ideal to be openly pursued for the common welfare was as yet almost unheard of.

Gradually, with the rise of the New Science, men's perceptions began to change. The New Husbandry especially came to be viewed as a potential means of transforming the nation and of bringing prosperity not only to the individual landowner but to society as a whole. In the 1650s enclosure and improvement of land gained a new moral legitimacy, and tracts began to appear with titles like Silas Taylor's *Common Good: or the Improvement of Commons, Forests and Chases by Inclosure* (1652), and Adam Moore's *Bread for the Poor ... Promised by Enclosure of the Wastes and Common Grounds of England* (1653). Sometimes literally and sometimes metaphorically, and with varying degrees of directness, the New Husbandry inspired such poets as Herrick, Marvell, and Milton to write new forms of georgic. Even the increasing vehemence of anti-georgic poetry written during the Civil War is strong evidence for the growing importance of the georgic spirit in England. Out of the Civil War emerged the Royal Society with its Georgical Committee, which, working in the tradition of Bacon and Hartlib, was the direct ancestor of the eighteenth-century agricultural reformers as well as of our modern agricultural ministries or departments and land-grant colleges.

The spirit of Christian reform, which for more than a millennium had expressed itself mainly through the Church and especially through the great monastic foundations, and which led to recurrent progress in agricultural technology and recurrent revivals of belief in the dignity of labor, necessarily took a new direction under the English Reformation. Secular control of the Church effectively eliminated one traditional source for the rebuke of aristocratic pretensions, and the influx of Calvinist theology militated against commitment to broad reform of society within the main body of the Anglican Church and the more conservative sects. Reform in England naturally meant Protestant reform—although a few innovators, such as Sir Richard Weston, were Roman Catholics (which may explain Weston's reluctance to answer Hartlib's several queries about his new methods of husbandry during the 1650s). On the whole the Anglican Church was broad enough to include many reformers among its members in good standing—Bishop Hall is an example—but seemingly the main work of reform was done by those who were inclined to give greater prominence to free will than the Thirty-nine Articles encouraged. Milton especially was a firm believer in free will, as is sufficiently evidenced by *Areopagitica* and *Paradise Lost* as well as the more technical discussion in *De Doctrina Christiana*.[2] Spenser, in spite of his emphasis on divine grace in *The Faerie Queene*, was also an evident believer in the importance of individual effort. In contrast, the Presbyterians, who were among the staunchest Calvinists of the day and at the start of the Civil War were in the political vanguard, quickly moved to the conservative side as affairs developed; there is little evidence that they played an important role in the development of science, agriculture, or georgic consciousness in general. The case may have been very different in other countries with other histories—Holland especially—but the manner in

[2] On Milton's Arminian position with regard to free will, see Maurice Kelly, ed., *The Christian Doctrine*, vol. 4 of *Complete Prose Works of John Milton* (New Haven: Yale Univ. Press, 1973), 74-86; and Dennis Richard Danielson, *Milton's Good God* (Cambridge: Cambridge Univ. Press, 1982). Spenser scholars have been divided as to how deeply Spenser was commited to a Calvinist theology of grace and works. Certainly he was committed to Protestant reform, but in my view *The Faerie Queene* presents an approach to history incompatible with strict Calvinism.

which the Reformation was introduced into England ensured that the Established Church would be slow to commit itself to any wholesale program of social, economic, and scientific progress.

How much the scientific, agricultural, and industrial revolutions owe to a Christian conviction that the world is an orderly system and how much they owe to a breakdown in traditional Christian views of the universe is an unsettled question. Curiously, a similar dispute is connected with the works of Virgil, for scholars are sharply divided on the question of whether Virgil believed in the gods who appear so prominently in his poetry. In any event, he lived in an age of transition between religious faith and materialistic skepticism that was rather similar to the seventeenth century. We find in his poetry the application of originally religious ideals to an essentially secular situation. Much the same is true of those English poets who were most prominent in the revival of the georgic tradition. Most late sixteenth- and early seventeenth-century poets divided their secular poems from their religious, or else they condemned the writing of secular verse altogether. Spenser, to the contrary, is notable for writing poetry at once deeply religious and deeply involved in the processes of secular history. So is Marvell, and so too is Milton. All three poets were Christians who were committed to working in the secular world. Bacon and Hartlib too were inspired by a vision of Christian reformation that would reach out into secular society and provide for the material as well as the spiritual welfare of the nation. Over the course of the century that Christian commitment tended gradually to break down—as we may see it breaking down in the later writings of Gerrard Winstanley—until the lessons that succeeding generations of English reformers were to draw from Spenser, Marvell, and Milton were almost purely political. During the period of its germination and first flowering, however, the georgic revolution combined the best elements of religious and secular reforming impulses and encouraged its supporters to work toward a hopeful vision of England's future.

CONCLUSION

Virgil did not live to see the failure of the dream he projected in the *Georgics*. The Roman Empire, instead of combining the enlightened political stability of an Augustus with the ancient republican virtues of a sturdy agricultural society, combined constant (if long-lived) political instability with an economic system of large estates worked by slaves and heavy dependence on grain imported from North Africa. Paradoxically, although Virgil was deeply in touch with the historical moment when he wrote the *Georgics*, the political vision he embodied in his poem proved in the end to be better suited to the situation in modern England than to the ancient Rome for which it was intended. Perhaps because of the growing disparity between the social vision in the *Georgics* and the course of Roman history, the early Virgilian scholiasts, on whom the Middle Ages depended so heavily, confined most of their attention to the *Aeneid*, and therefore Virgil came to be known largely as a poet of empire who told how the new Troy was founded in the West out of the ashes of the old Troy—a legend that nearly all the emerging European nations took to heart. The Middle Ages developed an extensive tradition of native georgic (and anti-georgic) literature, out of its own social practices, reforming impulses, and familiarity with biblical georgic. (It is, of course, possible that the *Georgics* were better and more directly known to the Middle Ages than has been thought; I have not yet had the opportunity to investigate that question.) The Renaissance revived Virgil in his original texts, but not until the late Renaissance and the seventeenth century were the English ready to understand the georgic spirit and its implications for their own historical situation. To put aside empty fighting and to subordinate leisure in order to build a nation: Spenser was the first important English poet to understand that side of Virgil. Milton was his chief heir and saw most clearly the radical implications that a dedicated work ethic might have for a modern society.

INDEX

Library of Congress Cataloging in Publication Data

Low, Anthony, 1935-
    The Georgic revolution.

    Includes index.
    1. English poetry—Early modern, 1500-1700—
History and criticism. 2. Pastoral poetry, English—History
and criticism. 3. Literature and society—Great Britain.
I. Title.
PR549.P3L68   1985   821'.009   84-26520
ISBN 0-691-06643-4